D0821433

Paths to Fulfillment

Paths to Fulfillment

WOMEN'S SEARCH FOR MEANING AND IDENTITY

Ruthellen Josselson

OXFORD
UNIVERSITY PRESS

Oxford University Press is a department of the University of Oxford. It furthers the University's objective of excellence in research, scholarship, and education by publishing worldwide. Oxford is a registered trade mark of Oxford University Press in the UK and certain other countries.

Published in the United States of America by Oxford University Press
198 Madison Avenue, New York, NY 10016, United States of America.

© Oxford University Press 2017

All rights reserved. No part of this publication may be reproduced, stored in a retrieval system, or transmitted, in any form or by any means, without the prior permission in writing of Oxford University Press, or as expressly permitted by law, by license, or under terms agreed with the appropriate reproduction rights organization. Inquiries concerning reproduction outside the scope of the above should be sent to the Rights Department, Oxford University Press, at the address above.

You must not circulate this work in any other form and you must impose this same condition on any acquirer.

Library of Congress Cataloging-in-Publication Data
Names: Josselson, Ruthellen, author.
Title: Paths to fulfillment : women's search for meaning and identity / Ruthellen Josselson.
Description: New York, NY : Oxford University Press, [2017] | Includes bibliographical references.
Identifiers: LCCN 2016035250 | ISBN 9780190250393 (jacketed hardcover : alk. paper)
Subjects: LCSH: Women—United States—Psychology—Longitudinal studies. | Women—United States—Identity—Longitudinal studies. | Identity (Psychology)—United States—Longitudinal studies.
Classification: LCC HQ1206 .J672 2017 | DDC 155.3/33—dc23
LC record available at https://lccn.loc.gov/2016035250

1 3 5 7 9 8 6 4 2

Printed by Sheridan Books, Inc., United States of America

To my women friends of forty or more years, with whom I have shared the challenges of finding, revising and fulfilling ourselves: Amia, Barbara, Bev, Connie, Dori, Ellen, Judy, Judy, June, Megan, Pam, Roberta, Sally, Sherry, Sue, and Susie.

You have won rooms of your own in the home hitherto exclusively owned by men. . . . The room is your own, but it is still bare. . . . How are you going to furnish it? How are you going to decorate it? With whom are you going to share it? And upon what terms? These, I think, are questions of the utmost importance and interest. For the first time in history, you are able to ask them; for the first time, you are able to decide for yourselves what the answers should be.

—VIRGINIA WOOLF, "PROFESSIONS FOR WOMEN," PUBLISHED POSTHUMOUSLY IN *THE DEATH OF THE MOTH AND OTHER ESSAYS*

". . . we all begin with the natural equipment to live a thousand kinds of life but end in the end having lived only one."

CLIFFORD GEERTZ, *THE INTERPRETATION OF CULTURES*

{ CONTENTS }

{ ACKNOWLEDGMENTS }

I have been working on this project, in one way or another, throughout my entire adult life so it seems like everyone I have known has contributed in some way to my thinking and understanding about women's development. I am grateful to so many people for their support, encouragement, and interest over the many years of this study. Here, I will acknowledge only those who have assisted me in this last round of interviewing and analysis. Most heartily, I wish to thank my colleagues and friends, Jane Kroger, Jim Marcia, and Ravenna Helson whose own work on identity has inspired me throughout my career. They, as well as June Price and Amia Lieblich, read all the chapters, talked with me at length about my perspective on these women, and contributed their own ideas. Many of my students at the Fielding Graduate University have helped me by transcribing and commenting on interviews, working with me on analysis, or commenting on chapters. In particular, I am grateful to Devon Jersild, Heidi Mattila, Janita van der Walt, Shari Goldstein, and Marti Spriggs. Others read and commented on interviews or chapters, and I thank Tova Hartman, Monisha Pasupathi, Paivi Fadjukoff, and my daughter, Jaimie Baron, as well as my colleagues in the Society for Personology who allowed me to present this work and offered me their insight: Jim Anderson, Jack Bauer, Sunil Bhatia, Mark Freeman, Gary Gregg, Jeannette Haviland Jones, Jen Lilgendhal, Dan McAdams, Dan Ogilvie, Mac Runyan, Brian Schiff, Todd Schultz, Jefferson Singer, Ed de St. Aubin, Paul Wink, and Barbara Woike. I also thank Jonathan Slavin for having lent me his apartment for a snowy winter week so I could do interviews there. I am appreciative of having had a research grant from the Fielding Graduate University to fund my travel to interview these women. And I thank my editor, Abby Gross, for her counsel and support. As always, I thank my husband, Hanoch Flum, for his wisdom and knowledge about identity development and just for being in my life.

Most deeply, I give my thanks to the women of this study who have, over the course of 35 years, opened their lives and hearts to me. They must, of course, remain anonymous. I hope I do them no injustice by how I have written about them. Immersing myself in their lives, I have come to love each of them as fellow travelers trying to grow and to make sense out of our lives.

{ PREFACE }

To observe a woman's life unfold is like looking into a kaleidoscope. Women's identities integrate multiple elements in an arrangement that changes over time as new pieces are added and old ones given more or less prominence or discarded. Each change makes the overall pattern shift but still resemble the previous one. The elements grow out of the childhood they had and the experiences and people they encountered later along the way as they go through life making choices. There is both continuity and change over time. I have been following the unfolding of 26 women's lives for 35 years, trying to understand how and why the college seniors they were became the women they are today.[1] My inspiration has been Michael Apted's "Up" series, but I use words rather than film to document lives, and I think psychologically rather than sociologically. Nothing intrigues me more than to witness change over time. I am interested in providing fleshed-out descriptions of these lives in progress rather than vignettes to illustrate a point. Rather than focusing on social class, as Apted did, I concern myself with differences among four distinct psychological pathways that I identified when these women were seniors in college. There are many ways for a woman to live a life, and some, in late midlife, feel more satisfied with what they have created than others.

In psychology, adolescence and old age are well-conceptualized, but we understand less about what occurs developmentally in the many decades of adulthood that constitute the middle years. This period reflects continuity as well as growth and change and has its own challenges and possibilities. The women I studied have forged lives very different from one another, yet there are commonalities among them.

I make no argument in this book; I have no axe to grind. My aim is to map the developmental paths of adulthood. I lay claim to charting the seasons of a woman's life and demonstrating how different inner arrangements at the end of college give way to different life courses. Because of these different launching patterns, generalizations about women, even college-educated women, become impossible to sustain. Women become themselves in intricate ways. Yet some women experience their lives in their mid-50s as more fulfilling than others do—and how they create that fulfillment has much to do with the form of identity they shape along the way.

Note

1. Although I have followed 26 women for 35 years, I report on 25 of them in this book. One of the women was in a marital crisis when I saw her at age 55, and she was in a rather traumatized state of mind.

Women and Identity

I sit in my rented car somewhere in the middle of nowhere. I have come to this rural area of West Virginia to meet Alice, one of the women I have been tracking, once every decade, for 35 years in my effort of learn about the development of identity in women. Alice is a woman who had seemed to me to embody promise and stability from the time I first met her when she was a college senior, and I am eager to know how her life has evolved. The winding rural road that I drove to reach this spot was paved but barely wide enough for two cars. I am early for my interview with Alice, and I had thought to stop for a cup of coffee. I drove past several lakes and looked at blush-of-spring green wooded hills but I saw no coffee places the past 30 miles in this remote area. Simple clapboard houses dotted large lots, never more than three houses in a half-mile span. Alice gave me detailed directions, but I am nervous about there being no cell phone service and I'm not absolutely sure I'm sitting in the driveway of the right house. I hear no sounds but the wind and the birds, and I wonder what it would be like to live here, to make a life here. It is spring now, but I suppose the winters are harsh. The women I have been following have crafted such different lives in such varying places. I wonder how life is shaped by the presence of this natural beauty and the absence of any real town life—or, at least, any coffee shop. What sort of person will I encounter here? I am relieved when a small four-wheel drive van pulls up next to me and gives forth a stocky middle-aged woman dressed in jeans who appears to be expecting someone. Alice. She acknowledges me with a smile, invites me in, and, mercifully, offers me a cup of coffee.

Imagine four groups of young women graduating from college in 1972. They exit through different gates. One group, which I have called the Pathmakers, has used their college years to transform the high school students they were by exploring other ways of being and believing, charting some path on their own terms for their future. Another group of women, the Guardians, are not much changed by their college experience. These women have held fast to the values and goals they derived from their families, and they plan to stay on the same course they have always followed. A third group, the Searchers, are uncertain, still unsure of how they want their lives to progress or the people they wish to be, but they are actively questioning and questing. And another group is, either merrily or despondently, moving toward the gate with little idea of where they might be headed but not troubling themselves about it. This group, the Drifters, are leaving their future to fate and circumstance.

What becomes of these women in adulthood? This is the question I have spent 35 years pursuing, tracing the evolution of their lives by interviewing them in depth every 10 years or so. I found, of course, that the women change courses and move into other groups. Nearly all the Pathmakers continue to make their own way, carrying forth the psychological strength they garnered in their college years and earlier. Some of the Searchers and Guardians and one of the Drifters eventually join the Pathmakers, facing forward in directions of their own choosing. Some of the Searchers gave up their exploration and went home again to the ways of living they came from, becoming more like the original Guardians. To my sad surprise, nearly all the Drifters continue to drift, unable to organize themselves into a purposeful and ultimately meaningful life.

My purpose, though, is not just to note these changes in path, but to track the *processes* of change in order to better understand how adult life unfolds for American, college-educated women. And this is a particularly fascinating group to follow because these women who graduated from college in the early 1970s are the ones who actually created the revolution in women's place in American society. Although few of these women declared themselves to be feminists at the time, they seized the new possibilities and definitions for women created by the feminist movement. Turning their backs on the traditional roles their mothers had occupied, they were determined to create something different for themselves. By shunning cooking, dusting, and ironing as their central tasks in life, they lived out the (at the time) new vision for women by taking up work in the wider world. The choices they made over the course of their lives were personal but, taken together, had political implications. They made contributions to the social good outside the home and, at the same time, raised a generation of daughters and sons who took for granted the right to equality for women. Although often only dimly aware of the larger social forces that made opportunities for them to create lives different from their mothers, they became part of the snowballing social processes that enhanced opportunity for women. Many of them became "the first woman" within their social contexts to do things—get a judicial appointment, be on a professional credentialing board, receive a particular award. They were the generation in line when professional worlds were looking for women to take positions formerly restricted to men. They did not set out to shatter glass ceilings, yet they were the ones to do so.

Although all of these women were college seniors when I first interviewed them, and all received college degrees, what they did with them varied widely. Some eventually made headlines (and Google searches unearth lots of photos and articles); most others have led lives unknown to search engines. Because I chose them at random from women who were graduating from four different universities in 1972 and 1973, they represent a diverse range of college-educated women from disparate backgrounds.[1] Some grew up in large cities, others in small cities, towns, and in rural areas—and there remains diversity in where they live now. Some were from well-to-do families; others put themselves through college by working while studying. Some had immigrant parents and are embedded in ethnicities that feel to them separate from the American mainstream. There is religious diversity—people who were raised as Catholics, Protestants, or Jews—although their religious affiliation and commitment has declined enough over the years that many now do not hold religious identity very important. Many were the first in their families to go to college, getting themselves there either by forming their own dream or fulfilling their parents' hopes for them. In midlife, most of them feel comfortable materially, part of the middle or upper-middle class, and most of them have a higher standard of living than their families of origin.

When I first met them when they were 21, about to take their college degrees, all envisioned the same outlines for the future. They would marry, have children, and work. But the particularities of the work they would do, the husbands they would marry, and the children they might mother remained obscure, as the future always is. I have been interested over the years in how they created these particularities and how they coped with the decisions and challenges along the way. By the time they were in their early 30s, the shape of the identities they would live out was firmer than it had been at the end of college, some of the details filled in. By their early 40s, they were actively revising what was in place—in their work, their marriages, and themselves. And now, in their mid-50s, they are reaping the fruits of the dreams they have been striving to realize in their lives. All but one of them have spent most of their lives in the work world, either in professional careers or having a series of jobs. All but one married at least once, and most, in their mid-50s, are still married to their first husband; just over half had children. They have fulfilled themselves in different ways as they have expressed their varied identities in the worlds they found and created for themselves to live in.

There is perhaps more that distinguishes these women from each other than what unites them. What they have in common is that all graduated from college in the very early '70s and have remained willing to talk to me over the course of 35 years. (Only two chose to drop out of the study between the ages of 33 and 43 and some I could no longer find.) I recognize, though, that with 26 randomly chosen women, I have obtained a wide range of lifestyles and life structures but cannot represent all possible life configurations.

I have had the extraordinary opportunity to follow these women's lives—most of whom are very different from me and different from the women I get to know in the ordinary course of my life. In earlier books about these women, I have described the ways in which they went about forming their identities from college to their early 30s (*Finding Herself*) and then how they revised their identities into their early 40s (*Revising Herself*). In this decade, their mid-40s to mid-50s, I was eager to learn if they continued to revise their identities and, if they are no longer in search of something different for themselves, what constitutes their sense of fulfillment.

Envisioning Women

Carolyn Heilbrun's comment in her book, *Writing a Woman's Life,* made a great impression on me long ago. Commenting on how courtship, with its flaming desire and anxiety, has always been the literary plot depicted as central in a woman's life, she wrote, "The rest is aging and regret." It may be true that this is the literary rendition of women's lives, but it certainly hasn't been my life story—or the life story of other women I have known. Part of my own quest has been to create a fuller description of women's lives, one beyond literature and certainly beyond the variables-based lifeless studies of women that my own field of psychology generally promulgates.

I have been interested in creating holistic, rich descriptions of women's lives—of "ordinary" women's lives—ordinary in the sense of not being victims of one thing or another, not necessarily heroic or outstandingly successful in the public world, women we neither feel obliged to pity nor to extol. These are the masses of women, and they have a psychology and developmental course as well. How do they go about creating their lives? And what else is there besides aging and regret?

The Social Contexts

Women's lives are, of course, affected by the social world they live in. These women came of age during a time when fetters were falling. They were to be welcomed into the work world although discrimination still persisted.[2] In that era, the early 1970s, women were actively questioning why all the household drudgery should fall to them just because they were women. They were each raised by a mother who could not escape the tyranny of traditional women's roles, and they were clear they were not going to follow her footsteps. They noted her dissatisfaction with her life—or their mothers loudly proclaimed it as they counseled their daughters to do something different with *their* lives. The world they grew up in was changing and not only in terms of women's roles. The late '60s and early '70s were anti-authoritarian times: "Don't trust anyone over 30" was the mantra. The war-mongering government could not be trusted; rampant racist attitudes were becoming anathema. This was the generation that would remake the world. (I know. I was part of it.) There was freedom everywhere. None of these women dressed the way their mothers thought young ladies should dress. The birth control pill, widely available since 1965, made sexual freedom possible and the insistence on virginity as a moral imperative began to seem antiquated (*Roe v. Wade* wasn't until 1973). And then there were the drugs that permeated college campuses. The music—of the Grateful Dead and Jefferson Airplane, Bob Dylan and Pete Seeger—that blared on campus spoke of states of psychedelic euphoria and of protest and political discontent. New possibilities were everywhere in the Age of Aquarius if one sought change. It was a heady, if confusing, time to be in college. Few of the women in this study were campus or political leaders, although many took part in political marches. But it was hard not to be touched by the spirit of the times, the collective desire to rectify the injustice and question the rigidities of the past.

At a more personal level, most of these women felt themselves to be bridging two worlds—the world of the families that they grew up in and the world ahead. Just in going to college they all had taken a step away from their mothers' paths. (Only two had college-educated mothers.) Their colleges were in the East or Midwest; they studied either in large state universities or one private woman's college. When I interviewed them as college seniors, all imagined that they would find a way to combine some sort of career with having a family—less out of ideology than from a wish to use their abilities and not to be bored. "I don't want to just sit at home," many told me. Most thought that they would probably marry shortly after college, work for a time, stop work to have children, and then return to work after their children were of school age. This seemed to be the generic fantasy that their generation fashioned. At age 21, however, most thought of having children as something they would definitely do, but far in the future, too far to really think about. They hadn't yet given any concrete thought to how they would combine being mothers and career women (and, in general, neither had the larger society). They were thinking about what they would like to "do" (meaning work), being on their own for a time, financially independent and free of the pressures of school. Their dreams were to get their own apartment, a nice car, to travel perhaps. Only five of them had plans to go to graduate school immediately after college, although some thought they might seek further schooling sometime later. Their goals were largely for the short term—what they would do for the years immediately after college—leaving the rest to be decided down the road. Envisioning the "rest of their lives," they imagined that their future would play out much like their mothers' except that they would also work, at least for some significant part of their lives.

By 1972, it was no longer radical for women to think of having a career; the media had been saturated with the right of women to participate in the work world. There was some tipping point in the early '70s when women could seriously think about and tell others that they planned careers without getting surprised stares. I remember being at a party with medical people in the late 1960s—I was at the time married to a medical student—and telling someone I was a PhD student, and the response was, "Well, when are you going to start having babies?" I remember being the only woman there with serious career plans; all the other women defined themselves as about-to-be-doctors' wives and treated me as rather freakish because I had other visions for myself. Only a few years later, the social climate had completely changed, and, by the later 1970s, women who were stay-at-home-mothers found themselves having to defend their choice.

Few of the women in my study were actively involved in the women's movement, although all were aware of it and could not but be bathed in the themes of feminist ideology. Some took up these matters at abstract philosophical or sociopolitical levels, whereas for others discussion of the issues raised by the feminists of the time emerged in questions about who should pay for dates, whether men should hold doors open for women, and whether or not they ought to do "wifely" things for their boyfriends like iron their shirts or cook their meals. Demands for full equality for women were just emerging, but the consciousness of gender-based assumptions was rising everywhere. Many of these women resisted, for example, the idea of seeing a woman doctor for fear they were somehow not "as good" as male doctors, but, at the same time, this thought made them uncomfortable. They were just beginning to question some of the gendered attitudes that were so deeply ingrained in them. The crux of the larger social debate at that time still centered around whether or not women were inferior to men. (One could still in those years say with impunity, for example, that a woman could not do this or that job because "what if she had her period?") Many of these women still worried about surpassing their boyfriends for fear of "hurting his ego," but most of them were working their way around to feeling that that was something "he'd have to deal with," taking their chances on being rejected.

If there was one political idea that united them, it was the idea of choice: that people, especially women, should have the right to choose, that no one should be kept from doing what she or he wished and was able to do because of race, class, or gender. And, personally, they balked at whatever seemed to limit them. Conformity was "out" and individuality was "in." The Human Potential movement had its effects in a prevailing ideology of self-realization. Students kept on the walls of their rooms the Fritz Perls' poster that decorated the times, a poster that said, "I am not in this world to live up to your expectations. And you are not here to live up to mine. I am I and you are you and if we find each other it's beautiful."

None of these women was a crusader. None had a cause or was out personally to remake the world, although many were highly critical of the world they found themselves in. They struggled to articulate themselves with the people around them. They wanted to have friends who were loyal and compatible, and most of them did. They agonized over their relationships with men, wanting a partner and worrying over the details of real relationships—how they wanted to be treated, how they wished to be loved. As college ended, several were engaged and one was married. And many were eagerly looking for the "right person" to be a partner, hoping to marry as soon as such a person could be found. Others regarded marriage as something they would likely do later in their 20s, after they had more experience.

Overall, these women were optimistic about their future, although few could imagine even the faintest outline of how their lives might look 10 years later. Most had a dim vision of themselves as married and working and perhaps having children, but the image was shrouded in mist. At the threshold of their adulthood, they were building flexibility into their identities by leaving some options at least partially open, preparing themselves for what might come. They varied, one from another, in how they anticipated using their freedom to choose—and the differences in how they chose or didn't choose is what I will explore in this book.

In Their 30s in the 1980s

Much of the sense of social ferment fell away when these women passed out of the college gates. The university, with its massing of peers, was no longer the social world. Leaving college, they had either to go home or situate themselves elsewhere. Where they went and the people they chose to embed themselves with constituted the first statements of the identities they would try to live out. By the time I saw these women again, in 1983, they had widely dispersed. They were now living in 14 different states and one foreign country. All but one were working in paid jobs at least part-time. While all had thought as college seniors that they would be married in 10 years, only slightly more than half had done so. Most who had married by age 33 did so in the first three years after college. A few had divorced and remarried.[3] Although all had thought they would most likely have children by their early 30s, only 8 of the 34 I followed were mothers at this time. Half had two children already; the others had one and were planning another. If we were to speak of a pattern common to them at age 33, it would be that they were working in some occupation and either thinking about getting married or thinking about having children. But identifying a common pattern is somewhat misleading because these women were already a highly varied group who were creating very different lives. Maria was trying to care for two babies and maintain her nursing career,

Debbie was roaming the country in search of mystical experience, Donna was part of a religious cult. They had been offered choice by their social world, and they were availing themselves of it.

In part because of the times—the Reagan era—and in part because of their own life stage, these women were in an acquisitive phase of their development. In the larger culture, awareness of "hippies" had been replaced by the dominance of "yuppies," a new word of the early '80s. The radical voices of the 60s had been stilled in the rush for material success. In 1983, *In Search of Excellence* was the bestselling book, and the movie "The Big Chill" was already waxing nostalgic for the idealism of these women's college years. People had turned inward. The women I had known as college seniors were now focused on buying, maintaining, restoring, or upgrading their housing. Concerned about "lifestyle," a popular word of that age, they desired the material things that would give them a good life. The health consciousness of the times led them to spend more of their energy concerned about diet and more of their time on exercise. Some still smoked, drank, and occasionally got high on pot. All had found some avocation—gardening, tennis, needlepoint. Many had traveled abroad.

By 1983, when I met them for the first time after college, the image of the "superwoman" was emerging in the public mind. These women were aware that newly wrought ideals of success for educated women expected them to "do it all" and "have it all." No longer a matter of breaking through barriers and proving that women *could* balance all the roles, "having it all" began to seem the mode. These women, then, had to articulate their personal life designs in this highly altered context.

Those who were not married were in search of partners while at the same time preparing themselves mentally for the possibility of life as a single person. Those who didn't have children were struggling with the sense that time was beginning to run out and they would soon have to decide to conceive or, if they were having difficulty conceiving, adopt. (At that time, 35 was considered "old" for motherhood. The widespread phenomena of 40+-year-old first-time mothers hadn't occurred yet.) Most still imagined that children would be somewhere in their future. Although two said that they had decided not to have children, it was with full awareness that this was a highly reversible decision.

Nearly a third of these women had gone on for further education, received post-baccalaureate degrees, and were working in law, medicine, business, or education.[4] The rest had found employment with their bachelor's degrees—as teachers, nurses, physical therapists, or systems analysts. Many were in the business world in various levels of administration or management. Few had plans for further education at this point in their lives, although many had taken specialized courses for certificates or credit related to their jobs. Although all of these women felt relatively settled in their jobs, most felt their lives still very much in the process of being made. Few had higher career aspirations. Most had set limits on how much they wanted to invest in career success. As a group, these women were struggling with how to get it all in—work, family, partner, friends, exercise, hobbies, reading.

By age 33, most of these women had moved away from the religion of their childhood. They had joined the more secular cast of the larger society. Politically, they were largely uninvolved and uncommitted. Many spoke of feeling that they had grown more conservative. Economics, more than anything else, had linked them to the political world. As working adults, they were aware of what they were paying in taxes and wondered where it was going. Eschewing the idealism of their younger days, they said they had become more opposed to spending for social welfare and had come to generally dislike government. Although most of these women felt themselves to be more allied to the philosophy of the Democrats, if they could define any political conviction at all, they were more in sympathy with Republican individualist values. Some women, through their work, had become concerned about a specific political issue—educational policy, for example. Or they had come to understand where the funding for their organizations came from and recognized that this was an aspect of political decision-making. Asked to name a political issue they felt strongly about, they most commonly mentioned their support for abortion rights, but few had taken an active stand here either. In general, these women were focused on their immediate concerns and were, if anything, even less politically interested than they had been in college.

Having been out in the work world for 12 years, these women were much more attuned to issues regarding women's status than they had been in college. Most were aware of discrimination against women, and many had direct experiences of being paid less than a man doing identical work or being given less responsibility or less acknowledgment for their skills. For them, women's issues felt real rather than theoretical, but they had found no venue or organization for complaint. Many protested on an individual level if they could; many more suffered silently.

For most, college felt emotionally very far away. Few felt that college had any lasting effect on their lives, and only a few retained friends from their college years. Their feeling was that college had been a life stage, an experience, a time in which they had gained some emotional and physical independence from their parents, but, in their developing narratives of their lives, real life had begun after college.

At this point in their lives, these women had, to me, grown more distinct from one another. Whereas 10 years earlier I could discriminate them mainly in terms of their backgrounds and their aspirations, in their 30s, they distinguished themselves more in terms of what they were creating in their lives. Andrea, for example, was a doctor, married, probably not going to have children. Natalie was working as a technical writer for a corporation, hoping to find a man to marry, intrigued by a parrot she enjoyed caring for. Helen had two children but continued her teaching career. And so on for each one. These were women who had fashioned identities for themselves, but all were still very much in process, with important decisions waiting ahead. All had built a life structure by this age, more or less tentatively. Those with children were the most settled and certain; the others by and large felt that they could revise as they wished. And most had a clearer idea of how their lives might be 10 years later than they had in college.

In Their 40s in the 1990s

By the mid-1990s, the image of the superwoman was firmly rooted, and these women were having it all—or at least trying. By now, half of them were mothers.[5] They worked out childcare—either by sharing it with their husbands, recruiting their mothers or aunts to help out, hiring babysitters, or finding day care centers. They didn't sleep much, and they packed their days. They found ways to do what they wanted to do. They were busy, tired, but, at least to me, not complaining about their life structures.

In these next 10 years, Fate played more of a role than it had before. Illnesses of those they loved, infertility, economic vagaries, personnel reorganizations in their workplaces, special needs of children—these were elements that many women had to integrate into their evolving identities. At this point, my group of women was more settled, more recognizably people who knew who they were. They had grown firmer, and they felt less likely to change. The contrast between who they were outwardly at age 21 and age 33 was much greater than the shift between age 33 and 43 even though many, in their late 30s or early 40s, had changed partners or careers. Most had made subtle and internal changes in this decade as they began to understand themselves and their own needs better. Still, they were more likely to emphasize the continuity despite the changes. Interestingly, most of these women remembered our interview at age 33 but had no memory of the interviews held in college. Again, I had the strong sense that, for them, life began in earnest only after graduation as they faced forward with their hard-wrought identities. Once their identity structures had been formed, the circumstances of creating the scaffold of their identities faded from memory. At this time, I began to understand that my possessing transcripts of the earlier interviews gave me a quite different view of their development than they themselves had in retrospect. I was not surprised that they had reconstructed the past because this is what people do as they age.

In 1993, "my" women were now living in 17 states, mostly in suburbs or small towns. (Few had the highly urbanized lives that the media so often depict.) At age 43, all but three were in marriages or committed relationships, including one who had come out as a lesbian and was living with a long-term partner.[6] Even though many were raised in large families, the majority of the mothers had two children, and no one had more than three. Of the non-mothers married or living with long-term partners, half of these had made clear decisions not to have children. The others remained uncertain or confused over this issue, still thinking "it might happen" or "we might adopt."

All but three of these women were employed outside their homes in their early 40s, and one of these was in graduate school. Only two, then, at midlife were full-time homemaker/mothers, and these had a variety of volunteer activities. Some women had outstanding professional success; others merely worked. Others were still casting about trying to find a career direction that suited them.

In Their 50s in the 2000s

When I found them again in their mid-50s, nearly all of these women were living in the same place they were 12 years previously, and few had made major changes in the central investments in their lives. The period from their early 40s to their mid-50s were the Bush years, but one wouldn't know that by listening to my interviews with these women. If they were engaged with the larger sociopolitical context, it was mainly in terms of how it affected their children. In comparison to the values they had been raised with, everyone had become more sexually liberal in terms of standards they might impart to their children, but the threat of AIDS loomed as something to worry about in their children's sexual behavior. If people had political passions, it was usually over local issues that engaged them or environmental concerns. They kept up with the news, but neither national nor international issues seemed to them to affect their lives directly. It was now a post-9/11 world, yet life went on. (No one mentioned it.)

Most of them had been having conversations, at least with themselves, about when they might retire, so the end of their occupational lives seemed to loom on the horizon, requiring a decision in the foreseeable future. For some, the pension structure dictated how long they would work, and the pacing of their husband's career was also something to take into account. Some of these women still had teenagers living at home, but most had seen their children off to college or into adult lives of their own. Most still had living parents. Some of these women had had health challenges in the intervening years, but none that necessitated that she change how she was living her life.

In terms of women's issues, the struggles seemed to them now to have been over long ago (except for vigilance about abortion rights, which was important to many of them). It seemed, by 2004, taken for granted that women could do what men could do and that men should be taking up a share of the housework (most of their husbands did). Most had not considered themselves feminists at any time in their lives, although nearly all remain passionately committed to the idea of equality and choice for women and tried to send their own children off into the world with a bedrock assumption about gender equality.

By age 43, most had acquired the things of life they felt they needed, and the majority said that they were financially secure. In their mid-50s, some worried about having saved enough for retirement but were otherwise uninterested in further material gain.

What continues to unite these women as a group is their common belief in choice. They bristle at the idea of coercion of any sort. People, they believe, especially women, ought to be free to choose their own way on their own terms. They eschew categorical statements, remain staunch in their refusal to impose their values on anyone else. These women live lives they chose, having taken advantage of the new freedoms to have a career or not, to marry or not, to have children or not. They made their own decisions about what it means to be a woman in this world. This book examines how they came to the choices they made, how they revised them along the way and what, for them, in late midlife, creates and signifies fulfillment.

The Research Project

How strange it must have seemed to these young women, back in 1972, when they received a phone call from me asking them to come and talk to me about their lives.[7] Back in those days, before all the concerns about privacy in universities, I was allowed to go through student lists and randomly select people for my study. I thumbed through cards (no computers then) and pulled out every 25th or 50th name. Hearing that I was studying women and that women had not been given much attention in psychology intrigued them—and I offered them each $10 for taking part, which was a nice bonus for college students at the time. Women's issues were gaining momentum on college campuses, and everyone was aware that a sea change was occurring in possibilities for women, so my project made sense to them.

They came to meet me with curiosity and some worry about who I was and what I would ask of them. But when they found me, just a few years older than they were, friendly and interested in them, most settled into the conversation. At the time, I could easily identify with each of them, and we were both highly engaged in the interview. Even then, these young women told me that they had shared things with me that they had never told anyone else. I was a "stranger on a train," and I seem to have remained so over the years.

I wrote about them, after disguising them fully, in my dissertation and in a published monograph which, some years later when I was a college professor, my students read. My students were captivated by the detailed cases and demanded that I tell them what became of these women. I had, of course, no idea. It was my students at Towson University, in 1983, who did the detective work to try to find these women again—and we succeeded in finding 34 of them who were willing to participate. (Women still routinely changed their last names when they married at that time, so, for those with very common last names, it was almost impossible to locate their relatives and thereby find them.) The group, now 33 years old, had spread geographically—across the United States and as far away as Italy. I was able to interview many in person. Others filled out lengthy open-ended questionnaires or recorded a tape in response to questions, both of which I could follow up with phone calls. At that time, I was more careful about thinking ahead to how I could find them in the future, and I easily located 30 of these 43-year-olds in the early '90s. At that point, I was teaching at Harvard and my graduate students did some of the interviewing, although I interviewed many myself. Again I relied on questionnaires, tapes, and phone calls for those I couldn't get to in person.

For this last round of interviews with women now in their mid-50s, I was determined to meet with each one in person. That took a long time, and I traveled all across the United States. Except for a few interviews I did belatedly through a video call[8] and one interview done by one of my Fielding University graduate students who lives in the same town as one of my participants, I managed to sit down with each of these women for at least 3 hours and hear about the development of her life since we were last in contact. It was important for me to see each woman in her own setting, to drive on the roads she travels, to sit in her house. A house, a setting, says a lot about who a woman is and what she has created as her nest. In some cases, we met in her office—or, as a last resort, in my hotel room if her home was not available for private talk.

Over the years, as I have talked about this study, many people have suspected that being in the study has strongly affected these women and that their participation therefore colors the lives I hear about. I don't believe this is so. When I called each woman to arrange an interview, there would usually be a brief pause when I said my name and then memory of who I am would click into place. "Oh, are you still doing this?" was the usual surprised, but warm, response. After *Revising Herself* was published in 1996, I had offered to send each woman a copy. This was a bit complicated by the fact that simply receiving this book in the mail could compromise confidentiality (i.e., "Why is someone sending you this book?" asked by a spouse or child), so not everyone asked for it. I didn't know who had read the book and who had not. So I began the interview by asking women about their experiences of being in the study, how it has affected them (if at all), and particularly if they read *Revising Herself* and had reactions they wished to share. Most acknowledged somewhat sheepishly that they didn't remember the book or even if they had read it or, if they had read it, what it said—as though I were a teacher asking for their homework. Some said, "Oh, I meant to read it before we talked, but I didn't find time." Only a few were interested enough in the study (or in what I had to say about them) to have engaged with the meaning I make of their lives.[9] They are occupied with their own meanings. Most did not remember the content of the prior interviews, but they did remember that they had liked talking to me. When I arrived, they all greeted me exceptionally warmly, as though I were a long lost friend, which is rather how I felt toward them. (For them, I appear for 3 hours or so every 10–12 years and then vanish. For me, they are an ongoing occupation as I spend hundreds of hours poring over their lives.) When I mentioned that some people asked me whether being in the study affected their lives, they laughed at the idea that they would make life decisions based on being in my study.[10]

The mid-50s interview was the most unstructured of all. I asked them to "bring me up to date on the years since I last talked to you." I thought that listening to them talk about what was most on their minds would give me the best clues as to how their identities evolved, and I was ready to ask about areas of life (work, relationships, health, political and religious views, etc.) that they may have omitted.

The narratives these women produced varied enormously. It was always interesting and important to note where they began their story because this reflected what was most central as they presented themselves to me anew. From there, their narration of the years went in various directions. Some women had many elements that mattered to them that they wanted to tell me about. There were some who got stuck in a particular preoccupation—a current worry about a child, for example—and everything seemed to circle back to that. As in the prior interview, I asked them for an outline of their whole life, organized into chapters, because I wanted to see how this changed over the years. Most of my participants had less interest in talking about this than about the present and more recent past. The distant past was clearly not something that they thought much about; the long story of how they got to where they are now seemed to them to carry less psychological weight than the short story that started more recently.

By and large and with some exceptions, these women are not very prone to self-reflection or pondering their own development. Mostly, they face forward rather than inward. They are not psychologists, and they don't think the way I do, always wanting to know how and why people are the way they are. Yet I think they enjoy the "stranger on the train" phenomenon, the chance to talk to an empathic, interested, nonjudgmental stranger who feels that their lives are worth chronicling. Some who have been in therapy told me that talking to me feels like talking to their therapist, although we both understand that I will say nothing therapist-like. But I *am* a therapist, and I listen like one.

Everyone seemed to trust that I can disguise them well enough so that no one can recognize them, but, of course, people can recognize themselves. I warned everyone that if they tell someone close to them that they are in the study, then they might be recognized. If I were to disguise that deeply, I would be distorting—and my topic is identity. Some have evidently shared my portraits of themselves with their husbands, but most keep the whole experience private.[11]

At the same time, I am well aware that it is impossible to depict another woman fully or to capture *all* the important aspects of her existence in terms that she would use. One cannot faithfully photograph the inner world. The portraits of these women I present are very much my renditions, based on what they have told me but organized through my own perspectives. I witness these lives through my own sensibilities as an upper middle class, Jewish professor, psychotherapist, wife, mother, (and recently) grandmother. I live an international life because my husband is Israeli, and I travel a great deal, doing work in several countries, but I feel profoundly American. I have always been passionate about my work, and my professional projects are an important part of my identity. My colleagues and friends, as well as my family, nourish me and are central to who I am.

I try not to judge the people I write about, and I am transparent about the observations and reactions that are mine rather than my participant's. I think I have discovered some truths about each of the women I have followed, but never the whole truth—as Debbie, one of the women you will meet, vociferously pointed out to me. I hope it is "truth" enough to enlighten us about the different life paths that these educated women follow.

Identity

I have been tracking identity formation in women—but identity is not something that one can describe directly. First of all, identity is a conceptual idea that refers to the integration of a felt sense of continuity as a person and aspects of one's place in the world that one has chosen or been given by others. So how could I have these women tell me about their identities? The lead-off question I chose at the very beginning of the study in 1972 was "If there is someone you wanted to know you, what sorts of things would you tell about yourself?" Their answers to this question were my first important insights into women's identity—but I didn't know it at the time. Most of them said something like, "I'd tell them about my friends and the people who are important to me." This is not the answer I was hoping for. I wanted to hear about what I then thought was real identity—their occupational and ideological commitments. This is what Erikson had theorized identity was about. In 1972, with the Women's Movement clamoring for equal opportunity in the world for women, I certainly didn't want to find out that women's identity was rooted in the people in their lives. But now, after following these women and studying women's identity for 44 years, I have come to understand their response differently. Indeed, most women's identity is grounded in relationship to others, but I have a much broader understanding of what relationship means and how identity is bound to these relationships.

From the very beginning, then, these women have been teaching me about how identity is formed and how it unfolds. I have been understanding these lessons in the context of the work of Erik Erikson. When I began this study back in the late 1960s, I was firmly allied with Erikson as a theorist because his concept of identity seemed to me to be central to psychological life as I experienced and understood it. Identity marks who we are in the world and links our inner self to our outer world. But Erikson never pinned down his concept of identity into some concrete, definable terms; rather, he depicted it through case studies and intensive psychobiographies that demonstrated both what identity might be and how it functions in a life. All of his case studies and biographies, however, concerned men—and that distressed me. Women, I was certain, formed and lived out identities, but differently from men. My project was to investigate how identity was created and revised over time in women.

Identity is both a psychological structure and a set of contents within that structure.[12] As an internal structure, identity is the integration of all the important elements of the person we are in the world, from the most public to the mainly private. As Erikson developed his concept of identity, he stressed its synthetic function—identity putting together in some unique combination the elements of who we are. Identity subsumes identifications, talents, roles, goals, psychological defenses, biological necessities, emotional responsiveness, and accidents of personal history, and it bridges these sometimes contradictory elements into some larger pattern. Identity, once formed, is the ineffable internal structure that directs the actualization of goals and values. It is a sense of who we *are*.

Another function of the identity structure is to preserve a sense of continuity over the life course. We trust that we will wake up today as the same person we were yesterday. Many people, after a great loss, report waking up feeling that they don't know who they are—once the reality of the loss comes back to them. Barring such experiences, we generally take for granted that our lives and selves are continuous.

The achievement of the identity stage is a sense of what Erikson calls "fidelity," that is, faithfulness to certain commitments and the abrogation of other possibilities. Identity choice always involves giving up some potentialities in favor of others. I chose an academic life rather than a career in business, and my fidelity to intellectual values makes me wary of the mercantilism seeping into the academy. This is an example of my own fidelity to certain values and of how my identity as a professor goes beyond the name of my role.

Change in identity structure reflects change in how one comes to respond to or evaluate input from the world about one's psychosocial identity. This is the experience of "I have changed as a person." We may recognize that we now have different goals, different values, or different ways of positioning ourselves in the world. An open and flexible structure is receptive to alternative views of the self and might try to integrate them. A rigid, closed structure will screen out discrepant responses with vehement denial, closing off possibilities for an enlarged view of the self. An example: A manager considers herself empathic and caring of her employees. If her identity structure is flexible, she will be able to consider feedback about times when she has been harsh, acknowledge that she might have impatient aspects to herself—and perhaps modify her behavior. If her identity structure is rigid, she will just become angry and blame others for misunderstanding her. If her identity structure is unintegrated, she will merely try to adopt whatever behavior is acceptable in this workplace ("I'll do whatever is required with no implication for who I am as a person"). This is but one small example of how the flexibility of the identity structure has consequences in even the daily experience of the world.

We can also look at identity in psychosocial terms, as a set of contents. In this sense, identity is a location in a personal universe. Identity marks our place in ongoing narratives that are larger than we are, mapping where we fit in the overall scheme of things. Depending on the context, different aspects of our identity are salient. When I am working in China, I am taken in by the people I meet there as a "Westerner." I had never thought of myself in this way before—as an American, certainly, but not as a "Westerner." It took me a while to understand that most Chinese don't differentiate Western people. It isn't meaningful to them whether I come from the United States or Norway—much as Americans often don't differentiate Asian nationalities. If I am among psychologists, it becomes mandatory to announce what kind of psychologist I am or what theoretical paradigms I am allied with, if I have a clinical practice or not and, if so, who I see. If I am traveling and meet someone from Baltimore, they want to know which neighborhood I reside in. All of these elements mark something about me; they locate me in the larger scheme of things relevant to the person with whom I am interacting. They place me in a world of meanings. One of the women I interviewed found it disconcerting that I did not immediately know the significance of her living in Huntsville rather than the neighboring town of Monroe because the people she usually associates with simply *know* how people from Huntsville differ from Monrovians. While the differences were difficult for her to detail for me, whatever they were explained why it was unthinkable for her take a job she had been offered in Monroe. In her world, her decision made perfect sense, but it was hard to move her knowledge into my context without explaining to me subtle differences that were important for how she locates herself in her world.

Everyone builds a personal universe in which meanings are apparent and anchor identity, and people depend on that identity being recognizable and articulated with others who have shared meanings. Some aspects of identity are ascribed as people learn over time how others view them, always in the terms salient in that social sphere. Much of adolescence is focused on discovering how one can be seen by others—as smart, pretty, or funny, for example. These attributions can be painful when they seem to be fixedly other than we wish to be. As we will see in some of the cases, being labeled as a "fat child" can persist as part of identity even long after the woman has become thin.

Identity, then, has many moving parts. It melds multiple aspects of the inner sense of self with the ways in which one is viewed and recognized by one's social world, maintaining some consistency over time. Identity, Erikson said, is the integrator that moves one toward wholeness.[13] In my kaleidoscope metaphor, identity is the overall pattern that results from the arrangement of the elements.

In the modern world, with its many freedoms, coherence of identity is no longer assured by the defining force of collective identities. Integration of one's *identities* into an *identity* therefore becomes the task of the individual. Identity construction involves, among other things, locating oneself, through choice, in an array of communities—nation, class, sex, family, professional guilds, or even imagined communities. Whole identities are not available "off the shelf," so to speak. Creating an identity, then, is a process continually open to change.[14]

Erikson located the "crisis" in identity in late adolescence, a time when developing internal needs for independence from the family of childhood meshes with the social demands for choosing ways of being in the world. Young people of this age leave the rhythms of familiarity that constitute home, and the college environment offers a panoply of other possibilities. Erikson noted that complex societies make available what he called a "moratorium" period in which young people are given a time-out to try on possibilities without the social world taking their choices too seriously. College environments are ideally suited for such a moratorium period. College students are given license to experiment—with different fields of study, with different groups of friends, with different political stances, with different ways of conducting relationships, and with sometimes extreme behavior. Students are exposed to ways of being and thinking that challenge what had been taken for granted. The social world broadens to include different subgroups of people than had been available before, increasing the possibilities of finding acceptance that may not have been offered earlier. Some people can insulate themselves from being too much in contact with what is new, either by seeking out like-minded others or simply keeping largely to themselves. Others actively explore, reaching for new experiences, adventuring into the as yet unknown. But this period of moratorium ends, usually with college graduation (although the moratorium period seems to be extending today into the late 20s). The young person is then expected to declare some commitments that will anchor her (or him) in the world and proclaim the place she will stake for herself in the adult world.

Stages of Adult Development

Identity as a "crisis" period moves from center stage at the close of adolescence and gives way to the challenges of adulthood, the later stages of "intimacy versus isolation," "generativity versus stagnation" and "integrity versus despair" in Erikson's model of development. Identity, however, continues to evolve and influence these later stages while, in a mutual patterning, intimacy, generativity, and integrity all have implications for identity.

In Erikson's model of adult development, resolutions of the identity stage scaffold the next stage: the search for intimacy, the making of a deep commitment to another person with whom to share one's life. Having a sense of who one is and wants to be in life leads to a need to partner, and the society also presses with this expectation. Successful resolution of the intimacy stage yields the ability to love, to experience mutual devotion and respect toward a partner or selected others. The "I" enlarges to the "We." Because Erikson's model is often understood to mean that one has to know who one is before one can commit oneself to another in a mutually interdependent way, I came to this study with a question about whether this is also true for women. How, I wondered, do intimacy and identity intersect in women?[15]

Following resolution of intimacy issues, around midlife, generativity comes to the fore in Erikson's model. At this stage, adults turn their attention away from the self toward care of the next generation. This can mean care of children or the next generation more broadly construed, such as mentoring younger people, contributing to one's community, or taking care of the environment for those yet to be born. The negative pole of this stage is stagnation and self-absorption. Erikson and his wife, Joan Erikson, enlarged this idea of stagnation to include the exclusion of others different from oneself or from one's focus of care, as well as the use of power alone for regimenting others. The virtue derived from successful resolution of the stage of generativity is that of "care." If these stages of identity, intimacy, and generativity are successfully traversed, the later life stage of integrity versus despair is resolved in favor of a sense that one's life has had meaning.

Although each of these issues—intimacy, generativity, and integrity—is the focus of progressive life stages, identity continues its influence, shaping and being reshaped. Identity influences how one is generative, for example, and how one is generative becomes part of identity. Each later stage involves a reformulation of identity as one responds to the demands and rewards of each developmental era.[16] Although there are sometimes dramatic transformations of identity, more often identity evolves slowly. Over time, identity broadens and deepens as the identity structure subsumes newly developed or newly realized aspects of the person.[17] Difficulties in resolving the challenges of the identity stage, however, may presage or even create difficulties in managing the ensuing stages of adult development.[18]

Identity and Narrative

Erikson's concept of identity has eluded those who would measure it. It is a dynamic integration of self and social world, in time, and manifests itself in a variety of ways, none very linear or scalable. No one can simply state what her or his identity is, although people can talk about how they locate themselves in the world in terms of group affiliation, actions, and beliefs. Newer scholarship has understood that identity is organized as a story, a plotline that relates our various ways of being in the world and charts its course from the past to the present and projects us into the future. Identity reflects the meanings we are making of our lives, our sense of unity and purpose, and this is expressed in narrative form.[19] As Kierkegaard famously said, we live life forward and understand it backward. Our life narrative, which encompasses our identity, both directs us forward and provides us a (more or less) coherent look back. Living involves continually constructing and reconstructing stories, revising the plot as new events are added, without knowing the outcome. Life progresses—the self and identity are not finalized[20]—until our story ends and others fashion a story of who we were.

We are each the central character in a life story we are creating and living, and our identity marks and reflects who we are in that narrative.[21] As we would tell a story or read a novel, we describe the central character in terms of roles, goals, feelings, wishes, important relationships, values, and significant events that might explain how the main character became who she is. We would expect the story to have links between past and present and to point to some as yet unrealized future. The unity of the individual life resides in a construction of its narrative, a form in which hopes, dreams, despairs, doubts, plans, and emotions are all phrased. Identity, wrote the sociologist Anthony Giddens, is "the capacity to keep a particular narrative going."[22]

Viewing identity as a narrative marks its dynamic nature. It is a process, not an entity. Identity, as an ongoing story, evolves to encompass what comes into a life and omits what no longer seems at play in that life.

The changes we undergo are metabolized slowly so that we preserve the illusion of sameness and stability in who we are. Nowhere is this process more apparent than when we view the changes in life narratives that have taken

place in these women over the 35 years I have followed them. The present creates the past as these women revise their life stories to be consistent with the
selves they have become.

I laugh when, digging through some old boxes in my attic, I find a feature
story about me in the school newspaper when I was in the 8th grade. I said
I wanted to be a psychologist. I laugh because what idea could I possibly have
had in the 8th grade of what a psychologist was? I never met a psychologist
until I got to college. And I know that I wanted to be a lot of other things in
between the 8th grade and my senior year in college. But I could narrate this
as a lifelong interest in people and why they do what they do—that would be
true. I can connect these dots and change my story to "I always wanted to be
a psychologist." Like most oversimplified life stories, it would be both true
and not true.

Identity is embedded in a multilayered life story. It is a story of "who
I am"—but it is told under very particular circumstances. Although our identities are lived out in storied form, the story as a whole is seldom put into
words. Rather, we narrate episodes in the course of our lives, sometimes surprised when people who know us well respond with something like, "That is
quite unlike you" when the episode seems not to fit with their sense of who
we are. Such a response usually compels us to, at least privately, reconcile the
episode with our ongoing sense of the narrative we are living.

To say that identity is organized narratively, though, doesn't imply that
people "have" a life story that can be downloaded like a file on a computer.
The synthetic work of identity is largely unconscious, holding all of the parts
together, although we can usually create some chain of causation if called
upon to do so (as in "how come you did *that*!?"). People construct a more
elaborate life story for someone else only rarely, and this is always tailored
to the moment of the telling. We might tell our life story in segments to a
new friend—in segments because few people have the patience to listen to an
extended account; we may create one for a job interview—only including what
may appear favorable in the eyes of the evaluator. Yet we have an internal life
story that we don't tell, a set of memories of experiences that are meaningfully
linked to one another so that we have a sense of having started somewhere,
lived through inner and outer events, and arrived at where we are, headed
somewhere else. Life stories vary among people as to how much they reflect
unity, coherence, and sense of purpose[23] in a life. Some people construct life
stories, for themselves and for others, with clearly marked paths, as though
the present were the inevitable outcome of the past, where all that led up to
this moment in time was prologue. Others have a fragmented life story, a
story with threads that never unite, as we will see in some of the Drifters,
and its fragmentation may or may not be recognized by the narrators, who
may not expect that their lives "add up" or have consistent themes. And many
people's stories lie between these extremes, with aspects of the story that have

coherent threads over time and others that have important subplots that seem to belong to some other story, that are not integrated into a central narrative.

Only in adolescence does a person begin to construct internally a story of her or his life.[24] The need to do so comes with a recognition of one's individuality, that one is the way one is and has the life one has for *reasons* having to do with personal endowments that differentiate us from others and social and economic circumstances that position us in particular ways. As childhood comes to a close, there are choices to be made, and the life story emerges to reflect and account for those choices, which grow in number and scope over time. The self is no longer taken for granted. We expect ourselves (and others expect us) to be able to give an account of ourselves, to explain—at least to ourselves—why we are the way we are, why we live the way we do, at various levels of depth of understanding.

Indeed, most of the women I have followed begin the *vital* part of their story some time in high school with a description of who they were and how they changed when they went to college. This period in late adolescence felt to them like the period of birth for the current self, acknowledging elements of who their parents were, the context in which they were raised only as it affected the self of that age. Childhood seemed to them to be simply prologue—for most of them, marked nebulously as "happy." Only in college did the real drama of identity begin.

As William James suggested long ago, people are more likely to have multiple stories of themselves than a single unified one. This I could see clearly as my participants momentarily sifted through their various senses of themselves to determine where to begin their narrative—with the self as a worker in the world or the self embedded in a family? Most women gave a brief "introduction" indicating that both of these realms were central in constructing their experience of themselves, that is, their overarching identity.

A culture, located in history, determines what narratives are possible for living out. Templates of possibility are considered master narratives, that is, social narratives within which one must embed and elaborate one's own life history. (In today's world, for instance, being an exorcist is not understandable because the master narrative of demons and dybbuks has been relegated to earlier times.) The women of my study came into adulthood when the master narratives for women were changing and new ones were not yet firmly in place. This gave them freedom to create their own life narratives—their identities—in creative ways, in contrast to the fading master narrative of a woman as only homemaker and mother that they had been raised with. Although there are shared understandings within a generation, people react differently to the times, so we can't assume that everyone in a cohort is alike. The life story, however, always takes account of the master narratives in the background and illustrates how these are subjectively integrated (or not) within personal experience.[25]

Identities are always unique to the individual. Identity is a very *particular* puzzle because each person has different elements to combine. Yet, if we think about types of identity configurations, we can witness commonalities and differences across individuals.

The Identity Categories

Jim Marcia, in 1966, found an insightful way to access Erikson's elusive concept of identity, and his paradigm has led to hundreds of studies in psychology since then.[26] His reading of Erikson noted that there were two fundamental aspects to the formation of identity in late adolescence. The young person (in industrialized society) is challenged by the alternatives available to choose a way of being in the world, to affirm what she will stand for as she takes her place in the adult world. This could be about occupation (what she will DO) or ideology (what she will BELIEVE). Late adolescents can make these commitments with more or less exploration of alternatives. If we are to think of exploration and commitment as two axes of the identity formation period, reasoned Marcia, then we can sort late adolescents into four groups: those who have made commitments following a period of exploration (Identity Achievements/Pathmakers); those who made commitments without exploration, carrying forward childhood goals and beliefs (Foreclosures/Guardians); those who were still in a moratorium period, still exploring (Moratoriums/Searchers); and those without commitments who seemed not to be exploring or trying to make commitments (Diffusions/Drifters).[27]

Identity Status Categories

(assessed as seniors in college)

		EXPLORATION	
		Yes	No
COMMITMENT	Yes	**Pathmakers** Identity Achievers	**Guardians** Foreclosures
	No	**Searchers** Moratoriums	**Drifters** Diffusions

I came to Marcia's work toward the end of my graduate school years in 1969. More than any other theorist, Erikson inspired me. Only he, at the time, seemed able to analyze the psychology of the individual squarely within a social context. But all of his case examples and psychobiographies were about men. Indeed, there was no psychology of women anywhere to be found at the time,[28] and I was determined to study and learn about women. Marcia's paradigm for identity categories seemed to ideally suit my purposes, and I could look at how women came to their identity choices in these times of social change.

Marcia's strategy was to interview college students and ask them about their choices and how they made them. Then he assessed the degree to which they had explored options and made commitments. He asked about occupation and (religious and political) ideology, the two focal points of Erikson's concept of identity. But there was a problem. When he created these categories with men, the four groups were distinct on a range of other measures, indicating that the interview-based classifications identified people with statistically significant differences in personality and behavioral characteristics.[29] But, alas, this approach didn't work with women.

What was important in assessing these identity categories is that the late adolescents be exploring and making commitments in areas that were important to them, that they prized in their lives. Therefore, if someone was uninterested in religion (or politics) and had little religious (or political) background, religion (or politics) was not given weight in assessing where he best fit in the categories. So what was central for women at the time in forging an identity? Clearly, decisions about whether and how to take a place in the occupational realm mattered to most women, as did decisions about religion in that most of them had been raised in fairly religious homes. Few had strong political ideologies; most had none at all. But assessment of identity status with these categories alone did not produce distinct groups. To solve this dilemma, one of Marcia's students, Susi Schenkel, reasoned that what challenged women at the time in terms of values was making decisions in regard to sexuality and relationships. Most women of the time had been raised with the idea that one must be a virgin at marriage and that not to be so was a source of shame and stigma—and great disappointment to one's parents. Women came to college with this stricture pounded into them and found on campuses an increasing pulse of sexual freedom. Sorting out how they would relate to the possibility of sexual encounters became a major test of their capacity to explore and decide—and the necessity to come to a set of values in regard to sexuality challenged them all equally. When Schenkel added to the identity interview questions about sexual standards and values, weighing this in with the indicators of exploration and commitment in the other areas to determine in which category a woman best fit, the categories for women became consistent.[30] I was able to make use of her modification of the identity status interview to determine the category placements in this study. (Later, the interview was expanded to assess values in relationships for both men and women[31].)

Over the years, I became dissatisfied not with the four categories, but with their names. In 1992, when I published *Revising Herself,* I changed the names of the categories to make them less pejorative. So I speak of Pathmakers rather than Identity Achievers because identity is not something one "achieves," but one can make one's own path; Guardians rather than Foreclosures because possibility may be foreclosed, but it is in the service of preserving what was; Searchers rather than Moratoriums, so as not to confuse the name of the status with the social permission and to indicate that what people are *doing* is searching; and Drifters rather than Diffusions because, although identity is diffuse, what these people are doing is drifting.

Following Marcia's model, I classified each of the women while they were seniors in college into one of the four categories. I am aware that any classification of people always involves injustice. People are broader and more complex than any typology can contain. I realize that the pathways I detail are imperfect and that people do not go along them in lockstep fashion. Yet they offer us a helpful way of organizing the ways in which women go through the years from late adolescence through adulthood and a means of thinking about different trajectories that women follow as they grow and develop. And their meaningfulness holds up over time. Indeed, the women who have read my work agree that they are placed in the right category, even if is not a category in which they might have wished to be included. One might think of these groupings as prototypes rather than rigid categories, and the women's stories are illustrative of the various ways these prototypes could be enacted in real life.

Having worked with these four categories for decades, I ask myself if they are still meaningful—and I think they are. I'm not sure on which areas of life one would best sort young people today, given the changes in the social times, but I do think that the categories reflect profound and enduring differences in psychological structure that presage adult lives. Even today, as always, young people grow up in families where they are ascribed identities and are, in late adolescence, given the opportunity to explore possibilities with the expectation that they will make commitments to ways of living their lives. That hasn't changed.

The Plan of the Book

I continue to organize the presentation of these lives within the original four groups even though people have changed categories over time. The Searchers, of course, were in a state of flux as they passed out the college gates, and we would expect them to change categories, either to make commitments along self-directed paths, to take up earlier ways of being, or to drift. Many women who, as college seniors, were in the other categories—the Pathmakers, Guardians, and Drifters—changed categories, and how this change occurred is part of the story and illustrates the differing courses these first identity formations may take over time. I treat the original categories, assigned as college seniors, as the starting places of adult identity structure. I then try to analyze, within each group, the various permutations of each identity trajectory as exemplified by individual women.

The life stories I present are lengthy, drawn from extensive interviews at each time period. These are, of course, *my* versions of these women's lives, based on life stories they created for me under particular circumstances. I have shaped the material to explore the questions of identity and adult development that interest me, smoothing out some of the edges so that patterns can appear in sharper focus. I organize the presentation by person rather than in snippets and vignettes so that the reader can see each life as a whole, as much as possible. I aim to find some larger truths about identity and adult development in women, making use of what these women have told me about their unique lives. I hope to trace the evolution of the eager, hopeful young woman to the mature, life-experienced woman she becomes. Each has a different history and has created a different world in which to live, but each world is uniquely her own, shared (and constructed) with those whom she joined.

Although the disguises are solid enough that no one will be able to recognize any of these women, each will be able to identify the portrait of herself. I hope they will each feel that I have captured some truth, even if not the whole truth, about her life.

As each woman has highly particular pieces to fit together in assembling an identity, the details are important. Where someone grew up, in what kind of family, with what quality of relationships to her parents, to her siblings, if any, what her experiences in college were like—these form the soil in which identity takes shape. Identity is an internal process with external markings. I could write about what someone did (career, marriage, children, other activities—like an obituary), but that would only be the public story. Identity is also how a woman thinks about herself and her world, how she makes choices, how she feels about herself in her private reflections, her outlook on life and the qualities of those with whom she peoples her life. Identity lies in the specific, not the general. I try to draw a portrait not only of the woman but also of the world she feels herself to be living in. Identity is manifest in voice; we sense a person's place in the world by her speech, by the words she chooses, by what she notices around her. Therefore, I try to use the actual words of each of the women as much as is feasible.

One other thing about what I am about to present: As I was interviewing two of these women in their mid-50s, I discovered that they had daughters, college seniors, the exact age that they were when I first interviewed them. I asked for permission to contact their daughters, recognizing that this would compromise the woman's anonymity. Both agreed, and both daughters were willing to talk to me about their own identity development. It was a rare opportunity for a researcher. So I include in this book this small window into how the identity of the mother (one a Pathmaker, the other a Drifter) impacts the identity formation of the daughter. For me, the opportunity to do once more an identity interview with a 21-year-old also gave me the sense that the fundamental challenges of late adolescent identity formation haven't changed all that much in 35 years, although the content sounds a bit different from the issues of 1972.

Notes

1. Some reviewers criticized me for not having racial diversity in this study. In 1972, there were few black women in college, yet two did appear in the original randomly drawn group. One died in her mid-20s, and the other I could not find in 1983. In current times, racial difference has come to signify diversity, but other aspects of identity mark crucial differences among us. Among these women, differences in class, ethnic background, and geographical location provide enormous diversity, in my view.

2. Gail Collins' (2009) book *When Everything Changed* documents in detail the social changes of the periods I cover in this book.

3. At age 33, 15 were married to their first husband and three had divorced and remarried. Of the rest, nine had never married, one was a widow, and two were divorced.

4. Two had law degrees, one an MD, one a PhD, one an MBA, one a master's degree in library science, and four had master's degrees in education.

5. According to Census Bureau statistics compiled in 1992, 24% of all white women between the ages of 40 and 44 who earned a bachelor's degree did not have children. For women with graduate or professional degrees, 32% were childless. These figures indicate that my sample, in which 36% have no children, somewhat overrepresents childless women in comparison to the base population (see Bacha, 1992).

6. Of the three not in committed relationships, one was a lesbian in an ambivalent and uncommitted relationship, uncertain about whether she might really be bisexual; one had never married; and one, who had been among those married at age 33, was divorced but engaged. All the rest of the women who had been married at age 33 remained married to the same partners except one who had divorced and remarried in this decade and another who had divorced at age 40 and was engaged at the time of this interview.

7. Please see Appendix A for details of the sampling and procedure.

8. By that time, 3 of these women were in their early 60s, which I note in the case studies.

9. Debbie is an exception to this, and I discuss her and her response to being in the study in the "Drifter Who Created a Path" chapter.

10. George Vaillant, who has conducted an even longer study of Harvard men, is also frequently asked about the effects on his participants of participating in the study

throughout their lives. He reports that he responds, "Alas, if only changing the course of human lives were so easy" (Vaillant, 2003, p. 35).

11. In two cases, I interviewed a woman and her daughter. Of course, they could recognize each other. Each gave me permission to use the portrait of her that I created, understanding that her daughter (or mother) would see it.

12. Many psychologists have written extensively and thoughtfully about identity from an Eriksonian point of view, too many to adequately reference here. For current reviews, see especially Kroger (2004) and Kroger, Martinussen, and Marcia (2010).

13. Much of Erikson's thinking about identity development in adulthood is in unpublished writings summarized by Hoare (2001) and also Kroger (2014).

14. Kraus (2006). Indeed, the current scholarly focus on intersectionality recognizes the multiple and shifting character of identity.

15. Erikson's paper, "Womanhood and the Inner Space," published in 1968, seems to suggest that the crux of a woman's identity is the partner she chooses (i.e., who she admits to the "inner space"). In this paper, much maligned by feminists, Erikson also recognizes that options at the time were limited for women and that this might only be the case until social opportunities for women broadened. Still, this paper led to all of Erikson's work being largely repudiated by feminist psychologists. Some research using questionnaires has demonstrated that the epigenetic progression of identity to intimacy holds for both men and women (see Kroger [2014] for a summary of this research), particularly in that those diffuse in identity are less likely to resolve issues of intimacy.

16. See Marcia (2010) for elaboration of this point. See also Erikson (1980) and especially Erikson, Erikson, and Kivnick (1989) for a discussion of how later stages are influenced by earlier ones.

17. This idea was also central to Jung's ideas about adult individuation. See Flum (1994) and Marcia (2010) for further discussion of the evolving nature of identity. Research has also demonstrated that identity becomes more stable over time (McLean, 2008; Stewart, Ostrove, & Helson, 2001; Whitbourne, Sneed, & Sayer, 2009; Zucker, Ostrove, & Stewart, 2002).

18. Marcia and Josselson (2013).

19. See McAdams (1997, 2001); McLean, Pasupathi, and Pals (2007); McAdams and McLean (2013); and McLean, Pasupathi, and Pals (2007). There is a vast literature on narrative and identity, some of which is reviewed in Lieblich and Josselson (2013) and Josselson and Lieblich (2001). Among the works I consider most important are Bruner (1990, 2003) and Polkinghorne (1988). See also Singer (2004), Kraus (2006), and Brockmeier and Carbaugh (2001).

20. The work of Mikhail Bakhtin (1981) develops the idea of the ever-evolving unfinalizable self.

21. Dan McAdams has developed this idea in a number of works (McAdams, 1988, 1997, 2013).

22. Giddens (1991, p. 64).

23. Scholars differ over how "good" this story has to be in terms of its unity and purpose and whether life stories require coherence. There is also recognition of the ways in which life narratives, like identities, are jointly constructed in relationship to important people and to social forces. See, in particular, Bruner (2003), Gergen and Gergen (2001), McAdams (1997), and Linde (2001).

24. McAdams (2013).

25. See Cohler and Hoestler (2003) for elaboration of this point.

26. There have been many integrative reviews of these studies (Kroger, 2003; Kroger & Marcia, 2011; Kroger et al., 2010).

27. I explain later why I changed the names of these statuses, but I give the original names when I refer to research that used them. To avoid confusion, I give them both here.

28. The exception to this statement was a book by Judith Bardwick that was largely rooted in biology. There was also some psychoanalytic writing about women but, being heavily colored by trying to elaborate Freud's penis envy concept, I didn't find it very useful. At the time, during the late 1960s and early '70s, I did have many arguments with psychoanalysts who wanted to dismiss women's striving for equality and the possibility of achieving in the world as penis envy.

29. Marcia (1966, 1993).

30. Schenkel and Marcia (1972). Research in the 1970s, however, showed that whereas for men Identity Achievement and Moratorium, the exploring statuses, seemed to be the "healthiest," for women, it was Identity Achievement and Foreclosure, the stable statuses. This suggested that, for women of this generation, stability rather than exploration predicted psychological well-being.

31. For a review of the assessment and patterns of identity status in adolescence and adulthood, see Fadjukoff, Pulkkinen & Kokko (2005).

2

The Pathmakers

Upon graduating from college, Betty was quite certain she wanted a career as a physical therapist. Growing up in an athletic family in northern California, herself a championship skier, she was interested in the body and how it functioned. Briefly, she had considered a career in medicine, but she was impatient to get on with things, didn't want to spend so much time in school. She was happy about her choice, looked forward to being able to help others return to good physical functioning, and had completed a demanding training program. She described herself as a person of many interests and only worried that she might eventually get bored in any one profession. Yet she felt confident that she could always find something else interesting to do. Through a period of exploration, Betty had staked out her independence from her parents and gave up the Catholicism of her family. In this, she had been much influenced by a charismatic professor who challenged everyone's beliefs, questioning many of the values Betty had always taken as universal truths. Intellectually, she felt windows opening in her mind. At the end of the process of arguing with him—both in the classroom and in her mind, Betty stoically gave up her belief in God and attempted to define her life in terms of feeling responsible for herself. It was wrenching to no longer pray to God for help but to come to feel in charge of her own fate. Along with this, she began to experiment sexually, which felt to her like "a tremendous breakthrough." For a time, she slept with anyone with whom she felt "a magnetic pull," rationalizing that "it's part of life, so why pass it up?" But when she met Dennis early in her senior year of college, she devised yet another perspective on her behavior. She began to worry that she had been promiscuous and was besieged by guilt. As she and Dennis came to care deeply about each other, Betty reworked her understanding of her college years. Perhaps, she thought, what she had been seeking all along, without realizing it, was a committed relationship. Perhaps sexual freedom wasn't so valuable or, at least, wasn't valuable for her. Sex with caring, she decided, suited her better.

By the end of college, Betty was standing firmly on her own ground as she looked at her self-chosen path. She was planning a life with Dennis in which they would both have careers but would center their lives in their shared enjoyment of sports and the outdoors. Eventually, she hoped, they would raise a family.

Like the other Pathmakers, Betty had authored an identity on her own terms. Unlike the Guardians, the Pathmakers did not claim the authority of the past or the counsel of their parents as the underpinning of their choice. They had done the psychological work of independence and crafted an identity out of what they felt they were and wished to be. They had taken the step of belonging to themselves. As they approached adulthood at the end of college, the Pathmakers seemed to be blazing a trail through uncharted territory. They carried with them the ties and talents of their past, but they faced forward, surveying the terrain, picking a path. At each step, they paused to consider. What are the choices here, where would I like to go? What is possible? If the underbrush is too thick there, I may not be able to go that way, but here I may be able to carve my route. And I must think about what I am carrying with me. Perhaps I could lighten my load, but there are some things I don't want to be without. In this manner, they made their way. Their path was not necessarily a revolutionary path or even, often, a highly original one, but it was clearly their own.

Within psychological theory, the Pathmaker identity style in late adolescence has been considered to be the most developmentally advanced: these are people who are "on time" according to the developmental clock. But we have known little about what happens to such people later in life. What characterized the Pathmakers at the end of college was their capacity to integrate aspects of themselves with their growing understanding of their world as they were both finding and creating it. This was an often silent cartography, deeply internal, partly unconscious.

Despite their differences in personality and the differences in their life choices, women who were Pathmakers as college seniors developed into adulthood along similar psychological paths. Entering adulthood, identity for these women continued to be an act of charting and balancing, stepping up to new challenges, backing off from what was too daunting. What they added at each turning determined what might be possible in the next step, one road leading to the next, leaving the other roads behind. Having made a path for themselves, they widened and extended it, planted aspects of themselves within it, for a time investing most of their energy in one part of it (while tending the other parts), later moving to focus in another region, all the while aware of what may lay beyond, of how they might enlarge what they were creating. Sometimes they stood still for a time, the better to know where they were. Yet they continued to look ahead, following an internal compass, picking their way with great care.

These are women who were confident and clear as college seniors—they scored at the high end of psychological tests of autonomy and self-esteem. All of the five women who remained Pathmakers from college to late midlife had attended a state university, with most working to contribute to their education. While they all seemed to enjoy talking to me about their lives, they were not very internally focused (unlike the Searchers), electing to work toward a goal rather than to examine their feelings. Self-analysis in itself was not very appealing to them. They were more oriented to action or to choice.[1] Many were rather uncomfortable with their emotional experience and did not linger long with it, preferring to present to themselves and to the world a rational front, a sense of self in control of matters. Unlike the Guardians, they experienced anxiety and guilt, the emotional runoff of taking their lives in their own hands, but they had a variety of means to defend against these feelings, to keep these feelings from overwhelming them or inhibiting their capacity to act. They made changes in increments. Theirs are odysseys of slow and progressive change rather than lives of turmoil or wrenching inner drama.

Over the years that I have followed these women, I found that they have grown into centered and capable women at midlife and beyond. They have become busy women, engaged in their lives, leaving only occasional moments for introspection or rumination. They were buffeted by the elements while they moved along their paths—most have been rocked by fairly strong winds; yet most held to their course, integrating the wind along with everything else. They made compromises along the way, but most ended up feeling that, in the end, they arrived where they had intended to go—even though their lives in their mid-50s are lives they could never have imagined at the end of college.

Five[2] of the women I classified as Pathmakers in college still, in their mid-fifties, continue to follow paths of their own crafting. All undertook new periods of exploration where they once again sifted through options and then chose anew. In the life histories of these women, we see the continual process of identity revision toward fulfillment in their 50s. They remain committed to the essentials of their path in life, although it may have undergone many turnings since they started out. At present, all of these women work full-time in professions or as managers (except Betty who works part-time). They vary in how close their careers are to the center of their lives. All are married (two to second husbands); four have children. Among them, they have created lives quite different from one another but alike in that each in her own way has mapped a life course that is uniquely hers.

Betty

When I met her in college, I was puzzled by Betty. She had strong opinions and seemed confident on the one hand, but she laughed anxiously throughout the interview, as though talking about herself seriously was an unfamiliar thing to do. Her interview was very long and rambling. While she seemed to relish the opportunity to talk about herself, each time she approached something emotional, she would veer away. I felt she didn't want to let me end the interview and, at the same time, didn't want to disclose too much about what was going on inside her.

The eldest of five sisters, Betty described a family life centered on the outdoors and physical activity. Her father, who had graduated from college, was a physical education teacher, and, when Betty was 8, her parents bought and began to run an all-year children's camp in Colorado where the family lived. There were always a lot of children and animals around, and family life was focused on outdoor activities. This, though, had its dark side, and one of Betty's few allusions to problems or disappointments was that her mother, who had four younger children and was busy with the camp, simply had little time for her. There was no one to "go to" for anything that troubled her. When Betty was 16, she was having "a lot of emotional problems" and developed a chronic cough that no one could diagnose, so her parents sent her to live with her aunt in Arizona. She said that this whole episode was "traumatic" for her father. If she had an "emotional problem," this would mean he hadn't fulfilled his proper role. She had been known as "Jesse's daughter" in their town because he was the well-known physical education teacher, so her difficulties caused him some shame. But Betty didn't linger long on this story. Clearly, she had learned to suppress her feelings.

Betty told me that had always felt sorry for her mother who hadn't had a chance to develop own professional interests because her children came so fast. Although Betty agreed that it was important to be at home with preschool children, she wanted a career as well.

Betty's steps toward independence centered on her giving up her belief in God, which she said had been "a security blanket" and defining an "essence" to her spirituality based in nature. The other was her taking responsibility for her sexuality—but this began with a rape. Early in college, "sex was forced on me" and she decided that she should go ahead and do it with someone she could enjoy it with. "If you fall off a horse you should get back on it," she said, so she decided to sleep with whoever she enjoyed being with. "When you're brought up as a Catholic, it's difficult, but it's a tremendous breakthrough." Once she was engaged to Dennis, though, her standards changed. She told me that it is hard for her sometimes to control her feelings toward other men, and this sometimes makes her doubt her feelings toward her fiancé. In line with this, she worried that marriage would "lock me in" and this frightened her.

Dennis, though, was the central person in her life at the end of college. "We grew up in totally different worlds. He grew up poor and caring for an invalid mother after his father left—he grew up very fast." She described him as, like her, very "outdoors-y." He had been in the drug scene for a while (of which she strongly disapproved). He was a year younger than she. She enjoyed watching him change and at times sounded even a bit maternal toward him. They pulled each other up when the other was down. It was hard for him to get away from his mother, and she was helping him with this. "He's very sure of himself and the way he feels about me." She valued Dennis for his support of her; they were good at lifting each other's spirits

When I asked her about her favorite daydream, Betty told me it was "building my own home." Her plans for the near future were clear, though. She would marry Dennis and work as a physical therapist. She had secured a sense of independence and seemed clearly on a Pathmaker course. That there was some emotional distress bubbling underneath this confident exterior seemed apparent to me, and I wondered how this would play out as her life unfolded. My worries, I realize in retrospect, were misplaced.

AGE 33

When I saw her when she was 33, I learned that she and Dennis had married as planned shortly after Betty graduated. She insisted that he finish college even though he was often chafing to get on with what he felt was "real life."

Betty worked in physical therapy to support them for two years, after which they decided to begin a whole new life together in Vermont, a state that both of them loved because of its ruggedness and wilderness. Betty found it difficult to find work that she liked there—there was not that much demand for physical therapists. While waiting for an opportunity to open for her, she worked in various jobs related to her expertise in skiing as well as secretarial work. Although it took several years for her to find employment as a physical therapist, she eagerly grasped the first opportunity. Dennis, meanwhile, set out to make his fortune in real estate—which he did in a short time. So short, in fact, that he was ready to retire when he was 30. He envisioned a life they had always daydreamed about, a life of travel and adventure rather than being tied to the routine of job schedules. But Betty had thought this was only a daydream—she didn't think it would come true.

The change in Dennis's fortunes, quite literally, meant that Betty had to drastically revise her vision of her life. Now Dennis didn't want her to hold a job that would tie them down. But she wanted to use her professional training: she loved her work. On the other hand, she also loved to travel, which they wanted to do for half of each year, arranging adventures in remote countries—kayaking, hiking, and diving in South America and Australia. Dennis suggested that Betty find a way to do her work "on call," substituting for others who were on leave, a solution that allowed her to have both her work and their travel. They built their house (which they designed) not too far from a Medical Center where Betty could find "on call" work opportunities, and the basic shape of her life was set. Half the year they spent in Vermont while Betty worked as a physical therapist. Half the year they explored the world. She valued this life structure. "Since I've never been totally immersed in my field for a long period of time, I do not suffer from professional burn out like some of my colleagues." This life structure left Betty time to pursue her many other interests in weaving, painting, and many sports.

Their son was born when Betty was 32 and still they continued to travel. Betty wanted another child, and this was a cause of some dissent with Dennis who would have been happy without children at all.

When I interviewed her at age 33, Betty's main challenge seemed to be maintaining a sense of her own identity in the face of Dennis's exceptional competence. She admired him for being able to make wonderful decisions—about what stocks to buy, what airlines to fly, how to build their house. "He certainly makes a major contribution to the decision-making process," she said. Their relationship had shifted from college, where Betty felt like the older, wiser one, to Dennis now having that role. Betty was trying to hold on to her professional aspirations as a way of delineating her own competence. It was a struggle not to feel overshadowed, but she said that they complement each other well. "He plans the trips; I organize and pack the gear." She felt completely satisfied with their marriage. Dennis offered her financial security, a home, and was her "best friend." If she could have anything different, it would be more sex.

Betty enjoyed mothering her 2-year-old son, William, even though it took Dennis some time to become fully involved with him. While she continued her part-time work, her decisions about work and travel took account of William's needs. She wished she had a full-time grandparent living with them to give her more free time, but she was managing.

Betty was satisfied with who she had become. She loved traveling around the world, and she loved having a family and building their house. She was proud of "having become known and respected in a town so far away from our roots." She recognized that she was creating a unique life and that her identity was an integration of her interests, her family, and her work.

Looking back at her college years, Betty said that college was important because she learned self-reliance, met her husband, made lifelong friends, and earned a degree.

AGE 43

Over this decade, fate generated some major hurdles in Betty's path. When William was 4, they discovered that their son was seriously disabled by speech and learning problems, a syndrome that no experts could precisely diagnose. Betty had to become his champion, understanding him when no one else could, finding schooling for him, being his companion since he was quite unable to relate to peers. His difficulty was, as she described it at age 43, "all-consuming" for her because Betty had to develop a whole new kind of expertise. Yet, still they traveled, even after their second child, a daughter, was born 5 years later. This child, too, had physical challenges and many illnesses, but even this did not interfere with their travel. They simply took the children with them (most of the time), home schooling them while away, and were gone on voyages half of each year. Sometimes she and Dennis left the children with her parents, who had followed them to Vermont.

Betty continued to work on an "on call" basis but, when they were in Vermont, she did a variety of volunteer activities in her children's school related to environmental concerns. She said that she thoroughly loved her work as a physical therapist and enjoyed helping people return to good functioning but did not see herself as "career-oriented." There were too many other things she wanted to do, so her "on call" jobs suited her well. She was hoping one day to do some PT work in an underdeveloped country but that would depend on her children's needs.

Betty's path at midlife was far from anything she could have imagined as she graduated from college. But her determination to choose for herself, to shape her own life, remained. At this time of life, Betty's life story was intricate and interwoven, focused on myriad relationships in her family and her effort to make peace among often warring family members, to find a place for everyone. Thinking back over what she felt were the main turning points of her adulthood, Betty described moments in which defining herself in relation to others were paramount.

One such moment came in the process of mediating between Dennis and William. Dennis was disappointed not to have the son he had fantasized, and Betty was absorbed in trying to help him to overcome his sense of loss and to love and accept William as he was. But Dennis persisted in thinking that punishment would at least help control some of William's more destructive behaviors. And so he would spank him, much as he had been spanked as a child. Betty found this intolerable. "I had to stand up in a very strong way. I had to physically intervene and say that this type of treatment of this child makes me so sick and I will not allow you to do this and I will remove the children from this. My intent was to make him wake up and see that this is just not the way to go. I'm not saying that he physically abused them on a regular basis, but his attitude toward discipline was spank and they'll straighten out. I had to be strong for a number of years on that issue. So I see that as a turning point. Because I'm a strong person, but not in an adversary situation. As soon as there is adversary [conflict], I'll sit back because I don't like confrontation. But it was really important to do."

Growth for Betty also involved standing up to Dennis in other ways. Several years ago, he found property on an island off the coast of Maine that he very much wanted to buy and live on. "It would have meant an absolute total life change. We would have turned all our money over to that property.

I couldn't decide where I fit into this. The land was absolutely gorgeous. You get on this island and you can't think of anything other than living there. It was like being in paradise. Finally, I said no, I couldn't do it. It took absolutely everything I had—because it was so awesome and so overwhelming to be there. I'd get there and I'd feel I couldn't even think about anything else. And I'd get away and I'd think what about the difficulty of getting out, what about not being able to get medical service for my son. . . . What about living so far away from my family?. . . We were about to change everything and I finally got the strength to say no, I couldn't do it. My husband was in love with this property and I was too. And I realized that this was just the wrong decision—for me."

Their marriage evolved over this decade. They still argued about decorating, but Betty knew better when to insist and when to yield. Their sex life was better than ever. The relationship was fulfilling in every way, and Dennis was still her best friend. But she missed the romantic sparkle sometimes—and here Betty made her most passionate statement about what she learned in this midlife decade:

"When you first meet someone, you fall in love because it's all new—new experiences and emotions that you've never had before or never were allowed to experience. Especially if you're involved sexually which we were. Then you spend time together in a marriage and initially it may be smooth and then you get those hard times where everyone is working so intensely to try to make a go of life and money and 'happiness' and you tend to grow apart because there's so little time for each other . . . and through time you come back together and look to each other again as the marriage matures and realize how much good you have in your own situation and you might not have that sparkle, that glitter that brought you together initially but you have an understanding and a comfortable relationship that is fulfilling. But you can't describe it as—in the same terms of the love of a new marriage." "Do you miss this?" I asked. "I think I miss it but I can do without it. I think a maturing relationship in which you are fully comfortable with your partner is much better in many respects than infatuated love. Instead there is the feeling of security and closeness and bonding that you can feel in a mature relationship."

How would you describe Dennis's importance in your own identity? I asked. "I have everything I have and am the person I am because of him. I was a strong person when we married but only in certain areas. But I was the type of person who saw life in a limited manner. Professionalism the major one—although I had many other outside interests, I didn't have the strength to pursue them. . . . If I had stayed in New York, I would have had a full time position as a PT and lived in a primarily medical world. Having left the area with my husband, all that I've seen—its broadened me beyond anything I could have experienced there. And financially—how many of us get financial independence. I worked very hard the first ten years. They were not good paying jobs and they were not always in my field. Through his encouragement and strength, I continued my education and got back in the field. He's always been supportive of whatever direction I wanted to take and that's been really important. The strength of dealing with a child with learning disabilities is pretty awesome and I've taken a major role in it. It's been a real focus for me. And having him try to change himself—he's been willing to make those changes within himself and it's taken a lot of work—to look at his son differently. He expected his son to be perfect. And his son isn't.

"When William was first born, it brought us very close—he was premature, delicate. But he had a son—it was wonderful. I was more realistic, knowing he was a preemie. And you could see it early that he had problems. And early on it was trying to get my husband in a realistic frame of mind, that this child is not going to be the scholar or the athlete. Have him love him for the child he is. . . . And I've had to grow, become strong. I believe that if he grows up with a good self-image, he will make it. William has been the biggest source of dissension in our household. His outbursts and how we handle them. And it's not like it's going to disappear in the next ten years. You have to do what you believe in. And sometimes it takes a long time to find out what you believe in."

Having children has changed her—especially that her children both had special needs. "The hardest part has been William and his abnormal relationships to others and the difficulty of being the middle person between him and his father. It's much easier to be the middle person between him and school. It's very draining and stressful. It takes everything sometimes. . . . I've changed in that I've had to educate myself in an area I would never have touched. I had no interest in or tolerance for learning disabilities. Having children allowed me to become more understanding of others—people in general and also patients. I always gave out advice people couldn't follow because I didn't understand the needs of parents. It's made me more generous of my time—giving my time to others, my money to others, material gifts to others. . . . I've become more nurturing as a person. It's made me less self-centered. You have children and your whole basis broadens."

Betty, like the other women who began as Pathmakers, continued through her adulthood to find and to feel her place—in the context of others' needs and interests, but not on anyone else's authority but her own. These women attained the capacity to approach their life by asking "What is the right decision—for me—in relation to all that I am and all who I care about?" Betty held to her work identity, she said no to her husband, she found resources for her son when none were apparent.

In her mid-40s, Betty was aware of how influential her husband had been in shaping her life—both his needs and his financial means. Yet she continued to try to define her own realms of competence and decision-making. She figured out and implemented the home schooling of the children when they were on one of their long journeys. She maintained her work involvement even when abroad by keeping up with professional literature. She took charge of their charity work and contributions, and she was engaged in a number of volunteer activities centered around environmental issues. She took care of her invalid mother-in-law. Her parents retired to a place in Vermont not far from them, and she maintained a close relationship with her mother and sisters. She continued her interests in weaving and art and made the gifts they gave to others. And she continued to ski, scuba dive, play tennis, and dabble in her other sports. In each domain, I could hear her defining herself based on her own needs and those of others, putting them together, not losing herself but interweaving herself. Despite her husband's strength of character, Betty was clear that when she looked at their life, she could see her stamp upon it.

While Betty said she was thrilled to have such a comfortable and exciting life, she also cried a lot during her interview at age 43. It had been a difficult year with lots of illnesses and deaths, mainly in Dennis's family, and she had spent a good deal of the year trying to care for these family members. The illnesses and deaths caused a lot of family dissension for which Betty tried to be the peacemaker. Over this decade, Betty became more aware of how important family is to her. Family, she said, had been the bulwark of her childhood. One very meaningful experience of the past decade was taking her parents to Lithuania, where their parents had come from. All those family members were closed off to them until the Soviet Union fell, and she took the opportunity to go with her parents to the village from which her grandparents had emigrated early in the 20th century. It was a profound experience for her to meet all this "lost" family, and she had since gotten involved in charitable work with this village.

One source of some pain was that she had never been able to have good relationships with her sisters, each of whom were out of control in some way. She tried to help where she could, but there was no closeness. She implied that her sisters suffered from the lack of attention from their parents, but now she saw her childhood, in contrast to her sisters' view, as rather idyllic—with the farm and the animals and all the outdoor activities. She told me at this interview that her father spanked them, hard, with a leather belt, but she didn't feel this mentally scarred her. "I feel we had a wonderful upbringing and, for whatever reasons, my personality survived."

Betty's tears throughout the interview, especially talking about the family struggles, suggested to me that Betty was more in touch with her inner life and her feelings than she had ever been before. This made her seem deeper, fuller. She was living a happy, fulfilled life but it was not without pain. She expressed some vulnerability even as she seemed so capable, earnest, and controlled.

Identity for Betty in midlife was still in activity, not in introspection. Did she have any regrets, I wondered? Only that she wished she had been less sexually promiscuous in college, something that still haunted her, but I could not determine why.

AGE 58

I saw Betty again when she was 58 under circumstances somewhat unusual for how I went about these interviews. She and Dennis had moved again, now to a rather remote part of Vermont, and I scheduled an interview with her in conjunction with a vacation I was taking with my husband. I had planned that my husband would drop me at their house and then return for me. But they lived in an area with no cell phone coverage, and Betty insisted that we both join her and Dennis for lunch before the interview. She suggested that after lunch my husband, who is an amateur photographer, could go take pictures on their land until we finished talking. I tried to explain to her about confidentiality and so on, but none of this made any sense to her, so I simply accepted her offer. As a result, I had a chance to see the new house that they had built and to meet Dennis. Indeed, Dennis was an impressive man. He spent most of the lunch telling us about building the house and about the land they occupied—its wildlife and flora. The depth of his knowledge and breadth of his interests were vast and yet I had the sense that these were unassuming people who reveled in living close to nature. I found Dennis captivating. Betty spoke little except to chime in occasionally. This seemed to be their pattern. I could feel her, though, taking my measure.

The house was a marvel to me—all logs and glass, with heart-stopping views in each direction. The décor was all natural objects, mainly Betty's weaving and masks from their travels. There was no television. The overall sense was both magnificent and simple. They had made most of the furniture. Nothing lavish in sight. The house seemed a statement of their shared identity.

Betty looked her age—still attractive, but she had a somewhat weathered look, the look of someone who spent a lot of time outdoors. Betty began the interview telling me how much she had looked forward to my visit. The last interview, she said, had transformed her. "I am not introspective and these interviews have been the most interesting self-study opportunity for me in my life. Because, I guess I am not that kind of a person. The last interview helped me go forward. I was struggling so hard, problems with my son, problems in my marriage, and actually evaluating where the stress is coming from going through all that. Just changed everything—how I was approaching and dealing with things. It helped me realize some of Dennis's problems at that time." This was a great surprise to me because Betty hadn't seemed that introspective in the previous interview—and I had offered nothing but a listening ear. Evidently, she is someone who does her reflection privately.

As a result, Betty began to evaluate differently what William required to grow and set about trying to educate the people around him—the teachers, his father, his sister—about his needs. Her main effort was to help him have a good image of himself, to reward rather than to punish him. Over the next decade, William was diagnosed with several mental health problems in addition to his learning disabilities, some of which could be somewhat helped by medication. As he began to improve, she began lecturing at local colleges and medical conferences, sharing all she had learned about managing someone with multiple diagnoses and difficulties. At the time I interviewed her when she was 58, William was in his mid-20s, and she had arranged to have him live independently in Burlington, quite far from them. She found work for him that he could handle. She was still very involved in his life—he still needed a lot of help, but Betty was delighted that Dennis was now doing more of the management than ever before.

Still, as Betty narrated her development over the recent past, she said that William has driven her growth. "I have evolved as his needs have evolved." And Betty told me at the end of the interview that others have commented on how well she has raised him. Unlike her sister, who also has a disabled child, she never succumbed to guilt; she just kept solving problems as they arose. Now that both of her children are less in need of their attention, she and Dennis have more options in arranging their own lives and have revived their old intimacy as a twosome, including a livelier sex life.

One big life decision that Betty had to make over the past 15 years was to move to the place where they now lived, far from her family. By this time, her parents, many of her parents' friends, and two of her sisters had moved close to Burlington, where they had been living—but now she and Dennis had moved several hours' drive away. After her father died, Betty began making many long trips to help care for her mother. But Betty felt it was worth it. She proudly elaborated the details of building their house, which the two of them did without outside help. She stripped the logs; Dennis put them in place. She helped him install the plumbing and electricity. They worked sometimes in three feet of snow. They collaborated on the design and negotiated if they disagreed.

Once the house was finished, they decided to take their building skills abroad and began organizing trips through Projects Abroad to underdeveloped countries to build for others. This they could combine with their travels and spend the time while at home in Vermont doing the organization for the next trip. "We had always loved houses. And felt that we had a wonderful place to live and we wanted other people to have what they could call home. Dennis had been a general contractor, so he was experienced in the building trade. We had traveled all over the world, so we were well versed in that. I have lots of experience in organizing things—that was an asset—and I had medical background and that was an asset. Dennis is a real talker—as you saw earlier when we were having lunch together. I have few words. He's the talker and that is important because he does all the interviewing for prospective team members. . . . So we take a team, usually one in the spring and one in the fall to different parts of the world. And we leave in two months for Africa and that will be our 19th trip."

Their lives, Betty explained to me, had largely been a series of projects, some, but not all of them, inspired by Dennis who has more projects in mind than he will ever be able to accomplish. Looking over her life, Betty saw herself as engaging in many such projects in place of a steady career. She still had a sense of the path not taken, a path of a career in physical therapy in which she might have earned a doctorate and taught others. She realized that she was talented in this work, given the ways in which others looked to learn from her skills. But she did not regret having had all the opportunities for travel and for volunteer initiatives, such as the Projects Abroad work she was now doing, as well as many others. Dennis, too, occupied himself with serial projects. There were times over the years, she told me, when money would be running low, at which point he would take on a project to build for someone else as a general contractor, and then retire yet again. Over the years, they had both independent and shared projects, but she saw them as a solid team, oriented increasingly to their "need to do for others."

As she looked toward the future, Betty was eager to become a grand-mother. Their daughter, who Betty said little about at this time, was about to marry and, although she lived far away, Betty wanted to figure out how to be a good grandmother.

Looking back, although she does not feel herself to be introspective, she thought that her upbringing taught her responsibility. With many children in the house—her sisters and those boarding at the camp during the year—she had many tasks to look after. Often, she recalled, she would get involved in teaching some of the younger children. And there were always animals to care for. She feels now that the experiences she had outweighed having to share her parents with so many others: "I think I learned a lot of empathy for people because of these children. They came from such broken situations sometimes. . . . We had a young woman who was legally blind and we had to learn to bathe her and walk with her. . ." I asked her who taught her to do that, and Betty replied, "My mom was not a teacher. She just expected us to be able to do anything she told us to do. We kind of made a face, and then kind of figured it out. You just learned yourself, because they just weren't there for you." I asked her how come she had come out so much more together than her sisters, but Betty had no explanation except that she always had a good self-image and worked hard. When there was too much commotion in the house for her to study, she got up at 5 A.M. to do her homework in the quiet. It seemed to me that the emotional hardship of those years had now vanished from Betty's life story.

The next biggest chapter of her life was moving to Vermont with Dennis. As she now narrates it, she wanted to move somewhere far from home, far from the expectations of her as her parents' daughter, which had felt constricting.

There were expectations that seemed to come from a social register kind of thinking influenced by her mother's city friends—how she fixed her hair, what kind of shoes she wore. She wanted nature and freedom—and Vermont seemed to promise both. "I wanted to be my own person. . . . Vermont proved to be a place where you could be whatever you wanted to be, make something of yourself. . . . Whatever you set your mind to, it was doable. No one would stand in our way."

From there, her life has been about adventure travel and building, making life as good as possible for William, and taking on projects. The only regrets are that she fears she didn't pay enough attention to her daughter, whose needs were dwarfed by William's. And she wishes she had had more friends. Friendship has always been a challenge because of their travel—and because Dennis has been her best friend. They do quite a bit of entertaining, for fundraising primarily and for what she calls "social bonding"—but this, to her, is not the same as friendship. She often wishes, and says somewhat tearfully, that she just had a woman friend to confide in when she has troubles.

As I was leaving, Betty took me on a tour of the house and showed me her weaving. She had done the large, rather dramatic woven pieces that hung on the walls, and one had won an international prize. There were also paintings and sculptures that she had created. So, I concluded, Betty had produced much in her life in which she could take pride, all within the framework of the relationship she had structured with Dennis. My early worries about Betty when she was 21 were for naught. She had managed well the challenges life brought her, keeping herself focused on doing rather than internal experience, and I had to admire the ways in which, at age 58, she had fulfilled herself.

Andrea

AGE 21

Andrea as a senior in college struck me as one of the most mature of the women I was interviewing. Tall, thin, with intense green eyes, she had a seriousness of purpose and clarity about herself that stood out among the group. She was tense during the interview, and this seemed a product of how unusual it was for her to reflect on herself. She thought a lot but seemed to put feelings aside, and the rather flat cadence of her speech made me feel distant from her rather than engaged. Still, her thoughtfulness about her struggle for independence and her passion for her intellectual goals drew me to her. Unlike many others, she seemed quite aware of her own developmental path. She knew she was breaking away from her childhood life and doing so deliberately while still maintaining her bonds of love. In terms of the identity categories, Andrea was an exemplary Pathmaker at the end of college.

Andrea's father was a lawyer and her mother a homemaker. Her family lived in Philadelphia, where she was at Temple University, paying her own way with some scholarship assistance. She had, over her mother's objections, moved into the dorms after living at home the first two years. Andrea had set her sights on doing biomedical research and wanted to earn a PhD. She had decided on this in high school when she was challenged by a biology course that stood out in a field of easy courses. While her father encouraged her intellectual interests and thought she should go to medical school, she felt her parents would have been content if she had become a secretary as long as she was doing something she enjoyed. (When Andrea described this in her mid-40s, she told me that her parents were prepared to pay for her brother's college education, but not hers, thinking she could just as well become a secretary. Evidently, Andrea had received some mixed messages from her parents but in college chose to see them as supportive of her goals. Only later did she think of herself as having succeeded despite their more traditional attitudes toward women's achievement.) In any case, Andrea was clear that she was going to follow her own desire for education. As she envisioned her future, she thought she would stay home for a year or two after having children and then resume her career.

Raised Catholic by a strictly observant mother, Andrea said her big rebellion was getting a scholarship to a secular university when her mother wanted her to continue her Catholic education by going to a Catholic college. Although she had been active in Church activities in high school, she had largely moved away from her religious involvement during college. Some of the Church teachings seemed "dumb" to her rationalist, scientific mind. She thought she would probably raise her children Catholic, but not strictly. What seemed most important was that "they realize that being Catholic is not the only right way to be." This statement seemed to reflect the most important psychological change in Andrea (and the other Pathmakers). At this age, the sense of there being many right ways to be was an opening to possibility, a path to liberation from the confines of earlier values and beliefs. Nowhere among the women of this time was this realized more than in making decisions about sexual standards and behavior. And Andrea had been having a sexual relationship with her boyfriend of 2 years, despite knowing that this would devastate her parents. "I figure that that's them and that's the way they are and I'm different."

Tolerance of difference from parents, even in ways that might perturb them, was, at this age, the hallmark of the internal psychological work that made independent identity creation possible. Where the Guardians could not free themselves from parental models or values and the Searchers could not overcome their guilt at doing so, the Pathmakers found a way to manage whatever guilt and anxiety they felt and move forward.

Andrea valued her independence of mind. When I asked her what sorts of things she would tell someone so they could get to know her, she mischievously told me that she wouldn't tell them anything. They'd simply get to know her by being with her. While I was a bit taken aback by her questioning my question (she was the only one who did so), I enjoyed her taking a stance on her own terms. She wasn't going to let others, including me, define things for her. She told me that she was "One thousand different personalities and the sum total of all those things. I can't characterize myself as 'what I am.'" (Indeed, of course, she was right.) She also told me "you are what others see you as." (Also true.)

In the past three years, her fiancé had been most central in her life. "He made me more sure of myself, more confident and willing to try new things. Just having someone you know is there and knowing someone else thinks a lot of me." Andrea was aware that she grew through his presence. This, too, seemed an important pattern for her. She told me of a recurrent daydream, "I'm in a castle out in the woods with dangers. It is spooky but exciting, with things there trying to attack me, but I was looking for the treasure. I was with a friend and as long as I'm with someone, I don't get scared. It was fun going through the tunnels, having adventures." What I learned from Andrea (and others) at this point was of the developmental importance of integrating adventurousness with secure companionship. The adventure is grounded in having someone along, perhaps in the shadows, but clearly present. Andrea had clear goals at this point in her life, but it would be a mistake to see her as a woman of ambition without noticing the importance to her of the person beside her.

Growing up as "the studious one" in her school, Andrea had just a few friends and, attending a Catholic school, no real challenges to the assumptions and values of her community. Going to a university opened her to different people with different ways of being, and she embraced the fact that she could choose her own way. She named many people, particularly teachers, who encouraged her intellectual interests.

As she thought about who she wanted to become, she contrasted herself with her parents. Although she admired her father intellectually and shared her ideas with him, she also felt that he was too much under her mother's thumb—at least when it came to standing up for Andrea in her clashes with her mother over hours (while she lived at home) and the friends she chose. She emphasized that her fiancé is very different from her father—he is strong and stands up to her when necessary. She said she loves her parents but resents them for trying to overprotect her. Like the other Pathmakers, her process of separating and individuating from her parents was marked by ambivalence toward them. Unlike the families of the Guardians, they are not portrayed as wholly gratifying. Leaving home internally is painful but promising.

AGE 34

I found Andrea at age 34 to be softer, warmer, and more engaging than she had been in college. She had married her fiancé and earned a PhD. in biochemistry and a medical degree. "Enough," she declared, about all the years of study and training; she was looking forward to being a professional in the world, doing both research and clinical medicine. Her career path evolved according to her interests in hormonal disorders, and she felt she needed both degrees to accomplish her goals. Andrea had found two important mentors—one male, one female—who helped her envision the kind of life she wants. Of the woman, "She is hard-working and she demonstrates that you can have your own set of values and goals, which may not necessarily correlate with those of others. She also proved to me that it's quite possible to work hard and still enjoy oneself without feeling guilty." I was struck by how these were such similar themes to the ones Andrea had stressed at the end of college—having your own values despite others' views, managing guilt over enjoyment. It seemed to me that she was indeed still the same, although the playing field had changed.

Andrea told me that she felt she had had a successful 12-year marriage. They married just after she graduated because "we thought we were compatible, we loved each other, enjoyed doing things together. He is independent enough and self-confident enough to be able to cope with being married to a professional woman and not feel threatened." They each worked hard and supported each other's professional goals, and she felt they had both grown and changed together.

Andrea was following her own path in her marriage as well, insisting on the possibility of extramarital relationships that her husband disliked but tolerated. She didn't feel that the two intense affairs she had had threatened the marriage. "We have deep feeling and a long history together, and so far he's always won over anyone else." She had one lover, who she still saw occasionally, for 10 years, and she felt this relationship actually strengthened her marriage.

Andrea regarded herself as the more independent and outgoing one of the couple and rather resented Arnold's dependence on her. Often, she liked to do things just with friends, but Arnold had a hard time finding other companionship or activities. And when he said he resented the long hours of training in her residency and warned her that he might not be there when she finished, she told him that that was a chance she would have to take. However, when she was offered a high-status job in another city, Andrea decided to stay in Philadelphia (where Arnold had a settled dental practice) and find the best work arrangement there that she could. She said she found the prospect of a commuter marriage unappealing,

Another important identity decision at this time was her decision not to have children. "I realized I am not going to be able to do everything. I didn't think I could take care of children and maintain my lifestyle and my work." She said she valued her independence and spontaneity too much and was focused on her career. "I do not feel the need to procreate," she said. Again, Andrea was choosing her own path, setting her own goals, and resisting the crowd.

Andrea's father died when she was in her late 20s and this mainly affected her through the need to be attentive to her mother. That was difficult, because her mother remained critical of Andrea's lifestyle and choice of husband (she wanted Andrea to marry a Catholic). Andrea set limits on what her mother could know about her life and tried to be dutiful in a caring way, bringing what pleasure she could to her mother's life.

Asked about how she is the same or different from her family, Andrea responded in terms of how she does not carry any of their traditional views, especially about women, but she is like them in concern for others. "I consider that the bond with other people is most important; career is low in the microcosm. My husband, other friends, how I'm interrelating—that's what matters most. Feeling close to someone, being able to talk to and understand someone, having people you feel comfortable with, who have a similar outlook on life—that's what matters most."

At this age, Andrea was regarding the future with a glint in her eye—another adventure. Research funding was unpredictable, so she could not be sure how her research goals would materialize. She expected to stay married to Arnold but acknowledged that perhaps some other man might seriously compete for her affections. For Andrea at age 34, the future still seemed fully open to possibility. Her identity commitments were solidified by a sense of increased confidence in her skills as a physician and a researcher, by her embeddedness in her marriage, her decision not to have children, and her privileging of what she called her "lifestyle"—working hard and playing hard. She reveled in her sense of independence and freedom.

Recounting her earlier life at this age, Andrea stressed more the "turbulence" of her late adolescent years. She described "major confrontations" with her parents as she fought them to loosen their control of her. I wondered (privately) at this point if this fuller picture was a reflection of her greater openness to her own experience, needing less at this age to keep things wrapped tightly as she had at age 21. She could perhaps allow herself a greater range of feeling and awareness of conflict. She also admitted to more pain at having been "the studious one" at school; she had wanted to "belong" more than she had been able to acknowledge while younger. Still, Andrea was not a woman who lived in her emotions or spent much time examining her inner world. She saw the risks in the decisions she had to make, and she tried to decide on rational grounds. I was surprised that she was so matter-of-fact about her extramarital affairs, explaining them with a simple "It's something I feel I need."

AGE 43

By age 43, Andrea had flowered professionally and gotten divorced and remarried. These were her main identity shifts. She spent much of the interview animatedly telling me about her work, which was marked by a lot of political struggle over grants. She took pride and pleasure in her clinical work, but research still intrigued her. She was proud of becoming the first woman ever to serve on her specialty certification board.

When I met Andrea this time, her mother's death was fresh and she was grieving—so she was a bit subdued and often tearful as she tried to rearrange her sense of herself without her mother. Indeed, they had become closer over the past 10 years as Andrea tried frequently to arrange outings that would bring joy to them both. A highlight was taking her mother to Italy, her ancestral home.

Andrea had decided to divorce three years after our previous meeting, even though divorce felt like failing at something. She said she had been unhappy but didn't really know why. Over the years, Arnold wanted to be more settled, and she wanted to travel and try new things and develop new friendships; Arnold resisted all these things. She had begun to connect her affairs to her discontent: "I may have gotten tired butting my head against the wall. I didn't like having other relationships. It was a way of avoiding the problem. I suggested therapy, and he wasn't interested. Then I met a friend who was getting divorced, and, in talking to her, I got more clarity." Arnold was angry and the process was stressful, "but I did it. It was nice once I was alone and could do what I wanted when I wanted. I even got both cats. I was surprised he didn't want one of them." She met Charles a year after leaving Arnold. Charles is a musician, very different from Arnold, and she found it invigorating to be in his world, a world quite far from medicine. Unlike Arnold, he was not dependent on her and shared her joy in the spontaneity of travel. She married him because he asked her: "I didn't really think about it. I said yes, and once I decide to do a thing, that's it." Andrea was still not very analytical about herself, but she remained decisive and determined. She felt that being with Charles made her more relaxed. They took more vacations. Coordinating schedules was a challenge, though, and they spent a great deal of time apart because his musical engagements were usually on nights and weekends when she had free time. She was now committed to monogamy: "I always felt guilty. And I realize now that it was all a way of avoiding the problem. I wouldn't condemn anyone else, but it's not what I want for myself." She said that she might have considered having a child with Charles, but she had had her tubes tied. Anyway, Charles didn't want children—and they were content with a puppy as "a surrogate child." They enjoyed doing things together, but Charles still allowed her a great deal of independence. Sometimes they went weeks without seeing one another, but this made for joyful reunions and gave her time to work and be with her friends.

Professionally, these were growing years, and she valued the autonomy she had in her academic research job. Still, there were intense struggles with a Department Chair that marked a low point of the previous decade. She continued to try to find the right balance between doing research and clinical work. She organized her professional life so that, working at an HMO, she could increase or decrease her clinical time depending on the vagaries of the research funding available. With her clinical work, she enjoyed working with patients, trying to solve their problems and help them, but she disliked the bureaucracy and loathed having to work with a boss who might try to control her. If anything, Andrea was even fiercer about never being controlled by anyone. But she appreciated the supervisors who supported her in trying new things. When I asked her about her future goals, she said she hoped to produce more publications and continue to see patients. She told me that she used to want to be Department Chair somewhere, but now that she saw what administrative work entails, decided that it was not worth the hassle. "I'm not interested in status. I like what I am doing."

It was striking to me that Andrea had only four people listed on her list of "people you are closest to" at age 43—while at age 33, she had 10 listed. She felt she lost several friends when she and Arnold divorced and hadn't really had the opportunity yet to create new ones. Charles topped the list. There was one colleague who remained with her over these years, one new friend, and her brother. But, she said, friendships had become "peripheral."

As before, Andrea had little patience for reflecting on her life or her development, but this time perhaps a bit more than earlier. She felt that she and her mother had parted well. Her mother liked Charles, and their puppy delighted her. When she got divorced, she expected conflict with her mother, but, to her surprise, her mother had been supportive. "I think we became more tolerant of each other," Andrea said. Looking back, she realized that her mother—and her mother's sisters—were all constricted by traditional views of what women could do. She thinks her mother might have liked to go to college and do something, but this just wasn't possible then. Still, her mother could never fully understand why Andrea was working and not having children. Andrea's brother, also a lawyer, married a woman with a PhD, but she had stopped working to raise children. Andrea had little but a formal relationship with her brother who had become a born-again Christian and was "very traditional." And she disliked the chaos that his children brought to her house on their infrequent visits. So Andrea continued to feel very far from her family's expectations—and it annoyed her that they all still addressed her Christmas cards to "Ms." instead of "Dr."

Narrating her life history at this age, Andrea again returned to her college years as pivotal. She stressed the importance of enlarging her world and learning new things, having the opportunity to get involved in scientific research, but she added that leaving home and separating from her parents was "traumatic." The main theme of her story was even more clearly independence, doing what she wants, on her own. She titled the current chapter, her 40s decade, "OK—now it's your call."

AGE 53

I was struck by how young Andrea looked when I met her at age 53. She was in good shape, and her large green eyes still dominated her face, which could change from very pretty to rather homely, depending on her level of animation. I found her this time to be quite reserved, showing little emotion except occasional excitement. Her life is steady, stable. She had no regrets and little passion. I found myself during the interview trying to enlarge and extend her, to inject some feeling into what seemed to be a constricted account of herself. But I thought she was trying to communicate and relate to me even though self-reflection was, it seems, even more distant from her than ever. It was as though she couldn't find the words to express her current state of being. We could chat comfortably and easily about medical ethics or a novel we both read, but the subject of herself seemed fraught. She remembered our previous meeting and had read my last book. Previously, she had told me that she liked the way I wrote about her, and I reminded her that she had been a major character in my reports of this study. She attributed that to her professional standing—often being the first woman to pave the way in her male-dominated field.

Much of her story of the past 10 years concerns houses. To her astonishment, her mother left her some money with the injunction to do something with it to remember her by, and Andrea and Charles decided to build a house on the Delaware seashore. At the same time, they bought an old house in Philadelphia which they were redoing. Their marriage had been doing well, but Charles's travel schedule became a serious problem. At one point, she threatened to leave him if he didn't arrange to be home more. This led to them seeing a marital therapist who showed them "how we were being dysfunctional." Charles was having an affair about which he was feeling extremely guilty. Around this time, he also stopped playing music and earning money, and he became very depressed. Then he tried several jobs to make money, but, as Andrea put it, "he hadn't yet found what he wants to do." It wasn't clear just how the marriage therapist helped, but Andrea has continued seeing her monthly.

From the therapy, Andrea got an understanding of herself as "rigid." By this, she meant that "I see things in my own particular way and that there are more than one way to do it and how Charles sees things is not necessarily how I see things." Her example was that Charles was going to buy a car with an alarm and "I feel pretty strongly that I hate noise and . . . we talked about it, but for some reason, I had this feeling that he didn't necessarily hear what I was saying cause . . . so I asked him to repeat, you know, what I wanted as far as the car goes, and it took a bit, but it was clear that he definitely hadn't heard what my concerns were and before I actually would. . . it would not have occurred to me to do that and basically I'd be fairly explicit without getting excited and understand that just because you see something one way that's not necessarily how it is or how other people perceive it. ... We clearly were not communicating. He wasn't hearing, and I thought I was being very explicit, but clearly not from his mindset."

What she feels that she has learned about herself in the past 10 years, and in therapy, is that what you need for professional success is different from what you need in intimate relationships, where things are less certain and defined, less good or bad.

This more shades-of-gray view seems to have dampened Andrea. There are clearly problems in the marriage that she doesn't know how to address, but she appreciates Charles's companionship. They enjoy spending time at their house in Delaware, although she reads and relaxes while he goes fishing. They now have two dogs and three cats, and their pets keep them occupied—and sometimes prevent them from traveling, which Andrea had always made a most important part of her enjoyment of life.

In addition, her investment in her work has taken a downturn. Research funding largely dried up, so she had to give that up and turn to more clinical work. Although she had always been gratified by taking care of patients, medicine, she told me had "become a business... which is most upsetting. When I started it, it was about taking care of people. I mean it still is, but you sort of have to do that in relationship to everything else. So... you know, I still work for the same HMO, but it's changed markedly. It's now run by an MBA and our department has become completely bottom line in what's important. So it would be nice to think about doing something else. Unfortunately, something else that pays as well and I don't have to restart over. ...." I was astonished to hear that Andrea could be thinking about leaving medicine, but she feels that the changes are permanent and intolerable. "Finances are a major issue in what people decide they can do or want to do and that's not something I'm all that happy about.... It's a business. Also, the physicians I know are so overburdened, and we can't work together on cases well and we get a lot of fairly sick people—so it's difficult." When I asked her what else she'd like to do, she was thinking in terms of opening a restaurant or a cheese shop, but these didn't seem very practical. She was not yet ready to retire so supposed she'd keep on doing what she had been doing.

Over these years, she began volunteering at two homeless shelters and was on the managing board of one of them. This is a place where, although she is not paid, she feels she can do some good for people "who need help and don't have a way of getting it."

Andrea maintains friendships with some old friends and extended family members, but these she is in contact with infrequently. She delights in how quickly they can pick up their connection even if they don't see one another for several years. And email now makes staying in contact easier. Her list of close relationships is nearly full again, and many are very old friends with whom she has re-engaged. But the sense of the lively community present for her in her late 20s and early 30s—the friends she fought her husband to go out with—that is no longer present.

Most of this interview was taken up by stories of crises in Charles's rather chaotic family, which they had to respond to. They caught her attention through their drama and tension. In these stories, Andrea positioned herself as trying to be helpful but not getting too caught up in the problems. But it was hard to tell how these family struggles actually impacted her. In one episode, the wife of one of Charles's brothers died leaving him with a 4-year-old child that he was unable to raise. Charles's parents decided to take in the child over Charles's vociferous objections because he felt his parents were too old and his mother was needed to care for his ailing father. This led to an estrangement between Charles and his parents for several years. I asked Andrea if they had considered raising the child, and Andrea said "Neither of us particularly likes young children, but he's even more vociferous than I am. It would have been really disruptive, but I would have been willing." I couldn't tell, though, how she *felt* about this. Did it evoke any feelings about a last chance to raise a child? Any regrets she may have had along those lines? Or perhaps she felt that there was really no choice to be made given how strongly Charles felt about it.

Andrea seemed most animated telling me about their dogs. But, in this meeting, Andrea was more interested than previously in tracing her life history. I was surprised that she spent a good deal of time detailing the story of her high school years that now seemed dominated by an ongoing battle with her mother about whether she should be a secretary or go to college. I asked her where she got her determination, and she attributed this to her mother, who she now cast as adventurous. "She had a fairly traditional life, but she liked to travel and she would do things. She wasn't necessarily set." So Andrea now sees herself as getting her own adventurousness from the very person who tried to thwart this in her. "It was clear to me that she wanted me to go to secretarial school, and it was clear to me that that wasn't going to happen. And I got a scholarship to a Catholic girl's school, and I just didn't tell them. If I didn't tell them, it wasn't going to happen." Here she laughs for one of the first times in the interview. I asked her where was her father in this? "He was fairly silent. I'm not sure where he was since he wasn't the vocal one." Her mother was very unhappy when she went to college. "I started going days and then I decided to move into the dorm. We didn't speak for six months sophomore year." Andrea now also stresses that she mainly put herself through college by working.

Her new understanding of her life is that marrying Arnold was a way of separating from her parents, although she says that she was "very much in love" with Arnold. But now she thinks that her decision to pursue a residency, and Arnold's opposition to this, was the turning point of their marriage. "He wasn't happy about it. He didn't like how much I had to study." She can't detail this further except to say that, eventually, she decided that she was unhappy and wanted to leave. Mainly, though, it seems that her unhappiness was focused on his not wanting to travel. Her story was not one I found very coherent. Her retrospective story of Charles was centered on being introduced to a whole new world, his world of music and artistic friends, adventurous travel and spontaneity—the opposite, it appeared to me, of Arnold.

The current chapter is one she feels she will stay in "until I switch jobs or something else happens. . . . I've been talking about it for a couple of years, but I haven't done anything." So Andrea seems somewhat blocked and stymied at this stage. All her preparation and early promise for her career seems to have stalled as the field of medicine changed. She thrives on challenge, and right now her field seems to offer few new possibilities. She is trying to rethink things and perhaps reinvent herself, still guardedly optimistic, but without her previous determination. Like the other Pathmakers, she is in her own way revisiting her past and rewriting it in some ways. Andrea, though, has always defined herself in terms of what she is doing and where she is heading. The inner world has never held much appeal for her. She realizes herself in action, and, right now, she is unclear what actions to take. Still, I didn't feel sad in interviewing her. There is something stoical and determined about her, and I felt she would figure something out, find a new path. Andrea's inner life, her emotional experience, continued to elude me—and it seems that attending to this, thinking about how and what she was communicating to others, had become a new horizon for her, only now in her 50s.

Alice

AGE 21

When I first met her when she was a senior in college, I was impressed by Alice's quiet determination. From a small town in Pennsylvania, her parents had not graduated from college and seemed not to have any expectations of her. She had done well in school so was set on finishing college. She described herself in high school as having been the "cheerleader, Honor society, student council president" kind of person. She was a success and had good reason to feel confident. She was majoring in physical therapy because she thought of it as "a selfish field. It's nice to get somebody up on his feet who couldn't do it." Her life plans were to make this a career but to stop work when her children were small.

Alice had been raised vaguely Unitarian but without any strong beliefs. She regretted that she felt she was an agnostic because "it would be nice to have someone to go to for help." Even at 21, there was something stoical about Alice's independence. She hadn't had any real emotional closeness with her parents, who were reliably present but shared little of their internal lives. She was a bit rueful of this. "I just never knew anything about their values and opinions. It's difficult to sit down and discuss things with them. There hasn't been the closeness that there should be." She hadn't really even considered the possibility of being emotionally close to her mother, telling her things, until she heard other girls talk about their closeness to their mothers, and she sounded a bit sad when she told me this.

When we talked in college, Alice had been through a period of experimentation that she was still a bit shaken by. After she had broken up with her high school boyfriend, in sophomore year of college, she "went to the other extreme" and began smoking pot and sleeping around. Then she had regrets, although she felt she had learned something from it. What she learned was that she felt she could understand people better and became more liberal, more accepting of people as they are rather than how she expected them to be. Still, she had a lot of guilt, especially about the sex, and she tempered her "wildness" in order to get her respect for herself back.

For Alice, college was an eye-opening time. She got to know different kinds of people while living in Philadelphia. She felt she was learning to think and analyze things. The major marker of her changing was breaking her engagement to her high school boyfriend, a boyfriend she had had for six years, who had gone into the Army, and, while she was changing, he did not. He was conservative and was "making a groove for me to fit into," a groove she resisted. But he had been the center of her life for so long.

Whatever else she was doing or exploring in college, Alice had her academic achievement to fall back on to give her confidence in herself. Some of this came from her long history of competition with her older brother. He was a high achiever, and she wanted to do at least as well as he did. She described herself as "always pretty independent, more of a leader than a follower."

When I tried to better understand Alice's history and the roots of her psychology in college, I found myself picturing her family like the "American Gothic" painting—the quiet father who rarely spoke, who watched TV and read his paper, the mother who stayed at home most of the time tending the daily chores. They never talked much, Alice said; she even had to learn the facts of life in school. They were solid, reliable, but "average," without characteristics or values she could define. "I always wanted to please my parents, I wanted them to be proud of me." But she felt cheated out of closeness to them. She had to fight her father for some for her independence, and this conflict was waged over her right to visit her fiancé when he was far away. It bothered her a bit that her parents seemed to have no idea of who she was—at least they knew nothing of the "wild things" she had done, but she wasn't tempted to tell them.

I asked Alice who she most wanted to be like, and I wasn't surprised when she told me that she is content with being herself. Her ideals were in terms of helping people as a physical therapist. She wanted to marry but not right away: "I want to be on my own and see things and do things before I settle down."

Alice told me at the end of the interview that I hadn't asked her about her bad points, and I realized I had underestimated how self-critical she was. So I asked her about this, and she told me that she was too domineering and wished she could find a man who could dominate her. She also felt that she was very rational and that she pushed her feelings down, often got angry when she felt like crying, especially if guys left her. At the same time, she is afraid she is caustic and can hurt other people's feelings. Very much the late adolescent, Alice was proud of her accomplishments but still taking stock of herself. I liked Alice. She was nervous talking to me about herself, she smoked a lot and seemed a bit to be trying to please me, but I was taken by her geniality and confidence, and I believed that this was a young woman who was solid and healthy and would likely realize her goals.

AGE 33

When I encountered Alice at age 33, she had, as I had expected, attained the goals she had in college. She was working as a physical therapist, was married, and had two young children. Those were the "facts" of Alice's life, but beneath the surface was some turbulence.

Although Alice had a successful career, she was increasingly disappointed with her work situation. Now living in a small town in West Virginia and working as a department head in a small hospital, Alice felt increasingly discontent with the administration and bored with her work. "I've had many gratifying experiences helping patients recover from injury and illness. I've met many, many interesting and fine people through my work. I've continued my education via seminars and mini-courses. And I can say with confidence that I have become a good therapist. But my job has now become little more than a paycheck these days. I job share the position, working three days a week. Administratively, the hospital is one screw-up after another. After six years of sticking my neck out to try to improve matters, I finally gave up because nobody else seemed to care enough to listen anyway. I'll probably stay with this job at least until the children are in school. I may then consider returning to school, possibly to get a teaching degree. I've often thought about teaching a good health course at the high school level. It depends on the job market at the time. It might be nice to do some mindless job for a while—like work in a retail store, though I probably wouldn't get that desperate." She and her husband Adam also imagined that they might create a business making wooden toys for children, something they enjoyed doing for their own children, so maybe this could happen some day as well.

In terms of her religious beliefs, not much changed for Alice. She attended Church occasionally for social reasons, because it is nearby and all the neighbors in this small town go, but she was not a believer. She wanted to raise her children in the Church but make sure that they understood that she has different beliefs and, when they are older, expose them to various churches so they have a choice. Politically, Alice was active in local issues, particularly those related to the environment. She also considered herself a feminist, more so now than in college, but moderately so, more a matter of attitude than action. She felt she had been discriminated against for a promotion in a previous position in favor of a man with less experience, and this still rankled with her.

Alice had married shortly after college, but she didn't want to say much about this marriage. Mark was a "loser," and she stayed with him for four years hoping he would get a job or do something other than smoke pot. She was the breadwinner, and, although she felt she loved Mark, she was growing increasingly frustrated with him. When he became abusive while drunk, she knew she had to leave him. But, as she described these years, it was clear that it seemed like the distant past. She felt that it had been destructive to her self-esteem, both the way Mark treated her and that she had to admit defeat. But she had largely shrugged it away by this time. It was a mistake, and she had moved on.

Alice's husband Adam had been one of her patients, and they met just after her divorce. At first, she viewed him as "someone I could share some good times with," and he got her involved in skiing, camping, hiking, "and some *very* good sex." She somewhat hesitantly allowed him to move in with her, and, a year later, they married "in a small ceremony on a perfect day." In contrast to her first husband, Adam was ambitious and had a good job. They equally shared household responsibilities, and she felt they had the same goals about home and family. With very few clashes, she delighted that they were able to work out differences constructively, and I could sense Alice's joy in her marriage. She described Adam as more high strung, but she could calm him down and whereas she saw herself as the lazier of the couple, he could get her going. "I have a wonderful family and my own home, which were major goals in my life. I have a life partner with whom I hope to grow old." Alice at this age was at peace, delighting in what she had created together with Adam.

Among their greatest creations were their two sons, both under two, the youngest still an infant. That was a major adjustment, having two babies, but she felt they were settling into some routines. They had decided on having the first, but the second was a "surprise" when their first son was just six months old. Alice hoped that, so close in age, they would be good friends, so it felt worth all the work right now. "Motherhood is wonderful," Alice said, and she felt so grateful that she had the chance to experience it. It seemed to her that, through her 20s, she hadn't wanted to ever have children. But now, "I've been either pregnant or nursing for the past three years and my career has obviously taken a back seat." Alice regarded this as a temporary situation and something that she could deal with. "They've added *so* much love and joy to my life—there aren't words for it." As she thought about her goals as a mother, she contrasted them with how she was raised. She wanted to raise her sons as feminists, with respect for equal rights and roles, and she and Adam wanted to spend more time with them than their parents had spent with them. She also wanted them to learn about sex at home, which she had not. Other than that, she said, she appreciated that her parents had "instilled in me a sense of independence and self-confidence" and she wanted to do the same.

At this age, Alice was occupied with the challenges of career and family. "The most difficult has been the lack of *time*—to be with friends, to read, to go to the bathroom, etc. I especially miss having time alone with Adam. Yes, I've heard of baby sitters but Roger is still nursing every three hours and I'm exhausted in the evenings so don't have the energy to go out. I wish I had as much time and energy to devote to being a wife as I have to being a mother. And the same amount again to devote to just being a woman. Oh, well. . . ."

All in all, Alice was comfortable living in this rural community where they had the means to live decently. And this led a positive glow to her reflections on her life to this point. As she told me her life story at age 33, Alice narrated a tale of success—in her early life, "the pride of my parents and teachers." In college, she felt, she had become herself, once separated from her home environment, and she developed her own morals and values. But, she said, "I guess I wasn't as independent as I thought since after college I latched on to a husband rather than strike out on my own." Meeting Adam changed things, restoring her self-esteem and creating "the best years of all as I've gained a family, a home, and the opportunity to grow in any direction I wish."

Adding to the generally positive glow, Alice felt she had become somewhat closer to her parents, with whom she was never able to have intimate conversations. They had an affectionate, if distant relationship. She liked giving feminist lectures to her mother, extolling her own independence, and she felt generally more assertive than either of her parents. With her brother, she no longer felt so competitive, but also not close. She remained emotionally close to her best friend from college, and, although she had local friendships, none seemed really intimate. But who had time?

I could do nothing other than marvel at how "perfect" Alice's life seemed to me at this age. She seemed to have achieved or created all that she had wanted—success at her job, managing the challenge of two babies, what seemed to be a very happy marriage, and no regrets. Alice seemed to be a woman who was flexibly in control of her life, easy to relate to. Yes, there was discontent with her work, but she seemed to have some plans for how to find something more satisfying—once she had time. Reflecting on herself, Alice felt that she tended to tolerate difficulties longer than necessary unless it became a matter of principle—and then she gets awakened to a passionate fight. And she "internalizes" feelings—walking away from a clash until she "cools down" rather than dealing with it. Adam had pointed this out to her; he thought she avoided issues. She turned to her projects—woodworking, knitting, reading, or running—to burn off inner pain.

In leaving Alice at this age, I was impressed with how well she seemed to manage the stress in her life. True, she wasn't very focused on her inner life, and when she told me about the blows to her self-esteem from her first marriage, I couldn't see the scars or even imagine how she would be with wounded pride. Alice was not a woman to wallow in *sturm und drang*. She was focused on the world outside herself—healing, tending, and creating. And Alice felt fortunate—and lucky. Lucky in her good family, her good health.

When I wrote about Alice in my first book, *Finding Herself*, I viewed her as a quintessential Pathmaker. She showed the distinctive pattern of exploration and commitment, clearly marked, and I could describe the ways in which Alice had gone about defining herself and the life she wanted to lead. It was easy in Alice to see the struggle for individuation from her family, her quest for independence, while at the same time grasping onto men for security. She had made a mistake along the way, marrying Mark and staying with him too long, but she extricated herself and chose a better partner. With Adam, she found someone who would offer her stability but also value her individuality and share rather than structure her dreams. At age 33, I thought of Alice as somehow finished with her growth. Indeed, Alice told me, "I don't expect to make the history book's pages, nor do I care to. I wish to be contented. I am now and expect to continue to be. That's all that really matters, isn't it?"

AGE 43

I was eager to see Alice again 10 years later. With the passage of time, I had rather idealized her. I found her still living in West Virginia, and she met me for the interview in my hotel in a nearby town, bringing me some food in case I hadn't eaten. Still attractive, what was most notable about her face were the prominent smile lines. She was warm and smiled throughout our interview, enjoying recounting the joys in her life. She was enthusiastic about her family, her work, and her house. At the end of the interview, she said, "It all depends on whether you see the glass as half full or half empty," but I wasn't sure just what she was missing in the empty half.

In the 10 years since I'd seen her, Alice had changed course professionally and become a high school teacher. Her sons were now 12 and 13, and she was proud of them for being A students and star athletes. Little League now took up a lot of her time. She described her husband Adam as "still my best friend."

The biggest change in Alice was a growth in self-reflection that involved a reworking of her personal history. She had come to label her family of origin as "dysfunctional," a popular construction of the 1990s, and this idea helped her make new sense of her history and of herself. She told me that although there had been no substance abuse or violence in her family, she felt kinship with children of alcoholics. The idea that something was amiss in her family began percolating when she was in college and discovered that other young women had closer relationships with their parents. She recalled going home and telling her parents, "Do you realize I don't know either of you?" Her father's comeback was to say, "Well, then, you couldn't pick up any of our prejudices, could you?" She recalled a roommate who told her that her mother was her best friend, something Alice couldn't even imagine. But these thoughts, like many unsettling thoughts that crossed Alice's mind, got put aside. By her early 40s, though, she had built a lot of resentment about the lack of communication in her family and the feeling that conversation was always on a superficial level. Although she smiled as she told me this, she recounted a time when her brother yelled at her mother, and her mother responded by telling him that he should see a psychiatrist for his "difficulties." Beneath the smiles, then, Alice was struggling with how she could appropriately express her anger.

To illustrate the lack of communication, Alice told me that although her parents lived just three hours away, her mother hadn't even told her that she had cancer until after the treatment was successful. This seems to have been generational because Alice's mother once told her that her own parents never spoke to one another at all. "Not until I had my own kids did I realize how little communication there had been. . . . When I got my period for the first time and told my mother, she said, 'Well, I thought you'd find out about that at school.'"

By contrast, Adam's family was very expressive, and Adam helped her "not to close up so much. I've known for a long time I had a really good denial system. I had learned to depress my emotions so much." This was a remarkable insight for Alice in this age period. She began to see that some of her strength rested on denying her feelings and was curious about if and how she could live more expressively. She relied on Adam to help her with this, to force her to acknowledge her feelings, even though his demand for emotional response from her often led to conflict between them.

She was most focused, though, on what her tendency to close up might do to her children. "Having this knowledge about myself and the family in which I grew up has made me concentrate on making sure that there is a closeness with my kids so I don't repeat that pattern. And I feel really good about what's happened so far. My 12-year-old son had a conversation with me about masturbating about a month ago, so I feel I must be doing something right. And I try to tell them that I love them, something I never heard in my family." Identity, at this age, then, seemed to expand into a focus on what kind of person she was going to be in the world, particularly in regard to expressing her feelings in her family.

Still, Alice's attention was primarily outward, in her work and her relationships. The career change was just what she needed. She had no longer been feeling challenged in the small hospital where she had been directing the physical therapy program, as she had said in her previous interview. Innovation was discouraged by the administration, which was chronically short of funds for learning new ways of working. She said, somewhat ruefully, that she had given up on the idea that she could do something to "save the world." Teaching was appealing because she saw it as a way to spend more time with her children, so she went to graduate school to earn a teaching certificate. Alice thrived as a high school teacher and was nominated for the state "Teacher of the Year Award."

The greatest joys were with her sons, and they spent a lot of time doing things as a family. Alice had played softball as a teenager and now devoted much energy to playing baseball with them and getting into coaching. When I asked her about the major good experiences over the past 10 years, she included the moment when her older son hit a home run for the first time. Another joy was fixing up their house, a long-term project she worked on with Adam. They seldom traveled—"we have all we need right here," she said. She loved gardening and being close to nature. "I don't ever want to move from here." Alice had wanted to live in the country where there were forests, lakes, and fields for her children to play in; the city held little appeal for her.

The most difficult moments in Alice's world at this age occurred when there were clashes with Adam, usually about her not communicating enough, often about their difficulty in getting sexual desire in sync. She was rarely interested in sex, and he took this as a lack of affection. While she was a willing lover, she seldom had the drive and this led to conflict. "It's my chemistry but he takes it personally." Adam was very supportive of her dedication to her teaching but sometimes resented her bringing work home, wishing she had more time for him and their relationship. While she thought Adam might be going through some kind of midlife crisis due to physical challenges and stresses in his work, there were no fissures in the solidity of their marriage. Alice still felt fully determined to grow old with him.

Alice was animated talking about her teaching and her students. She delighted in coming up with interesting special projects for them, getting involved in revising the curriculum to make it more student-friendly.

Envisioning the next 10 years, Alice said that she toyed with the idea of getting a PhD but couldn't even think about this until her children finished college—she couldn't afford to stop working. She supposed she'd still be teaching, hoped to be in the same house—finished. She felt content, all in all, and thought she was "more realistic" about what she could accomplish. There seemed to be no big push for change. Alice felt she had gotten where she wanted to go. And she gave Adam the credit. "He's like a soulmate. He gives me a compliment every day which is good for my self-esteem. He is my solidity and my roots. I like where I am and if weren't for him, I wouldn't be here. I can't imagine not having him in my life. He's been so good for me."

At age 43, Alice's political or religious views had not changed. They did not press religion on their sons; she thought she could teach them values and morals by how she lives. She continued to identify strongly with feminism and took action locally by writing a harassment policy at school and insisting on non-sexist speech. She monitored pay scales to make sure that women were treated fairly. Alice got active politically around the local school budget, an issue very close to her.

Alice was at this age blessed with good health but was a bit overweight and thought she should probably exercise more. Their financial situation was manageable. They could pay their expenses while living simply and had little saved. They wanted to build an addition to the house so each of the boys could have his own room, and this was their next goal.

There were many friends in Alice's community, and she was heralded by her former students. She had just one intimate friend, the same friend from college days who lived far away but with whom she stayed in close touch.

After talking to Alice, I was taken by her calm steadiness, her sense of fulfillment. I realized that talking to me was a bit stressful, although she wrote me later and said she enjoyed it enormously. The stress came from reflecting on herself, something that doesn't come naturally to Alice. She told me that her biggest worry was about her outlook on her feelings. She wondered whether her way of managing her inner world was because of something inherent in her personality or a result of what she grew up with. She said she often felt confused about her emotions and how she expressed them—not so much anger, but love. It was the expression of love that Adam seemed most to be missing from her, and she was very confused about this because she loved him so completely.

Alice had the sense of having arrived at the place she aimed for: "I'm at peace. I have a wonderful family and my own home, which were major goals in my life. I have a life partner with whom I hope to grow old." When I asked Alice about her goals for the next 10 years, she said, "I look forward to getting older, having more time to do the things I really want to do—puttering in the garden making trails in our yard, be like Rachel Carson. Simple things—just being, so I can keep learning. That's what keeps me going—becoming closer to the Earth."

AGE 56

When Alice drove up in her van, to my great relief, I was struck at how middle-aged Alice now looked (as though I hadn't aged as well!). She was now at least 20 pounds overweight, dressed in jeans although she was coming from school. As before, she was warm and welcoming, even though, with my city clothes and demeanor, I must have seemed quite alien to her. Still, especially as I had written so positively about her in the age-30s book, *Finding*

Herself, she was happy to see me. Alice said that she hadn't been affected at all by being in the study and didn't even remember what I wrote, but there were times during the interview when she referred to comments I had made about her. She had given Adam the book to read the parts about her, but no one else, since she was sensitive about having revealed her pot-smoking and promiscuity during college. She was a teacher and had a reputation to guard, after all.

For my part, I was happy to see her as well, but found it hard to talk to her. With all her experience on a single plane, I could find no edges to grasp. After an hour, I felt that my energy had sagged, and it was hard to engage with her. She was living a fulfilling life, but a simple one. I am too much of a city girl to imagine how one could live with so little stimulation and too much of an introvert to imagine living life so externally.

What Alice was most enthusiastic about was having moved to a new house, the one where we were meeting. after she had told me—and herself—that she'd never leave the old one. She was very proud of this new house, which they just moved to a year ago. They have 30 wooded acres, and they are excited about the possibilities. She wants to plant a large garden, grow their own food, build paths to the river. They had already remodeled the kitchen. The house is furnished very simply without much decoration, but there is a lot of light and a small swimming pool that she says they didn't even know was there because it was covered by snow when they bid on the house at auction. They have a friendly Golden Retriever who joined us, and we enjoyed her together.

Again, or perhaps more so, Alice smiled throughout our talk. Her smile seemed to be one of fondly observing herself, like one would narrate someone else's life that one is pleased about. There wasn't a lot of feeling, but feeling had never been a major part of Alice's psychology.

Alice's sons were by now off in their own lives in Pittsburgh, but they kept in touch and visited reasonably often. Now that she and Adam were on her own, she was even more appreciative of his love. She wanted me to really hear how special her marriage is to her. "He tells me each day that he loves me and most days that I am beautiful." The only real crisis that Alice told me about concerned her marriage. Adam's resentment about the lack of sex boiled over and, 10 years ago, threatened the marriage. This led them into counseling, and things got much better. Alice realized that she had to pay more attention to this aspect of their relationship; the thought of losing him was too much to bear. With her usual stoicism, Alice shrugged it off, "Just a bad patch, I guess. Now we're best friends again."

The contentment that Alice aimed for and achieved at earlier ages was still very much present. She was still teaching, but getting tired. "It's a lot of work. Emotionally, paper work, staying on top of it. The pressures of my being held accountable for how kids do on assessments. It doesn't matter to the kids, there's no consequence." She has a couple more years before being eligible for a pension, and she was looking forward to retirement. Perhaps, she thought, she'd teach part time, but what she was most hoping to do was work on her house and garden. When she mentioned her hope to have a root cellar, she told me that her father used to do that, and I was interested that the path seemed to be coming full circle, back to what was positive in her early years. There were still satisfactions in her work; she still joined the students in efforts to make life at school more equitable, more just, but she sounded weary of this. She told me that she had always had the role of mover and shaker at school, and students came to her when they saw changes that needed to be made. But demographic shifts have brought more immigrants to the school and made teaching more difficult, and she was worn out from clashing with the administration. Throughout her career, Alice resisted offers to become a principal; she didn't want the hassles.

It took me some time to understand that moving house had been a major turning point for Alice. "I had said for years that I didn't want to leave the other place—that was our family's history in that house. We had our babies there and I had marked off their heights and the idea of leaving that. . . . But it was a difficult house to maintain. Adam would do the stuff, he's good at that, but it gets to a point where it was more of a chore for him and I didn't want him climbing up on top of a roof to paint. He had been talking for a couple of years about moving." "He wanted to move more than you did?" I asked. "We had gotten that place because I liked it, and he did all that work over the years, but he wanted something else, so we looked for a few years. . . . I decided to let go. That was good. I drive by the place when I go to work. Most of the time, I don't look at it. Every once in a while, I get a pang. But we love being here. . . . We have fun just sitting home. We'll have a glass of wine and walk around and talk about the stuff we want to do with this place. What we want to do with the cellar, what will go where. We've hired a landscaper. We both like being outside, working outside. We've been clearing some of the land. I'll get to retire first, and he will retire a couple of years after that . . . and we'll keep working on this place."

With something of a start, Alice realized that she was like her mother who has lived in the same place for 60 years. But Alice seemed not to mind this similarity; she was just noting it. In her family, communication was still a difficult issue. Several years ago, one of her brother's children died, and the family could barely speak about it. "He's just like my father. When the family is together—at holidays, he just turns on the TV." She reminded me that I had used the word "stoic" in describing her family, a word she thinks fit exactly. "I'm a lot better than I was, mostly because of my husband. I think I told you before that if we had any kind of conflict, my approach would be to shut out those things and if I got really angry, I'd go for a walk—I'd just leave. And he would say, you've got to stay here because shutting me out is worse than anything you could say." So Alice was continuing the battle with her tendency to close up and move on.

Looking for some layers of experience, I asked Alice again to review her life as chapters or transformative moments. Here, she astonished me by elucidating in very clear and straightforward terms the phenomenological essence of the theory of identity formation: "It wasn't until I got away from my parents in college that I started experimenting and being more independent and looking at some of my values and were they really my values or were they my parents' values and pulling out the stuff that was more me and letting go the stuff that was more them." I asked her if she remembered doing that specifically. "Yes. I remember an English prof I had as a freshman talking about God and religion and pretty much saying that we created God as a way to explain the natural world, and one of my classmates was debating him about this and the prof said 'Is this something you believe or something your parents taught you to believe?' And that may have been a trigger for me to examine some of my beliefs and were they really mine?"

So this is the moment from which Alice dates her independence—this and her decision made on her own, to go to college over her high school boyfriend's protests. Indeed, her identity was formed on her own terms.

From this vantage point of late mid-life, Alice sees more clearly that the biggest, and perhaps best, decision she made was to go to college over her high school boyfriend's objections. And she did this on her own, with no encouragement from her parents who gave her complete freedom to do whatever she wished. College was an eye-opening time of experimentation. But she fled from her freedom out of fear of being alone, grasping for Mark who, unlike her high school boyfriend, at least didn't try to control her. She was grateful to him for "letting me be myself" and eventually married him. But then, when this marriage didn't work out, "I didn't go very long without a man in my life because I started dating my present husband before the divorce was done. I thought I could have a good time with this guy for a while. He made me laugh. We had fun. And it stuck." Having her babies was the next major chapter, a "fun" chapter, she and Adam doing things together with the kids while they grew up. And what follows is a chapter called "No kids," in which they miss their sons but keep in touch and make plans for their garden.

I commented to Alice that she indeed seems to have created the life she wanted, and she replied, "It is. Better than the life I thought I would have, I think. I think I'm more affluent—we have more money than I thought we'd have. I never thought I'd end up in a place like this—much nicer than what I had pictured. I have a very good, very strong marriage to my best friend and I'm incredibly grateful for that because I see so many marriages that are really not happy. And for my sons being in the position in which they are. It would be nice if they were in positions where they were using their college degrees and making enough money so that they could have a little more free time for their music, but as long as they say they're happy, that's what's important. I feel good about the careers that I've had. I enjoyed being a physical therapist while I was that, and I learned a lot that I have used just personally and with family members with health or medical issues. That was good in taking care of my kids' medical issues, the few that they had. I feel good about the professional growth. I really feel I made a difference with a number of kids. Influencing their career directions. There was a young girl who was dating a boy who was very controlling. It was like my high school relationship. She was brighter than he, and they didn't seem to fit and I took her aside and I knew I was sticking my neck out. And so I had a conversation with her about this boyfriend and talked to her about my relationship and about respect and that kind of stuff, and she just nodded at me and I thought all right. And then several years later, she was in the school as a community member and she pulled me aside and she said, 'Do you remember the conversation? You pulled me aside. . . Well, I want you to know that on the morning I got married, you were the first person I thought of when I woke up because I thought, if I hadn't had that conversation with you, I would not be marrying the great guy I just married.' The story still gives me a chill every time I say it. So often we have little conversations with kids, and we never know whether or not we're getting through but we do, at least sometimes. That's one of the really cool things about being a teacher. Over the years, I've taught close to 2,000 kids." Indeed, I recognized how many accomplishments Alice had to be proud of, but she didn't seem proud. She just seemed to take it all in stride.

Perhaps sensing my boredom with the placidity of her life, Alice told me directly that her life isn't very exciting. In fact, the only thing she does for excitement is something that embarrasses her, and she told me about it only hesitantly. Recently, she had gotten interested in past lives that can be contacted through séances. This she did with several friends. She became quite passionate telling me about the people, mainly strangers, who they have met, people from different centuries. Alice was a bit sheepish about this because she realized that it didn't fit with her usual level-headed down-to-earth self, but it seemed to be a somewhat quirky part of herself that she was enjoying. Indeed, she had been very skeptical at first, but gradually came to believe in the reality of this experience. I wasn't sure what to make of her stories of having a keeper, to whom she was married in a past life, who will greet her when she dies, of having been married to Adam in two other past lives, of helping people who died long ago. "If you don't do this, I know you must think it is wacko, but it is amazing!!!! And the older I get, the more open-minded I get for things like that." So now Alice could trump me in open-mindedness and access to the unseen. I asked her if this was some kind of spiritual belief and tried to have her explain it to me.

So Alice tried. She talked to me about energy fields, forces, and Chi. I couldn't make much sense of it—and neither could Adam or her children or her other friends. "We're not as well-defined as we think we are. I love this stuff. My husband thinks I'm nuts. There's a force—I'm not sure about the origins. I'm pretty sure we live many lives, and I think we connect with people again and again that we have known in previous lives. I think we knew each other in a previous life. I've always felt a very positive connection with you, so I think we probably knew each other in a previous life. According to the information I have found, there is someone who is always with us. They're known as keepers. They are sort of like teachers, and they're just sort of there."

I tried to stay with this by asking Alice what she had learned from her keeper. "I asked my keeper, and he brought up the idea of teaching and he said what's important is that you help your students achieve their own potential. He also told me I need to kind of relax." I asked her if these were things she kind of already knew and she replied, "I think it was new as far as paying attention to individual kids' potential more. . . . I have a student now who is a senior, a special ed kid, he's really high strung, always in a hurry, difficult to focus on anything for a long time. He always hurries up to do something and hopes its good. We have conversations now."

I'm afraid I lost Alice at this point. It seemed to me that she was attributing her own good intuition and teaching capability to an unseen keeper. But I was happy she had something to be passionate about in her life—it just didn't happen to be something that I could relate to. She worried that I would think she had gone off the deep end, but I had no worries of the sort. I was rather delighted to know that there was a corner of her life where she could be less rational, less in control. Erikson would have cheered her for this because he prized play and wonder as aspects of adult vitality.

So Alice brought me into other worlds in more than one way—the world of rural self-containment and the world of a kind of mysticism, neither of which I could understand very well.

Alice was, in her word, content. "I love my life. I can't believe I'm as lucky as I am to have everything go as well as it is. I'm just waiting for some disaster—not that I think about that a lot. It's just the fact that we were able to pick up this place and the fact that we were able to sell the other place—in a month, in this market. And we had a contractor who wasn't busy because of the economy. We were able to get people to come in who normally you couldn't get in a long time and bang, bang, everything just fell into place. It was incredible. I feel like my whole life is like that to a large degree. I don't have to work real hard at things that I want, it seems."

This, too, was hard for me to understand. By the age of 59, Alice had created exactly the life she had hoped for. She was a highly successful teacher, had raised two independent sons who were doing well, and had a marriage that was thriving. All of that took work of some sort, but she seemed not to know how to account for it.

When I pressed her about a future, there were some glimmers of unrealized possibility. Maybe she'd get a PhD in something completely different, Alice thought. Or become politically active. She didn't *really* think that gardening would be enough for her, but she never had so much free time before. "If it is meant to happen, it will happen," says the fatalistic part of Alice. And then she tells me her overall favorite saying: "it is what it is." In these phrases are the key to Alice's personality, I think. She makes things happen but is also ready to accept what fate brings her, both at the same time. She is independent in spirit but has always needed a man to depend on.

Alice's ways of dealing with internal conflict feature suppression, a defense mechanism that George Valliant found predominant in healthy, successful men. It's not an approach to life that psychologists generally recommend, but, in Alice's case, it seems to work.

Maria

As identity unfolds, a woman's sense of her own life history changes. The present creates the past. Andrea enlarged the story of her determination to go to college, amplifying her parents' resistance to her wish to be other than a secretary. Betty revised her view of her early life from one of parental deprivation to one of the opportunity to learn responsibility. All these reworkings of life history served to buttress the identity of the time. Without having followed these women from college to midlife, I would have a murkier view of their development because, as they age, their past gets cloudier, more packaged, and they forget not so much what they did as what they felt. Nowhere is this clearer than in Maria, who had a clear self-defining identity memory that transmutes dramatically as her identity evolves. In tracking this memory, we see both the processes of change and continuity in her identity.

AGE 21

Maria grew up in an immigrant Italian family in Philadelphia, surrounded by relatives and embedded in Catholicism and old-country values. Consistently over time, she described her mother as emotional, giving, and loving and her father as reserved and strict, the harsh disciplinarian. Maria was in the Pathmaker status in college, and much of her crisis and commitment was centered on a relationship she had with an African-American boy that lasted for six years, from high school through college.

When I met her as a senior in college, Maria described herself as in love with Jack and intending to marry him. She was in the process of individuating herself from her family, and, while going to college and planning a career as a social worker were an important part of her goals and the process of growing into her own person, Jack was emotionally a more central part of her staking her independence.

As she told it at the time, at age 20, she had taken seriously all the Church teachings about loving one's neighbor and had expected her family and friends to accept Jack. She described him adoringly as "intelligent, very independent, as unemotional as I am emotional, athletic, plays semi-professional basketball and interested in going to law school."

The relationship affected her way of thinking about her values, which she also formulated as a breach with her family and community. She said: "That was a decision I had to make. With religion talking about love thy neighbor and all men are equal, and it was all right until he asked me out. Now, after six years, my family has accepted it." She intended to marry him. "It's a decision I've thought about for a long time, and it still bothers me. But when I think about it, I know it's going to be my life, and I can't go against my own ideas for my parents."

Jack was to be Maria's badge of differentiation from her family and her traditional background, a position from which she could create a distance from her childhood self. But she remained fiercely loving of her family. Her sense of individuality did not undo her ties to them. Still, she was determined to live her own values and make this life that seemed incomprehensible to her family. It was the site of her identity formation.

AGE 33

Maria's early adulthood was quite different from what she had envisioned. When I met Maria again when she was 33, I found her to be less vivacious than she had been in college. She was married to George and had two children. I was eager to learn how she had gotten from where she was in college to where she was now.

Maria began the interview by commenting that, of course, I wouldn't recognize her since she had gained 50 pounds since college. Even more startling to me, this Maria seemed weary. Gone was the sparkle, the idealism, even the determination. Her life had gone through many revisions in the intervening years, with burdens greater than she had expected. I met her in her office—she had retrained as a nurse and was working in a rehabilitation facility, a job she chose because the hours and demands worked with being a mother. She was proud that she was a working mother, something her family thought was impossible, and she was proud of her success at work even though financial concerns made it necessary to work more than she wished. Working was now a form of differentiation from her family. "I feel like my whole extended family—the 10 mothers I had growing up—is watching me, asking in subtle, indirect ways if I am sure I am doing the right thing." But, not long before, she had overheard her mother telling someone else, "Maria is married and working and her kids are okay." At that moment, she felt that she had triumphed—on her own path.

Still, her life was centered on motherhood ("no stronger love or bond exists for me as the one with my children")—and Maria emphasized to me that, in many ways, she had become more "traditional" than she had been when I saw her last. Only physical problems kept her from having more than the two children she had.

At age 33, Maria again narrated the story of her relationship with Jack, but this time told it very differently. Jack mainly appeared as a foil to her husband, George, a white man. As she told it at this point, Jack would not have been a good life partner for her. What was centrally important to her was a stable life focused on family. George was a friend she had known for many years. Although she never "fell in love" with him in an intense way, she knew George to be "sensitive, caring, handsome, somewhat shy and responsible." He loved children and had the same values as she, and she felt that they "fit together" well. They married shortly after she graduated from college. At this telling, Maria described Jack as involved in the drug culture, selling drugs. She said "I didn't want to have to cope with that. . . . He was not motivated to finish school or to work. He had a big circle of friends that didn't include me, there were lots of times he wasn't there for me. I ended the relationship—I needed to see what else was out there. He wasn't interested in marriage or children."

Maria remembered that there had been a lot of emotional pain with Jack and contrasted this with the steadiness of her husband. I hadn't seen Maria during what must have been a time of turmoil as she let go of Jack, but evidently the sense of standing by her own values apart from her family had strengthened her enough to take yet another step toward living a life on her own terms.

Paradoxically, Maria's life structure at age 33 brought her closer to her family of origin, again with Jack as a central foil. "My father pretended my relationship with Jack didn't exist. But he likes George. The relationship with Jack was a real struggle knowing my father disapproved of it so much. As I became more traditional, we visit back and forth a lot. He adores my children." At this point, the now more "traditional" Maria portrayed her college self as more misguided than anything else. Jack represented the self that Maria might have become, and, in not becoming this, she could feel more clearly the boundaries of who she is. Maria expressed her valuing of George's stability and devotion to fatherhood by remembering Jack who didn't even want children. Perhaps, having made her point with her family and assuring herself that she could decide her life on her own terms, Maria was free then to adjust the content of her identity more in line with other aspects of herself—the part that she calls more "traditional," more in line with her upbringing. Her sense of differentiation was now anchored in her ability to be both a successful professional woman and a successful mother. She felt she was raising her children with similar, but more liberal, values. She thought she was less restrictive with them and teaching them to be more tolerant of others.

At this age, she had discarded the value-driven self who also needed the excitement of the relationship with Jack in favor of the self who wanted to raise a family with a man who she felt would be a good father to their children and a reliable husband to her. She hadn't exactly retreated from the independent identity she was forging in college. Stressing the importance of her being a working mother in her highly traditional extended family, she still saw herself as shaping her own path. Evidently, the turbulence she had experienced with Jack threatened her dreams of having a family, and she reached for George as a partner who could join her in this. At age 33, she was living a life she had chosen clearly and carefully. The main stress came from there never being enough money, even though they lived fairly simply. And she was aware that she coped with stress by eating. Beyond this insight, though, Maria wasn't very interested in self-reflection. She seemed to me to be solid, a good problem-solver, focused on the well-being of her children. She had made her choices, but I missed the sparkle I had seen in her earlier.

AGE 43

Life wasn't kind to Maria, and when I saw her again at age 43, she was, with good reason, even more beleaguered. She had been feeling that her life was running smoothly when, three years before this interview, George, at the age of 42, developed a brain tumor. Although he survived a very risky surgery, he was left with multiple disabilities, and Maria had to take on herself the support and management of the family. There were many losses of family members, so for Maria, "the last ten years have been an extended period of trauma."

Maria was at this point even more deeply committed to George. She said, ". . . I have such respect for him—how he would never accept the limitations that others kept putting on him. And I think he also saw a strength in me. I held things together. I worked. I took care of the kids, visited him in the hospital every day. It brought us closer. We care about each other. We care a lot about our kids. We are committed to each other. We've been through some rough times together, and I can see where this could drive people apart." Reflecting on her marriage, Maria feels that it has turned out much as she expected. "I wanted someone who is very family-oriented and that's what I got. . . . There were times I wished we had more financial security and I could take golf lessons or belong to a gardening club and not have to work as much as I do." Maria cannot look to George to be the traditional breadwinner, and this is a source of disappointment that she bravely bears. Although he still can work part-time, she had always been the more ambitious one of the couple.

"All this trauma . . . does make you reevaluate some things in your life and what's important—your friendships, your relationships with people are more firmly cemented by these events, or you realize some relationships weren't as strong as you thought. You see who is really there for you and who isn't. I look at things a little differently. My family has always been very important for me. It's even more important to me now... everything else really falls by the wayside, and that becomes the real core of your existence and when you are faced with that kind of thing, nothing is more important—not your job or your financial situation. I think someone's health—it's such a basic, basic thing. I had more aspirations professionally. Now I'm not so sure I want to keep climbing that ladder. Maybe I should be content pretty much where I am and not always try to move ahead and take on more. Personally, I'd like to develop more personal interests and take more time for myself than I did in those first 10 years. George's mother's death was particularly difficult for all of us because it was very sudden. She was young and healthy and just dropped dead one day of a heart attack. She didn't have the time to enjoy her life that she really deserved."

These years, though, were years of great professional success as she became Director of Nursing at a large hospital, and Maria was proud of what she had accomplished. "Professionally, I've grown. I've been in the same position I've been in for 14 years as a manager. But I did go to graduate school—that was positive. I was nominated as Nurse of the Year one year. My program got an award from the AMA as one of the outstanding programs. I've done a lot of community work with this program, and I'm well-known in the community. So professionally I feel that I've done well and I've been recognized for it. I feel secure in that. There's been times I've thought it would be nice to keep moving up the ladder administratively. The hospital here has gone through many administrative changes in the past few years and I jokingly say that if you climb that ladder you can fall off. That top layer changes frequently, yet the people who are department heads and are closer to the patients and do the nitty-gritty work have stayed more stable. So I've kind of re-evaluated how far do you want to go? Do you really want to move on? Sometimes I think I should try something different, and I may some day but it's not—it won't be—because I want to become president of a hospital. It would be because I want to expand my horizons."

Maria was aware of the irony that although her mother and aunts had regarded her work as self-indulgent and dispensable, it had now become a necessity. Although she took pride in having been able to become the breadwinner, she also lived within the constraints of that responsibility. When she toyed with the idea of applying for a higher position, she feared losing her livelihood, which was no longer a matter of discretion. The massive administrative changes in the hospital made her worry in a new way. "I have to decide whether I want to stay at this job or move on to something else. There have been times when I've really struggled with that and continually chosen to stay where I am although I have sometimes been very tempted to try something different. I [now] have some fears about losing my job because they have tended to let go managers here who have a lot of seniority. A lot of people say that's an economic decision because you are at the higher end of the salary scale, and people who I worked with here as long as I've been here have been fired. And I don't know how I am going to fare. I think before my husband's surgery, I would have been. . . . Now I say if it happens to me, it happens to me, I'll find another job. We're not going to starve to death. I may not like it as well, but it may turn out well. I can't stay up nights worrying about it. Maybe having been through what I've been through, it gives me perspective. I don't know who they can find within the organization who has the experience or community contacts that I have, but you never know. Sometimes that gives me maybe a false sense of security."

Maria had always valued George for his devotion to the children and his willingness to be a full partner in their family life. She admired him for the recovery he made. "He had major determination that I'm not sure I would have had in that situation. He has had a lot of fight from the beginning and has exceeded anyone's expectations in terms of his recovery. I just don't think that I have personally that kind of determination and fight. But I also don't think that you know until it hits you. You know, I've seen so many patients—that human spirit kicks in, and you don't want to die. But I've also seen the work he put in and the struggle. I don't know if I ever would have had that stamina. I'm a more laid-back individual, more introspective. My husband is very concerned about his appearance, always had been. For him not to be able to talk and have a paralyzed body—whereas I may have been more accepting of it. I have such respect for him—how he would never accept the limitations that others kept putting on him."

As Maria detailed for me all the pain and struggle in her life, I did not expect Jack to appear at all in her narrative. Clearly, Maria no longer needed the Jack episode to construct a self independent of or differentiated from her family or to define George by contrast or to justify her choice of him as a life partner. But Jack *did* appear, and her memory of him served quite a different function, again to buttress a current center of her identity. In this autobiographical telling at age 43, Maria was most ardent in the interview when discussing her daughter, Linda, now 17: "I'm having a tough time dealing with her. She has been dating a boy for over a year which I am having a real hard time with. And what's funny is that I was involved with this guy before I got married for seven years and I was at my cousin's for Easter and we were talking about our daughters and I said I don't know why she'd want to stick to one guy and my cousin turned to me and said, 'Sounds just like her mother.' And I thought, my God, you're right. And the more I try and discuss it with Linda, the more she digs her heels in. She's always had a stubborn streak but we've always had a good relationship, and this is the first thing that we've hit that we just don't see eye to eye on at all. And I'm not particularly fond of him. He's not a bad kid, but I think he has some real problems and I think she sees herself as a helper. I never drank as a teen and neither does she, but she went to a party the other night and all the guys gave her their keys to hold and it was like looking in the mirror. I was called the 'Mother' of my high school. And I see Linda—she is the dependable one, and I look at her and I think, 'She is me.' Yet it's making me angry to see her in this long-term relationship at this young age. She won't even let me open my mouth about it. I've used all the skills I have to talk to her about it. This is the first big struggle I'm having with her. She's a very bright girl, does well in school, has never been in any trouble. She's a child most parents would die for. Talking to her about college is a real struggle—she could care less. She's got so much potential, but she is so caught up in this relationship."

So Maria sees a ghost of her earlier self in Linda. And I wondered why it would make Maria so angry to see her daughter repeating her own pattern. "Because I look back and know why I rebelled. Because my parents were so strict. But I've let her do almost everything. I feel like I've done just the opposite of my parents in bringing her up, and here she's doing the same thing. I didn't expect it from her. I expected her to be a little more worldly and not to get caught up intensely in a relationship. She's seen her mother be very independent and work. I've supported the family for three years, I've always worked outside the home. The different awards I've gotten. She's come to the dinners, so she's seen her mother. So I always felt she didn't have the same role model as I did, you know, a mother for whom marriage was almost arranged and was very subservient. . . . I just don't understand why she's had that need to get so involved in such a monogamous relationship at such a young age. . . . It's been a major struggle."

In this long narration at age 43 are many complex signs about Maria's current and past identities and their relationship to one another—and all are entangled with the meanings she was currently making about her late adolescent identity, represented by her relationship with Jack. It was noteworthy that she told me that she didn't even make a connection between her relationship with Jack and Linda's relationship with her boyfriend until her cousin called it to her attention. Thus she indicated that the self with Jack had been buried somewhere, suppressed, repressed perhaps, but not alive in her consciousness. Once her cousin told her that Linda "sounds like her mother," we might expect that Maria would call on this old self to better understand her daughter. This would be a way of making her life narrative consistent, drawing on her past to illuminate the present. But, instead, Maria reconstructed her adolescent self as "rebellious," a construction she had not offered before in her interviews. Now, she depicted her earlier self as engendered by the strictness of her parents, as an oppositional, rather than a principled self, a self that was fighting her parents rather than a self fighting racism or groping for independence. She had lost the self that was in love and could not even imagine Linda as a girl in love.

Maria's current identity was anchored by her effort to be a certain *kind* of mother to her children, a central theme of her identity that she may not have even been able to articulate before Linda posed a challenge to it. Core to her identity was seeing herself as a good mother, in contrast to her own overly strict mother. Her current identity narrative now portrayed herself as having been in rebellion against overcontrolling parents, and Maria was astonished that, having tried hard not to be overcontrolling in her own mothering, Linda nevertheless rebelled against her wishes. An intense love relationship now signified rebellion, which implies a failure of mothering.

A third aspect of her identity that is apparent in this narration is the self that Maria remembered as "the dependable one," a self that seems continuous but now is viewed with some ambivalence. This is the element that leads her to say, with some repulsion, that "Linda is me." She finds in Linda aspects of a self that she wishes to disavow. And what she wants to disavow is the adolescent self who was devoted to steadying an impulsive boy. She doesn't mention the racial issue. She reshapes her remembered adolescent self to correspond to her view of Linda.

That her relationship with Jack was once a way of defining herself as principled, independent of her family or a means of discovering the importance to her of a devoted, family-oriented man are all no longer part of her remembered self. The discarded self that she remembered at age 33 now took a different emotionally meaningful role—as one not only to be gratefully put aside but now to be actively disavowed.

AGE 53

At her interview at age 53, Maria launched immediately into the lives of her children, now in their 20s. Although her son was living far away and she missed him, her daughter had married someone different from the boyfriend she had had in high school, someone from their small town whom she had known a long time, and they lived on the same street. Maria was very involved emotionally in the decisions her children were making in their lives, although she tried hard not to interfere. She said that her greatest joy was having raised them to independence, and she was gamely trying to hold to her primary identity as a mother. "The hardest time of being a parent, I think, is letting the kids go." A conversation she related with her father showed the intergenerational gaps as well as Maria's struggles. When her daughter, after her college graduation, decided to move across the country with her boyfriend, Maria's father said, "'She's *what*? You tell her no!' I said, 'Dad, how can I tell her no? I mean, she's 22 years old, she's graduated from college—How can I stop her? Lock her in her room?' [Chuckles.] He said, 'Well you just tell her she can't.' I said, 'Don't you get it Dad? I can't tell her she can't anymore; she's an adult now; she can do what she wants. I can tell her I don't like it and I already did—but I have a feeling she's going to do it anyway.' I would just never want to be in the position of estranging myself from my kids. I couldn't bear that." Still, what was emotionally prominent for Maria were the events in her children's lives, events about which she had strong reactions and struggled with deciding if or how to offer her views.

Occupationally, Maria left the hospital just as managed care was strangling her department; she had one short disastrous job with a new health center that failed, then she settled into managing a large medical practice, building its administrative structure nearly from the ground up. The job has been a huge challenge and a lot of new learning, especially about technology, but Maria is glad to have taken on the challenge and grateful that, for the first time, she and her husband are free of financial worries, given that the private practice pays her much more than the hospital ever did. At the same time, she feels there is a lot of the new technology that she does not want to learn—that she is tired and less interested, wants others to do these things. She feels her energy flagging at this age.

In describing her experiences at work, Maria presents herself as an organized and strict manager who can get systems in shape and people to shape up. She isn't very tolerant of laxness in those she manages.

Her husband had retired the previous year and spends his days bored. Maria was struggling with his dependency on her and finding ways to encourage his doing things on his own.

Maria has had some health problems in the past few years, including a mysterious illness that partially incapacitated her but then went away. Through it all, she did what she could to maintain her demanding work schedule. This was a very frightening time because she was very aware of being the family breadwinner and feared not being able to work.

As in the previous decades, Maria looks back at who she has become and what she has done with her life and stresses that "I've had many jobs over my lifetime, but none compare to the satisfaction I've had from raising my children." Her successful career, though, seems to have been in the service of the family. "I've been reading a lot lately about the moms of today and *Newsweek* had a thing about you really can't have it all and how women are just falling apart trying to be these super moms and have a career. And I think, you know— I did go to college, I did get an education, I did get a graduate degree so that I would have the skills to work. And I have always worked, and I have gotten a certain amount of fulfillment out of my job. And I look at what happened to us as a family, and I say, "What if I hadn't gotten a career? Or, what if I had a lower level job or a low-paying job? My God, what would have happened to our family?'"

Since George has retired, Maria thinks more about her own retirement, but is calculating this in terms of having enough money to live on. She doesn't see that as possible for another decade.

As Maria looked back on her life from age 56, she sees herself as having an "ordinary" life, which rather surprised me. I didn't think of her as in any way ordinary. The picture she paints is of growing up in a large, extended Italian Catholic family and being the first to go away to college. In this sense, she was the pathfinder of the family. And it was a battle with her strict father to do this. Maria remembers threatening to join the Peace Corps if he persisted in opposing her. "I was going to get out of that house, one way or another. Because of his rule. I mean, he was very very strict. I mean, you know, no dating, he didn't want me to wear nylon stockings, I mean a very old-fashioned kind of father. And, um, I guess—I rebelled in a quiet way—being sneaky and doing things my father wouldn't find out about, or kind of out of his line of vision. But I was determined to go away to school and so I went away—30 miles away [laughs]. But to me, that was away. I went through college years where I had fun but now, again, looking back, I wish I'd had more fun. I wish I'd dated more; I wish I'd experienced more; I wish I had traveled more, uh, seen more of the world like the young people are today, like my kids have. You know, people are not settling down so soon these days; they're not getting married as soon as they did when I graduated from college. You know, I graduated from college and, you know, almost everyone was engaged or engaged to be married when they graduated from college." Here, I was waiting for her to tell about Jack, but she did not.

Then, as Maria pursued her compressed life narrative, there were the years of balancing work with maximizing her time with the children, working out a schedule so that either she or George were with them all of the time. "We spent all of our time with the kids, all of our time with their activities. This is the life we wanted." Then there were the difficult years with George's illness and rehabilitation, and Maria now recounts her gratitude to her mother for coming to help her, sometimes staying with them for months. Now Maria is thinking about how to repay this debt by taking care of her mother who is slipping into dementia.

The strict Catholicism of her childhood had simply dropped away, and religion no longer had any significance for her. Particularly when George was ill, she felt that the Church community was not supportive, and the sense of community had been the last thread that had tied her to religious observance. Religion, then, was not defining of her identity except in terms of her roots.

The move away from her ethnic and religious foundation has characterized her generation in the family. Of the 18 cousins, all married out of the faith and the Italian community, and the parental generation simply accepts this, even, Maria emphasizes, tolerating a gay couple.

Maria makes the theme of her life perseverance. "I think you have to just kind of get up and do what you have to do and get through today, and tomorrow you get through tomorrow, and the next day, and pretty soon you kind of realize you're getting through it. But if you think of it, if you think too much about it, you try to take it all in or you try to think Oh my God, you know, how'm I gonna, I don't know— I think if you look too far forward you'd get bogged down with thinking I'll never make it or I can never do it."

Asked where she thinks this perseverance came from, she replied, "My parents were never quitters. Again, my parents were first generation in this country so my grandparents, who I knew, came to this country with nothing, like a lot of immigrants. And my grandfather started, you know, three or four businesses that failed before he started a business that was successful. My father, I saw him graduate from college when I was in eighth grade: He went like 10 years at night to get a college degree. So, again, I think it's kind of what you're brought up with and what you're made of, and what you see around you—that you absorb all that as a child." Above all, her parents wanted their children to have a college education, which they all did. And Maria told of being moved to tears when she attended her son's college graduation—the family dream carried to the next generation.

She tries not to push her daughter too hard to give them a grandchild, but this is what she now yearns for. The future she envisions is about being a grandmother and having the money to travel. She also wishes to take more time for herself—to exercise, to relax—but as I heard this, I realized that she has been saying this for the past two decades. The caretaker identity is just too strong—and there is always someone in her life—her parents, George, other family members—who needs her care.

Jack did not appear in Maria's spontaneous life story at age 56, but because I had been so taken with her account of her relationship with him as a touchstone of her development, I planned that, if Maria didn't bring it up, to ask about it at the end of the interview. When asked, Maria responded, with a small laugh, "That's funny cause I was thinking about it the other day. . . . He, uh, that he was my first sexual partner. And, I guess, George and I have been together now 33 years and, you know, intimacy has, has never been his strong suit. But, you know, I've come to terms with it. . . . And it's not that we don't love each other or he doesn't love me, but in terms of the fire or the passion kind of end of things, um, you know, it's, I don't want to say— It's just been a long time that we've had those kinds of feelings. And I think, when I think of that, or me, or the fact. . . . I, I think thank God I had that first relationship because, from that perspective, I felt really desired. You know, that someone really desired me, or wanted me, or. And . . . I'm glad I got to experience that. Even though for a lot of other reasons it didn't work out. . . . And it's not that I, I really wish it did, or that I have fantasies about that it should have, or— Cause I know that it shouldn't have, we were moving in, in different directions. . . . But I think back, in terms of, you know, kind of the, the ideas you have about, uh, romance and passion and all that, that, well, yeah, I experienced that."

I was intensely moved by Maria saying this. It seemed to me to demonstrate a profound integration of the various parts of herself, something she could not have done earlier. Her remembered relationship with Jack became the container for Maria's passionate, sexual self, a self with which Maria enjoys dialogue or reminiscence. There is something poignant about her saying "I experienced that." This is a self that exists enshrined in memory because Maria does not imagine that she will ever realize it again. But it is still very much part of her (private) sense of identity. "I am a person who experienced that."

Maria's identity, if we can try to talk about identity as unitary, has been rooted in caring for others, and the fruits of all her work are symbolized by the children she is so proud of. I feel, though, for her continual absence of interest in her own pleasure. She says that she has stopped going away on yearly trips with her old high school friend since George retired. She feels she can't leave him all alone when he is already so lonely. And when she says of the absence of sex in her marriage, "the lack of intimacy. I mean I missed, miss it. And, uh, I guess I had to, I had to come to terms with it on some level. What was I going to do about it? I talked to him about it, you know, um. He wasn't willing to do anything about it. So then I said to myself, have to decide what am I going—I wasn't going to go out and have an affair. You know, that just wasn't in my nature. And it's upsetting on some level and disappointing on some level, but like I said, I look at more than that in terms of our years together and our relationship. And, you know, he's always been a great father and he's, I can never say, you know—He's never run around, he's never had problems with drugs or alcohol or anything. He's been a good husband."

Like many women, Maria lives with disappointment. But she is aware of having made her choice—choosing a man for his potential as a good husband and father rather than a lover, and when she says she appreciates him and the children and the life they have made together, I believe her.

Notes

1. In this sense, the Pathmakers in this study were very much like the people Gail Sheehy (1981) identified as Pathfinders. She was also surprised to find that they were action-oriented people, not very much given to introspection or self-analysis.

2. There were eight Pathmakers from the college-age sample that I found at age 33. One woman who seemed to be a Pathmaker in college developed after college more like a Drifter in the sense that she experienced life as happening to her rather than herself making choices. In later follow-ups, she seemed to have commitments, but weak ones and commitments that were hard to assess in terms of whether she made choices or allowed herself to be claimed by circumstances. These commitments also morphed

into different ones at later follow-ups. She did not seem to follow any pattern that I could discern, so I do not include her in this book. Another woman, Nancy, I discuss at the end of the next chapter as someone who lost her self-direction. Another woman did not want to be interviewed in her mid-40s, so I dropped her from the study and did not contact her again.

3

A Pathmaker and Her Daughter—And a Pathmaker Who Lost Her Way

The Pathmakers I have described so far tended to be doers rather than internally focused and highly self-reflective. Clara was, among the Pathmakers, at the other end of the spectrum. She was quite psychologically minded, very much aware of the various parts of herself and her own complex feeling states—and this has been true throughout her life. I think she articulates some of the inner experience that some of the other Pathmakers can't quite get into words and sheds some penetrating light on how parts of the self and parts of a life are brought into balance. Because I am so taken with her ability to do this, I quote her at length, especially in the later interviews, so the reader, too, can get to know her in her own words. In addition, I had the opportunity to interview her daughter at the same age Clara had been when I first met her.

At the end of this chapter, I summarize what I think I have learned about the Pathmakers, in part through contrasting them with a Pathmaker who could not maintain her direction and began to drift.

Clara

AGE 21

As a college senior, Clara talked fast and with so much self-assurance that I was suspicious about how confident she really was. It was as though we were having some kind of job interview and she was trying to sell herself, but the anxiety was clear to me as she spoke. In my notes at the time, I wrote that Clara "came on like a steamroller," and I began to understand that she was managing her anxiety with an overlay of hyperconfidence. A student at the University of Illinois, Chicago, she had taken a year off after her sophomore year and went to Chicago to work and think about her future. She enrolled at the University of Illinois in Chicago because, as she put it, "it was the only place I got in," and she didn't want to go back home to the small college where she had begun her studies. Majoring in English, she was planning an academic career that involved pursuing a PhD. This was a lofty goal for the time, unusual for a woman, as I well knew.

Whatever she did, Clara was evaluating herself, worrying about measuring up. With two older brothers, one who did everything better than she, she felt she could never best him. "My whole life, my brother was always going to do better than me." But he was interested in science, a field prized in her family, so choosing English as a field seemed a way of staking her own ground and excelling. Clara saw her mother as incessantly critical of her, never satisfied with how Clara looked or what she did.

Like her brothers before her, Clara, who was raised in Detroit, attended boarding school from age 14 and there fell under the spell of a "perfect girl" whom she tried to emulate and imitate in every way. Clara recalls her parents' irritation when she came home with the manners and sophistication of this special friend and used them to distance herself from her family. She dressed like her, spoke like her, and listened to classical music like her. And, from junior year on, she began following her friend into sexual adventures with boys although she was so concerned about doing well in sex that she never slept with anyone she liked for fear of falling short. She worried a lot about popularity, and following her friend seemed the safest course.

After her freshman year of college, where she did not do well, Clara decided to enter therapy and focused on her fears of not being the best. She said that this intensive therapy made it possible for her to come to terms with "just being myself," and she was able to return to school with less anxiety and less sense of needing to prove herself at every turn. She said that through therapy she "got it" that she didn't have to be better than her older brother. This allowed her to engage in her studies with less pressure, to discover "interest" (rather than success for its own sake) for the first time. She felt that she opened herself to people she met and enjoyed encountering their ideas that were different from her own. She relinquished the goal of perfection and tried to find herself rather than imitating someone she believed to be perfect.

Unlike most of the women I have been following, Clara became very involved with the Women's Movement. Already sensitive to feeling put down and belittled by men, Clara adopted feminism as a cause and was making it a central part of her identity. She was determined to have a serious academic career and doubted that she would ever want to have children. Never would she be submissive to a man. As a college senior, Clara was living with a Catholic man, his Catholicism somewhat troubling to her Jewish parents although religion had never had any importance in their family's life. She told me with pride that they shared all the household chores equally, overcoming any assumptions about who should do what based on gender. Ralph had been her teacher at her first college, and she felt comfortable with him. Early in their relationship, she was relieved to move away from the indiscriminate sexual experiences that had become customary for her. Still, Clara was very sensitive to "being dominated" by other people and worried that marriage might threaten her autonomy and independence.

In part a reflection of the intensive therapy she had had, Clara was well able to articulate her inner struggles. Musing about religion, she regretted not having a "protector." "I was on a plane between Chicago and New York and I had a moment of crisis about God. I was alone and I realized that the plane was not going not to crash because I was on it. No one was protecting me. There was no one there that made me special, and even if I was a good person and didn't sin, it didn't matter."

Clara had clearly made identity choices at this age on her own terms. She chose her field, her religious beliefs, her political commitments, and her sexual values after a period of experimentation or thought. The cornerstones of the nascent identity she was shaping were, in the order she named them, the Women's Movement, literature, and Ralph. But I wondered about why she was so anxious, so deliberately confident. She told me about getting over trying to be perfect, and, indeed, she described to me a lot about herself that she didn't feel was perfect, but she remained very competitive and set her goals high. She saw herself as "independent," able to define things on her own terms, but she felt she had to anxiously guard this and resist others' influence.

AGE 33

Twelve years later, I found Clara living in Italy. During a sabbatical I had taken in Europe, I went there to interview her. Now 33, Clara was married to Ralph and pregnant, living a life she could not have imagined when I saw her 12 years earlier. She filled me in on the many changes in her life she had made since college. After graduating, through a friend, she was offered a job in a private girls' school. She thought it made no sense to pass up a good job, especially because, in retrospect, the transition after college was "scary," so she taught English there for three years. While she liked the girls she taught, she hated the atmosphere of elitism at the school. She felt that she was in a "very small world" at the school and "I felt I would rot." During these years, she took a course in book-binding and found that she loved it. When she had the opportunity to get a job restoring old books, she left teaching and devoted herself to book-binding full-time. Meanwhile, she and Ralph married, and he had an opportunity to teach and do research in Italy. There, she had discovered two women who were experts in book-binding and who took her on as an apprentice; she was relishing her time with them and all that she was learning.

Clara now seemed to me to be content and comfortable, no longer selling herself, but instead enjoying the life she was pursuing and looking forward to the future, just a bit worried about what bringing a child into their lives might mean for them.

In terms of her occupational identity, Clara now saw herself as a book-binder. "I think books are special, and I think working with them is wonderful. I'm passionate about it." Part of her enchantment was with the women she was working with and how much faith they had in her and her skills. Sometimes she couldn't tell if what she loved was these women or the work, but she told me that the work itself was very satisfying aesthetically. She took such pleasure in a finished product. She had a few commissions, but saw her time in Italy as a time of pure learning in that Ralph's income was sufficient to support them. She dreamed of having her own book-binding studio when they returned to the United States, but told me that she wanted it to be a studio with others. The one thing she did not want to do was work all alone. Although Clara was not sure she could make this into a reasonable profession, she felt she had a good chance of making it happen and wanted to try. She hoped to recreate in the United States what she was doing in Italy—and make a living doing it. But, she worried, the Italians were so much more sophisticated about all of this than the Americans—could she transplant her skills? Perhaps she would work part-time in some book-related institution just to stay "part of the outside world."

Like nearly all the other Pathmakers, Clara had made a change in the occupational identity she had committed herself to at the end of college when this path didn't actually suit her. Psychologically, having made choices on their own terms seemed to have made possible making a different choice. The process of matching interest and talents with the realities of the world and its opportunities played out for these women in subtle ways as they discovered that what they imagined they would be doing occupationally was at odds with how it actually felt to be doing it. In Clara's case, she didn't so much struggle with relinquishing her initial plans as stumble upon something that she hadn't even known about in college and then used her determination and resourcefulness to develop her interest in book-binding. She had always loved books; she was, after all, an English major hoping to be an English professor. Now she found a different way to engage with books.

In 1982, when I interviewed her for the second time, Clara still felt strongly about the Women's Movement, was intensely opposed to some of Reagan's policies, but had become inactive politically, even before their move to Italy. "I realize how much more complicated things are. In the '60s, everything seemed so clear and simple." But she didn't feel her political views had changed, nor had her views on religion. In terms of sexual standards and values, she articulated similar ideas to those she expressed in college. She thought that premarital sex was good and healthy but should be combined with caring and affection. "But I understand that people have such different needs. So I say that for myself and wouldn't impose it on others. But I'd impose it on my daughter—that caring and love are a part of a sexual relationship, but I'd hope I could accept that she might need to go through a time where that was not so and she had to experiment if that were important." All the "buts" in the preceding statement seemed to reflect the complexity of Clara's thinking. She had her values but was still sensitive to one person imposing ideas on another.

Central to Clara's sense of herself at this age was her marriage to Ralph. She emphasized that he and their couplehood gave her a cherished sense of stability. He was supportive of her, loved her work, and cheered her on in whatever she was doing. "He takes me seriously intellectually and as a human being." Again she contrasted him with the "oppressive" men she had been with before him. They had now been together for so long she couldn't imagine life without him. "I admired him. He is brilliant, came from a poor family, and did everything on his own." Ralph's level-headedness balanced her emotionality, she told me. I asked her about clashes, and she said that she tends to be more neat and compulsive, but they fight and fuss very little. Although they didn't have great financial security—there were always questions about his contract being renewed—everything else had been "stable."

I asked about how she felt her marriage had changed her. "It's a process of softening," she said, "You mellow out. Things are so much more intense when you're 20." Indeed, Clara here put into words exactly what I had experienced of her—she had mellowed. Again, she emphasized that Ralph had given her security and stability. She felt so fortunate that she was free to do what she enjoyed rather than to feel the pressure of earning money. "Ten years ago I would never have said that I'd allow myself to be supported by someone else, but I realize now that working is not necessarily a lot of fun and it has actually meant a great deal to me to play a very feminine role—cooking, entertaining friends, having that be a rich part of our lives—and having time to pursue my own interests. Our lives are so much what we've chosen. We've both grown and moved without interference from one another. What was most basic and important has changed very little—support and closeness."

Clara warily regarded the future, with a baby on its way. "We decided that's it's now or never. We started talking about it two years ago and wanted to wait for financial stability, but who knows when that may come. So far it's worked out. We were intellectualizing the decision so much. Neither one of us wanted to take responsibility for the decision. One summer we got a cat and we got obsessed with the cat and realized what was going on. I like the idea of having a baby in Italy. Also, it's far from my mother, and it's a good idea to have a baby far from her. But having a baby is the one thing you can't change your mind about so it's very scary. I'll have to give up my work for a period of time. I'll have to wait to see what it's like to see what I will do."

One of the most interesting things to me in this meeting was that Clara filled me in on her earlier history, told me things that she hadn't wished to tell me earlier. As she reviewed her life from age 33, she marked an early chapter of being a "gawky, fat, freckled and frizzy-haired child" who fought with her brothers and played with her friends. While her father doted on her, her relationship with her mother was always troubled. "She was disappointed that I wasn't beautiful, that I wasn't all the things she wanted me to be, and she didn't like me very much. That my father doted on me must have felt to her like competition." Clara called the second major chapter of her life "Turmoil," a period that extended from the time she went away to boarding school until she entered college. A time of "profound unhappiness," these were the hardest years of her life. She remembers fear and insecurity, hating herself and hating everything around her. "I wanted to be a million things that I wasn't." She felt rejected by her family and fought bitterly with her mother. She remembers her high school friend, whom her mother hated, who "tore me away from my family" and taught her about music, art, literature, sex, and men. (She also told me that this friend had later made three suicide attempts.) She still recalled this friend with some fondness as having been an influential "teacher."

The final and current retrospective chapter she called "Stabilizing," and it encompassed the time of college when she was in therapy and met Ralph. "All sorts of things became possible. I lost 50 pounds and began to feel good about myself and capable of doing things. Before that, I felt I was rubbish." At this interview, Clara credited her former therapist as one of the most central people in her life, ranking her ahead of Ralph in terms of importance. Clara now viewed her therapy as transformative in terms of her working through the old struggles with her mother and coming to self-acceptance.

Reflecting on herself, Clara felt that luck had played a role in that there were no traumas, no deaths. She felt lucky to have found her current mentors but recognized that their relationship was also a function of her being good at what she does and their appreciation of her passion for the work. Luck, she said, "keeps disaster away." The only regret Clara expressed at this time was being far from old friends and having little time for new ones. Having the intimacy she had with Ralph, she no longer found friendship essential in the way it was before they got together. She wondered if people sensed how self-sufficient their couplehood was and stayed at some distance.

I asked Clara how she felt she was a product of her family and how college affected her. She said she felt that she hadn't fallen that far from the tree—still middle-class Jewish in outlook, wanting a house, family, and dog. "Most of my values come from that world." But, she felt, her choices were less materialistic, more open to things like premarital sex and smoking pot. College, she felt, affected her little, but the times, the '60s, were very important in terms of her participation in political movements, particularly the Women's Movement. She regretted not choosing a more serious college and being more serious about her studies. Looking back, she wished she'd had a more classical education. Therapy and Ralph were crucially important during these years, but she had little sense that the university itself had much lasting meaning to her.

Clara said that, in difficult moments, she tried to remember that she has control over her life and that she can change things. She tried to keep things in perspective. And I felt this sitting with her. Here was a woman who had created an identity on her own terms with sufficient flexibility that she could make the changes she needed to make when she needed to do so. She was basking in what was a very satisfying marriage, one that supported both her sense of identity and self-esteem, and she was now at the cusp of another identity piece, becoming a mother. When I asked about her hopes, dreams, and plans for the future, Clara again emphasized stability. "Settling down and having a family, working in a serious way and having a peaceful life." I asked how she might like to change as a person. "That could go on for hours," Clara said. "Always. I want to be different in lots of ways—less emotional, more rational, stronger intellectually and physically. I want to feel capable of competing in my profession." So Clara was content with herself at this age but was still self-critical and not finished with growing.

AGE 43

In 1993, I was teaching at Harvard as a visiting professor for a year and had some very talented graduate students eager to participate in my research. With no research grant, I allowed some of them to do some of the interviews, and one lived very close to Clara. Although I regretted not seeing her at this point, I allowed Kathy to interview her. I followed Clara at this age through the taped conversation.

Clara started by emphasizing that the important changes in her life occurred in her 20s. Since then, the path seemed smoother. But, as she had more or less expected, the transition to motherhood was a major shift—and a difficult one at first. "It's funny that I can say that I think I've changed so much less in the last ten years when in so many ways my life has changed so much. The most significant change is that when I was interviewed 10 years ago, I was pregnant with my first child, so of course shifting into parenthood after having been a couple for over a decade was difficult. . . . It was not an easy transition. Being tied down, the responsibility of becoming a parent seemed very hard. The first few months I was very depressed and very weepy, and it took me three months to work myself out of that and then I shifted into being a mother and found myself wishing I had started early enough to have a brood. And although we stayed on in Italy until Rachel was a year and a half, we decided that, having made the decision to have children, we did not want to stay in Italy so we came back to the States. It's funny how you can't wait to get out of a place and then, when you have children, you suddenly come back around to feeling that having family close is real important." Ralph got offered a job at Oberlin, and they realized that they wanted a home. "Having children made security seem more important. I came back pregnant and I had a miscarriage in my fifth month. That was one of the worst years that we had because that was so painful. I was lucky enough to get a wonderful part-time job in the Art Museum preparing exhibits, and I worked with three people who I just adored and who really kept me going for that year. It was a fluke—I saw this ad in the paper and even though I was pregnant and had no future, I thought why don't I try for this. They interviewed me—and because I had been trained as a bookbinder, it was love at first sight. They hired me instantly. I worked four mornings a week—Rachel was in daycare. That helped me bounce back. . . . By the spring of that year I was pregnant again and Roni was born."

Clara broke down in tears describing the most painful episode of the past 10 years, which occurred three years ago when her middle brother's 14-year-old daughter died in an accident. "It was horrible. It marked us tremendously—it happened the summer before Ralph came up for tenure—it helped us realize how insignificant these things are. I always think if something happened to my children, you could just shut me away. I can't imagine bouncing back from something like that. These are the sort of things that you think happen to other people. . . .

"I remember wanting to wrap a cocoon around the four of us. I guess what one takes away from that is the importance of supportive people. One of my friends had cancer and has since died. . . . I was so grateful that I was working part-time and had time to be with her and then even when I was working full-time I could still take off a few hours. It just seemed like the sort of thing you'd do for a good friend. One of the things that troubles me about the way the world has evolved is that women have so little time anymore to give to their friends, and I have these moments of having nostalgia for the '50s when women had time. I can't even think of anyone to put down as an emergency backup person on my children's school cards. I was lucky at the time to have a job that was flexible. I feel like my family responsibilities and my professional work eats up all the time and I don't have time for my friends. I remember them asking me at my job if I could do some traveling and having to say no, I can't take on any more right now. I know that as the children get older, that energy comes back and you can place it in different ways."

Clara had returned to school to get a library degree that qualified her for a job as a humanities librarian at the college, giving her the sense of moving ahead professionally. They still went back to Italy frequently.

"Professionally, coming into my own has been really significant, and that was possible because I became a mother. . . . I felt like I was floundering a bit. I was a book-binder and worked part-time, but I wasn't very focused. It came as a kind of counterpoint to the family and partly because taking care of small children is not the most interesting thing in the world. Intellectually it's deadening, but there is such a huge emotional satisfaction in nurturing and caring and loving. It was like this strange way in which I could let go and allow myself to move forward. It was like I've done this, it's wonderful, I have wonderful children and a phenomenal husband, and somehow that fulfillment let me move ahead and do things that are satisfying intellectually and professionally. Ralph is wonderfully supportive and has encouraged me to do what I wanted to do. I wanted to be the primary force in my children's lives up to a certain age, but now one is in fifth grade and the other in third grade. They are going off in their own directions, and I have the right to do that as well."

Clara managed to balance her work ambitions with the needs of her children. When her children were small, she had part time jobs to make "time for me and time for them. But I found the toddler period deadening, and I had a great need to be out. I needed some sense of purpose. I think the periods of my life that were most depressing were periods when I didn't have a sense of myself or a sense of direction. I feel great to have myself on my feet professionally—finally, in my 40s." Clara was working as a librarian and had responsibility for choosing material to add to the library collection. "Sometimes the politics gets to me, and I hate dealing with the insanity of the institution. But I feel a great sense of accomplishment. . . . I feel like I've ended up at the right place at the right time. I've always loved books and loved to work with books, and the question for me was how to work in a way that would pay me. The hard struggle for women is not always keeping yourself at the bottom of the ladder. And I knew that without a library degree, working as a book conservator, I would always be an underling, so it was clear to me that what I needed to do was to go get this degree, which was like a union card, and at that point I would shift. That made it possible for me to have a real job with benefits."

Clara was hoping to specialize in archives, special collections, and preservation. "That is what I am most suited to do, and everyone knows that. In part I see this as a holding pattern, but a healthy one. What's most enjoyable is working with students and faculty members—I love the public side of it. People come to you with problems and questions, and you have to solve them. The down side of it is that the library has been a dysfunctional place. A lot of people despise each other and undercut each other. The new director is ambitious and insensitive—working for her unnerves me. She's one of these people who tells you 10 minutes before she wants something. It's a hornet's nest. Some of the people wouldn't support me for the position because I was friends with someone they didn't like. I was so naive—didn't realize I had enemies.

"I've always worked with old books and have a personal collection. I enjoy messing around with computers, but my heart is really with the past. When

I find old papers, I find it very moving—the sense of history and the past and continuity. Taking care of pieces of our heritage and our history. It seems very important to me to be able to look back. Books are so unique. A series of different people have handled them—they seem so human, something that connects, that seems very emotional.

"I'm not looking to move up. I'd like to move sideways into what I like to do most. I'm not interested in administration." But she left open the possibility that she might get worn down by the institutional politics, and, 10 years on, we might find her back in her studio binding books.

Clara offers a finely nuanced example of how some women balance work and family. For her, having a family actually propelled her to take her professional ambitions more seriously. She derived different kinds of satisfactions from these two overlapping and intersecting areas of her life. At age 43, she still remembered her ambivalence about having children. "My brothers had these broods of boys, and it seemed so unappealing. Ralph and I were living this wonderful life, living in Italy and traveling, and I would look at my brothers, bound to their families and crying children in diapers and we would visit them and leave and wonder how people could do this to themselves. For so long, we weren't at all interested in having a family. But it's probably that clock—I was 33—I was going to have children then or not. I don't know—it just shifted. I remember even being pregnant, wondering why am I doing this? Even just before I delivered, I remember saying to my husband, if I could just back out of it now and go back to my studio. For the first few months, it totally floored us—the dirty diapers and snotty noses—you just do it. You derive such pleasure from the positive things."

Reflecting on her marriage at age 43, Clara said, "I can't think of any way that our marriage hasn't fulfilled me. . . . He's always been there, supportive and loving. I know he thinks I'm wonderful and beautiful. I know he cares enormously about the children—he plays an active role. He's a wonderful companion, intellectually, emotionally. My emotions are very on the surface—I cry very easily—he's always been very indulgent. I feel so grateful to have this relationship which is so wonderful, this best friend that I live with, who I can talk to about anything.

"The children get so much better. I found early childhood very demanding and intellectually stultifying. I find this age wonderful because they are so easy and are such friends, and I feel I can talk to them about everything and I do. But they're still kids and I can tell them to go to bed. For a long time, we always had dinner with them and then we had adult time for an hour. We needed our time."

So, at this age, Clara had created the basic structure of her identity and was engaged in developing its details. She was on a new career path but still had in mind what her basic goals and values were, and she accommodated the shifting demands of her ambitions and her wishes to mother in particular ways.

She took on a lot, but reflected that "the times in our lives when we've been most frantic and most busy, we get the most done."

The identity of "mother" is not unitary, and one identity challenge for women is how to mother. Therefore, there were a lot of questions in the interview about the experience of children and their development as mothers. I was in part interested in how well women differentiated their children and could describe them as separate people with distinct personalities and needs. Clara offered finely nuanced stories of her children and her intersection with them. Her overarching principle was "to respect *their needs and my needs at the same time.*"

"I have a very difficult mom. I always thought it was just me, but this has been confirmed by others. She is very negative about life, and I always thought that was being negative about me. So I spend a lot of time trying to encourage my children. I knew my mother loved me and still does but I always felt she didn't. It was always clear to me that she preferred and adored my oldest brother who was brilliant. She's never felt good about herself. In my late teens, when I dropped out of college, I decided I was not going to follow in her path. She never takes responsibility for things. She rewrites history with herself being victimized or someone else being at fault. It's very complicated and very exhausting. I admit when I'm wrong—even to the children."

Having children has felt like "an overwhelming sense of responsibility which is there every minute every day. There is always something nagging at your mind and your heart. Aside from the tedium of keeping up with the daily chores and responsibilities, it's the emotional responsibility. That fear of something happening to my children. The rest is just details."

The hardest time for Clara as a mother were the early years. "The challenge of trying to figure out how to keep a newborn baby happy—this feeling of being sucked dry. I nursed a lot—the exhaustion, sense of being overwhelmed. Sleep deprivation had a lot to do with it. But it's overwhelming to be a parent. It's an enormous responsibility to have to keep another human being happy—it's the hardest thing I've ever done. You can't walk away from it—you can't walk in one morning and say 'I quit.'"

Asked to describe her children, Clara said, "Rachel [age 11] is a terrific reader, very fearful, hates transition. It took me a lot of years to get my feet on the ground, and I'd hate for her to have the same problem. She's got a terrific brain, has the ability to be successful, aware of what others are thinking, very on the mark, sees through people very quickly, has things so together it scares me—but she has a side which is terrifically sensitive—takes her weeks to adjust to changes at school." Her younger daughter, Roni, Clara described as "artistic, much more daring, very distracted, kind of flaky. I worry about her a lot. Rachel is so strong and successful and smart and having followed a brilliant brother, I worry. They resent each other's strengths at times. I don't know a way to make it not hard. I just think it's life."

So Clara is, like all mothers, seeing in her children aspects of her own history that are still troubling or remembered as difficult. She worries about Roni in terms of her own experience of having had a very successful older sibling, and Rachel's fears of transition remind her of her own struggles to find herself as she grew and the world enlarged.

Only at this interview did Clara fill in more of the detail of that difficult period in her early college years. For the first time, she said that she had flunked out of her first college and the "hard time" she was having included drugs as well as "promiscuity." Perhaps she has at this age made peace with this old troubled self enough to be able to acknowledge it.

In other aspects of identity, religion, and politics, there had not been much elaboration. "Being Jewish means eating. I'm attached to the Jewish connection to food with family and friends. Ralph is Catholic—we have a lot of friends with mixed marriages, sometimes we get together and do a Seder or something. We have Christmas, but not as a Christian holiday." Clara felt there was simply no time in her life for political action, although she felt strongly about pro-Choice, worried about AIDS, and cared about the world, especially the human tragedies of Bosnia and Somalia that were in the news at the time.

Her sexual standards and values became somewhat more complex in light of AIDS, especially as the question about "what would you tell your daughters" had begun to feel more immediate. "I'd like them to be aware and conscious of what they are doing, to understand both the dangers and the pleasures of it. It seems like there is danger lurking out there, and I want them to understand it, but I don't want it to compromise the pleasure. As an adolescent, I made a lot of mistakes, but it was no big deal. Now that's all changed. I want them to be able to enjoy the pleasures of a sexual relationship with someone they care about, but I don't want them to be so free-spirited that they don't also take into consideration the dangers." In her accustomed style, Clara was trying to balance her views, opting for managing the complexity rather than seeking simple imperatives.

At age 43, it seemed to me, the uncertain bravado of Clara's late adolescence had evolved into mature self-confidence. She retained her openness to experience but also prized stability. Her ambitions were strong but tempered; she had clarity about what she would and would not do. She had integrated motherhood into her identity, profoundly feeling the sense of responsibility to her daughters while insisting that her own needs to express her ambitions in the world were to be taken seriously. And, at the root of her identity construction was her embeddedness in a supportive marriage. Clara attributed her identity development to both her own abilities and luck. She had grown confident about her talents, but remained humble, aware that bad things do happen out of one's control.

AGE 53

I was eager to interview Clara 10 years later when she was 53. I had some special feeling for her, partly because of all the trouble I had taken to interview her 20 years earlier in Italy. But more, I felt identified with her. I found similarities in our attitudes toward work and family and in our cultural Jewishness. I felt we somewhat shared a background and its assumptions, and I had found her personally engaging. In addition, I had come to think of her (and write about her) as a kind of poster child for psychotherapy, demonstrating with her unfolding life story the benefits of early intensive work in therapy to remove the blocks to continued growth. I had been taken by her insight, years ago, that "luck keeps disaster away," and I was hoping that nothing untoward had befallen her, confident that she would continue to pursue her path if disaster kept its distance.

Clara was vaguely waiting for me to contact her. She had never told anyone of her participation in the study and said she never thought of it between these times that I contacted her. Yet I could sense that she also felt a strong connection to me, interested as she was in how people grow and develop.

I asked her to bring me up to date on the last 10 years. Narrating her life now, it seemed to Clara that she was just setting off on a professional career 10 years ago, a career she felt she hadn't really had. This surprised me because it had seemed to me 10 years ago that she felt well launched on a career path. But such are the vagaries of our life stories as we review and reorganize them. At this age, 53, Clara's life was changing as her daughters were in college and setting out on their own.

Professionally, as she had hoped, Clara managed to work on the special collections in the library, a dream occupation, marred only by having to work for a difficult director. When this director left, Clara was made acting director of the library and participated in a search for a new director, quite clearly deciding not to apply for the job "in part because I sensed that there was some reticence on their part . . . having to do with my background not being in technology and this powerful sense that technology was the future of the library and we needed to bring someone really strong—and because I knew that if I had applied for the job and didn't get it, it would be very hard for me and hard for the person coming in, and it would change my relationship with the college, which I didn't really want to do. And my daughters were still . . . the idea of the family and the family unit trumped everything for me. And so I thought it's not worth it. The responsibilities of being library director were huge. The pressures of having to worry about 25 staff members and . . . it was exhausting. So I didn't apply for the job. . . . We hired someone we were quite excited about, so I went back to being the special collections person. The new director was great, but after eight months, she resigned to take a better job. And so the administration came back and asked me to take over as interim director and I said no. At that point, we had done two searches in two years, we knew who was out there, and if they wanted me to be library director, they had to give me the job. Not so much that I wanted it, but it was clear to me that another search would get us nowhere, and it was incredibly hard on staff. At that point, I agreed to do the job for three years after which we would renegotiate. I had just sent my older daughter off to college, and the extra income was very welcome. This is my third year. They are currently doing the review. I stood for promotion and was promoted last year. I insisted, for this review, bravely, I think, that they get reviews from all levels of campus. I felt either the campus was supportive of what I was doing, or, if they weren't, I was better off leaving. Truly, I didn't feel threatened by it because I know the feedback I have gotten has been incredibly positive. I know that a lot of the same people will write letters who wrote letters for my promotion. So I thought I would rather learn from this about ways in which people thought the position should be changed, an opportunity to learn as an administrator.

"I think it would be hard for me to step down right now since I have too many things under way and there are many people I have hired that I feel protective of and want to see through the various personnel reviews. The money still is . . . we have two girls in college, so that's welcome. There are plenty of days I go home and wonder why I am doing this, with all the pressures. Personnel, budget, building. And I've got this whole place. I've got to worry about clean bathrooms."

Although she didn't seek a job with this much responsibility—indeed, had said earlier that she did not want an administrative position—Clara takes great satisfaction in it. "Part of it is doing a good job. I know that people just love this library. It's never done such a booming business. I know the students just love this place. We've done some great things—afternoon concerts. We served cookies and tea. I ripped down all the 'Do Not' signs in the library. No negative messages. To feel you can make decisions and have some effect, and you get caught up in feeling good about what you are doing. Positive feedback and people want you to stay. One thing that was hard for the person who came in is that I got the President's award that year, and it was the library staff that nominated me. It doesn't mean that everybody supports me or that everyone even likes me. I'm not dictatorial, but I have become more and more decisive as time goes on."

Is that a change? I asked her. "Yeah. The library faculty meets every other week, but there is a certain point at which I just have to decide, and I'm much more comfortable with that than I used to be. It can't always be a majority either. Sometimes you just have to make a decision about what is best for the library or the college. And then it's a matter of how much time it takes. I end up sitting down and explaining to everyone the reasons so they don't feel that their voice didn't carry weight or no one cared. I think no man would ever do that."

I commented to Clara that her career has taken an unexpected direction ... more toward management, away from books, and she said that it had been hard. She's continued to work with the special collections and often does classes about the history of printing or finds bits of time to work in her bookbinding studio on personal projects.

She saw herself as on a trajectory that would take her to retirement. Although she had little time for her own research, she anticipated the next 10 years as "overseeing what I expect to be an enormous change in libraries." With some regret, she realized that she had to give up the goal of being what she considered to be "a true academic who gave papers with enough depth to be respectable. . . . I'd love to have time for it. I am burdened by the pragmatic aspects of my life."

There is still a small part of Clara that is aware that she never did a PhD. "If I had gone on to do a PhD., this would be a natural part of my life. But I don't feel frustrated by that. I feel grateful in a way, because my life would have taken such a different path. So part of it might be just proving to myself that I am capable and worthy in that academic community. . . . I want my voice to carry weight on this campus. I don't know if there are really those expectations. I think they are my own. Part of it is—I really think it's a balance just spending so much time fretting about administrative details. Wanting to step back and contact the intellectual part of me. But I wouldn't want to do that all the time either."

I realized in talking to her that, despite her accomplishments and success, the part of Clara that was self-critical and feared that she was underachieving was still hovering in the background. This, clearly, has been a lifelong struggle that she has largely mastered, but there are still moments of feeling that she didn't achieve all she could have.

She feels it has been important to be a successful professional role model for her daughters. While work has given her success, the family has brought her happiness. "It's been really hard giving up being a full-time mother. It's what I like most. We are so amazingly close, it's kind of pathetic. I finally told Rachel that she could no longer call every day from Rome because it is getting too expensive. But she has so much to share. It started out being neediness on her part because it was insecurity—and her difficulties with transitions—and then it turned into excitement. She just wanted to share the story of her day, and she's so used to being able to share that with us. And then seeing Roni off this fall was hard. In between, the dog died." So the family experience has changed, and Clara has had to change in tandem.

For Clara, being a mother has been a road of "endless ups and downs. Rachel is very insecure. They're both insecure. I can't understand it. Maybe it's a female thing. Rachel was made in my mold—I see all my insecurities in her. I used to blame it on my mother, I blamed all of my personality flaws and insecurities on my mother, but now I see them in Rachel and I don't quite—could this have been hard-wired, just a part of who we are? This has been very sobering for me, cause, you know, it's a way of taking it on myself—not her flaws, but the things that make her life so hard for her. And she's brilliant, beautiful, and talented, and she feels, sometimes she feels one or another, but more often, she feels she has none of it. The same is true of Roni. She's incredibly talented in a lot of ways, but . . . Roni could wake up any day and feel that she's ugly. There's a great obsession with how she looks. Um, and feel like she's inadequate. I think Rachel feels that way a lot. They're never crippled by it, and Rachel, for awhile, I genuinely worried about her. Ralph and I used to talk about her going into therapy. I had been in therapy when I was in my 20s for two years and so there was no shame in that. But she's always functional, just she panics about things. That is what it was like when she left for Europe. Feels she'll never be able to do it. I feel like I've been a full-time therapist. Hours on the phone, just consoling her. And I think what happens is that she gets off the phone and just gets on with her life. . . . I just try hard to be sympathetic and tell her she's not the only person who worries."

Clara seemed to share my wonder that Rachel seemed so much like she had been at this age, and I asked her to talk about the ways in which Rachel reminded her of herself. "Even when I went into therapy, I thought the big issue in my life was my mother and how crazy she is and was and how irrational. And I suspect her endless levels of insecurity about herself which always made my brothers and I feel that we were inadequate. Cause that was the message we always got from her. And even if we did something well, she wouldn't praise us. She might brag to a friend about it. But then it would be so exaggerated that we'd always feel like we fell short anyway. Certainly never had any sense that anything I did was right or that she was proud of me." This continued into adult life, and Clara told me a story about her mother ranting at her recently because she got their fax machine instead of the voicemail. "I had an incredibly violent reaction to it. I was just furious. Like can't you ever just leave me a nice message saying 'How are you?' instead of a rant accusing me of not having lived up to my responsibility?. . . So I just assumed that my problems in life were because of my mother and my insecurities. When I moved to Chicago when I was 18, and I remember getting on the bus and I was too afraid to get up and pull the cord on the bus because I thought the bus driver would get angry at me for requesting the stop, so I would ride the bus until somebody else pulled the cord, even it meant I had to walk a half mile back to where I was going. So I think I was really pretty insecure. Rachel has difficulty with transitions and new things, and I did too. I can still go off to a professional conference and feel very uneasy, like everyone else will have someone to have dinner with and someone to talk to. So I see in her much of what I see in myself, that I've passed down."

I asked Clara how she thought she "passed down" these insecurities. "I have no idea. Cause I think children see their parents very much for who they are, and we compare insecurities often, and I do remind them that I have managed to get on in life even with all those incredible character flaws. But it just surprised me. Like wait, you've grown up in this incredibly supportive and loving family, with two parents who just adore you, and you still feel all those feelings, reticence or insecurity. I think what cured me of much of that was being a parent. You just have to take action. So I would never hesitate at this point to ask someone for directions. I hope she'll outgrow it. And Roni, who I thought was always our happy-go-lucky girl, the separation was really hard . . . she cried all through dinner. A lot of it was that she realized how hard it would be to have us all leave. She just felt so bereft, and I'm such a believer in tears. I cry all the time. I never discouraged them. We're a very weepy family. I'm hoping next year will be an easier year. Fewer transitions."

At work, Clara is able to put her worries about her daughters aside as she focuses on her work. "I can put things in perspective. I remember once when Rachel was younger, this was the first time we thought about putting her in therapy. She was just in third grade and just unhappy, and I remember saying to her that she has to be very careful about not wearing unhappiness like a cozy quilt. You really can wrap yourself up in it and make it your life." Although Clara doesn't make the connection, the image of her unhappy, disappointed mother is clearly in the room at this moment.

"No one else seems to see Rachel's problems. She's very good at disguising it. It reminds me of myself to this day. I always marvel that people think that I'm unbelievably together. Very grounded, very strong and solid."

"But inside it doesn't feel that way?," I asked.

"No. . . . No. I mean sometimes. But sometimes completely not. And I certainly know that that was true well into my 30s and 40s. And, you know, I feel like every decade, I feel like thank goodness, I get stronger." As time goes by, the doubts become less pressing, and she feels less like a fraud. She agonizes less over how she is doing.

The dominant theme in Clara's life—managing what she calls her insecurities—had now extended to the next generation. The need for support and reassurance was always with her, and slowly, over the years, she gained confidence and was now taking up her authority to make decisions and braving the inevitability of criticism. This, for her, was a major step in personal growth. In addition, she had to bear the insecurities of her daughters and provide support for them. That she saw so much of her own struggles in them, despite her commitment to provide at home, as in the library, no negative messages, led her to a profound insight and rethinking of her life. She now realized that her "insecurities" were not a product of her mother—and that her mother didn't dislike her but disliked her own life.

Mood has always been a problem for Clara. She can easily get very sad and weepy. She told me at this meeting that she had had a postpartum depression after Rachel was born (she had alluded to this 10 years ago but not emphasized or labeled it) and was, as we talked, frequently on the verge of tears speaking about Roni's recent leaving for college or the dog dying. She told me of a time when Roni didn't get a part in a play that she wanted and "I fell apart. I lost control, breaking down crying. And it was such a triviality, and she was much more resilient about it than I was." She has tried various medications to try to take the edge off these sad moods, but the side effects have been worse than the problem. She is never "nonfunctional."

Her marriage to Ralph is "still unbelievably close. . . . We talk too much about work. And I work too much, that's another thing we talk about. There used to be a limit because the girls were home, and knowing they were home would pull me out of the office. We always had tea together every afternoon, the four of us would just settle down for a late afternoon tea, and I'd hear about their day and that was my downtime, and I'd find the energy to cook dinner or whatever. Part of it was I couldn't get home at 5—I come to work at 7:30 every day. I get up at 5:30 and walk."

And still Ralph is the bulwark of her life structure. "I can't imagine life without Ralph. We are so much a part of one another. He's been the best supporter I've ever had. He believes in everything I do."

Again, as in the previous interviews, I asked Clara to tell her life history as she now thinks of it, and her telling this time was of particular interest to me. In part, she frames it through the lens of her daughters' experience, but she includes many aspects of her life that she had left out previously, especially aspects that she might have been ashamed of in earlier times, but that now have lost their sting.

Looking back at her life, Clara stresses that she feels she has been "unbelievably lucky"—but now using luck in the sense of privilege rather than the absence of disaster. "Well, it's funny because I persist in thinking that my mother is an incredibly difficult person. So it's really hard for me to look back and think that I had this idyllic childhood cause I didn't. But certainly my family must have been close enough to give me some sense of family. And it wasn't that my father wasn't a loving father—he was just very busy. And my brothers were there, but they were boys and I was their chubby little sister, so neither one was particularly interested in me. And then I went away to school when I was 13, hated it, switched, went to another school when I was 15. I was just not happy with myself and not happy with my life. I wasn't perennially unhappy. I made friends, I did fun things. Had my nose fixed when I was 16. Did hard things. Went away to Israel the summer I was 15 even though I hated it, felt so insecure about everything. So every one of those transitions was a big thing, like this transition for my daughter, but I still did things even though they were hard.

"I think I must have been so torn between desperation to leave and get away from home and just holding on for dear life." "What did you want to get away from?" I asked. "Probably" my mother. And the sort of middle-class Jewish suburban life I was leading which I found really deadening. It was the '60s after all, so I think about my adolescence as being very turbulent. Lots of smoking dope. And, in a lot of ways, I think Ralph was the miracle of my life. And I think that goes back to the first interview I did with you. I met him my first semester at UMass. He taught my Italian class. He had a girlfriend at that point, and we didn't start going out, but we became very good friends. It was very hard for me to work that relationship into my life. He was short, for one thing, and I always felt fat and big. That was such an issue in my life. I was chubby as a kid, then in my 20s I was quite heavy, then I lost 60 pounds and kept most of it off until my late 40s. My 50th birthday present to myself was to join Weight Watchers and lost 40 pounds, just because it crept on. So that's self-image. So committing myself to a man who was small, short, and slender as he was in those days, and he was Catholic and very working-class, not refined and cultured—almost the opposite of what would have been carved out for me. But so exciting and dynamic and smart. It's interesting—I sort of anticipated that when the girls hit adolescence, that somehow they'd be embarrassed by this weird couple—and one of things I realized about my girls is that they very much want to be living the life that we are living now. So I think that Ralph was my miracle.

"We're so unlike the parents of their friends. We're not out there playing tennis and golf. Ralph is so not handy around the house, not at all interested in building things. All of that. I thought kids would find this strange, but I think it's really the opposite. Sometimes I tease them by saying that we've made life difficult for you by making home just too much fun. Having dinner parties and sitting around the table with artists or writers just seems so interesting to them.

"Anyway, so then Ralph—that's that middle section of my life. Then we go to travel and go to Europe and live abroad and that was pretty thrilling. We had the sense to do it before we had children. And then sort of mothering, I think, and then realized even when my children were very small that I needed to have a life of my own other than mothering. In part because I needed a little piece of a world that belonged to me and I couldn't do that to them, that I'm such a dependent character that I couldn't do that to them, to be that way to them, for them to be too important. I don't know how I could say that because I don't know how they can be more important than they are, but I think that if I had had nothing but them in my life, it would just have been really harmful for all of us. And it was really important for me to have this whole other world out there and for them to see me in that context and to have friends. And I think they revel in the affection people have for Ralph and for me. When it's made visible, like awards we've gotten."

Again, I wonder about how Clara credits herself for the design of her life. As it had been previously, her answer is multilayered.

"I pride myself, strangely, on my daughter's lack of ambition because I actually think that's how I was, strangely enough So I feel that I could have done everything that I did and there might have not been a job opening here, or the crazy library director could have stayed forever. All of these steps could have been different. That said, I think I do my job well, and I can say that not with infinite arrogance. I know the things I do well. I can make decisions that people hate, and I can accept people hating me. I can not renew contracts when I have to, even of senior members of the department. All of these things I know I am strong enough to do, and I know I couldn't have done it at earlier points of my career. And I can hire good people and help them along. Ralph could have not come along and I could have met someone else and fallen in love. And even my children. We have these sweet conversations where they say that they think that Ralph and I are amazing as parents, and we always say that they make us look good. We have no idea how this happened, but they are so terrific. Ralph and I talk about that all the time. We feel unbelievably lucky. We know wonderful people who have horrible children. Maybe that's folded into who they are. I know *everything* about what happens with them. I always said to them, 'When you are ready to have sex, you are the first person to know, I'm the second, and the guy is the third. You have to push me in there, so we can tend to what needs to be tended.' And I was gleeful last summer when they had sex for the first time. I felt genuinely happy for both of them because I thought it was such an important piece of feeling confident about who they were as women and about their bodies and being able to love some-one enough to share—that seemed so important to me. They have each given me their email passwords so I can see each day who has written to them—and what they write to one another. We share everything."

I asked Clara about her turbulent time in the '60s and what effect she thought it had on her life, This produced a deep sigh.

"Actually, what I remember of that time, because I was stoned so much of it. . . . I feel as though there are huge chunks of my life that I've either blocked out or forgotten. I remember those years as being excruciatingly hard. I remember being amazingly temperamental and sad and angry a lot of the time. And I'm sure that's not because of the [VietNam] War, I think it was because of the chaos of my own life. And I sort of went straight through it, eyes wide open, took so many risks and that's another way in which I feel I was so lucky. I took ridiculous risks—hitchhiking in horrible parts of Chicago alone at night, you know and being picked up by all sorts of people. Things that send shivers down my spine now. One thing that amazes me about my chil-dren is how prudish they are about drugs and even drinking. Whereas I could get stoned every night. It's just sort of what I did. So I just think about them as hard—directionless. I didn't know where I was going or what I wanted to do."

This seemed so anomalous a chapter in Clara's life that I asked more about how she now understood it. For me, it was a clear description of what Erikson calls the moratorium period, but in Clara's case it was tinged with depression. "Some of it had to be adolescent rebellion, which again I see in so many of my girls' friends. And I went off to college, from boarding school, college being a bigger version of boarding school. I know I went into a real depression. I stopped going to class and that's when I dropped out of college and really didn't know what to do. . . . I thought I might go to a school near home. So I think I was both wanting to stay close to home and yet needing to be far away. And my mother was humiliated at the idea of my going to a state school. My older brother went to Harvard. I don't even know how I ended up making the decision to go to Chicago. I think a friend called, wanted a roommate, I had no place else to go, and said okay, whatever, made the decision to go, realized once I got there that the person didn't need a roommate anymore because she got a job that gave her room and board. So I was on my own needing to find a roommate, which got very complicated and it was really, really hard. They were just chaotic years. Roommates I didn't get along with or did for awhile and then didn't. And then a series of . . . adventures with different guys, not one of whom I really cared for. I can't say I was promiscuous cause I wasn't sleeping around endlessly, but certainly had a series of very unhealthy relationships with guys. I got involved with a med student who then dropped out of medical school, who treated me quite shabbily. He wasn't abusive, but clearly didn't care for me, clearly to him it was a physical relationship while to me it was everything else in the world. When I finally broke it off, he said, 'So you finally decided to stop being masochistic.' But I remember taking to my room and just crying for days and days and days on end. I remember my roommate coming in and saying, 'You've got to get over this and get on with your life.'

"And all through that time I was in therapy. It was an acknowledgment on my part that I absolutely didn't want to spend the rest of my life being miserable. It was such an important decision. Because I could have ended up like my mother. I really think if I hadn't gone to therapy, I would have ended up like my mother, just feeling sorry for myself, feeling like I could never achieve what I wanted to achieve and it was always someone else's fault. And I do feel like it did take me decades to work out of that sense. But I think that was the pivotal moment.

"I do feel that even had Ralph not come along and had I not done therapy, I wouldn't have then been in the position to let someone love me. My sense of myself was so low, that I think the idea that anyone could genuinely be in love with me was inconceivable at that point. I think I blamed a whole lot on my mother. I think mothers do take the lion's share of blame, rightly or wrongly. My brothers agree with my vision of her. She was very unstable and very angry a lot, screamed a lot and yelled a lot. I'm sure she has obsessive compulsive sides, so the untidiness of children was really hard for her to take. She had a master's degree in education, but she worked in my dad's accounting office and was never actually paid. So I think she aspired to so much but accomplished so little. To this day, my parents, who are in their 80s, own two huge houses, both getting shabby because they can't keep them up anymore and they're too cheap to pay people to keep them up properly, but my mother complains bitterly. She has more money than Ralph and I will ever have. She has lost more money over the years than Ralph and I will ever have. And I think that's just a measure of her disappointment with life and with herself. So there was definitely some sense that there was something wrong with me and there was something wrong with my world cause she was angry all the time and unhappy. . . . My daughters now protect me from my mother. They don't like her either. I forgive her nothing at this point. She is the only person who makes me hate myself and when I'm with her, I turn into a brute. And I'm so patient and forgiving and understanding of everyone but my mother. So . . . I'm 53 and she can still get under my skin, and I can still be angry and temperamental and difficult with her. She's 82 years old. And I still forgive her very little at this point. And the girls just get between us. They really understand that the dynamic is so complicated, that the only thing they can do for me is to get her away from me.

"I adore my older brother, and I think its mutual, but he married a woman I have a really hard time with and who Ralph just can't abide, so we see very little of him. My middle brother is more complicated because he's a lot like my mother and he sometimes provokes in me a similar response and he also makes up rules. Roni had the chutzpah to refer to herself as not Jewish to my mother—and since then, he stopped inviting us for Jewish holidays."

Clara still feels the absence of close friends in her life, but work and family consume all her energy—and Ralph remains her best friend. "Sometimes I have a nostalgic longing for the '50s when the men would go to work and the women would sit down over coffee and just get to talk. I love the concept of a crew of friends that got together just to talk. And for some people that was satisfied by roommates in college that they've stayed friends with, but I have no associations from college at all. One friend from high school, who, if we're lucky, we see each other once a year. For me, what I wanted was a sister."

For the future, in 10 years, Clara was hoping to be closing in on retirement, having grandchildren, working on the special collections without the administrative responsibilities of a director. "I feel that this is my peak professionally, I would like to feel that I hit this plateau and then start to scale back. I don't see myself moving on. I don't want to take on a bigger job. At one point, Ralph was called about a position in Florence and we had a brief fantasy about moving abroad. When I thought I wasn't going to have a job, my fantasy was to take my administrative skills and apply them to a nonprofit organization. I felt I had a set of skills, strong administrative skills, and I would love to apply them to something a little more involved with the real world and less with the ivory tower, academia. But it seems that I ended up in a place that seems like such a logical place for me. Part of my mission is to get students excited about books and I do—when I take them to the special collections and show them something by Virgil . . . I would love to be able to go back to that. . . . And pass that on to a younger generation that has more energy and vision. And I'd like to think that Ralph and I would have enough money to spend a couple of months in Italy every year."

As before, I marvel at Clara's self-reflectiveness. She is aware of—and often just tolerates—her own complex inner life. Proud of her successes, she still struggles with her lifelong self-doubts. Her values are to be accepting of others, not to criticize people, but she cannot forgive her mother for being who she is. Being with Clara, I felt the glow of her joy in her husband and children and in her work. Her goals at this age were firmly generative, animated by what she wished to pass on—to her library, her students—and her daughters. Personal ambition remained in the shadows—although success accompanied her efforts to do well at what she was engaged in. Her identity at this point was an extension of the work and family goals she had been pursuing and was completely entwined with intimacy and care for the next generation.

Clara's development was so intricately intergenerational, a story of painstakingly extricating herself from the self-doubt instilled by her critical mother and trying so hard not to pass this on to her daughters, that I could not help but be curious about how her daughters experienced her. I obtained Clara's permission to interview Rachel who was, at the time, the same age, 21, that Clara had been when I first interviewed her. And indeed, Rachel showed herself to be much as Clara had described.

RACHEL, CLARA'S DAUGHTER, AGE 21

Rachel, a senior at Princeton, was attractive, poised, articulate, and comfortable talking about herself, but quickly became tearful when speaking about how overwhelmed she feels when she fears she can't live up to her own expectations. Although Clara had masked this at age 21, Rachel was expressing what Clara described having felt at this age. Rachel spoke of feeling herself to be moving toward independence while relying on the "security system" of her family.

Rachel was in a exploring phase and would have been classified as a Searcher in the identity status categories. "I sort of went through my whole life assuming that I was going to be a professor, because I grew up in the middle of academia and I didn't really picture myself anywhere else, but um, I'm not really so convinced that's the right path for me anymore." She was intrigued by many possible career options and trying to sort through them. "There are a lot of things that I'd like to try, but nothing really seems like something I want to settle on." This included everything from cooking to film to comparative literature to computer programming. Rachel felt that she had largely followed her father's interests academically, and, although her parents encouraged her goals of becoming a professor, they were always "incredibly supportive of everything that I've ever come up with." Although it felt safe to simply follow the path she knew best, she felt herself doing the "scary" thing by considering other possibilities. "I feel like I always had these sort of paths of theirs to follow and now I have to go do my own thing."

Religion and politics have not been sites of identity formation for Rachel. She described herself as having been raised with no religion and does not identify as either Jewish or Catholic. Politically, she feels aligned with the left-leaning views of her parents and the academic community she grew up with. The larger question she was dealing with was how much to coordinate her future plans with her boyfriend of two years. She might like to go to Italy after graduation. This was the place of her birth, a place she has visited with her family many times over the years, a place for which she feels a ". . . weird homesickness. I feel like my mobility is really lessened by having to sort of coordinate with someone else, and I don't think that, especially because I'm so undecided about my future, it's a good idea to be tied down to something because I think I might end up resenting the fact that I'm being bound and not able to fully explore all these options that I have. I am hoping there's something that would let us do things we would find fulfilling and still be nearby—but I don't know that it's possible."

Narrating her life in chapters, Rachel made the first chapter her life in Italy, followed by a chapter called "my sister." "I'm almost three years older than she is, but when we moved into the house that I grew up in in Oberlin, where my parents still live, it was so that they could have a second child and really put down some roots. So I think that sort of the arrival of my sister and this home that I grew up in coming together sort of really sealed what my childhood was going to be like and she's still my best friend. . . . All the time I ever spent with my family was wonderful and full of companionship that felt really intimate in a way that probably wouldn't have if it were just me and my two parents because it's really kind of symmetrical, the daughters and the parents and the four of us get along really well and each pair does, too."

Rachel makes the next chapter "School" and told me that this is how she discovered that one thing that is central to her is a love of learning. "I always really liked school and sort of discovered very early that I was pretty good at it, and that gave me pleasure and I really liked learning, which was really exciting for my parents because they both loved teaching, so that was really nice. . . . I always kind of want to know the extra little bit. . . . I think that my appetite is just greater than most people's for learning, and I like to talk to people about it. . . . It really orients my relationships with people I think, this love I have of learning and talking about it. So I think that kind of blossomed early. . . . That is exactly how I define myself. I was always kind of the smart girl, and I always really liked it. I've always been a big nerd, so, but it never,

I mean it was never, I really enjoyed being a nerd, too, and it never was really a cause of strife, it was just an extra enjoyment I got out of school. I know that sometimes it's a burden for people, but it wasn't for me, I just liked it and it made me feel good. I had a really supportive group of friends who were the same way, so I think I was really lucky in that sense, and I think the way that the school system was organized was really helpful, too, because we could all go through it together and we just felt good about being in those advanced classes."

Another important chapter was learning to play the oboe, something she found without her parent's directing her toward it, and playing in orchestras has been an important part of her life and a source of friendship and community. "I think I sort of broadened their classical music horizons through my playing of the oboe, so it became really special and that was huge; because they introduced me to so much, I was really excited to share something with them from my side."

She had a lot of trouble making the decision about where to go to college, but feels she made a good choice. Still, she remembers that it was agonizing to decide. And it was difficult to be far from home. "I feel like, in my family, there are all these things and here there's a friend that I share a love of cooking with and a friend that I share a love of music with and it's like really segmented, so I think it was hard for me to get used to that."

It was less difficult to decide to spend her junior year in Rome, although this, too, was a challenging transition (as Clara had recounted). "In Rome I learned to like being alone not as sort of a default, just to prize the time I spend by myself doing things, whereas before I think I always secretly thought that it was better to be doing it with someone else, so I sort of think of that as the main lesson I learned in Rome, to really like that, being on my own. I mean, I'm really glad that I learned that, because it's been liberating in a lot of ways. . . . I mean I still consider my family to be close friends, to be a security network, but I don't need them or rely on them as heavily as I did. I think I was just worried that I would not be able to do it. I'm really not very good with transitions, I always think it's gonna be the end of the world, and it wasn't in Rome, so that was really helpful, cause it seemed like this kind of impossible undertaking to just go by myself for a year."

So Rachel at this age told an identity story of weaning herself from the security and pleasures of her family and learning, despite her "insecurities" to rely on herself. She was very much in the process of charting a path, and it seemed that the decision-making was going to be grueling for her. Her family had clearly given her the tools to manage it—as well as the continuing support. But it struck me that Rachel had not yet done the hard work of loosening her emotional ties to her mother, a process that would likely be difficult—and lengthy—for both of them.

In Rachel were echoes of Clara, but cast in a different tempo and phrasing. Unlike Clara, she felt herself to be growing out of a supportive home without nearly as much turmoil as Clara had experienced. But the struggle with self-doubt (what they label in the family as "insecurities") carries on.

For Clara, the identity-defining story was her troubled relationship with her mother, a relationship that led her, as a college-age adolescent, to try to wrest free of the debilitating criticism that she had internalized from her mother. Mired in self-doubt and self-hatred, she teetered on the edge of self-destruction, failing out of college, soothing her inner pain by staying stoned. Clara was rescued by intensive psychotherapy and a loving relationship, and she moved far away from her mother, to a place where she could get her grounding in a craft that drew on her talents and a husband who emotionally supported her. At this period of time, her early 30s, she saw herself as finding herself and freeing herself from her mother's disabling hold on her. By her 40s, she had some perspective on her mother, saw her as an unhappy, angry woman who took her disappointments out on her. But Clara felt she had freed herself, although she still saw her battles with her "insecurities" as a direct consequence of her mother's treatment of her. With her experience of Rachel's similar self-doubt, by her early 50s, Clara was questioning her life story. If insecurity could result from continuous loving treatment, as she saw happening in her daughter, perhaps her own story was not just a story of her mother's mistreatment. Perhaps she had to refashion her story and claim her self-doubt as her own inner demon, one she had battled and largely triumphed over all her life. It is this shift in self-understanding that most clearly marks Clara's identity development even as she takes on ever more responsibility at work and struggles through the anguish of letting her daughters grow out into the world.

Lessons from the Pathmakers

These five Pathmaker women have lived very different lives and realized distinctive identities. They have each woven together different aspects of their lives into a flexible whole—lives of accomplishment and relationships. The shapes of their lives have been cast based on the people with whom they have intertwined themselves, and, in this sense, their identities are fundamentally relational. They are who they have become for others and who others have become for them. One could not adequately describe any of them without the (very particular) people who surround them—at home, at work, and in their larger networks.

Across the time that I have known them, the Pathmakers are pragmatic women: they are doers. Their lives are built of multiple investments—career, partners, children, parents, siblings, friends, charity, sports, exercise, travel, reading—in various orderings, all in delicate equilibrium. But they are practi-cal, down-to-earth. There is a hard-headed sensibleness about these women.

None retains religious connections, although most were raised in a strong religious tradition. They rely on themselves and those with whom they build their lives. They are women who started adulthood trying to feel in charge of themselves and making choices about what happened to them. They thought, by and large, that if they could plan a life, they could realize it. All have learned to temper this sense of control, to recognize deeply how much they can't control. Many now (in midlife) see their lives as marked more by "luck" than they ever had before. "Luck keeps disaster away," as Clara put it. Many felt lucky in finding the partners or job opportunities that they did at the right moment. None made their lives come out just the way they imagined. Necessity and circumstance refracted their lives, yet all have realized some essentials of their own desires. All feel that they have pretty much arrived where they had intended to go.

They tend to speak of difficulties only in looking back, after they have tra-versed them. They acknowledge how scared they were at various times—as they took on new work roles, embarked on marriages, faced life alone after a divorce. But fear is clearer to them in retrospect. They rise to what they decide to do, quelling the anxiety. The Pathmaker mothers also speak about the strain of their transition to motherhood, the doubts about having made the right choice when they were sleepless and exhausted by their infants. In their 30s, they recounted being overwhelmed by young children, longing for some time to themselves. In their 40s, they are busy with their children's lives and activities, but less pressured. By their 50s, they are reinvesting more in their careers and other interests, varying in how much they stay closely involved in their children's lives. The Pathmakers feel life's stresses—but they are psy-chologically stoical. They don't allow themselves to be governed by a need to escape painful feelings. Nor do they wallow in them.

The Pathmaker trajectory for these women stayed constant over these 35 years. Heading into life with this particular psychological structure led to a renewed and revised, but solid, identity at each stage of later life. They expanded and revised themselves while the fundamental capacity to integrate identity elements and withstand challenges remained. So it is worth attend-ing carefully to what was taking place internally during the college years that afforded this fundamental capacity to find and renew themselves as life progressed.

Making one's own path seems to require, above all, the capacity to toler-ate uncertainty, doubt, anxiety, and guilt. Most of the women who finished college as Pathmakers had a profound sense that they were skating free, hav-ing let go of the external supports that sustained them through childhood. Relinquishing this inner certainty, they had to find validation in supportive others—husbands, friends, bosses, mentors—and in increasing recognition of their own capabilities and values. Most of these women, as I interviewed them, narrated their stories with a sense of conviction in the basic meaningfulness of their lives and choices. Self-doubt was present but not disabling— they were aware that they might have made other choices, that some of their choices had led to pain or to dead ends, but these women had the capacity to rally themselves and choose again, hoping to do so with better understanding and insight.

Betty, Alice, and Clara live away from where they were raised. Where they have chosen to live (in part determined by their life partners) forms the grounding of the identities they live out—in small villages close to nature (Betty and Alice), in a college town (Clara), or in a city (Andrea and Maria). Maria chose to stay close to her family. The choice of place to live shapes and reflects their expression of themselves. It forms the boundaries of the world they inhabit and the opportunities available to them. More important, their relationships to particular others are the immediate framework of the identities they create. Their life courses are shaped inexorably by the people they choose as partners and by the exigencies of those they love. Yet, in the way these women apprehend their decision-making, painful choices between self-interest and others' needs don't arise. They devise a creative strategy before the problem is ever phrased in either-or terms. To use Clara's words, "You have to flex and improvise and compromise." The nature and needs of partners and children simply become part of who these women are.

Each Pathmaker began with different pieces to shape into an identity. And the needs of her life partner have often been an important aspect of determining the way in which she could put the pieces together. As other important people have been joined to her inner circle, their needs, too, have been added to the plan, revising its details. So the Pathmakers' story is not only one of amalgamating aspects of who she was with who she will be, but also a story of putting together who she is and will be with who the others who are important to her are and what they need. It was striking to me that the "we" of identity dominated the "I" in each of these women's life stories. Their identity was embedded, part of a unit as small as a marriage or as large as a community or work group, in which individual achievement and interests nested and flourished and were, in turn, reinvested in the relationships.

Many of these women described their husbands as their best friends. Their marriages were not without difficulties or disappointments, but they counted on their husbands for emotional support, even cheerleading, for their endeavors outside the family. Their husbands also expanded their social worlds, bringing them into areas of life they may never have discovered. For those who are mothers, there is a range of continued investment in their children's lives in their mid-50s, but all have launched their children into independence. Even Betty, the one who has the most compromised child, found it a major task of her 50s to see that her son could live on his own.

When I interviewed them in college, most of the Pathmakers spoke poignantly about having wished for more love or approval from their parents. In the interviews when they were in their 30s, this pain still rankled, was still a source of distress in their lives. But by the time these women were in their mid-40s, the wounds seemed to have healed—or been put aside. They remembered their old grievances, but the pain was replaced by bemused resignation. Adulthood has offered them another chance at relationships with their parents—relationships of attachment and roots rather than relationships defined by dependence or needs for approval or righting the wrongs of the past. They found new ways to maintain meaningful connection to their parents. Most of these women had reworked their relationships with their parents in their late 30s or early 40s as a major theme of their internal growth during this time. Making peace with their mothers, in particular, made it possible for them to make the transition to being caregivers, both physically and emotionally, to their aging or dying parents. In her 40s, Alice began for the first time to see parts of her distant unemotional parents in herself and took note of her own reluctance to discuss her feelings and her shying away from physical expressions of affection. It was only in her 40s that she began to think of herself as having come from "a dysfunctional family" in which there was no communication. She began reading about adult children of alcoholics and felt she had much in common with them. Although her redefinition of her family life did not change her relationship with her parents, it did provide Alice a new version of her own history, one that made it possible for her to make some changes in herself. She gained a new perspective on herself. "I'm learning more and more about myself all along. I've known for a long time that I had a really good denial system. For example, I never even cried about my divorce until about two years later. I've learned to depress my emotions really well. My father never expressed any emotions at all. My husband has been really good about making me open up and making me start expressing feelings more, which was not part of me in the past. And having this knowledge about myself and the family in which I grew up has made me concentrate on making sure that there is a closeness with my kids so I don't repeat that pattern." Working through this realization continued over time, into her 50s, when it took a crisis in her marriage for Alice to open still further. So Alice's trajectory of emotional identity has been to bring more of her feelings into her life; Andrea has had a similar challenge as she has just been learning in her 50s to communicate more clearly what she wants and needs. And Maria continues into her 50s to try to take some time for herself while she takes care of everyone else.

By their mid-50s, these Pathmakers, secure in the personal authority of their own identities, are the most interested of all the groups in forming adult relationships with their parents through knowing their parents as people with their own histories. Internally and emotionally, they have struggled to detach and distance themselves from their childhood anger over their parents' failings, but, at the same time, they have come to be able to appreciate their parents for what they are able to offer. By their 50s, they have come to know their parents better, to accept them and to forgive them. Maria, working with disturbed young people, has had to come to the painful recognition that both she and her brother were physically abused as children. She hadn't wanted to see her "ideal" family in this way, but she has also, in midlife, come to a complex understanding of her father. "He'd get out of control—it was beating. But I see it more as a cultural thing. I knew it didn't come from hate or wanting to hurt a child. This is the way Italians disciplined their children. It's difficult culturally for people to find other ways to deal with their kids. I always knew it didn't come from hate and was just my father's way." Only when she had her own children who could drive her to extremes of frustration did Maria realize she also had such rage inside her, rage she learned to manage quite differently. Except for Clara, whose struggle with her mother has been lifelong, the Pathmakers formed in late midlife an affectionate but no longer pained relationship with their parents. For Andrea and Betty, taking their parents back to their own place of origin was a meaningful experience that located them in the cycle of generations as well.

Over the course of their lives, their differences from their parents had to be tolerated. The Pathmakers' political liberalism, their lack of religious practice, their career commitment, their philosophy of raising children—all these were aspects of them that their parents, and often their siblings, are at pains to understand. And these women had to accept that their families will never fully know them. By their mid-50s, with their children raised, these differences with their families were now thoroughly recognized and were, for the most part, no longer a site of dissension.

While they are all satisfied with their career choices, their career decisions have been shaped by multiple forces of which ambition and talent were only a part. All of the Pathmakers changed their plans from what they had envisioned as college seniors. As they got into the working world, they became more sagacious—and sometimes more cynical—about what was out there and, with greater knowledge, could better match their own needs and interests with what opportunity offered them. In their 30s, they developed confidence in their abilities as they moved on to greater responsibility in their work roles, and, by some time in their 40s, felt they had nothing left to prove about their capabilities. By their 50s, they were satisfied with their work careers and were enjoying exercising their skills. Alice, Maria, and Andrea turned down advancement because the administrative work didn't look appealing; they knew what work they wanted to do. Clara took the director role because she had things she wanted to accomplish, but she had another route in mind that would have suited her just as well if she hadn't been offered the position. And Betty organized a life of projects that appealed to her. In their mid-50s, their ambitions are largely fulfilled, but, for some, this involved further changes. As Maria's occupational world changed around her and she was no longer able to work in a way that was meaningful to her, she found a new place to use her skills; Andrea seemed to be approaching the same dead end in the medical world.

Although all of the Pathmakers have taken up responsible professional or managerial occupational roles, all share a sharply realistic stance in regard to the rewards that are available in the working world. Much of their learning and growth in their 20s and 30s—and even into their 40s—involved coming to terms with what they could reasonably expect to gain from their occupational lives. For most, their learning here came through disillusionment or what they describe as "eye-opening" experiences. Work itself, they discovered, is not always meaningful. The real joys of working come through the relationships they have with those with whom and for whom they work. Moving ahead is not always the wisest course. The workplace is not always fair or reasonable. Don't trust institutions too much. Bureaucracies are dehumanizing. These are the hard-won occupational lessons that put their occupational identities in perspective. Nevertheless, they found great satisfaction in being able to accomplish reasonable goals: helping others, building things, nurturing the next generation.

Fulfillment for these women has emerged through the other lives that they have touched. Alice speaks of the students she has influenced. "I had a kid who is now applying to medical school. She told me that when I had her in anatomy and said she was going into nursing, I said 'Why don't you go all the way and be a doctor'", and I didn't remember saying that and she said, 'Here I am, I'm on my way.'" Alice has received public recognition as a superior teacher, but the satisfactions lie in the small moments like these. I think of Clara looking happily at the students using her library or Maria caring for her staff and her patients—or Betty building houses for people in faraway places. These are opportunities for expression of identity that their mothers never had.

As they contemplate the future, they think about retirement and doing something different. They rely on their Pathmaker stance; many possibilities seem open, and they are confident they will choose well—and integrate aspects of the person they have already been. Alice said, "I want to do something different that will make a difference. Maybe I'll become politically active. I've always wanted to make a difference. So I have to do more than just sit back here and work on my garden." Clara sees the future, after she has finished with her new role as library director, as a return to work she put aside. And, although I can't really imagine Andrea running a cheese shop, I wouldn't be completely surprised.

Nancy: The Coasting Pathmaker

Nancy provides a contrast to the other Pathmakers. Although she, like the others, continued to revise through her 20s and 30s, she found herself, in her

40s, dissatisfied with all aspects of her life, trying to reorient herself and find her way again. At age 43, she was in a period of searching, rethinking herself, not sure what to preserve of what she had been and what to create anew. I left off with her at age 43, uncertain, as she was, about how she would make her way forward.

Like the other college-age Pathmakers, Nancy was moving steadily toward independence through college, questioning the values of her childhood, flirting with left-wing political activity, preparing herself to become a high school math teacher. She had had no deep involvements with men by the time she was a senior, but was intensely connected to a group of women friends with whom she compared herself and yet tried to maintain a sense of distinctiveness. It had been a challenge to learn to live with people so different from herself and "to stand up for my own rights." Beset with worries about her adequacy that had been with her since childhood, Nancy worried a lot about her "worthiness" and wanted to be special in some way or at least to do "well enough." Above all, she deeply feared failure and humiliation. Throughout her school years, she had been at pains to leave "the security of my seat" and perform in front of others. She was very sensitive to what she experienced as pressure from others and was looking forward to finishing college, escaping from her conflicted relationship with her demanding, critical mother and "being truly independent."

In retrospect, I could see these worries foreshadowing Nancy's first major hurdle. Despite finding a teaching job just after graduation, Nancy could never feel comfortable in front of her class, and, after two years of struggling each day with her anxieties about teaching and the uncertain security of her position, she decided to choose another career.

She worked for a while in low-level jobs in the business world that made her aware of the necessity of having an MBA. So she went back to school to earn this new degree, and, when she finished, she began work in a purchasing division of a large retail sales company. Through several promotions and carefully timed job changes, by age 33, she had become a high-level manager. Although she continued to fear competition and to doubt that she was doing enough, she took on more and more responsibility. She enjoyed the challenges of her work, the problem-solving and the sense of accomplishment she derived from it, even though it was often frustrating to be limited in her authority by rules and bureaucracies.

Nancy married early in her 30s. Her husband, a systems analyst who was as ambitious as she was, was a man with whom she felt a great sense of security although there were conflicts in her marriage. "Marriage has met my needs," Nancy said at age 33, "in that I am no longer lonely, I have a full-time friend to talk to and to be around. I thought marriage would be easier than it is; it requires lots of work and time and, unfortunately, my job takes a lot of my time and energies."

Negotiating the demands of her marriage and the demands of her job became an ongoing source of difficulty for Nancy. To meet the pressures that emanated from her work, she was home little. In retaliation, her husband would get overinvolved in his work and be less available to her when she wished to be with him. At age 33, she couldn't see how she could make room for children, although she did want to have them. She was putting off the decision, worrying that the decision would be made for her by default because she couldn't bring herself to make a "yes decision." Early in her 30s, though, Nancy still felt herself steering her own life, creating her path, having many decisions yet before her.

By age 43, however, Nancy felt that life had gotten away from her. She worried that she had become a "workaholic" and that her husband had, too. They had so little time for each other, and, when they were together, it seemed that all they did was criticize and undercut each other. Their fighting escalated, sometimes into pushing and hitting one another. They had separated twice, but each time decided to try again. In the midst of the last, recent separation, Nancy lost her job in economic cutbacks and then felt that she had nothing at all. In addition, her mother died suddenly, without her having a chance to feel that they had resolved the more difficult feelings between them. At age 43, Nancy was in crisis. She had found another job but she hated it and felt pessimistic about her job prospects in the poor economy of the time. She felt herself clinging to her husband, but not too hopeful of making it the kind of relationship she wanted.

But the "age-40 crisis," as Nancy termed it, led her to rethink her life. With the help of a therapist, she began re-examining her childhood and discovering the roots of her lifelong doubts about herself. She began to understand better how her relationship with her mother had affected her. "When she died it was very stressful because I hadn't resolved anything. She loved me but she didn't make me feel confident and secure or have a high self-esteem. She had all these goals and expectations, but I always felt inadequate because no matter how much I did, I never felt it was enough," She learned that she had married a man much like her mother; he always seemed to be very critical of her and "did not help to build my self-confidence and make me strong."

Neither Nancy's work nor her primary relationship offered her the security she needed to flourish. In times of intense stress, she turned to both alcohol and to overeating to soothe herself, but both only contributed to her criticism of herself. At age 43, she felt blocked, was wondering if she could persuade her husband to start all over again in another city, maybe far away.

Nancy's Pathmaker beginning was disrupted by a combination of circumstance and her inner self-doubting. At times, she seemed to have been stepping on her own toes. At other times, her world offered her little support. Throughout her early 30s, she was much like the others who took this route out of their adolescence, but disappointments in her marriage and in her work led Nancy to a dead end.

When I saw her at age 53, she was a bit more grounded, but still, in her words, "coasting." With the help of a series of "life-changing" self-help workshops and then continuing self-help classes, she was able to change her attitude toward her husband, finding ways to appreciate the good that he provided her and thereby improve her marriage. Internally, she felt she had given up blaming her mother, accepting that how her mother treated her was not perfect and recognizing that "I'm on my own now, I'm the responsible party, I've got to get over that and move on, you know, at least for now." She still had checkered employment, getting dissatisfied or getting fired, but had now been in a job for six months that seemed like it fit her. At 53, she was thinking about what she could do to "give back"—was thinking about volunteering to read to children. She had some regrets about not having had children but realized that the marriage had never been stable enough—and she and her husband had never felt confident enough—to do so. As she retold her history at this age, the struggle to feel a sense of worth in the face of her mother's ongoing criticism and control was still the dominant theme. What had changed for her by her late 40s was "becoming more content as to what one has rather than what you don't have."

In some ways, Nancy's history echoes Clara's in terms of the lifelong struggle with an internal critical mother. While Clara's therapy in late adolescence helped her work this through enough to make a loving relationship with Ralph, Nancy chose a partner much like her mother. With Ralph's support—and good work experiences—Clara developed enough confidence in herself that made it possible to battle the recurrent worries about unworthiness. But Nancy, without such supports, succumbed. And until she found a healing intervention (her "life-changing" workshops) in her late 40s that promoted her self-acceptance, she floundered, much like many of the Drifters. Nancy's history, then, counterpoints and emphasizes the importance of others in sustaining the fulfilled Pathmaker path. Having found supportive others in her workshop, having gained greater acceptance of her husband and appreciation of some of the strengths in their relationship, Nancy, at age 55, seems to be in a period of renewed exploration in search of identity.

{ 4 }

The Guardians

In contrast to the Pathmakers, the Guardians in college during the late 1960s and early 1970s were either oblivious to or resisting the waves of change crashing around them. Surrounded by the backlash against traditional authority that greeted them on arrival at college, they clung even tighter to the familiar, wanting to retain the emotional comforts of their childhood at all costs. They were Guardians of their childhood selves, foreclosing on the possibility of forming an independent identity by seeking to preserve ways of being that had always been. Preoccupied with security, they chose what felt safe. Although they may have heard the call of liberalizing sexual attitudes, of possibilities for experimenting with other ways of believing and being, they felt morally superior to those who partook of impulse and risk. They flourished in the stability that came of moving along the tracks of others' expectations of them. They had learned, growing up, to silence inner wishes that did not meet others' approval, orienting themselves to please, to be "good," but they remained, at the end of college, quite unconscious of having done this. Only much later, sometimes as late as midlife, could they look back and see how they had been fettered.

Mired as they were in tradition and obedience, these were quite personally rigid college women.[1] Many had been introverted or socially isolated as teenagers and had exempted themselves from the confusions and distractions of adolescence. They told themselves that they didn't *want* to be part of what they considered to be teenage waywardness; that wasn't for them. A deep longing for security and safety kept them from ventures that might imperil the inner certainty they had. If impulses of any sort might emerge—to consider being sexually active, to question their religious beliefs, to join a political protest—they were firmly clamped down. These women lived their moral sense: right and wrong were givens, unquestionable, and provided them the backbone to stand their ground. Erotic and moral freedom were out of bounds, but academic achievement or wishes for career success could, given certain family values, fit well into their basic orientation to life.

These young women had always been "good girls," and their self-esteem had all their lives rested on submission to exacting regulation. The liberalizing of attitudes that usually takes place during these years was a process they dogmatically resisted.

Psychologist Roger Gould long ago pointed out that the transformation from childhood to adulthood is marked by giving up certain childhood beliefs—among them, that (1) "I'll always belong to my parents and believe in their world," (2) "Doing it their way, with willpower and perseverance, will bring results . . . [If needed] they will step in and show me the right way, and (3) "Life is simple and controllable. There are no significant coexisting contradictory forces within me."[2] But the Guardians had given up none of these beliefs. They clung to the security of their parents' world and their belief that life is controllable and responsive to their efforts.

Years of research on college women in this identity group has shown that they tend to have exacting parents who severely discourage unacceptable thoughts, feelings, and behavior. As a result, these people become authoritarian and approval-seeking, but sure of themselves. They are attuned to what they "should" do, think, and feel, and they follow along.

The bulwark of security to which the Guardians clung was the authority of a parent (or a long-term boyfriend) who structured life and set standards for them to reach toward. Their own sense of identity was merged with this idealized other person who seemed to know best. All goals, striving, and sense of self were phrased in terms of earning and maintaining that person's love or approval. And from this blessing, the Guardians derived profound strength. They felt secure and certain of themselves, safe against dangers that might arise both from within themselves and from outside.

The Guardians idealized their families and experienced them as warm havens, places filled with love and appreciation of their goodness. Their self-esteem was high, and their anxiety was low. Secure in knowing what was right, secure in their family's approval of them, they could press forward on their path, undistracted by temptation or inner crisis. They worked hard, studied hard, did what they were "supposed to." Whether earning high grades, going to Church or synagogue regularly, respecting their teachers—whatever they did they did because they experienced it as "right" rather than springing from inner desire. Or, perhaps more precisely, their effort was to make their inner desires identical to their sense of the right. These were idealistic and perfectionistic women. They had a clear vision of the mold into which they intended to pour their life. They were planners, conscientious, pledged not to leave anything to chance.

Being a Guardian did not mean having been raised to exclusively traditional female roles. These bright young women were often the hopes of their families—the ones who were groomed to achieve, to make something of themselves as well as to carry on the family heritage. Usually, their achievement dreams were rooted in childhood and not subjected to the doubt and rethinking of adolescence. Feeling a sense of destiny, their occupational choice had long been a part of them and not open to question. Fern, as a child, had been the only one in the neighborhood willing to play with a little girl who had cerebral palsy. Right then, she decided that her life work would be to help such children, and she had only to learn of the profession of physical therapy to make a firm and unwavering choice. Harriet, Helen, and Gwen all looked up at their grade school teachers with adoration and decided that there was no more wonderful role to take than being where their teachers stood. Both Grace and Emily had fathers who were fascinated by law, and their childhoods were marked by feeling close to and special to their fathers through sharing these interests. Their choice to enter the legal profession was, in part, a way of maintaining this unique bond. All of these women in college, then, knew exactly where they were headed—for their childhood professional dreams, for marriage, for children, and for recreating the family harmony and closeness that they had felt as children and wanted to keep forever.

On matters of religion, these young women were similarly unquestioning. Their beliefs were the same as their parents'. For the Catholic and Protestant women in this group, this was a matter of holding firm to ritual and dogma. For the Jewish women, family traditional observances and ethnic solidarity formed the core of religious identity. All of these women expected themselves to carry forward the heritage they had inherited.

Sexuality posed the more stubborn quandary. Here is where the line between childhood and adulthood is most dramatically crossed. Here is where the little girl becomes a woman, and this is the place where the Guardians were most likely to apply the brakes. To be sexual meant to be without their mothers, for they knew their mothers could not approve—or, if they would approve, at least, they could not go with them. So the Guardians held back, cited morals as a reason for remaining virginal. "My mother thinks the world of me," said Helen, "I couldn't break her heart."

What the Guardians were most trying to sustain was their childhood selves. They had an identity—one that had been ascribed to them or that they had taken up early on—that made them feel secure and certain. Internally, they were directed by a sense of right and wrong that they internalized from childhood. They vaulted over the developmental phase in which the harsh tone of conscience is tempered and in which ideals are reshaped in line with reality.

The push to experiment that occupied the Pathmakers and the Searchers was squelched, if they experienced it at all. They already felt firm in their commitments. This certainty gave the Guardians a somewhat dogmatic air.

When I interviewed them in college, I had the feeling very often that they were instructing me in how life *ought* to be rather than telling me about their own individual choices. They were strong women, that was clear, but I wondered if they were also brittle, if their intense need for security and certainty wouldn't perhaps lead them to be less resilient in life, less able to bend and adapt to the inevitable twists and boulders that awaited them on their paths.

Psychologically, the Guardians were unwilling to notice and to mourn the end of childhood. Either they grew up in families where they felt insecure and clung tightly so as not to lose their moorings, or they were raised in intensely close and comfortable homes that were so gratifying that they had no wish to move on. The dominant motif of the Guardians as college seniors was fear of change and a wish to retain control at all costs.

When I spoke about this group of women at psychological meetings, I found that psychologists were more critical of the Guardians than of all the other groups. Doing what they were "supposed to" do all the time, they were not doing what psychologists thought they were "supposed to" do—that is, to try to rework their childhood selves and achieve adult autonomy. They were getting older, my colleagues would point out, but they didn't seem to be developing. They seemed to be undertaking the impossible project of remaining little girls. Perhaps they would put on adult clothes and impersonate adult roles, but that is not the same as the inner restructuring that goes with real adolescence. Surely a crisis awaited them down the road, and they would have to endure the torments necessary for growth.

When I reported on these women when they were in their mid-30s and found them still to be rooted in the same basic psychological structure, my colleagues said knowingly, just wait 10 more years. By then they will have changed. They can't stay the same forever.

In fact, this group of women *did* change—some more than others. Of the five women who were Guardians at 21, three have remained so while two engaged in identity searching later and became Pathmakers.[3] Even those who maintained the same Guardian identity structure over time opened themselves to experience, but later in life and in more circumscribed ways, than women in the other groups. They became more insightful, more self-aware. As they approached middle age, they became less in thrall to security and learned to recognize another kind of strength in themselves. Into their mid-50s, there was no evidence that they were brittle. None has fallen apart, and all have fulfilled—at least most of—their life dreams. Among them are the highest achievers occupationally in the whole group. But those who became mothers were, by their mid-50s, the most likely of the groups to have struggled mightily with their children, as though the rigidity of their psychological structure had its primary effect on the next generation.

Guardians Who Remained Guardians

FERN

Age 21

Fern had always seemed to me to be the epitome of a Guardian, almost out of the Victorian Age. When I first met her as a college senior, she was wrapped tightly in her Catholic faith and her sense of family mission. She was filled with resolve and purpose and couldn't comprehend the commotion that her agemates were making around her. "I don't understand people getting high on drugs," she said, "I can get high on life." In many ways, at age 21, Fern seemed to be already "middle-aged," full of scorn for those who were still try-ing to get a handle on how to live.

Fern's father had been sick throughout her life and died when she was 11. In many ways, life had not indulged Fern the luxury of an adolescence. Her childhood had been organized around caring for her father; his health limita-tions kept the family from venturing far from the neighborhood. Her mother's Catholic faith provided solace and structure, and her mother's greatest wish was to have Fern's father convert to Catholicism before he died. She enlisted her daughters in this enterprise, and Fern joined her mother and sister in fervent prayer, fearing that without her father's conversion, they could not all be reunited in Heaven.

After her father's death, her mother sought work for the first time in her life, and house chores and care of her younger sister fell to Fern. Her fam-ily was relatively isolated. There were no cousins or aunts to cushion some of the tension. And Fern was not very successful in making friends. When some of the Protestant neighborhood children taunted her as a Catholic, she fled home in tears. Her mother counseled her that there were mean people in the world and that it would be best if she stayed at home. "I became aware of what kinds of things exist," Fern said in her college interview, justifying her retreat from what had the potential to hurt her. She idealized her parents: "I don't think I could pick parents who have given more to their children than my parents did to me." They expected a lot of her, and she was proud that she could always succeed in school. But she was jealous of her younger sister who was "manipulative" and always managed to get clothes and privileges that Fern wouldn't dare even ask for. As a teenager, after her father's death, Fern developed a fantasy relationship with a patron saint who she felt protected her and found things for her. She turned to her faith when she felt fearful and found security there.

In high school, a teacher noticed her shyness and her loneliness and invited her to join the drama club. With his patient guidance, she began to come out of herself a bit, to join the other kids and to gain some feeling of connection to others. She adored this teacher, imagined him as a kind of substitute father. But she remained wary of others, even through college, sensitive to what people said, easily offended. She was very attentive to "creating an impression" on others and felt unable to be spontaneous or playful.

Fern chose to attend a state university near her home. It was all she could afford, but she expressed no wish to go elsewhere. She was already set on becoming a physical therapist, and the local university had a good program. Through college, she continued to live at home and to avoid much of the student life. She had "several acquaintances, but no real friends." She was often a "shoulder" for others' problems and tried to engage with others by taking care of them when she saw the need. Wary of others, she was oversensitive to criticism or rejection and easily shocked by others' actions. One woman whom she liked and with whom she was developing a friendship began cutting classes. Fern was confused and judged her friend harshly, tried to persuade her not to do this. But when she didn't change her ways, Fern found that she couldn't tolerate her friend's "dishonesty" and distanced herself. She began to date for the first time in her junior year, but the relationship broke off because the young man thought that she was "too critical." She knew she lacked confidence in her femininity, but more, she worried that she would not be able to find a man who would live up to her standards. "I'm not willing to change. Someone will have to like me as I am—respect my standards and beliefs." But she feared that she might become a spinster.

At the end of college, then, Fern was very clear on what was right and wrong, on doing good and being good. "I'd never question authority," she asserted proudly. She wanted to be as close to an earthbound saint as she could. In this, she looked to her mother as a model, rhapsodizing about her good sense, her devotion to her family. Fern wanted a life of giving to others. The world seemed to be one of sorrow and malevolence, and she wanted to make it better.

Although I admired Fern's tenacity and fortitude and recognized the trauma she had suffered in the loss of her father, I worried for her personality constriction. So much of life seemed to be ruled out for her, and she seemed to be imprisoning herself. I thought that if she wasn't depressed at this time, surely she would be someday.

Age 33

When I met Fern again when she was 33, I found her, as a person, quite unchanged. Still, she seemed relaxed and confident, sure of herself, in control. In her life, she was fulfilling her wish to "serve others" as a physical therapist, and her dedication had led her to a position as department chair in a large hospital. She carried enormous responsibility and was enthusiastic about her work.

In her first job, Fern had met a man who seemed "compatible" and they married a year later. Like her father, he was not Catholic and Fern was intrigued with the idea of converting him. She appreciated his understanding of her "need to help," and he was willing to allow her freedom to engage in her professional commitments as well as a number of charitable organizations to which she offered her time. They had two children, and he was willing to be equally involved and helpful. But Fern was disappointed in her marriage in some ways. "Fred is not as affectionate as I would like and his morals aren't as high as mine." Separation, of course, was not a consideration, and she sought help through prayer. "This must be life," she said, "and with all the happy times, sad times and hard times, I wouldn't change it because through every-thing we have always had each other." At very least, Fern had established a new base of security.

Fern took delight in her two sons, although she had had a hard time with them as toddlers. Then they were "daring, defiant, and mischievous," quali-ties Fern had never been able to experience in herself. But with them, she was able to express and receive the open loving that she missed with Fred. She worried about not always being there when her children needed her, but her dedication to her career—and the good she felt she could do for others—was unwavering.

Fern was deeply invested in her work. Again, she had found some "fatherly" men who were willing to teach her and challenge her. One helped her expand her abilities as a therapist. Another showed her the art of managing. She felt herself in a period of intense professional growth, gaining deeper and broader skills.

In the 12 years since college, Fern had also made some women friends, people from work whom she felt she could confide in and share with. She also described herself as having "become more accepting of superficial friend-ships." In general, Fern seemed to have become a bit less demanding of oth-ers. She remained close to her mother who, having retired, came to live with them for several months a year.

At this age, then, Fern was fulfilling her dream of serving others and was certainly not depressed. She had dealt with some disappointment in her marriage, but there was much else in her life that was developing as she had hoped. Reflecting on her own history at this time, Fern was recognizing that she had never had an opportunity to be an adolescent. "I missed a lot," she said wistfully. "I was a mini-adult." She could see, from the vantage point of age 33, that she had been racked by inferiority and insecurity in her teens, and seemed to wish that she had been able to have had more fun.

Age 43

Not until she turned 40 did Fern have her first real "identity crisis" (her words). Then a job crisis led her to risks that she could never have dreamed of undertaking. The management at her hospital changed and, under pres-sure of tight economic circumstances, services were reorganized and her department was to have far fewer resources. Fern gradually began to realize that, given the new limitations, there was no way to provide the quality of service to which she had devoted herself. She framed this as a moral question and decided that to continue in her position was unethical. "I couldn't compromise myself any more," she said. It was simply wrong to hold herself out as a physical therapist when she was not able, as a therapist or a department chair, to provide what she considered to be adequate service. So she resigned. Her new dream was to establish a private service that would function independently and be able to serve disadvantaged clients who were being turned away under the hospital's system. With her husband's agreement, she emptied their savings, procured a new mortgage on the house, and invested everything into setting this up. Fern was frightened: she was putting her family's welfare in the service of her scruples, giving up a secure paycheck that had been the majority of the family's income. (Fred was working in a low-paying government job.)

Fern prayed. But the reality was more turbulent than she had imagined. Business partners reneged on their commitments. People she shared an office with left without paying the rent. For the first time, Fern had to be careful about what food she put in her grocery cart. "But it was not just the pressure of not having the income, but knowing that if that business failed, I would have lost everything of the family's." Fern described these as having been "the insane years, the unsettled years, the radical years—what most people go through in college." She weathered it by relying on the strength in her family and appreciating that. They supported her, didn't bemoan their changed lifestyle, endured deprivation without complaint.

When I saw her at this time, Fern had organized her business to a point where it was afloat, although not yet thriving. She was feeling a bit less terrified, but wished she could worry less about the income. Where she had hoped to be able to work fewer hours, she was in fact working many more. But the gratification was that she was doing it her own way. "I really felt I was going to be in a better position to provide for families—not cranking out numbers and bringing in dollars. I didn't realize then that it would really be much more like missionary work. Our practice goes beyond providing the concrete physical and occupational therapy modes. We end up being counselors of a sort, dealing with family issues and financial issues and school issues for their children. Knowing that the holidays are not good for them because they don't have money. We put together food baskets at Thanksgiving, organize clothing drives. . . . Its missionary work. We work with a population that no one else wants to work with in a place where no one else wants to go. . . . You have a responsibility to provide." What drives her to this? I wondered. "Knowing that I have two healthy children and a commitment to knowing that I'm supposed to give back and to do it in a way that I am gifted to do it." And here Fern got tearful, choked up. Her thoughts then turned to her father.

The commitment to serve was consistent with how Fern had been all along, but the venturesomeness was new. And much else was new as well. Fern had, in her 30s and into her 40s, evolved into a more open and insightful woman. Where her life had been dominated by "shoulds" and formulas, she had, in midlife, discovered feelings and psychological complexity. She was struggling to make sense of this fluid sensibility and had, in the process, learned to regard herself with a sense of humor.

Part of what initiated her revision of herself was her success in bringing about her husband's conversion to Catholicism. As part of this process, they renewed their marriage vows and embarked on a series of "marriage encounters" through their Church. "I hoped it would change him. *I* didn't have any need to change. I was the perfect wife," she said in a tone of self-mockery. "So it was a revelation to find that there were things I needed to change as well." She learned a lot about feelings and about communication, things she had missed in her relative isolation while growing up and in her supercilious contempt for others in college. "There is no education for becoming a couple—no education that prepares you to make a relationship with someone you are going to spend the rest of your life with. How can you be responsible to each other? For a lot of us who grew up in families where it didn't happen or was much more mechanical or superficial, [we had to learn about] having that depth and really being able to communicate things and being able to look at each other and know what is there."

Fern began to understand for the first time the way in which she substituted caretaking activities for relating to people. She began to take some emotional distance from herself as a caretaker and to recognize the way it kept her from deeper engagement with others. Coming to see herself as "a caretaker" in the self-deprecatory form of that word, she began to understand that it was more important to empower her patients than to take care of them. She realized that she had been being "a caretaker" in her marriage, and she eagerly took up new modes of communication. For the first time, she was able to allow herself to be emotionally vulnerable. "Sometimes I have periods where there is no energy and I feel discouraged. Sometimes I have significant mood swings where I can be very quiet and introspective. And Fred instinctively knows that it's not a good time and he can sort of cheer me up. I think we offer each other a good balance."

Even more rethinking of herself followed upon her mother's death seven years previously. Although deeply saddened by her loss, Fern reviewed her past and found herself rethinking her life history. No longer viewing her mother through a glorifying lens, she began to be able to tolerate an awareness of some of the more negative aspects of her upbringing, something she could not do at all in college or in her early 30s. Now she could see the unfairness of the caretaker role she was thrust into. She realized that, throughout her adolescence, she had been the parent and her mother the child, but she had been too dutiful to allow herself to know this. She hadn't been permitted an independent self, hadn't been granted the right to her own feelings. "Feelings weren't discussed in my household. It was neat and orderly—the Ozzie and Harriet family ... so feelings didn't enter into it. If your parents said jump, you said 'how high?' So I don't think I had the independent ability to evaluate my own self-esteem. But looking back on it now, knowing what self-esteem is, I know now I didn't have it. Because I was too preoccupied with being too much to other people to have had an independent life myself."

Fern wasn't dwelling on her anger about this but was trying to be vigilant and change those parts of herself that she felt were damaged. What she most resented was the way in which her mother always made her feel not good enough. "I think it was her way of trying to push me to be as good as I could be, but I always felt I was held up to be like somebody else or as good as somebody else. . . . I felt terrible because it was never good enough. I think that's part of what drives me to be as intense as I am—its always are you good enough? And I don't have to prove it to anyone but it's still a part of me. I'm not really sure who I am proving it to. And I worry about that with my children." Jim, her older son, at 16, often did less well than she thought he could. "I know he is not producing to his fullest potential, that he's just being lazy about that stuff but I am terrified of speaking those words, of saying 'Well, what did X get on his report card?' and holding up to him what was held up to me. And I really am terrified that I will become my mother, that part of her that always made me feel that my best wasn't good enough." She recognized that she got her strength from trying so hard to be good for her mother, but she was now becoming aware of the price she had paid. In some ways, Fern said she was glad that her mother died before the crisis in her work. "I'm glad she never had to see how hard we struggled. Knowing me as the person who could do it all, I think it would have killed her."

Fern seemed to be in a never-ending battle with herself to keep her perfectionism modulated. And the fight to be less critical and demanding than her mother was an arduous one, requiring an ongoing capacity to observe and understand herself. The previous year, Jim's school class took a trip to France which Fern, despite their financial difficulties, didn't want him to miss. Her need to feel like a good provider to her children led her to juggle expenses to pull together the money for him to go. "So he went on that trip to Paris and I was so angry at him because he came home and the main thing he wanted to talk about was leaning out the hotel windows and hollering up to the girls above and talking about other experiences that I could have arranged in the seedier parts of town here for much less money. He wasn't talking about seeing the Mona Lisa. His first recounts were of adolescent experiences and I was furious ... I wanted to say, 'I didn't work for the last six months for you to come home and talk about this stuff'. So I just didn't say anything. I know my expectations were different than his, but I still have a hard time letting go of mine. Because that was my dream, too, that went and what came back was not the dream that I sent." And here, with the poignancy of that statement, she laughed. I was deeply touched by her insight, admiring of how far she had come to be able to have that awareness.

Dealing with the adolescent challenges of her children when she hadn't had these experiences herself continued to puzzle Fern. Again, she responded not with the rigidity of her college-age personality but with an effort to remain open, to respect her sons' selfhood. Sex had been a difficult issue to talk to her sons about for it had never really been discussed in her family. "But his father isn't doing it, and he has to hear it from one of us. We've talked more about AIDS than the mechanical things but then you go up and find a wasted condom under the mattress and *Playboy*s. I sort of die. So it's been an awkward thing for me. I wish I had had girls, I think it would have been easier. And we've talked about *Playboy* and how that's not what a relationship with a woman is about and that's not what sex means." She still had her religious scruples but wanted her sons to decide for themselves. "I think I have evolved to allow them to be what they want to be and do what they want to do instead of just feeling that it has to be my way." Mainly, she was trying not to turn into her mother, who was full of expectations of how her children should be.

Coming into awareness of her own emotional life led Fern to be more respectful of others' feelings, less demanding that they live up to her principles. Fred had always kept his feelings to himself, sometimes not talking for days. Their new "tools" for communication, however, opened the floodgates of feeling, both loving and angry ones. And Jim, in Fern's perception, was much like Fred. "I am not a confrontational person, but I am more so than I used to be. I used to be a peace at any price person. You never saw anything that wasn't nice." (Here Fern seemed to be accurately describing how she appeared to me at the time of the college-age interview.) It was a challenge to manage—rather than squelch—the feelings that erupted within her family. "Jim stores things and then something stupid sets him off and he starts screaming at the top of his lungs and then he and my husband will start screaming at each other and I will have to verbally separate them and make them cool off. I don't like that, I don't like to have to be the one to get in the middle of that. I don't like the fact that they don't deal with their anger in a more appropriate way. Is it all right for them to have it? Of course. Because I'd rather have it come out than have it come out in some other way. Do I like that stuff? No thank you." But she could bear it. She could allow others as well as herself to feel what they felt.

Fern had also developed more openness and comfort about her sexuality. This, too, had improved with time. If anything, she was sometimes rueful about having missed out on some of that, too. When asked the interview question about experiences of sexual harassment, Fern laughed and said, "I wish I had the body that someone would want to harass. At work, I get described as Mother Superior—so sexual harassment doesn't fit with that role." (Fern is quite overweight and not very attentive to her physical appearance.) She wished she were sexier, and fantasies along these lines came easily to her. In contrast to the fear and moralism of her 20s and early 30s, Fern at 43 was vibrant.

Fern's faith was still what sustained her. If anything, Fern said, she had become more prayerful and her faith was deeper. Part of this related to her concept of service, of giving to others, of being called. And part was about having something "larger than myself" to fall back on in times of stress.

Fern at 43, then, seemed to be taking the reins, designing her own path. She seemed to be rethinking herself, revising herself, reclaiming parts of herself that were locked away or disowned, and she was shaping a more complete sense of herself. She continued to live her vision of moral purpose and self-sacrificing mission, but in an enlightened way. This woman who would never question authority in her 20s was finding a way in her 40s to reach and understand her own authority and to be more empathic of others as well.

Age 56

Remembering my excitement about the changes in Fern from college to midlife, I looked forward to seeing her again and learning about what more she had done with her new insight and self-awareness. I met her in her Victorian house, furnished to be serviceable and comfortable with what looked to me like family heirlooms.

Again, Fern surprised me. Although still warm and immensely articulate, she seemed more like she had been at 33 than at 43. What had claimed her attention—and the center of her identity—in the past 13 years had been problems with her son Jim, who did so many things she had never expected. He left school, left home, and got in trouble with the law. Much of her interview at this age was focused on detailing the struggles with him, and many of her stories were not very coherent, reflecting, I think, the degree of distress she felt trying to control his behavior for many years. She felt on her own. Her husband had been distancing himself from Jim's hanging out with "the wrong kind of kids," although once Jim got arrested, Fred began to engage with the problems of keeping Jim out of jail. "We lived in terror," she told me, "until he got a suspended sentence and probation." Prayer helped some. Fern tried to explain to me the causes of Jim's troubles—and, in part, she blamed herself for having worked so much when he was small.

At the time of this interview, Fern was hoping that Jim had turned himself around. He had married, had gotten a job, and, she told me joyfully, "I am expecting my first grandbaby." To ensure the success of this new family, Fern and Fred had decided to move across the country, where Jim now lived, to build a house that would accommodate all of them so she could be there to "help." There had been some years of complete estrangement from Jim, who had left home without even saying goodbye, but Fern was optimistic that they could create a three-generational living arrangement that would work. She prayed for this.

Her younger son, John, was doing well, "the complete opposite" of Jim— and although he had some misgivings about the new family plan, she didn't take them seriously. "It was a difficult adjustment," Fern told me, having the kids out of the house because "dealing with the kids was and is my passion."

There is a need for health care workers everywhere, Fern reasoned, so she and her husband could find work in California. Fern had given up the private practice she had worked so hard to build in her 40s. She couldn't make it profitable and had gone to work instead in home care, which was evolving in the 1990s and allowed her a salary without compromising her ideals. This work situation she felt she could find anywhere.

While visibly relieved that Jim seemed to have settled down, she still described him as "impulsive and headstrong" and mistrusted his wife who was not raised with "an attachment to faith." Fern wanted to make sure that the new baby was brought up correctly. "This child should know its roots from the beginning." And "Hopefully we'll be able to model some behavior as a husband and a wife and as a mom and a dad."

Although Fern berated herself for having put Jim in daycare, for not having been more attentive to his early learning difficulties, she still couldn't understand what went wrong. She believed that she and Fred had provided a completely loving family. I had a glimmer of some insight from a conversation that Fern reported with her daughter-in-law when she first met her. "We were meeting in the airport, and I hugged her and I said, 'I love you.' And she said, 'You don't even know me.' And I said, 'My son loves you. That's enough for me.' And she could not get her head around that concept at all." Fern told me this story to illustrate how they are loving in a way that the daughter-in-law's parents (who are divorced) are not—but I thought that it reflected the way in which love, for Fern, is connected to duty rather than feeling.

"We need to be there," Fern said, so they were selling their house, quitting their jobs, pulling up stakes to go. "Our mission here is finished. We need to be there for them." She never mentioned how Jim felt about this. She thought that it was perhaps "God's plan" for them. Fern also told me that "the void" of being empty-nesters was almost unbearable for them, but she did not connect this to their plan to move to California.

Looking back on the private practice venture she had devoted herself to in her 40s, Fern thought that "the whole experience was a tremendous burden on my family . . . and it was, in some ways, a huge mistake." It was never financially viable and she had to give it up. "Jim was 12 to 18, and I think if I had not been so involved with the business or not having to keep it going all the time, maybe who knows? He wouldn't have ended up making some of the choices or having some of the difficulties he had . . . and I'll never know. . . . If I had it to do over again, I would be poor and not work. I would have stayed home with them." And she regretted being away from John who has done well but perhaps not as much as he was capable of doing. "If I had directed him, who knows where he would be?"

I thought, but didn't say, that Fern was misplacing the blame. From the way she talked about Jim in the interview, it seemed she was too close to him rather than too distant. It was hard for her to describe him as a separate person, with his own needs and wishes. She seemed to see him only as someone who lost his way because she wasn't with him enough. For her, the defining moment was when he got a car . . . and if he hadn't gotten that car, perhaps none of this would have happened." I heard this as implying that without a car, he would have stayed home and obeyed—as she had at that age. When I asked Fern how, overall, she understood the difficulties between her and Jim, she said simply, "He just didn't want to listen to reason," a statement I thought said a lot about Fern. She felt herself to be the holder of reason, reason buttressed by her uncompromising values and her faith. She believed (and exhorted her sons) that the good things that happened in life were a result of miracles resulting from prayer, and she took comfort that John shared her faith and was therefore a beneficiary of many miracles, including being saved in a tornado.

In many ways, I felt that Fern had reverted to the person she had been earlier. The self-awareness and insight she seemed to have developed in her early 40s were nowhere apparent at this age, replaced now by self-blame. At the age of 56, prayer, duty, care-taking, control, responsibility, and self-sacrifice were again (or perhaps had always been) at the center. She told me that what had changed most in herself over the past 10 years was a deepening of her faith and an ability "to bring to the surface in the children the presence of God in their lives." Indeed, deepening of faith is what Fern had identified as the major change in herself at each interview. At this time, it was more focused on her son and his family.

Fern's life-altering decision to move to California is born of regret and hope. She hopes to redo what she regrets, to manage this new family according to her values, a new "mission." I reminded her in this interview of the wonderful story she told at age 43 about sending Jim to Paris and his coming home with a different experience than she intended. (I thought she had told that with great insight, insight that might have served her.) But she didn't remember either the story or having told it. Nor could she understand why I thought it significant.

The preoccupation with their children in their mid-50s appeared in other Guardians as well, both more so and differently than in the other groups. It seemed to me that the project of needing children to reflect oneself was part of the Guardian orientation to tradition and "the right way." Psychologically, it was rooted in the incomplete separation and individuation from their own families of origin, located in a relationship with their mothers that was not resolved, even into the later part of midlife.

HARRIET

Harriet spent most of her life tied to her mother and only at midlife was able to perceive herself as shackled by the bond and to make an effort to loosen it. But it repeated itself in her relationship with her daughter.

Age 21

The only daughter of middle-class Jewish parents, Harriet had always wanted to be a teacher. Her parents thought that she could aspire to more than being a classroom teacher and encouraged her to try special education. Her mother had started working as a nursery-school teacher after Harriet and her brothers were all in school, and this seemed to be an excellent model for her own life. When she was in college, her dreams for the future were to have a life exactly like her mother's.

Harriet had been a happy, popular child, but it seemed to her that when she entered high school, everyone else changed. She found herself unable to "connect with the other girls who were preoccupied by themselves and not willing to open up to others." They seemed only to want to show off. They got involved with smoking and drinking, and Harriet balked at such behavior. She retreated to her mother's support and tried not to care about her increasing loneliness. "I used to go home and cry every night, I was so unhappy. But I still felt I was right."

College was better. She began to date and had more success in finding friends. She found that she could open up to others. In school in Chicago, she still called her mother in Detroit daily to talk over the events of the day. At the time of the college interview, Harriet, although highly articulate, could not describe her parents as people separate from her with their own lives and inclinations. She missed them, but could only depict them to me in terms of who she took which kind of problem to. She wished at this time to have more confidence in herself and tried to put herself in situations where she would have to cope. But Harriet was hesitant, afraid to venture far. Even in her senior year of college, she was often homesick and looked forward to returning to the comforts of her family.

Age 33

After college, Harriet returned to the suburb of Detroit where she was raised and began studying for a master's degree in learning disabilities. She wasn't yet sure enough of herself to begin working. Her success in her graduate program gave her the boost of self-confidence she needed, and she began her career at a school she considered to be excellent. Surrounded by children all the time, Harriet said "you almost forget what it's like to be an adult." She thought, at age 33, that she wouldn't feel fully adult until she was married with children.

Throughout her 20s and early 30s, Harriet had been eagerly in search of marriage. But looking back at age 33, she realized how "naive" she had been about men, sex, and relationships, especially through college. She had been frightened about sex, which had not been much discussed in her home, and she had internalized her mother's moralistic stance against sexual experience before marriage. "I grew up not knowing much of anything and bit by bit, I've learned a lot more, relaxed a lot more and feel much more comfortable in the area."

But "more comfortable" to Harriet at this point was still "not very." She had, at age 33, spent seven years with a man who had serious sexual problems, and she remained a virgin. "I felt very insecure about my functioning as a woman," she said. She clung to the hope that if they married, the problems would resolve themselves. This, at least, was her mother's opinion. He was, in both Harriet and her mother's view, "perfect" in other respects. Harriet spent most of her 20s struggling with this relationship with Zachary, unwilling to give up the feeling of "having" someone. More than anything, she needed to feel not alone, bonded in the intense twosome she had felt with her mother. "I need to know that I'm needed by another person and that I can need another person. I don't mean dependency. I just mean to know that if I needed another person, there would be a person there for me. I'm a strong person and used to having others depend on me and I need the security of knowing that I, too, could fall to pieces and have someone there." Her greatest fear was being alone. "If something happens to me, who is going to be the person that really cares? I used to make Zachary swear that if there was some sort of nuclear attack, he would come look for me. I had to know that there was one person whose main goal would be to look for me and to take care of me if I were in a time of need."[4] When she was 26 and in a period of estrangement from Zachary, she had a serious appendicitis attack and her parents cancelled their vacation to take care of her. "Thank God I had my parents, "she said. "Who else would have been there?"

By the time she was 30, it became clear that Zachary was not going to marry her, and Harriet broke off the relationship. Her mother thought she should have given it more time. "The few times I stood up to my mother were in regard to him. But I was always afraid of doing something she would not approve of and what I finally came to realize was that I will always hope to have her support but I will not always have her approval. I was a long time getting to that point," Harriet said at age 33. But the end of that relationship drove her back to the comfort of her mother, and she had still to wrestle for her independence. "When my engagement with Zachary broke off, she was there when I needed to depend on her, and when the time came for me to pull myself back together, we had gotten into this pattern and she was taking charge of a lot of things and I was afraid to break away from that for fear of hurting her. It's only been in the last two years that I've been able to stand up to her."

Shortly before I interviewed her when she was 33, Harriet had become engaged to Len, a man she had met eight months before. She was delighted by their growing love for each other. "He fulfills a lot of the ideals that I have been looking for. He makes me feel so good and wonderful and secure. And it's a really passionate relationship." But when I asked her to list the people she felt closest to at that time, she couldn't choose between Len and her mother for the top of the list. She hoped that once they married, Len would be the clear first choice.

The hope and security she derived from her engagement to Len led Harriet to rethink her life from this vantage point. "I have a regret that I grew up to be such a goody-goody. A lot of my life has been geared to pleasing my mother. And I probably didn't even know that until the past five or six years. I remember—as a child, if my mother and I would have a disagreement about what I'd wear somewhere—she'd say one thing and I'd say another and she'd say to me, OK, do whatever you want and I would always wear what she said."

Harriet's dream at age 33 was much the same dream she had had since childhood. "I look at other families and see a close-knit family and I *long* for something like that—where families get together for the joy of it. It does give them some direction." She wanted to have children as soon as possible and was ready to abandon her teaching career with no regrets.

Age 43

Finally getting the home and family that she had always wanted indeed prompted growth and revision in Harriet by age 43. As fantasy evaporated into reality, Harriet found her own voice and began to make her path more her own. When I asked her then what had been most significant in her life over the past 10 years, she said, "Marriage was a wonderful change, but having children was most significant and not the storybook image I expected. I remember thinking, 'Is this what I've been waiting for all my life?' It hasn't been easy. I'm a working mother. I took two years off after our son was born. But I was very isolated, exhausted, and tense most of the time. I didn't know how fatiguing it could be." She was relieved to go back to work, and, in any case, it was a necessity if they were to be able to afford the comfortable suburban home that Harriet also desired. She amazed herself that the decision to have a second child "wasn't automatic." But she wanted her son to have a brother or sister (not to be alone, the old fear). With their second child, Harriet took off six months, then Len took a leave from work for the next six months. Harriet was on her way to effecting new definitions of family. Life became child-focused, and Harriet was rethinking how she wanted things to be. Their son was born a year after they married, and she regretted that she and Len didn't have more time alone together, more time to be spontaneous and to have fun. She missed the passion and romance that they didn't have time for, but she tried to content herself with his being her best friend.

Harriet didn't begin taking charge of her life in a more considered way until after she had battled her way out of the disillusionment and disappointment she felt after her son was born. Her sense of "Is this all there is?" punctured the idealized balloon, and she had to make a dream of her own. At age 43, she was still in the same teaching job, still family-centered, and, outwardly, her life looked to be much the same as her mother's had been. Inwardly, however, she was thinking in her own terms about how she wanted to construct her life. She had recently thought about changing careers, often feeling "burned out" by teaching, but, assessing herself, she felt that she is "not a go-getter," didn't have the energy to give up the sense of competence she had in her work and undertake something else.

Her mother was still ever-present, but Harriet had a new view of this relationship as well. She had a perspective on her mother's intrusiveness and made choices about what to speak up about and what to let go by in order to preserve harmony. She had asked her mother, in a kind way, not to come into their house and change the curtains, for example, but she let her mother give advice without getting angry at her. She still saw her mother nearly every day, but felt that it was for her mother's benefit rather than her own.

The deep emotional mother–daughter knot seemed, though, to be passing to the next generation. Harriet had a hard time with her daughter, Louisa, age five, who was stubborn and oppositional and had many fears. She found herself losing patience, yelling at her. Her daughter would not be controlled, and she was considering taking her to a psychologist. Harriet did not connect her experience as a mother with how she had felt as a daughter. And she was still, in her own daughterhood, grappling with how a loving relationship between a mother and a daughter can also have boundaries. "My mother created me," she said. "But she brought me up not able to say how I feel." Harriet still couldn't confront her mother very much, but she was now able to know what she feels. "There are a lot of positive feelings—and the resentments I push aside." Accepting the limits in her relationship with her mother paralleled Harriet's accepting other struggles in her life—with her children, with balancing work and family, with accepting that she couldn't do it all and having Len take over the cooking. "It isn't a TV family. It isn't ideal." And, for Harriet, accepting that it is not ideal was an enormous stride toward maturity.

Age 53

Harriet seemed to have aged quite a bit. She looked plain, unconcerned about her appearance—kind of the stereotype of the middle-aged schoolteacher. She said she had read my earlier books, found herself, and thought I had depicted her as "needy"—but decided not to let this bother her and didn't give it much thought. (I wasn't sure what "needy" meant because this was her word rather than mine, but it was interesting to me that this is how she thought I had described her. Indeed, I had not used this word or described her in this way.)

Her interview began with and was dominated by the struggles with her daughter, Louisa, which have claimed her attention for the past 10 years. Louisa was diagnosed with depression in the eighth grade and had been repeatedly hospitalized; she was anorexic, she cut herself. "That certainly sets you on edge," Harriet said. She frequently in this interview referred to herself as "you" in what might have been an effort to gain some emotional distance from what has clearly been highly distressing to her. "My life has turned into a total roller coaster," she said somewhat flatly, and she spent most of the interview describing for me, without much visible feeling, the ups and downs.

"I never dreamed that parenting would be as involved as it is. I don't think I was a difficult teenager, per se, although I know as an adult that a lot of the reason I didn't go through that is that I was raised to be this goody-goody compliant child and so, if I had anger, I kept it inside. . . . It was only in adulthood that I was able to separate and identify it and try to deal with it. In the relationship with my mother, I've come to terms with the fact that I can't really deal with it with her. The times that I've tried to bring things up to her, she's not the least bit receptive. And we have a relationship on the surface where we talk every day, just to check in, we spend some time together socially and my mother has no idea that I still have a lot of anger inside of me. Cause I was never able to express it. One of the things with my daughter, as much as you hate to go through it, I think its healthier that at least she gets it out of her system and says it and then it's over and done with."

Separation is an important issue, which they have worked on in therapy, but it remains. "She's still very, very clingy. She's 16. Yesterday she had a horrible, horrible day and ended up coming to school with me. She wanted to be home by herself, I told her I didn't feel comfortable leaving her by herself and I asked her if she wanted to come to school with me which she did. . . . And she still says to me, I'd rather be with you than anybody else. And that breaks my heart, you know. As a mother, obviously there is a certain loveliness to know that your child likes you and wants to be with you, but she needs to be spending the time with friends. . . . I don't know how much to foster that she needs time with me and how much to try to push her away toward friends and there's always this fine line." In Louisa's school, she has been branded as the "sick" one, which distresses both Louisa and Harriet. In this, I hear echoes of Harriet telling me at age 21 about how she was the different one in *her* high school—and how this propelled her back to her mother.

Harriet still thinks of herself as having always been "a goody-goody," although she learned in her professional role to say the difficult things

that were necessary to say and not always "to go along." Her work, especially with the children she teaches, has remained a source of satisfaction
although she is so fed up with the bureaucracy and paperwork that she
would walk away if she could afford it. She remains the primary wage-
earner and her husband, who has a lower paying job, still manages the
cooking and cleaning. Her work has become "my source of refuge.... At
school, I get letters and phone calls and accolades from the parents, principal and my supervisors. But you want to have the same sense of surety in
your home life and I don't. I think to myself that other people must have it
so much easier or better, and I've spoken with lots of people and I've discovered that a lot of people I know are going through all kinds of problems.
So—is it that we grew up in a period where you had this idealistic image
of home life and what it should be—Donna Reed—that that's not there for
me, so what's wrong? Is this just reality? I don't know."

Their son, Charles, also presented problems with drugs and alcohol and
some scrapes with the law, but Harriet's husband, who thought he understood
teenage boys, kept her from over-reacting, and Charles went to college and
seemed to settle down. "It's difficult when you feel you are in control and you
have a certain view or values and your child's not following those values. It's
very hard and it was very upsetting and I had many tears over it." In the end,
they paid for his lawyers. "And I feel bad that he has to come for Thanksgiving
and we have to deal with this issue of the law." Indeed, Harriet is very far from
Donna Reed and her ideal picture of family. Harriet feels that her marriage
is strong, but she and Len disagree on handling the children, and Len often
pulls back with Louisa for fear that Harriet will object to how he responds to
her. Although Harriet says that they talk through their different approaches
to the children, it seems like Harriet takes the lead with Louisa while Len
manages the problems with Charles. Their relationship is dominated by the
children. Out of fear of leaving Louisa alone, they cannot go out as a couple—
and it has been this way since Louisa "had anxiety issues" and would not
allow them to leave her.

In contrast to her professional success in modifying the behavior of special
needs children and instructing their parents in how to deal with them are
her own frustrations in getting her own children to do what she thinks they
should do. Harriet realizes that it is a different matter. She has been grateful
to Louisa's therapist for saying to Louisa what Louisa can't hear from her. In
her approach to others, Harriet's emphasis on control, rather than empathy,
seemed prominent to me.

Harriet does have some pleasure in her life—a yearly weekend trip and
occasional theater days with some old friends. "It's the most wonderful time
because I'm not a mother or a wife." I was struck by the irony of this, because
being a mother and a wife is what Harriet had most wanted to be. Harriet, if
she was aware of the irony, didn't say so.

By age 53, Harriet felt she had made *some* progress in her relationship with her mother. "It's her being critical and my allowing that to take such an important role in my life. That I can't get away from that teenager who had to be the goody-goody and not make waves and not upset the parents. . . . Is it her fault? It's just as much my fault for allowing her to affect me that way." This seems a testament to Harriet's continued growth. She can now recognize her own role in her enmeshment with her mother. "I'm not going to change her at age 83." It is nevertheless a source of embarrassment in her family of origin that "I have a child with the reputation of being a difficult kid." In the family, she feels, Louisa reflects badly on her. And there is a complicated three-way relationship among Harriet, her mother, and Louisa, as one might expect. When Harriet got the courage to leave Louisa alone for the day, Louisa called Harriet's mother to come and get her, which she did. So the tangles are now three-generational. Harriet thinks, though, that her growth has been that she no longer dwells as much on her mother's criticism of her, that she has separated enough by this age—age 53—to be less wounded.

Looking back on her life to tell her life story from this vantage point, Harriet stresses the influence of her parents, particularly her mother. Her father was quiet and in the background. From her mother came the strong moral values and ideals of family, an ideal she still feels her mother achieved with the family meals and outings and everyone doing what they were supposed to do. College she remembers as a wonderful time, having friends, developing her teaching skills, being happy. Then there was the period in which she gained professional self-confidence and "had the strength of character" not to marry the first man she was involved with but to wait for "the right one to come along." She now understands herself as having stayed with Zachary out of "neediness"—the need to have someone to rely on in her life. (So, I thought, there is the neediness she felt I had seen in her.) But, recalling this self, Harriet felt it was like a different person, disconnected from the person she is now. The current chapter of her life, marriage and family, is where she locates herself, and it is of one piece. She titles this adult chapter "You do what you have to do."

Despite their wide differences in background, Fern and Harriet share psychological similarities. Both had psychological structures that were governed by moral dictates derived from their mothers. Whatever anger they felt at having their independent wishes squelched was suppressed and channeled into serving others. Harriet was both repelled and intrigued by Louisa expressing this anger that simmered over the years inside of her—and neither Fern nor Harriet could see that their children's acting out reflected some disowned parts of themselves. Harriet's problems about separation and individuation from her mother were carried into her relationship with her own daughter. Fern had to confront difference up close when her son literally slammed the door on her, leaving her hurt and mystified. Both women had a wish to create ideal families, but the personality structure that kept them immune to the growth-promoting possibilities of their college years seems to have created too constricted an environment for (at least one of) their children to be able to separate and individuate comfortably in his or her own developmental course. And the revisions of early midlife (mid-30s to mid-40s), the greater self-awareness, evaporated when put to the test.

HELEN

Helen seems to have had somewhat more success with her Guardian identity project, but she, too, was struggling with disappointment in her children at age 53. For Helen, identity lay in caregiving, and, indeed, I had never been so generously and warmly taken care of. She picked me up at the airport and prepared a lovely lunch for me, and I felt I could accept this from her because she so genuinely wanted to provide for me. Helen told me, at age 53, that I would probably think she had a "boring" life, but indeed I thought that she lived out what I had thought of as an archetypal Guardian path. She remembered reading *Revising Herself* and remarked with a laugh, "I think I was one of those that pretty much did what was expected of me and … probably still do."

Age 33

When I met her at the end of college, Helen was finishing a year early so she could marry her high school boyfriend and teach in order to put him through school. They wanted to start a family as soon as possible. When I saw her at age 33, I learned that this is exactly what she did. Having had fertility problems and teaching a bit longer than she expected, Helen earned a master's degree and found that she was taking her career more seriously than she had supposed she would. She voiced some disappointment in her marriage. She was the one who dominated the relationship, who had energy. She described her husband as passive—he helped with chores, but lacked ambition and mainly liked to watch TV. Early in their marriage, he had a brief affair and Helen found it hard to forgive this betrayal, but she didn't even think of breaking up their family. Helen's life was centered on her large, extended, culturally Jewish family that was, in various combinations, often together. She described her life at this point as very happy and just like all the other women in her family except that she had a career. Looking back, she felt she had been touched very little by her college experience because she lived at home and was focused on her goals and her fiancé. She felt at this time that I asked very personal questions and wondered why she answered them. Perhaps, she thought, she wanted to do some soul-searching, although beyond her struggles with her husband's affair, I couldn't see that she was searching very deeply.

Age 43

By age 43, Helen had her "dream house" and her life was centered on her two children and all their activities. But she was finding their teen years challenging and missed their babyhood when they were just sweet and lovable. Her husband had developed spinal problems, and his many surgeries were unsuccessful, making him a semi-invalid. He could work, but, when he was home, his constant pain kept him in bed, suffering, uncommunicative, and not much help to her. "He doesn't talk to me much," Helen said, and sex had become too pain-inducing for him. Helen did activities with friends and family members.

Working with special-needs children, she could get to know them quite well over several years and teaching them was gratifying. She enjoyed gardening, exercising, and baking. Helen was not psychologically complex. The only thing that troubled her about herself was that she had a temper and yelled at people when she was stressed and they frustrated her.

Age 53

Helen indeed had changed little by age 53. What troubled her was that her children hadn't quite done what she had intended. Her son, at age 29, was still living at home, which she rather liked, but this was because he had gotten deeply in debt and found it hard to control his spending. In addition, she really didn't like his girlfriend and felt she would not fit in the family. What occupied her was worries that he would marry her. Helen spent much of the interview telling me about this woman and all the reasons she doesn't like her. Helen's daughter was living far away, and Helen worried she would not come back. She likes her daughter's boyfriend but was troubled that he was not Jewish—and he might want to raise their children Catholic—which might be all right as he seems to have "family values." So Helen's worries were mainly that her children would not carry on the family tradition that she had—that they would, in a way, break the chain. I noted that she did not tell me anything about her daughter beyond her effort to accept her boyfriend—but she did show me her picture, proud of her beauty.

As she always had, Helen spoke to her mother (who is in good health) several times a day "You wouldn't believe it, many, many times a day. Like, if I talk to her four times a day that would be, I'd say the minimum. If I have one sentence to tell her, I'll call her. She does the same. I'm very, very wrapped up with my mother." Together they were trying to deal with her father's increasing loss of cognitive capacity. If any family members needed something, Helen tried to provide it—trips to the doctor, meals when they are sick. "I'm pretty wrapped up, meeting other people's needs, taking care of everybody." She enjoyed baking things for her aunts and cousins, for her brother and his family, since she liked to bake but was watching her weight. (Indeed, I can attest that she bakes very well.)

I learned much about Helen just by being with them in their beautifully designed house (done by a designer, she told me) and having lunch with her and her husband. Both are notably attractive people, and I felt a bit like I had walked into a magazine. Not wealth, just attention to detail and a refined aesthetic sense. It was clear to me that looks matter.

Helen's husband had become unable to work, and he spent all his time at home, still in constant pain. His physical problems limited him almost completely, obviating the possibility of travel, even going to local events. He had become more withdrawn, and they often communicated through email, even in the house. (I did not see any of this because he seemed to me quite charming and available.) He knew I was coming to interview Helen but seemed to want me to be interested in him as well. Helen told me he did not restrict her in any way—she was free to come and go as she pleased. "I keep busy," she said. Helen did not voice particular disappointment about their marriage—and the issue of his early affair did not appear in her account of her life this time. She seemed to have adjusted to the situation, limited as it was.

Helen kept herself busy with the extended family and friends and did whatever she could to be out of the house. Given the structure of the school system, it would make financial sense to retire in two more years, and Helen was considering what she could do to stay active.

I struggled to create a picture of the world that Helen inhabited as her inner life seemed so focused on others. Her interview was filled with interpersonal crises among family members—conflicts with her sister, her mother-in-law. These were marked by approval and disapproval—of how people treat one another, who does what for whom or didn't do something for someone else: Helen doesn't approve of how her sister raises her children and clashes with her about this; she holds decades-old grudges against her mother-in-law, but treats her kindly nonetheless. They are a family that struggles together, albeit lovingly. In my world, I would call this being enmeshed with one another—but to Helen it is her way of life, and it seems to work for her. Helen realized her dream of family for a time, but, at age 53, she fears that it is in danger if the next generation does not carry it forward. Her daughter may be following a different direction, and her son is either clinging to them or acting impulsively. She is ready for grandchildren, but they have not appeared, despite her suggesting this avenue to her daughter.

The story Helen told me that made her saddest was going shopping with a friend whose mother had died and whose daughter was estranged from her. Helen found herself saying to her friend, as she usually did going through the goods on display, "This would be good for my daughter, this would be good for my mother" -- and then realizing that her friend had neither. This story also seemed to epitomize Helen—looking out for others, giving to them, sad to think there would be no one to buy for. It's what has been the center of her life.

When I asked her to tell me her life story in chapters, Helen couldn't do so. It's all one chapter, she told me, a chapter about "family values, the importance of family, staying in touch with family and being together on special occasions and looking out for each other. . . . I was born here and never left and never went away to school. My mother had three sisters and each of them had three children, and everybody's here in town. And we are a very close family and I would say that's been the biggest thing is family closeness. It's just a lot of family stuff." It's all Helen ever wanted.

Synthesis: Guardians Who Remained Guardians

The similarity among Fern, Harriet, and Helen is their intense ties to their mothers, ties that they did not loosen in their adolescence, ties that stayed firmly with them throughout their adulthood, even, in Fern's case, after her mother was no longer alive. In addition, they all married men who went along with their projects, passively "helping" them with children and chores, under their direction. Their marriages stand in high contrast to the vibrant partnerships described by the Pathmakers. These Guardians are all strong women in the sense that they know what they want, and they want to exert control over how their goals are achieved. Oriented to doing things "right," they are rigid in their psychological structures and arrange their worlds so they can be the directors. Their values are centered on care of others, but this is nurturing rather than empathic care—evident in contrast to the Pathmakers, who are curious about others and accept difference, more able to tolerate ambiguity and uncertainty, more aware of internal contradiction. The implications of this particular Guardian identity structure are manifest (in their early 50s) most clearly in the fate of their children. In both the Pathmaker and Guardian groups are conscientious women who have achieved in their careers. The impact of their different identity structures lies in their approaches to intimacy and generativity. The Guardians want to care for others—this is what forms the center of their being—but on their own moral terms. And these terms are sometimes so rigid that their children suffer, and they are left feeling helpless and uncomprehending, which leads them to tighten the reins, only making matters worse.

Guardians Who Became Pathmakers

All of the Guardians carried their preoccupation with being good and succeeding into their career planning. All except Fern have advanced degrees, and all have enjoyed professional acclaim. Two of the five women I classified in this group while they were in college became lawyers, and both eventually became the first female judges in their states. The Guardian capacity to doggedly stick to a path and to work hard served all of them well. For some of them, career success became a new base that allowed them enough security to explore and to dare in other aspects of their lives. Only after being professionally established did some of them reconsider themselves and begin to chart courses based more on their own wishes than on their need to be "good" in others' eyes. This involved sometimes wrenching changes in their psychological structure on their way to becoming Pathmakers. For both Emily and Grace, a time in psychotherapy initiated after they were unable to make others in the world act as they wished was a catalyst for their growth.

EMILY

Age 21

Unlike Fern, Harriet, and Helen, Emily was beginning to explore during her years at the small women's college she had chosen. She was leaning over the edge a bit, seeming to be making a transition to a period of testing. But her central identity was rooted in her closeness to and identification with her father, and she answered most questions with reference to his opinions and wishes. It was for this reason that I classified her as a Guardian. Emily's father, who had run a successful business, had entered law school just as Emily was finishing high school. She joined him intensely in his new project and avidly listened to all that he was learning. For Emily, this represented a shift in her own personality organization, but she seemed to have moved from intense involvement with her mother to a similar kind of involvement, though about different issues, with her father.

Raised in a well-off, liberal Jewish home, Emily had no religious strictures to govern her behavior. Until she left for college, she had been very close to her homemaker mother who was concerned that she have "the right clothes, the right friends, be in the right crowd, and be a cheerleader." All of this, Emily did; she was pretty, popular, and successful. But when she got to college, all of that seemed to her silly in retrospect, and she grew closer to the more serious pursuits of her father. He led her to an interest in politics, and all of her opinions were just like his. She found that she could derive the same sense of approval and well-being that she had gotten from her mother by intellectual involvement with her father. She intended to go to law school and perhaps even to join him in his practice.

Like the other Guardians, Emily idealized all aspects of her family and growing up. With four siblings, they were a close unit, traveled together, played sports together. Emily felt she had a secure place that she was reluctant to leave. She imagined that she would have a life much like her mother's, presiding over a warm, close, large family but having a place in her father's profession as well.

Age 33

After college, Emily did go to law school, put all other considerations aside and buckled down to study. By the time that I interviewed her when she was in her early 30s, she was proud of having become the first woman state's attorney in Missouri (where she was raised). She had what she described as a "Camelot" job.

Once settled in her career, Emily began to experiment with herself in earnest. She began to consider more who she was in relationships and what she wanted from them. She let loose and allowed herself to have some "wild times." She had become comfortable with her sexuality and examined how she felt about sex with love and about sex without love. Her first serious involvement ended when she realized that she could not abide being with a man who was less ambitious than she was. Feeling "no doubt about my attractiveness to men," Emily intended to select the right one. In her late 20s, she lived with a prominent attorney whom she loved but whom she left when it became clear that he didn't want to marry. When I interviewed her in her early 30s, Emily was in love with a man who lived in New York, and she was hoping to make a life with him. She was prepared to give up the job that she found so perfect to follow him once they decided to marry. She would simply begin again in New York. She had confidence in her professional skills and felt she could transport them wherever she went. Her main concern was to get on with the project of marriage and family.

At this time in her life, Emily retained her closeness to her father. He "was tremendously supportive of my career and he remains an inspiration to me. He has always been encouraging and helpful to me and has been a wonderful adviser whenever I have to make important professional decisions." She also stayed in close touch with her mother who worried with her about the ups and downs of her romantic involvements. Emily had, at this point, attained a part of her dream—the professional side—but the more personal vision was harder to settle and realize.

Age 43

There were big changes in Emily's life in this decade. The main one, she told me, was her husband, who "contributed more to my happiness than any-thing." And she had also become the first female judge in her court.

She did not marry the man she had hoped to marry when last we met. He had balked at a final commitment. Crushed and depressed, she entered therapy to better understand what she was doing in her relationships with men. When she was 35, she drew closer to a man who had been a friend and began to think of him as a romantic partner. When he asked her to marry him, she accepted.

And they created what she described at age 43 as a "fantastic" relationship, filled with sharing and travel and mutual support, the joys of which she told me about exuberantly. "Everyone in the world adores him, "she exclaimed, "everyone in the world is in love with him. He's charming, handsome and has a great personality." But, being 15 years older than she, her husband did not want to have children—which meant that Emily had to revise the dream she had always carried. She hadn't quite known how adamant he was about this. "We didn't really discuss it. I just thought that we would. But if he had told me, I would have married him anyway," she said. Emily described having gone through a process like grieving, giving up the family she always thought she would have. "It's a life experience you don't have, and I'm one of those people who wants to try everything. It sort of makes me feel left out at times, it distinguishes me from my friends who do have children, you have less in common. But I can't say I've been devastated by it." She "adopted" her brother's two children as substitutes and enjoyed indulging them and taking them on trips.

Emily was challenged by her work as a judge and strove to be the best judge she could be. Still, there were always losers as well as winners in her court, and she found it difficult to bear the anger of those she ruled against. She didn't see herself as staying a judge forever; perhaps when her husband retired a few years hence, they would move somewhere else and she would do something completely different. This was, for her, a happy thought.

In mid-life, then, Emily set about building a life for which she had no clear models. When she was in her late 30s, her parents divorced, and, in the bitterness of her parents' struggle, Emily became estranged from her father. They hadn't spoken to one another in five years. Her mother later remarried and moved to Florida, where two of her siblings lived. This left Emily in a prominent position in her home town but with none of her family there. But Emily was by then on her own feet, making a life out of her marriage to "an incredibly special guy" and her career success. She was revising her view of her mother, whom she had come to realize was unpleasant. She credited her therapy with having helped her overcome her need to form a relationship with a man that recreated trying to make a rejecting person love her, the situation, as she now understood it, with her mother. This, she felt, made it possible for her to accept her husband's love—and marked growth in self-knowledge as well as internal change. But she missed her family and was thinking about moving to Florida in several years when her husband was ready to retire. She wanted to be with them for the warmth and closeness—but security she had found now on her own.

Age 53

I met Emily at age 53 in her federal judicial office, to which I was ushered by security guards after gaining special permission to take along a recording device. In her massive wood-paneled office hung several judicial robes, and I waited for her to emerge from her private bathroom. I was impressed by all the trappings of office, even a bit intimidated, and I was delighted by the friendly, warm woman who greeted me. Emily was still petite and beautiful. She acknowledged that she was a bit distressed because my coming to interview her meant that another decade had passed. Asking about the other women of the study, she wanted to know if everyone was still alive. She couldn't imagine that she was the age she was. She still felt—and thought that she looked like—she was 30, maybe 40 at the most. "I'm still healthy and active. I have a lot of fun, I'm still a party girl, I still am wild and crazy . . . and I don't feel like—I don't think people would know I'm as old as I am because my attitude is so young." Laughing, she told me that if I was going to title this book, "The Golden Years," she didn't want to be in it. Aging to her meant loss—of capacity and of loved ones. Soon she would be eligible for retirement, and she did not want to retire. She told me that her 20-something-year-old staff like to go out with her, go shopping with her, treated her like one of them. "I can still throw a party for 30 people and do all the cooking myself. I can still go out at 10 P.M. or stay up until 2 A.M. working." She only felt her age when friends of her own age died. Then she was reminded that the future was shorter than she felt it was inside. Of all the women I interviewed, Emily was most trying to hold on to a sense of her youth.

"I am a judge," she declared, marking this as a central anchor of her identity. She was now in a different, more prestigious court than previously. Her appointment to the position was politically fractious, and she detailed for me the strategies of the fight to be appointed 10 years ago, the political enemies who tried to block her and her strategies to outwit them. Being a woman was a disadvantage, she felt, because the old guard feared that she was "prejudiced against men." Still, she triumphed and reveled in her position—and couldn't imagine who she would be if she stepped down from her role. "I do love what I'm doing now. This job is just, is the greatest thing that ever happened to me." She felt a confidence in her work born of experience; she was interested in the cases and issues that came before her to decide and enjoyed the respect that attended her seniority on the bench. She loved the fact that "every new trial is a learning experience for me."

What was most changed in Emily at this time of life was her view of her family. Now the history she related to me was of having a "dysfunctional" family and a "witch" mother who was never kind to her. Her description of her "difficult, moody" mother at age 43 had now burgeoned into a view of her mother as impossible to please. She sees her life as having been a triumph over the early mistreatment in her family, particularly by her mother. "I could never make my mother happy, no matter what I did." Her sister had become a devout Christian and one of her brothers was in jail, thus proving that one either reacted to the family misery through rebellion or learned to cope with it, as only she and her younger brother had. College she remembered as an ideal time when she could finally get away from home and be free of her mother's control. Emily's parents, who were still healthy in their 80s, entered her life story in recent years primarily when they argued about who gave money to help the siblings in distress and their children. She no longer seemed to expect much from them.

Indeed, Emily had made her own path, far from her origins. Yet she retained a binary sense of life, good and bad. She was still quite judgmental of people, which undoubtedly served her well in her work role—she was, after all, a judge. I was struck that as she told me about her life, people were either idealized (like her husband and her friends) or vilified (her mother, her political enemies). In all of her interviews, Emily habitually spoke in superlatives. At this phase, in general, Emily celebrated a "wonderful" life that she contrasted with a childhood "dominated" by her "mean" mother. From what I could tell, Emily had no sense of having revised her account of her history over the years she had told it to me. (At age 33, she had told me that she was very close to her mother who had always made her feel loved.)

Emily felt she had succeeded in the other main goal she had. "I needed so desperately to live in a home that was happy . . . we have such a great marriage, we're just, we're very, very happy with one another, because we respect each other a lot, and that's what it's all about. . . . People come into my house and they always say, 'It's just—there's such a good feeling in that it's a happy home.' And having lived in one that isn't, you can really tell the difference." Although Emily had chosen to meet me in her office, she said she was sorry I didn't get to see her beautiful home in the woods that had been designed in modern style by a well-known architect. She was very proud of it.

As I reread Emily's interviews over the 35 years I have followed her, I had the eerie sense that she has remained exactly the same person, despite the changes in her roles and her family relationships. She has always kept herself optimistic and happy, satisfied with herself and free of internal conflict. I was not surprised, then, that she did not experience her own aging and, at the age of 56, was just starting to recognize that she might not be able to move forward just as she always had.

GRACE

Age 21

Grace shares some elements of both Fern's and Emily's stories. Like Fern, her father died when she was 11, and, like Emily, she became interested in law through him.

Grace adored her father who adored her. He was a Greek immigrant, full of humor and "incredibly smart" with a passion for politics. "He was a really fantastic individual. He and my Mom existed for us kids. He used to take us on vacations, had high expectations for us. I think I was his favorite. We both read constantly, and I was sort of a tomboy. We used to talk politics, and I would impress the kids at school with what he thought. He took a lot of time with me." He was a barber and wanted Grace to become a lawyer. After he died, her mother became withdrawn and bitter. But Grace, in her college interview, venerated her "determination and strength of character. She doesn't give up." Grace began to work at age 14 to help out with family finances. She was paying her own way through the local state university.

Although she was raised in a strict Catholic environment, she seldom attended Church, finding no role for organized religion in her life. She had decided that it was "useless to sit around and worry about the nature of God." Grace's focus was elsewhere.

Throughout high school, Grace had felt different from the other kids at school. The necessity to work to help support the family kept her from teenage activities, and she felt more mature, less interested than they were in pranks and mischief. She studied hard, but questioned nothing that felt part of her unshakable bond to her father, which was still the source of her sense of security. Grace had a boyfriend whom she described as "really nice, not very attractive, but intelligent and nice." She felt comfortable with him because he "lets me do what I want and doesn't try to dominate me." She wasn't interested in marriage before she had established a career. Horrified at the thought that she might get pregnant, she was also deferring sexual behavior. She wouldn't take birth control pills because her mother might find them. "She really thinks I'm something and I wouldn't want to do that to her." She felt at this point that sex just wasn't an important part of her life and that "my boyfriend doesn't feel deprived or anything." Her sexual reticence suggested that she was trying to stay her father's smart, political, favorite tomboy—and "really something" to her mother. But Grace was clear on the path she wanted to follow.

Age 33

Grace stayed in this Guardian position until her early 30s, when a crisis in her marriage led her to reconsider what she had put together in her life and how she might rearrange the pieces. This became an acute period of searching from which she emerged with a very different sense of her identity. In recounting her life story at age 33, Grace told of how she had finished law school in her mid-20s, passionate about finding ways to have a positive impact on the world. At this point, she married her college boyfriend and followed him to West Virginia, where he had had been accepted for graduate work. She won a highly competed-for job as a state's attorney and was intent on trying to be helpful to the disadvantaged. While focusing intently on refining her professional goals, she had, along the way, settled into marriage, given up her Catholic religious beliefs and practices out of deference to her husband, and decided to delay having children until her husband had his own professional life under way.

In retrospect, from age 33, Grace could see that she had not given marriage much thought. "We were like a couple of old shoes," she said. They had been together for eight years—getting married seemed a natural next step. "I didn't feel passionate about him, but I didn't think that was important at the time for a successful marriage. I was very comfortable with him." But the marriage didn't work out. As she became more successful, he became more childlike. He refused to help with house chores, didn't work consistently, spent most of his time playing golf. Worse, he offered her no emotional support, wasn't interested in her experiences at work, and was very likely threatened by her mounting success. (Grace was often in the newspaper.) They began to be "at each other's throats" constantly. Being dogged about what she wanted and having been raised with Catholic values opposed to divorce, Grace wanted to try to continue to make things work, but, eventually, he decided to leave the marriage and Grace found herself on her own for the first time since early in her freshman year of college. "I was very upset," she said, understating her pain. Up to the point of the dissolution of her marriage, Grace's story of her development is much like Fern's. But her husband leaving her sparked a process of revision of her identity.

Far from her home, Grace had developed few friends and, taking stock of herself, felt she had lost a lot of her spontaneity and gregariousness during the marriage. She felt lonely again, as she had throughout high school. Her husband, old shoe that he was, had been her bulwark, the pillar to which she had clung to make much of her achievement possible. She sought psychotherapy that, she said, "helped me to face forward and get on with my life."

"The divorce," Grace said, "is what made me develop. It forced me to get out again, to make some friends, get involved in social activities, even rethink how I looked." Her dark hair had been long and straight, emulating Joan Baez, and Grace, in remaking herself, emerged with short curly hair and learned to use make-up. For the first time in her life, she began to think of herself as "okay-looking, maybe even pretty." She hadn't ever really dated, so this was a whole new avenue of learning. She bought a house and set about decorating it. She took a vacation alone. When I interviewed her when she was 33, she doubted that she would remarry. She regretted giving up the hope of having a family, but she thought that "the question of children for me is pretty much an outside shot." Divorced two years at the time of this interview, Grace said, "I found, through my divorce, that its nicer to be happy by yourself than miserable with another person. I'm happy to think that I'm the type of woman who does not need a man, however unappealing he may be, rather than be by myself." She had just ended a year-long relationship with a man who had tried to "dominate" her, finding it hard to accept any signs of her independence. "I couldn't tolerate his jealousies and recriminations." At age 33, then, Grace was occupied with making a life alone and with friends. Her mother and siblings, although five states away, were the people to whom she felt closest, so there was still a core of attachment and old connection to fall back on. She was rethinking her assumptions and understanding about marriage, but putting most of her energy into her work, which served to "compensate." Grace was forced to forge a path that had not been charted for her, a path she had to create on her own.

Having remained internally close to her roots, Grace could draw strength from the part of herself that had preserved her family's heritage. Rethinking her family, she could see in herself and her brothers and sisters a kind of "oddness—none of us would blend into the mainstream. None of us are big on conformity." Her siblings had become artists and musicians. She had distinguished herself by her education and achievement. The ethnic Greek in them still felt very strong. "We love each other very hard, scream at each other very hard and protect each other very hard." Far from home, she had the least responsibility for looking after their mother. This was a relief to her since she realized that she had become the family leader after her father died, the "strong one emotionally, the one who fixed things." She still had the role of being the arbitrator who resolved disputes, but she was called upon to do this less and less. Her sense of family remained a bedrock of continuity in the midst of all the change. Thoughts of her father, for whom she had set her course, had faded from her consciousness, however. Her goals now felt like her own.

Age 43

Between her mid-30s and mid-40s, transition and revision in Grace's life proliferated in ways she did not foresee. Grace in her mid-40s was married with two children and became, like Emily, the first woman judge in her state. During her election campaign, she fell in love with the lawyer who managed her campaign finances, and they married shortly after she won the election and took her new position. With age 40 approaching, Grace set about having babies. This was an intensely busy and stressful time, taking on the new duties of a judgeship and motherhood at once. After her second child was born, she developed a massive infection and came so near death that she had been given Last Rites. When she recovered, with the acute vision emanating from having been near death, she took stock of what she was doing with her time. She hugged her children to her with reawakened intensity, cut back her work hours to have more time with them—and painfully allowed herself to acknowledge that her husband was an alcoholic. At age 43, Grace seriously feared for the future of her family as she regretfully contemplated the possibility of another divorce.

Professionally, Grace's goals were sharper, more defined. Working in a court of general jurisdiction, she heard cases that ranged from murder to

small claims. The work load was immense and the intellectual demands for-
midable. She had just triumphed in her election to a second judicial term.
Vociferous about women's rights, she had become a leader in the Women's
Movement. Her life was full, rich, challenging and of her own devising.

But Grace longed to spend more time with her children. They had given
her "a dimension of joy" that surprised her. She wished that she and her husband could attain the economic security that would allow her to resign and
to work part-time. This had been their plan until she had recently begun to
worry about whether they would stay together.

Hopeful and confident when her marriage was new, Grace had appreciated
the intellectual and emotional companionship that she and Garrett had. She
had also found the first really fulfilling sexual relationship of her life. And
this time, she had thought about marriage, scrupulously, trying to learn from
her first mistake. They lived together for a time, and Grace found that "you
are able to be a lot more flexible after you have been through one marriage
where maybe you expected too much." She decided to take the risk and share
her life a second time. They had fallen into "the yuppie pattern of a bottle of
wine with dinner and then maybe a drink or two after." But she gave up alcohol when she got pregnant. After their second child was born, she began to
resent the emotional distance and increasing verbal abuse that came from her
husband's drinking. Having children strained their marriage. "Children add
stress to the family—it gives Garrett more things to become short-tempered
about." He agreed to get psychological help. "I love Garrett and I feel very
committed to him. So I will be flexible to a certain degree, to be understanding and encourage him in his efforts to gain control. But I'm certainly not
going to put up with it for any great length of time."

Being flexible was an ongoing struggle for Grace who had always wanted
things the way she wanted them. The limit of flexibility was what she had to
revise continually. In her mid-40s, it was her children that lit up her life. "I
could listen to them all day long," she said. As they grew older, she enjoyed
their maturity and their ability to articulate themselves. "They're wonderful
kids, creative, smart, funny." As she had grown older, Grace felt her goals
becoming more personal, less directed at saving the world. "After being so
sick, my focus changed 180 degrees. My personal life has been so enriched.
And being a mom has also made me a more compassionate judge."

Pulling again on her roots, Grace also returned to the spiritual side of
her life and decided to raise her children in the Catholic Church. "I want
to raise them the way I was raised. I think that if the children are going
to grow up as moral and responsible adults then a spiritual home life is
only going to contribute positively to that. So, in that respect, I'm like my
mother. But I don't think I'm as structured as she was. My mom was a
widow raising six children by herself. So she was pretty frantic, and she
could be tremendously emotionally abusive to us. I see that now looking

back on it. And I think it was because she was isolated and frustrated and alone. She used to threaten to put us in orphanages and what did she do to deserve such mean rotten kids. And I don't let a day go by without telling my children how much I love them, how good they are, how smart they are. In that respect, I'm different. But I don't want to paint a grim picture of my mom. She really overall was a good parent, and there's a lot about her that I would like to achieve in my parenting skills. But I want my environment to be an A+ loving environment. . . . I think I am a good mom but I think I make a lot of mistakes. I yell at them and I shouldn't do that and I try not to."

Giving up the unquestioning certainty about the perfection of their families of origin that characterized the college-age Guardians, by mid-life, Grace, like Emily, no longer idealized her childhood or her parents. This left her free to take from her early life what was useful and served her, but to revise other aspects of herself and chart her own course. She learned to live with less control over things, poised to adapt to the future, shaping what she could, but more humble, more philosophical about forces that were beyond her.

Late midlife

I learned that much had again changed for Grace when I met her in late midlife (at this point, she was in her early 60s). She was delighted to tell me about her life, a life that she was very pleased with, and she recounted to me her considerable accomplishments. An activist judge, she had succeeded in changing laws and policies and had received much public recognition. But a complicated series of circumstances—a serious illness just before she was to be re-elected, a political battle in which she was embroiled, and the details of the retirement rules—led her to retire from being a judge at age 55. It was both financially and politically the best decision, she told me. When I saw her a few years after her retirement, she was doing some very part-time substitute judging, a bit of teaching, but living a fairly isolated life. She told me it was a great relief to be outside the public eye. Her children had left to get on with their lives; she idealized them, they were wonderful in every way, and she passed the time waiting for their visits home.

Just a couple of years after our previous interview, Grace's second marriage had ended in divorce. Her husband's alcoholism had gone out of control, he left the family, and she raised their sons largely on her own. "I think that families that have one parent out of the picture end up either super dysfunctional or super close and we ended up super close. I think that motherhood is the coolest thing I've ever done. Overshadows everything else." This was not an easy task for Grace. When her ex-husband would reappear, there were some near-disasters to manage and a lot of fear—until he got sober some years later. And until her children were in late high school, Grace was still a prominent judge working full time.

Much of this interview was spent with Grace telling me with evident pride about the work she had accomplished over her career, for which she had received many awards. She said that she missed the structure of a work schedule, but felt relief at having a private life in which she could read the classics, study history, write stories, exercise, and see a few friends. One later romantic involvement ended in a tragic loss when her fiancé was killed in an accident, and she had given up on trying to find another partner. This occurred just as she was planning to retire, so just after her retirement, she had a period of depression that she weathered by steadfastly trying to keep her children from seeing how depressed she was. At the time I met her, she was no longer depressed, although her life sounded somewhat empty to me, especially in contrast to all the drama of her time as a judge. But Grace seemed to be contenting herself, amusing herself, and enjoying her sons' successes, if from some distance. To ease her loneliness, she got a dog.

Unlike Fern, Harriet, and Helen, who struggled with their children, Grace idealized her sons. She spoke of them reverently, but she said she did not take the credit for their accomplishment. "They have done everything right, and they've done that themselves. They are really wonderful young men." The best times in her life were when her sons were both home and they all laughed together for days.

I was interested at this point in Grace's reflections on her life. Her mother now having dementia made her "nicer," and this led Grace and her siblings to recognize how critical she had always been. "It was always sinful to be critical of your mother, but the reality of it was that she was very critical when we were growing up. Critical of us, critical of other people. . . . She was really good at telling you what you were doing wrong. We always knew her as a strong woman, a woman who survived a lot of very difficult things that life had thrown at her but I don't think that any of us remembered her as a particularly happy woman. I think that after my dad died, I think all of us were needy but eager to please and placate her and figure out a way to make her happy, because she's never been a happy person, prone to negativity. After my dad died, it was horrible. She'd cry all the time and she'd say terrible things to us—I can't take this any more. I'm going to leave and I'm never coming back. And of course we'd all get real scared—we believed her. And we'd think orphanage, orphanage. So we had to pay special attention to her. We all kind of lived for the little tidbits if she ever said something nice."

Raising her own children had also given Grace new perspective on her own growing up. "I was the good kid in a lot of ways. I was the hippie, the rebel, the peace protestor but I always figured out a way to get her to go along with stuff. That period of life where mothers and daughters don't get along—we never had that. . . . I had gone to work when I was 14. Since I was 14, I took care of myself and never asked her for money. This was part of my effort not to be a burden to her. Which was stupid. Looking back on it now, that was a big mistake. She had a duty—and it was hard for her. She had horrible, demeaning jobs, and she worked really hard and after my dad died, she scrubbed floors—but she had a duty there. And I could not have admitted or seen that even 20 years ago. I think that raising my own kids is what changed it. I felt that my kids would never be in doubt about how I felt about them. I mean, a conversation doesn't go by without the I love yous and I'm constantly telling them that they are the greatest things since sliced bread. I don't want them to feel the remoteness that I felt from my mom. It was a struggle to find a place through her remoteness and negativity to feel that I was loved."

With her sons, she "had what I always wanted to have with my mom. My son Kevin would tell me everything—even things I didn't want to know, like when he smoked pot. I said, okay, what did you think? My communication with them is extraordinary. I always want them to think I had their back, but their job was to be confident and independent and go out into the world. There's never been difficult times. They've made good choices." I was impressed. A judge responding to a child's pot smoking in this way is remarkable. And Grace was determined to provide for them everything she could. "I made sure my kids never had a sense of financial insecurity. I grew up where worrying about money was what you did. It was like a job that every one of us had. It wasn't enough that we had to be poor. My mother had to make sure we knew we were poor. 'We can't have this and we can't have that.' If there was conflict with my ex-husband, it was over what financial responsibilities the boys would have growing up. He wanted them to pay for things themselves, and I disagreed. I thought their education should be the first priority. Plus, when I was in high school, there were a lot of things I didn't get to do—plays I wanted to try out for or clubs I wanted to join, and I missed a lot of things because I was always having to work. I wanted my boys to have the full high school experience. In fact, I moved house so they could live near their high school so they wouldn't have to take the bus with me working, so they could stay after and join the clubs. . . . My next big goal was that they wouldn't be debt-ridden when they got out of college."

With some regret, Grace wondered what her career would have been like if she had had the financial capacity to go to a first-rate college and law school. Although she then mused further, "I don't even know what I mean by that. I couldn't be any more successful than what I've achieved. And yet I look back and think, there was another thing I might have done, you know. I just don't know that I ever got the full advantage for my talents." She had always suffered, at least privately, for not having had the Ivy League credentials of some of her colleagues. "The confidence I had along the way was the confidence I had in my innate abilities as opposed to any credentials I might have. I was always acutely aware of my extreme blue-collar roots and the poverty of my background, and I never felt I could present myself as a distinguished and cultured person. All of that was a matter of acquiring." She wished that there had been some adult along the way to guide her.

I admired Grace's pluck. I liked her stories about being the first judge in her state ever to have a baby while a judge and how being a judge made it so easy if one of her children were sick and couldn't go to daycare or school. "I had a private office with a big couch and I'd just bring them with me to work and they could watch videos and lie on the couch. My secretary would bring them juice while I held court in the next room. It was a great deal. And the other judges were all really cool about it."

Grace still practices her Catholicism, but in an idiosyncratic way and particularly if she can get involved in some political issue. She supports abortion rights, and this puts her in conflict with Church dogma. And she hasn't found a priest nearby whom she likes. "It's in my DNA," she said. But "the faith is what I love and the Church is what I don't love. . . . I don't think there's a God out there that micromanages us and if we say the right prayer we're going to get the prize at the bottom of the Cracker Jack box. I don't believe that. I think that if God exists, he's something that's hard to understand. I like there being a spiritual component to us as humans, and I like the meditative quality of going to Mass and thinking about those kinds of things rather than the things I normally think about—the everyday things of life. I like the idea of the core values that most religions do teach—love and joy and helping other people. Those are all good things. And I like the idea there could be a God. But all of that has nothing to do with practicing a religion. I'm comfortable living my life as if God did exist and wanting to achieve good things—because maybe that's one of my reasons for being alive." Grace had clearly crafted, at this point, her own ideological view of life, taking into account what she considered her religious DNA.

Grace credited Alanon with the important personal changes she had made during this period of her life. "There is no way I can say how extremely life-changing it was for me. I think I was much more of a controlling person before Alanon. It was a process . . . but after years of meetings and really incorporating the 12 steps into my life and learning there are three things you don't control: I don't control other people, other places, and other things. And the way I grew up, it was kind of fate that I should be kind of a controlling personality. And Alanon helped me let go of it. Not to say that I'm completely free of it. But I'm much happier not feeling that I have to be in charge of everything and in control of everything. And in terms of fulfilling my goals as a mother, to not try to direct my children's lives and let them make their own decisions—to be there for them if they stumbled but not to stop them from stumbling, I went to Alanon in great pain. I was just very in need of some kind of help. I was going to a psychologist, I was taking my kids to a psychologist. I was afraid at the time that Mike was going to die, and I took my kids to a psychologist to help prepare them in case their dad died. And I was a screwed up mess with sorrow and grief, failed marriage. At the height of his alcoholism, Mike was physically abusive to me—which was humiliating to me. How can you be a judge and be an abused woman?

"There was one day that he was coming after me, screaming, aggressive, and I'm grabbing them up and racing to the car to get them out of there because we weren't safe. And I remember going to a park and letting the kids play and sitting in the car sobbing. I did not know what to do. But I knew I had to get divorced, and, you know, there was the psychologist, and it wasn't until after I was divorced that I found Alanon. I wish someone had told me about it when we were still married. It might have helped a lot. Because I was doing all the wrong things. I had my part in the demise of that relationship. I wasn't just the victim. Because I was nagging and I was trying to control him. I think that Alanon really saved my life. I regained a wonderful sense of myself. I regained that old personal confidence. Meanwhile, I had this façade to the world and nobody knew I was going to Alanon. Anonymity is important to this group. Everyone kept my secret. . . . I haven't gone to a meeting in years and years. But I still read material that helps to reinforce the 12 steps because I know I have to fight against the urge to be controlling or to think that somehow I'm responsible for every outcome and to move away from that. If anything accounts for the sense today of being content, it might really be that."

Grace's life has been value-driven, but giving up trying to control everything has been her hard-won achievement. She became a Pathmaker through overcoming a slew of hardships. For the future, she told me, "I think I am fresh out of big goals. I like the peace and quiet of being by myself." She was surprised at how much she told me about herself, more than she had ever confided to anyone. "I don't trust many people, but for some reason I trust you." She had a few close friends, mainly at a distance, and was close to her sisters, who were also far away. I worried about what I thought was her loneliness, but she insisted that she enjoyed being alone. This was her choice for now.

The Guardians as a Group

There are no dire outcomes for the Guardians; they feel as fulfilled in their identities as those who were Pathmakers at the end of college. For those Guardians who became Pathmakers, it took some wrenching disappointments (and therapy) to revise themselves. Both Emily and Grace had to give up aspects of the future they had imagined for themselves in college (job, marriage, children). The life lesson these renunciations entailed was a coming to terms with a loss of control—or, more precisely, a growth in flexible control. For the others (and for the Searchers who became Guardians), their identities and lives follow a course set for them early on, and their life project is to make this template a reality. And they primarily succeed.

The Guardian personality style is more rigid and moralistic, more authoritarian, more suspicious of change, than the other groups, but in this rigidity is also strength. They are convinced of what is right and wrong (derived from their mothers), do not question or experiment, and believe that if they just try hard enough they will succeed in whatever they choose to do. Their sense of security and confidence lies in an unshakable inner tie to their mothers, a fantasy from early childhood that pleasing this powerful being will keep them safe. Even as adults, they remain less self-reflective, less psychologically complex than (most of) the women in the other groups.

Guardians insist on their wishes by framing them as ethical concerns, and this frequently leads to clashes with those they love and those they work with. Conflict is experienced as between themselves and others rather than as internal debate. They experience themselves as being on a single plane (although the planes may change) rather than having parts of themselves struggling to express themselves.

Being judges and teachers suits them well (although they could well be found in other occupations); these are roles that embody tradition in society and maintain order. The Guardians rework their proclivity to control themselves into an effort to effect social control. But they have to stretch for flexibility as parents and as spouses; compromise and sharing the moral high ground are less habitual responses. Harriet, for example, reports that the only thing that she and Len argue about are morals since he was raised so differently. Recently, on a family outing, their daughter found a bracelet in a museum. Len's impulse was to keep it. Harriet insisted on returning it to the museum office. Harriet saw this as a matter of the values they were teaching their children. Len saw it as a lost bracelet. They, of course, returned it. Still, this was an upsetting enough matter for Harriet to tell me about.

Into their marriages, the Guardians carry their adolescent sense of certainty and conviction and are unlikely to be the partner who gives in. Some, like Fern, Harriet, and Helen, have found men who are relieved to have a wife to structure their lives—or, at least, men who don't resist too much. In this arrangement, these women are the dominant force, the more ambitious, often the larger wage-earners. As mothers, as we have seen, they struggle about control. They want their children to be well-disciplined and to do what they tell them to do. Some more or less perceive their own authoritarian proclivities and more or less try to combat them.

Some who began as Guardians were likely to look to their husbands primarily to replace the security they felt at home, a hope that succeeded for Fern, Harriet, and Helen, even though their marriages felt unsatisfactory in other important ways. For Emily and Grace, working their way out of unhappy relationships was a primary trigger for reworking their own identities.

Revision for these women who began their adult lives as Guardians was wrenching but relatively invisible to the casual eye. The external markers of their identities changed less than the internal frame of reference from which they operate. Revision involved coming to take some distance from themselves, to see themselves as people with a history rather than people who evolved just as they "should." Some discovered emotional experience they never knew they had, some claimed their sexuality; some began to acknowledge imperfection in both themselves and in their families of origin. These shifts in the middle of life allowed them a new freedom to choose, to try to become what they are rather than to fit themselves into an idealized mold outlined by others.

College was an experience that barely touched most of the Guardians. They got their degrees as entrees to professional fields but did little reworking of their inner sense of themselves. Only later, usually after some aspect of their life planning went awry, did they begin to grow internally. Either professional success or a comfortable marriage could offer a secure base from which they could look into themselves and see that they were more than they thought they were. That moment arrived for the Guardians much later than for the Pathmakers— not until their early or mid-thirties or even later. From that vantage point, they assessed themselves and found inner aspects of themselves that they had buried long ago. What was silenced was given voice as they learned to live more on their own authority. The strong convictions of their youth, opened to question only much later in life than was the case for many other women, paved the way for more independent decision-making in midlife. But, as we saw in the cases of those who stayed Guardians, profound disappointment in their children's direction set them back in their 50s to the older, narrower ways of constructing their worlds. The dangers of the wider world indeed proved too great, and safety lay in reverting to what had always been right and wrong.

Notes

1. Kremen and Block (1998) found that ego overcontrol in late adolescent women, which is how the Guardians seemed in their interviews with me, was associated with parenting that was rulebound, highly structured, and insensitive to their daughters' inner life. "Over time, these daughters developed premises regarding the world as a place of inelastic rules in which a high level of performance and behavioral propriety would ensure continuation of crucial social relationships" (p. 1072).

2. Gould (1979, p. 40).

3. Kroger (1995) differentiates between "firm" and "developmental" foreclosure— that is, those who maintained their foreclosure status over the college years and those who had not yet undergone a period of search and exploration. Firm foreclosures had higher nurturance-seeking scores and more themes of need for security in their early memories.

4. Clara, one of the Pathmakers in the previous chapter, narrated a similar episode of awareness of her existential aloneness in the universe. How she dealt with it, as an awareness of her need to live life independently, contrasts in an important way with Harriet's resolution—a demand that someone find her.

5

The Searchers

Still in quest of themselves when college ended, the Searchers' adult passages toward identity are more varied than those of the other groups. In contrast to the other groups, the Searchers make more changes, both internal and external, as they try to match what the world offers with what they discover about themselves. But this is not surprising since the searching state is an unstable one. It *should* lead to one of the other possibilities—either making commitments, returning to the secure structures of childhood, or drifting.[1]

The world of work was one that each woman was eyeing somewhat warily. They were often full of ideals but confused about how they might translate these into reality and uncertain how or where they might be able to succeed. Only a few of these women had any real idea of how to enter the work world or match their talents and interests with occupational demands. Most "fell into" first jobs and either decided to stay for lack of a vision of what else to do, or they began bouncing from job to job. Hard workers, they were ready to apply themselves to a task, but they were lacking in information about the opportunities and politics of the workplace for educated women. This generation of women was, after all, breaking new ground and role models were few.

Unlike the Pathmakers, few of the Searchers had made relationships during college that could help them secure and support their quests in the wider world. This made the struggle to individuate from their parents much more onerous. They felt too alone to exert much effort in the service of their own shaky desires and often tried to cling to a man to support or guide them—a strategy that was successful for Norma, Teresa, and Regina, but less so for Marlene and Millie. They needed a holding environment that could "be there" for them while they grew. Some, sooner or later, were able to find the support they needed. Marlene found a women's support group to back her and cheer her as she gingerly tested her right and capacity to claim a path of her own. Millie found strength through reclaiming her faith and sense of community in religion. More self-conscious and self-doubting as young women than the Pathmakers or the Guardians, the Searchers required that others be there to buttress their ventures. They could dare, but not for long, not without support. Lacking this, they crept to safety or drifted aimlessly.

Throughout their lives, the Searchers have lived closer to their emotions than the women in the other groups. They are more expressive and more reactive, which leads them to more intense joy in small pleasures and greater pain at frustration. The abundant emotionality of this group of women may in part account for their having more psychological symptoms and physical problems than the women in the three other groups combined.

Unlike the Pathmakers and Guardians, who had envisioned a path to follow, most of the Searchers were in a lot of psychological distress at the end of college. They were, by and large, more introspective, more emotionally open than the Pathmakers and Guardians, more sensitive to the winds of their own changes, and more upset by them. Many were taking big risks with themselves, venturing farther from home psychologically, trying on more guises, throwing over the principles and certainties of their childhoods. All this was both exhilarating and frightening.

The Searchers, at the end of college, were still engrossed in the maze that the Pathmakers had found their way through. Or perhaps their mazes were— or seemed to them to be—more complicated. They were in an "identity crisis," filled with conflict, torn between the demands and expectations of their parents that were firmly inside of them and the wish to extricate themselves and to make their own choices. But they were caught in these dilemmas. Unlike the Pathmakers, they felt unable to choose, to integrate the warring sides of themselves. Perhaps they were still on the road to choice, still in the midst of the struggle, still stumbling through the period of exploration that was already largely settled for the Pathmakers. Or perhaps they were stuck, caught in ambivalence and angst, their fear growing as the end of college loomed.

As I got to know these women, it seemed that they had more at stake psychologically than the Pathmakers. They were trying to restructure themselves more, to emotionally separate from their families more completely, and to feel more independent. They watched themselves closely and took self-realization seriously as a goal. They worried about whether their values and choices were truly their own, trying to analyze themselves down to some basic core. Living closer to their feelings than either the Pathmakers or the Guardians, they were reaching for a deep form of authenticity. But they experienced themselves as a gathering of inner selves in conflict, pulling in different directions. To resolve this internal warfare, they were in search of some unassailable place to stand in relation to the world, a place that they couldn't undermine with their own questions and doubts. But whatever they did, they were critical of themselves, pointing out to themselves that another way of being or believing might be just as legitimate and possible.

In some ways, the women in the Searcher group seemed to be asking more of life than the other women—or, at least, life seemed more complicated to them. They sought Answers to their relentless questions, and they were more responsive to the cacophony of voices that surrounded them. They wanted their choices to have the feel of some larger sense of Rightness, but, unlike the Guardians, they did not accept the authority of their parents as an imprimatur of goodness. And, unlike the Pathmakers, they were less ready to compromise or to be pragmatic. They were more idealistic and unready to accept less.

In part because of their questioning and self-awareness, I found the young women in this group to be enormously engaging. I was moved by their often painful self-examination and by their honesty. They were the most mindful, the most animated, and the most self-reflective of all the women I interviewed. They took themselves very seriously and worried about everything. They talked on and on. Their interviews were very long: no question had a simple answer. To any query, many sides of themselves had a response. Here is what I am doing or what I believe, they would say, but here is the other side of that, here is where I am not comfortable with it but I can't find another way. If I did or believed this other thing, then there would be other problems. So there is no Answer. There is no right way. There is no certainty. "In a minute there is time for decisions and revisions which a minute will reverse." What on earth shall I do?

Erik Erikson described the ways in which societies make available a "moratorium" period during which young people can explore and choose. At the end of this time that society allots, society then expects that the young person will declare herself and the path she will follow. The Searchers were in the midst of such a period, but the time for society to call them to account had arrived. Sooner or later, this opened-up conflicted state had to end. And, as psychology has understood the process, it should eventually lead to making a self-determined path. But there was no telling how the Searchers might do this or how long it would take. Would they resolve their enigmas by turning away from the conflict, by going back to be the people they had been earlier in life? Or would they move forward to meld the contradictory aspects of themselves and create a life course that was truly theirs?

The Searchers in College

The search, for the women in this group, took many forms. Although some had made tentative occupational choices or formed political stances, the larger questions of how to "be" remained. They worried about how and where they might find a place for themselves in the world, who they would connect themselves to and how, what it meant to be a woman in a world that was rapidly changing around them, and how to make a life when they spurned whatever models they saw.

Sandra made it clear to me when I interviewed her in her last year of college that she was just in college to please her parents. "In my house, I'm expected to please my parents more than myself. I think I'm living my father's life for him. I'm going through this because my father didn't have an education and he wanted me to have an education. He wants me to be a doctor, but I know my capabilities and they are not medical school. He just won't admit I have limitations. I feel I am disappointing him." Living at home, Sandra's life was dominated by her struggle with her father. They argued about everything, but she couldn't disengage from him. To spite him, she majored in philosophy, simply because she liked it but recognized that it would have no practical impact on her life. She longed for escape from these conflicts, which permeated her life. She thought of going to Europe after graduation, perhaps working for an airline, anything that would take her away. Unlike the Guardian and Pathmaker groups, whose lives felt charted to them, Sandra was filled with conflict and uncertainty.

As Sandra constructed her life at the end of college, it seemed to her that she had to find someone on whom to pattern the new self she wanted to create. She looked to others to show her other ways to be. When she made a friend, she would find herself trying to be what that friend wanted her to be until she resented it so much that she would break off the friendship. She found herself "growing out of people" and worried about that. "I sort of bend toward people," she said, "but I have such varied friends that there is always opposition pounding at me." She was in search of someone to define her, but she fought whoever tried.

Sandra wasn't sure what in herself felt real. Having grown up as an obese child, she felt rejected, isolated, and mocked. After she lost weight in high school, people began to respond to her very differently. Now men were attracted to her, and she had to learn to manage advances from her professors and her boss. But this was a complicated process for her. On the one hand, she enjoyed their attention and desire for her and often couldn't bring herself to say "no." On the other hand, she often felt like "just a sex object" and worried about the men who seemed to have no interest in talking to her and only seemed interested in sex. "I used to want a lot of attention and now I've got it and I'm not sure I want it." She had been in an abusive relationship with one boyfriend who treated her as "a sex slave," and although she knew this was wrong for her, she couldn't firmly break off the relationship. Another boyfriend she rejected because he "didn't discipline me enough." Whatever she did he accepted, and this confused her. These are the sort of knots the Searchers found themselves trapped in during college.

Uncertain of their own worth, the Searchers were unsure what to ask for themselves. Many were drawn to relationships with men who seemed sure of themselves and wanted to define them as well, but often these were men who also treated them badly. Then these women would agonize over whether to stay or leave. Millie used a boyfriend to help her separate from her parents. "I used to be very sheltered and narrow-minded and never did any thinking. I used to let everyone else do my thinking for me. He changed all that. He made me a lot more open-minded. He was a freak. He was very messed up." This boyfriend led her into drugs and sexual experimentation, beat her occasionally, and abandoned her frequently. But he seemed to her the means of staging her independence from her parents. They hated him. She was obsessed with him. She didn't recognize, of course, that she had merely substituted one source of external control for another. "I was torn between my parents and him, and I couldn't condemn them for their motives because they only wanted the best for me, and everything I did was wrong and everyone was always mad at me and there I was in the middle. I really don't want to hurt my parents or to make them feel they've failed as parents, but I have to live my own life."

These conflicts about the right to live one's own life were central among the Searchers. As Millie stated it so well, their fear was that living their own lives involved harming their parents, disowning or discrediting them. This idea filled the Searchers with intense guilt and anxiety. But, despite the pain, they propelled themselves forward. Millie again speaks for the group: "The more I think about it, the more confused I get as to what I want to do with myself, where I think I'm going. It's scary in that sense, but it's good in the sense that I'm not living a life that's already been made for me—like I'm not just falling into a rut that I just didn't even question—that I'd just go to college, get married, live in suburbia, and be a housewife, and naturally I would be a virgin until I got married."

Many of the Searchers I interviewed came from working-class homes and were the first in their families to go to college. Their parents could not really imagine what they were experiencing in this phase of their life, and many were threatened by it and responded by pulling on the reins. The Searchers wanted something else, something beyond what they had seen at home, but did they have a right to it, were they good enough to deserve it, and what was "it" anyway? They had an intense sense that there were many possible ways to live a life but weren't sure how to choose.

All of the Searchers had deeply questioned their religious beliefs, disdaining what they felt was the hypocrisy of organized religion, but they gave up their religious practice with a lot of guilt. "These things are ingrained in me," one said, so they were haunted by the rituals they had disavowed.

Many had been somewhat politically involved during the late 1960s—the marches, the student strikes, but this, too, led to disillusion. Millie again: "I was believing what people were saying—that you can give up your grades for people who were over in Viet Nam dying. You can make a sacrifice for them and I felt 'Yeah, that's what I'm going to do' But there's no correlation between me not going to class [during the student strike] and them dying over there.

Its not doing them any good. And I got really screwed. And nothing ever came of it. The summer came and everyone went home and that was it. And I had three incompletes."

The effort to define themselves in terms of achievement and career fared no better. The Searchers kept changing their majors, losing interest in one field, hoping for better from another. Or they would define an interest and then not be able to bring themselves to do their work at a level that would get them accepted for the program of their choice. Lacking in self-confidence, they were often in search of a field that would adopt them, make them feel that here was something they were "good" at. Some handled this anxiety by putting career questions on hold, hoping to travel or explore before making a choice. "I think I'd like to be a bum," Millie said. "I'd like to start doing some traveling. I don't want to settle down in a job right now since I've been settled down in school for so long. I'd like to do something before I start." They all wished to "do something" but were finding it hard to define what that "something" might be.

Those who *had* made career plans were in conflict about how important they wanted to make their careers in their lives. Really, they thought, it was perhaps more important to marry and raise a family, so career was just a way station until they got on with the real business of life. On the other hand, just being a wife or mother looked very unappealing. Theresa, for example, wanted to be a teacher, but her Sicilian parents thought, "What is a woman who isn't married?" Similarly, Natalie was hoping to have a career as a journalist or a writer. But, she averred, if she married someone who objected to her career, she would give it up. Teresa and Natalie, like the other Searchers, weren't sure, couldn't know what would be expected of them—and they weren't yet able to think of themselves as the ones to define things.

The Searchers usually phrased their identity questions in very totalistic ways. Confronted with difference, they felt they had to make an either-or choice, to stay as they were or change completely. Teresa said, "I feel confused. I'm in the middle of two societies—a liberal one and a very, very strict one. I don't want to go into the liberal one, and I don't want to go into the strict one. I don't think I can decide ever." Throughout college, Theresa continually classified herself as being similar to or different from everyone she met and then pondered transforming herself to be more like those who were different. "I believe that every person you meet, you become like them in some way. In my senior year of high school, I felt more like my friends than I was like myself. Then, in freshman year of college, I met a group of hippies and had a hippie boyfriend. I was in a different world. I had never before seen anyone with a beard, long hair, and without shoes. It was confusing because I wasn't sure how I fit in with them because I was so different and I found myself becoming like them. I was leaving my old life [and entering] into a new life. Before that, I wouldn't go to a guy's apartment or smoke grass or go to a demonstration. I was doing these things because they were doing it." But Teresa was unsure whether these things belonged to her as well. Just as Sandra wasn't sure if she was in college for herself or her father or whether she lost weight for herself or for other people, Millie couldn't tell whether she was doing things for herself or her boyfriend. In college and after, the Searchers strove to be clear about who is in charge of their decisions and actions, but they often felt muddled about it. (This is in sharp contrast to the Pathmakers who, once having formed a sense of identity based on the experience of their own initiative, simply don't raise such questions.)

The Searchers came from families that clearly defined their values and expectations of them. But, unlike the Guardians, the Searchers did not want to carry on family tradition or meet parental demands. In contrast to the Guardians, the Searchers were more adventurous as college women and less preoccupied with security. Unlike the Pathmakers, however, they couldn't assert their right to separateness and modify themselves. They felt caught by the pulls of the very past they wanted to escape. All had parents that they found to be unsuitable models for one reason or another. Marlene was the daughter of Holocaust survivors and knew little of her parents' history except that their lives could in no way provide examples for her own. She spent her adolescence embarrassed by their age, their accents, and their foreignness. Theresa, daughter of immigrant Sicilian parents, learned English in school. Although she idealized her mother for being kind to everyone, she saw that her mother had never really found a place for herself outside the home. And, being an only child, she grew up in the shadow of her father's unmasked despair and anger that she was not a boy.

At the same time, many of the college-age Searchers grew up feeling exceptional, unlike others in some special way: Marlene, because of her parents' background, felt different from everyone else; Sandra and Leslie were fat; Laura had been born with a deformed foot; Theresa's mother treated her "like a princess"; Millie was especially good. Carrying this sense of specialness, they often romanticized their future. They felt that some sort of prince was on his way to them, not necessarily a man, but something out of the ordinary. Some had dreams of remarkable achievement—Millie imagined finding a cure for cancer, Natalie wanted to write a bestseller. But their goals were phrased, even if only unconsciously, as attainment of an ideal. They often set impossibly high standards for themselves. In that sense, they frequently seemed quixotic.

But, at the same time that they were reaching for so much, they were also frightened and craved security. The tension raged within them: stay with what's safe—no, reach out for what might be Right. They were vehemently leaving home but feeling stranded and abandoned. Where the Pathmakers were engaged in building and modifying, the Searchers seemed to throw everything in the air at once. They were constantly fearful about having burned the bridges that could lead them back home. They loved to argue and discuss issues, but needed a lot of reassurance and approval from someone that their views were acceptable. It often took them years to learn to hold on to safety with part of themselves while exploring and reworking other parts. And they varied in the amount of time and struggle it took them to settle on a path.

After college, the Searchers pursued their exploration in directions quite different from one another. While they resembled one another in college, they evolved into very different women. There is less commonality among them in midlife than within the other groups. Some had protracted searches, not really finding themselves until their 30s or even 40s. Some found a path that suited them shortly after college but cycled through renewed periods of questing in midlife. Others were overwhelmed by powerful inner demons, old and tenacious conflicts from childhood, demons that they needed therapeutic help to contain before they could move ahead. Still others found the road intolerably bumpy as they left college and found a psychological return ticket back home.

By the time they are in their mid-50s, the women in this group are leading very different lives depending on how they ultimately resolved their identity searches. Some, like Marlene, became almost indistinguishable from the Pathmakers at this age, their earlier identity struggles fading into the recesses of graying old history. Others, like Millie, are barely holding on to a life structure and trying not to drown in disappointment. Still others, like Norma, simply went home again and live out identities structured much like the Guardians. Yet others gave up trying to define themselves and just tried to keep afloat.

Revision over the course of life for these women had often been focused on tempering impossibly high standards for themselves in the face of which they could only feel inadequate. As they age and grow, they learn to accept themselves as less than they might have dreamed they would be and still to value what they have made of their lives.

Searchers Who Created Their Own Path

MILLIE

Age 21

I cherished Millie as my quintessential Searcher as a college senior. She seemed to step right out of the pages of Erikson, giving personal voice to what he had described theoretically. I talked about her frequently in my lectures over the years because she was so able to articulate her confusion and doubt as she contemplated a highly uncertain future. Raised in a suburban New England town in a Catholic milieu, she was drawn to all the possibilities of other lifestyles that dominated her college campus. Her torn bellbottoms and long, frizzy hair stated her distance from the conservative values of her family. When I met her in college, she indeed looked like a "hippie" of the times despite her round face and blue eyes, which made her rather cherubic-looking. She was perky and lively and talked for twice the amount of time I had allotted. I thoroughly enjoyed listening to her.

Millie was actively questioning everything but finding no answers. There were many things to do or believe, but nothing felt like it really fit her or couldn't be doubted. Millie told me then that she had no self-confidence and that it made her "very dependent" on other people. She described herself as "insecure." "When I take an exam, I am sure I will fail. When I go out with guys, I am sure they will break up with me." She felt she set such high goals for herself, she could never meet them. When she thought about her future, she thought that what she really wanted to do was find a cure for cancer. Her occupational dream was formed when she had worked in a nursing home one summer and got involved with a cancer patient who was dying, and "I couldn't stand it, so I decided that's what I wanted to do." She was majoring in biology, but killing frogs in her biology lab was so upsetting that she was beginning to realize she couldn't go into any kind of biology or medical field and was feeling somewhat lost.

Although her parents had not gone to college, her mother went to work to earn money for Millie's college tuition and Millie felt they had high expectations of her but were disappointed that she did not seem to be "normal." She talked of her parents only in affectionate terms. They loved her but were overprotective and wanted their version of the best for her. They couldn't understand who she seemed to be becoming. Millie wasn't even sure she wanted to get married. "I guess I will eventually. I don't like to think of myself as 40 and unmarried. But right now I can't imagine it. I can imagine loving someone or living with someone but as soon as I know there's a legal bond—that this is the way it's going to be, I get scared." Although she was glad that her mother was not a working mother while she was growing up, Millie said that she imagined that she would always work because she couldn't stand doing housework all the time. "I don't want my life to be my children. I want my own life. I've seen too many parents—like mine—who have put their whole lives in their children and then when the children grow up, they're lost. You've got to realize from the start that eventually they're going to leave."

Millie had been raised Catholic, but was now exploring Zen and Eastern religions. She was acutely aware of what she felt was the hypocrisy of church-goers and the wars in the name of religion. "I do want to believe. Because just to believe in reality is not so nice because there are a lot of things in reality that are not so nice." When she was younger, she had wanted to be a nun, and her disillusionment in the Church was painful. "I know my parents would like me to go to church and I'd like to do it for them, but I couldn't because I'd be a hypocrite and I'd be deceiving them into thinking I'm a good Catholic girl again when I'm not." She was trying to develop a personal, ethical system, having given up on organized religion. But even this was confusing. "I went to Catholic schools and those things are ingrained in me. Like I can cut down the Catholic Church, but when I hear someone else do it, I get really defensive."

I began to understand in this interview that behind Millie's doubt and cynicism was a disappointed idealist. Her foray into political commitment met with similar disenchantment. In opposition to her conservative parents, Millie had gotten involved in the student strikes and marches of the late 1960s but, as we heard from her earlier statements, she became disillusioned. ". . . And I had three incompletes. I'm apathetic now. I really did get involved. And all I could see is I was getting screwed and nothing was coming of it. And I really believe my emotionalism duped me, and I was really disillusioned."

Millie was a passionate young woman who wanted to embrace something completely. She was able to tell me, "Things aren't the way I'd like them to be in my ideal society." What she could fully endorse were the new sexual values that were permeating her campus. She could say definitively, "Someone who is 22 and a virgin is perverted. . . . You have a sex urge and you have to make love to someone before you're married." I noted that Millie defined her own values in these universal terms—not what was right for her, but what seemed right for her had to be true for everyone. Her conservative upbringing gave way to a man who she was involved with through much of college. "He changed my ideas—because I used to be so inhibited. He changed my whole way of life because I used to be very super straight and close-minded. I had to get over the idea that if you have sex before you're married you'll go straight to hell."

Trying to reflect on herself in this interview, Millie was mainly aware of how disappointed she was in herself. "I don't think I act my age. I think I act like a kid. Maybe it's that I don't act the way I thought I would act at this age. I used to think that at age 20, I would walk around discussing Plato or something." Indeed, Millie was laboring under her own high expectations.

What had been most prominent in her life in the past few years had been her relationship with Marvin, a growth-promoting but also traumatic love affair. "He was very messed up. He was a freak and my parents hated him. I used to be very sheltered and narrow-minded and never did any thinking. I would let everyone else do my thinking for me. He changed all that. He made me a lot more open-minded. He taught me by shocking example what I didn't know how to cope with." Of course, what Millie could not see was that, in some ways, she simply allowed Marvin to do her thinking for her. I thought she was alluding to a lot of drug use, but didn't learn until years later that indeed this is what she meant but didn't say. Marvin had recently left her, and she was obsessed about whether he would come back to her. Her inner conflict had been expressed by what she felt were the pulls between

Marvin on one side and her parents on the other. Now the challenge was to define herself.

"The more I learn, the more middle of the road I become, and I learn that there are two sides of every story and its hard that way because I like to have the answers. But it seems like that's the way it's going—that you just can't say that this is right and this is wrong. It's hard to make decisions about things because there are so many avenues to go down." This last statement seemed to be the clearest I heard from anyone about how it *felt* to be in a searching phase of identity development. Millie articulated the uncertainty, the doubt, the guilt, the wish for something that felt right even though it was not ideal. I could hear Millie being torn between the security and sense of rightness in her childhood and the new possibilities that had opened for her in college. And Millie helped me understand the anxiety and guilt that accompanied this process, the sheer pain of it.

Despite Millie's charm, I was worried about her at this point in her life. She could articulate her struggles so clearly, but she seemed swept up in a vortex of confusion without any clear exit to smoother ground. And I wasn't sure she had the inner resources to get on her feet.

Age 33

At age 33, Millie again entranced me by telling me an early memory that was so startling in its evolution over the next decade that it captured the inner psychological changes of adulthood. The memory was this: "Being in kindergarten. We were cutting out shamrocks. The teacher asked me to cut out the shamrock, and I was so impressed that she asked me to cut it out. This was going to be the best shamrock the world had ever seen. I was being so careful that I was going too slow and she ended up coming over and taking it out of my hands and saying, 'OK, we'll let someone else do this.' I was crushed."

Earliest memories reflect the deep dynamics of the present psychological organization, and, at age 33, Millie did indeed feel as though her idealism had slowed her down and her life was being taken out of her hands. When I saw Millie at age 33, she was nine months pregnant with her second child and about to move to the South with her husband. The previous decade had been one of somewhat aimless exploration with trips across the United States, brief stays in various places with friends or friends of friends, numerous brief jobs, and generally little direction. The longest of her jobs was driving a cab, unusual for a woman at the time, and she enjoyed being unusual and having a lot of camaraderie with the other cab drivers. But she eventually tired of this. At one point, she studied to be an Emergency Medical Technician so she could drive an ambulance, but that didn't work out because she didn't like the 12-hour shifts. She had taken computer courses, worked as a medical secretary and an administrative assistant at the American Meteorological Society—a whole gamut of jobs and interests. Mainly, though, her focus was on describing the people she found in these various spheres of the world. In those few instances where she liked the people, something about the work demands put her off and she moved on. She said she still didn't know what she wanted to do.

As Millie saw herself from this vantage point, it seemed to her that she had had a clear goal at the end of college—to do cancer research. But her first job, which she took after six months of "bumming around," was in a biology research lab that exposed her to asbestos dust. She remembers starting her job with a feeling of "Look out world, here I come," and her eventual awareness of the dangers in the experiments she had to conduct was as deflating as the shamrock being taken out of her hands in the early memory. She also resented that the men were being paid more for the same work. When she complained about these things, the management of the lab was infuriated, regarded her as "hysterical," and she was forced to quit. "I had the wind knocked out of my sails," she said.

Disillusioned, she impulsively moved to Florida where a friend of hers was living, and she worked as a waitress and a sales clerk—whatever work she could get. But she detested the drug-infested neighborhood where her friend lived, and, fearing for her safety, she returned home to Long Island. Still feeling lost, she began to drive a cab. At least in the short run, she could know where she was going. She drove the cab for four years, enjoying people's surprise at finding a woman taxi driver. But she found herself often angry at the way people treated her and again feared for her safety. At those times when she stopped and asked herself what she was doing with her life, she found herself longing to have an important, responsible position, but she couldn't envision taking the small steps that would be necessary to get there.

Finally, she decided to get some training in being a paramedical technician. "I really don't research things very well before I do them," she said ruefully, looking back. Working in an ambulance, which had seemed exciting and challenging, turned out to be overly demanding. The hours were too long and the stress was overwhelming. She quit and took a job as a secretary in a hospital coronary care unit. "I was not working up to my potential in terms of intellect, but it was fascinating." She felt appreciated and valuable. She stayed two years, during which she was taking computer training. In search of more responsibility and more money, she got a job at the American Meteorological Society but felt the work environment there was "oppressive, demeaning to women and filled with stuffy people." When she became pregnant at age 30, she opted out of the work world.

Millie's story of relationships with men had been equally checkered. Throughout her 20s, she had many relationships, each unsatisfactory in different ways. She had met Phillip when she was 28, and they had a stormy time together. They sort of "backed into" living together because both were afraid of making a commitment. Worried that they would "chicken out," they married hurriedly. Once married, though, Millie could allow herself to feel "crazy about him." She felt that they were "linked psychically." She described Phillip as a "very solid kind of guy" who helped stabilize her emotional swings. She felt more future-oriented, more responsible. Although it had been difficult to make a commitment, she felt herself settling down in a contented way. But after their daughter was born, Millie felt the relationship teeter. "I feel more defensive about me as an entity, as a separate person. I find myself backing off from responsibility and decision-making, especially about how money is spent since I'm not working. I feel weird being dependent on someone else."

For the next three years, ages 30–33, Millie had been channeling all her energies and aspirations into their daughter. (Their daughter, unsurprisingly to me, had been born through careless birth control rather than a decision to have a child.) "I worry about each stage, afraid I won't be able to handle it. But it's so nice to have someone who really needs me." She found a new self as a mother: "No one could have told me the joy I would experience as a mother. It makes me feel good about myself that I'm capable of feeling such strong emotions. It makes me feel like a good human being." She missed working, but didn't know what work she wanted to do—and anyway couldn't bear the thought of leaving her daughter in someone else's care. She felt transformed by motherhood, more responsible, more conscious of her behavior, eager to set a good example. And her fantasies of success were threaded into imagining what her daughter might grow into. "I want her to excel in something. She's very bright, and I think she could really do something, really make a contribution to whatever she wanted to do." These were hopes that Millie had not managed to realize for herself.

Although during college, Millie had stopped practicing the Catholicism in which she had been raised, she was planning to raise her daughter in the Church. "Religion is a good thing to have in times of need—a strength you can draw on."

Her world at age 33 was limited to her family. She had become closer to her parents, her brother, her cousins, and her aunts. In some ways, to me, Millie seemed very much back where she had started from, largely by default. She seemed to have drifted back home, a place she had never wanted to go back to. Her parents no longer even regarded her as "the weirdo of the family," although they still worried about the side of her that might "cut loose." Millie had had many disappointments in friendships and reflected that she had expected friends to be like family. "It's like when you find out your parents aren't perfect. I believed that some of my friendships would last forever, and I was really disappointed."

Millie described herself as settled into her life at age 33, filled with wonder at the intensity of her love for Phillip and her daughter. She was defining herself by the strength of her love. It was a quiet life, not much money for what Millie called "diversions," so their options for where and how they lived were limited by Phillip who was working hard at a commission-based sales job. Still, Millie's narrative was peppered with the words "disillusioned" and "disappointed," and she was mourning her failed occupational ambitions. On reflection, she wasn't pleased with who she had become, so far from her dreams of specialness and accomplishment. Her quirky sense of humor and quick wit were much muted. What worried her most at this time was that Phillip had been talking about moving to a different part of the country where his company felt there were good sales opportunities. Millie worried that although she regarded him as her "predestined other half," they might have to separate. She didn't want to leave the town where they had settled, to be on the road again. But she was frightened to think how helpless she had become, "tied to my daughter's needs and Phillip's schedule."

Looking back, Millie put a rosy glow on her college years. They were times of freedom and happiness, being a hippie believing in peace and love. She seemed to have forgotten all the pain and anguish. "I felt in tune with myself, could do whatever I wanted. I was free to express myself and I could be crazy." She feels that, in the past decade, her encounters with real dangers—driving a cab, living in impoverished neighborhoods—taught her that the world isn't filled with peace and love. Still, despite anchoring herself in her love for her husband and daughter, Millie seemed to be drifting, adapting herself to necessity.

Age 43

At this age, Millie retold her memory of the shamrock without remembering having told it before. But this time, she phrased it differently: "Cutting out a shamrock, I think, out of construction paper in kindergarten. I was trying to be very precise and my teacher took it away for someone else to finish because I was going too slow." Although the story is the same, this time Millie tells it without either the despair or the grandiosity. It no longer had to be "the best shamrock the world ever saw" nor was she "crushed" by having it taken from her. Both the passion and poignancy are gone. At this period of her life, Millie felt that she was actively engaged in a life she had chosen—perhaps not the best possible life, but a meaningful one. I was delighted to see the change in her. She had traveled a rocky course to get there.

Shortly after our prior interview, Millie (then nine months pregnant) and Phillip moved to a remote rural area of Louisiana where Phillip had what he thought was a good job offer. It was a very insular town suspicious of "Yankees," and Millie felt totally isolated. She described this time in her life as "pure hell." And the job was not as Phillip hoped. With great tension between them, they stuck it out for three years until Phillip was fired. Desperate for connection to people during this time and wanting to have her new baby daughter baptized, Millie began going to the Catholic church. Slowly, she felt faith growing. And that changed her life. "I felt like I'm really being drawn down a certain path. I feel like I'm being led and like I'm trying to open myself up to follow it." Millie did not sound fanatic when speaking about her faith, but it pervaded every aspect of her life that she talked about. It was a bit difficult for me, though, because she had entered a world completely foreign to me, and I lost her completely when she was speaking of miracles she had traveled to witness. Her faith, she told me, had made her whole and "brought me home." She had become the director of religious education in her church. In terms of identity, she was occupied with differentiating herself among different types of believers and belief categories, none of which I could follow very well—Contemplatives and Charismatics, all evidently important distinctions within the church community and important to someone focused on religious education. Contrasting herself with her college self, which she now saw as "wild," she said that her commitment to her faith is the first real commitment she made to herself and the people around her. There were many of her past actions that now troubled her, for which she felt terribly guilty, but she found solace in God's forgiveness and tried to forgive herself. And, I noted with pleasure, her sense of humor was back.

The Church also bound her family. She and Phillip were closer than ever. "I think sociologists think that religious people never have sex, but it's not true. It's a wonderful thing between a man and a wife." They were enjoying their two children who were "growing and getting real funny." They were a wisecracking family, she told me. She had some worries about adolescence—and her talking about this gave me some insight into her worldview and her sense of her place in it: "I worry about adolescence, not so much from within, but from without, from society and school handing out condoms and stuff like that. That's nuts. Don't do it but just in case you can't help yourself, here it is and we won't tell mom and dad. The logic is completely. . . . Those people are nuts. It is so detrimental to the family. I never in my life considered home schooling until lately because that would be extremely tough and I'm not to that point yet. And you get someone like Jocelyn Elders as the Surgeon General,[2] and they think that this is what the kids need. That's what I'm scared of mostly. Seems like I ought to just lock them up in a closet."

Throughout this interview, Millie spoke of becoming "less egocentric"—then laughed and said of course no one thinks they are egocentric. "This giving of yourself and, I sort of hate to use the term, sacrifice, is really rewarding. It's a way to find yourself, giving yourself away. You keep looking for yourself some-place in the mirror, you are not going to find it." It seemed that, indeed, Millie had found herself in this decade. She was more centered and proud of herself than I had seen her before, and I thought she had become a Pathmaker at last.

Age 56

Traveling to Raceland, Louisiana, to find Millie at age 56, I felt myself very much in a foreign country. The only music on the radio was religious. On the four-lane highway, the scene was repetitive: a Kentucky Fried Chicken, then a

Burger King, a McDonalds, Wendy's, a gas station, then the procession begins again. A Chevrolet dealership breaks the pattern, but then it soon reasserts itself. It goes on for miles. When there is a break, there are houses and many churches, each with a sign.

Millie wanted me to meet her in her office in the Church, where she had some donuts waiting for me. She was about 30 pounds overweight and looked her age, her face varying from animated and pretty to kind of distorted and odd. Knowing that I had recently returned from Israel, she asked me about the Middle East situation. When I asked if she had ever been to Jerusalem (where I live part of the year), she signaled that something was amiss by responding sadly, "No, I've never been anywhere."

Millie was eager to meet me because she said that "Being in the study gives me an opportunity to reflect on where I've been. It's like a stopping point to reflect on where I've been from the last time." She was warm and welcoming, but she seemed to regard me as someone from another planet, which is rather how I was regarding her. Still, we did manage to connect again, as best we could.

Our worldviews are so disparate, though, that writing about her involves stating clearly where I am looking at her from. To make her more familiar to myself (and my profession), I could write about her as someone who was finally diagnosed with bipolar disorder and is taking medication and seeing a therapist for it. Or I could describe her as someone whose life just went off the rails somewhere such that she lives in a spiritual world, having given up on the earthly one. I try to resist both these stances and to understand her as she understands herself. But Millie, who had always been exceptionally articulate, spoke rapidly and interrupted herself during the interview, which makes it a challenge for me to piece together a coherent account of what she had made of her life in the past decade. It seems that Phillip became so involved in the Church and his own spiritual life that he stopped working and Millie was overworking even though she was earning little money. "I had a, nervous breakdown six years ago. It was a culmination of everything. My husband was out of work and . . . I spent most of my time trying to be the perfect wife, the perfect mother, tried to save souls, be on God's team, take care of my husband. Phillip was spending most of his time reading about the saints, about Catholicism. . . . I guess he figured that God was leading him this way, so I figured, okay, if that's what you want, you know, I'll just work even harder, but in the meantime, things were very difficult for us financially. My older daughter started going into puberty and started becoming very rebellious because all the sudden, I was all the time over at the Church and just being very submissive. . . . And while all of this was going on, the pastor was having his own nervous breakdown and was not, he was a bully, and the parish secretary was a terrible person, and I was trying to support a family of four. Phillip lost his job and I asked for medical insurance, and no one wanted to give it to me because 'you work for the church—you're supposed to give to the church, they're not supposed to *give* to you.' And I kept this all on my shelf, trying to placate everybody, and God will you give the strength, and I'll just keep moving forward. You just put your nose to the grindstone, and you just keep, you know, one step in front of the other and things got progressively heavy for me to bear. . . . I never took it really as a job, it was always a ministry. . . . Emotionally, it just broke my back. I could not reconcile warring factions . . . I couldn't reconcile good and evil. I couldn't save anyone's souls. I couldn't support my family. I wasn't being a good mother because I was spending so much time trying to make the world a better place for my children that I wasn't spending time with my children to make them better people in the world. It was like everything that I was trying to hold these loose ends, and it just broke my back. I couldn't sleep, I couldn't eat, I would just wring my hands. . . . It was just . . . from a psychological point of view, a nervous breakdown, from a spiritual point of view, it was a dark night of the soul. . . . I failed everyone. I failed God and what I was asked to do. I couldn't take communion. I just felt like I would defile it with me as a failure. I'm not really describing exactly what I'm trying to say. You don't really realize . . . it's like being in a tornado, things are swirling so fast, you're not thinking clearly. And my parents called . . . I talk to them every week. And my mother has suffered from bipolar for 45 years and because she had been through this, she knew exactly, it went right to her heart. She called her psychiatrist and he said, 'Well, we can't let her suffer.' I didn't hear it from the church, from all the people I had been praying for, that I had been offering up things for. It was somebody from the outside who didn't even know me that said 'We can't let her suffer.' My parents came down and got me." In the aftermath of this crisis, her parents began helping them out financially, and the Church changed her job status to a slightly higher salary and included medical insurance.

Her family life was now quite a shambles. Her children were angry at her for not insisting that Phillip work. Her older daughter was drinking, and her younger daughter had gotten herself to college and was keeping away from the family. With the children grown and out of the house, Millie was feeling that perhaps she was beginning a new chapter in her life. She still wanted to do good, was thinking of doing more speaking and teaching through the Church. "I know that I have helped individuals . . . deal with life, deal with God, deal with life not making sense. I want to send people down the right path. There's always something more to be done, which is good, because if there's not more to be done, what would we do?"

When I asked her if her sense of her calling had shifted over the past decade, I quickly realized that this was not a good question to have asked. Millie began to describe in great detail intensely spiritual experiences having to do with being in the eye of God, or having her heart pierced by light while sleeping in front of a particular statue or talking to St. Peter—all experiences that, to my clinical psychologist mind, sounded outside of reality but seemed to make perfect sense to her in her spiritual worldview. I understood that what animated her most were moments of powerful spiritual awareness with both physical and emotional intensity. Still, I realized that I was no longer able to understand her experience.

In vain, I tried to redirect her back to our shared world. "I was not available to my children's emotional needs," she told me. This may have been true or it may have been her self-criticism. "My daughter wouldn't talk to me, so I'd get mad and she'd go stomping off and I'd feel terrible and go try to save some more souls. I was trying to make everything nice." Her children have left the Church. "Phillip and I were so wrapped up in it that they didn't want to have anything to do with it. . . . They don't practice their faith. Isn't that wonderful? I save all these souls, but my own kids—I can't get them to go to church."

Among the things I couldn't understand was her determination to see herself as submissive to her husband. Was this a religious tenet? I asked her. "Husbands are supposed to be the heads of the household, and I ended up becoming extremely submissive. He would walk around like the king." She told me that most of what she talked about in her therapy was Phillip. He spent money that they didn't have, and she just submitted, not saying anything. He was still a dreamer, and she worried that he would again move the family pursuing some job that seemed to promise what he always wanted. I gathered from what Millie said that she was trying to rethink her marriage and her behavior in relation to Phillip.

Millie was not without hope. She said she felt that a new window was opening, a new stage beginning. "I feel that I can stretch my wings a little bit. I don't have to kind of hover so much worrying about my children. Not that they listen to me all that well. I feel I have a little more breathing room, and this is the beginning of a new chapter. I'm standing in the doorway right now of a new chapter." What would be in that chapter? I asked. "I'd like it to be a lot happier than it has been. Not that there haven't been good times. But I would really like to . . . uh . . . I feel like I'm standing in a doorway to the outside looking out and almost salivating thinking and seeing that there's a whole world outside. I had been so uh . . . narrow in what I could do. Work has been all-encompassing. I like to be competent in what I do. I'm not going to make any more money. I like working. I've been thinking lately that what I'd like to do is go out on speaking engagements. That's a good thing about SSRIs—they make you more calm [laughs]. I'd like to get out of the house. I go to the supermarket, I'm at work, long days and evenings and when I'm not doing that, I'm reading books on it. I would just like to get out of the house and do something . . . for me . . . I would like to . . . do something to add to the world."

Poring over the early interviews, I tried to find some straight line between the Millie of 21 and the one who I just now encountered. She has always felt her emotions strongly; that was part of her charm for me. Was she always bipolar? Did this somehow "explain" her? At age 33, she had spoken of Phillip stabilizing her, being able to contain her moods. When he stopped being able to do that—and in fact, seemed to develop his own problems with emotions, did that upset her balance? And what of her involvement with the Church, which seemed to have settled her identity quest in her age-43 interview but became an involvement she lost control of? Was there some identity thread here? I suppose I could say that Millie had always wanted to do something grand that helped others. As a late adolescent, she had a dream of finding a cure for cancer to save people, a dream she could not put into real attainment, and, at 53, she is rooted in trying to save souls. To the extent that she feels successful in what she has become, saving souls is what she prizes of her accomplishments. So, amidst all the pain and broken dreams, I would say that Millie has realized her identity project. She has effected her identity in her spiritual life, with the pained sacrifice of her children and perhaps even her own mental well-being.

MARLENE

In contrast to Millie, Marlene was someone who felt familiar to me. We share a Jewish background, and there is something about her style and way of expressing herself that had always made me feel like I was talking to a friend. She has always been a warm, calm, articulate woman with a gentle, ironic sense of humor.

Age 21

Marlene was the only daughter of immigrant, Holocaust survivors, but she didn't tell me this right away. Rather, she stressed that her parents were older parents who spoke Roumanian at home, had only passable English, and so could give her little guidance about how to be within the wider culture or how to pattern her own life. From childhood, Marlene had to become adept at "fitting in," although she always felt different as the child of immigrant parents and one of few Jews in the small suburban town where she was raised. As a teenager, she became sensitive to the views and style of others, regarding everyone she met as a potential source of patterns for her own life. Successful at reading what was expected of her, Marlene in high school lived the life of an A student and cheerleader, although she didn't date much, wanting to date just Jewish boys. She chose a small women's college because friends a few years older than she went there. Marlene said that college had been such an epiphany that she could hardly remember the "innocent and unaware" person she had been in high school. She chose to major in political science because she liked the people in the department. Feeling that "everything is debatable," she had no clear beliefs—but she agonized about everything. Not religious, she felt a strong tie to cultural Judaism and her roots, but wasn't sure what this meant except for some draw toward maybe going to Israel some day. Although she had flirted with left-wing politics—SDS, socialist ideas— she came to dislike the people in the movement and disengaged herself from these groups.

Marlene acknowledged in her senior year interview that she had "trouble expressing her feelings" in her life. She thought deeply and questioned most things, but it was hard for her to tell where she stood on most issues. In a period of feeling depressed, she had begun to see a counselor. But opening up issues frightened her, and she "dropped it like a hot potato."

Somewhat by accident, she joined a women's collective that ended up raising her consciousness about being a woman. She recounted trying to justify to a friend the fact that she ironed her boyfriend's shirts, but realized that she had no rational explanation. This confused her. Marlene couldn't get clear on how to think of herself at this stage. "I feel the image that my friends have of me is not the image I have of myself, and I felt I was being pushed into their image of me as nonemotional, practical, independent, reliable, trustworthy— a strong, cold image—and I didn't know if there was another side and if there was, how to show it." Her search in college, then, was about how to *be* and what aspects of how she presented herself in the world really belonged to something core in her.

She felt bereft of models. She had gone through a period early in college of anger at her parents for having "ruined" her. They hadn't taught her to communicate with others. They gave her "hang-ups" that made her feel isolated. Worse, they couldn't know her or who she was becoming. In a moment of courage, Marlene told her mother that she was sleeping with her boyfriend. This was an act of trying to disavow the fictional view she felt her mother had of her. At the same time, Marlene felt she burned her bridge to childhood. "I could be a child as long as I could preserve my mother's view of me a child," Marlene said. But now her problem, having declared herself an adult, was what kind of adult to be.

Marlene had turned to her boyfriend to guide her and teach her. Having met him in her freshman year, she credited him with opening her to all sorts of new experiences. Over time, he increasingly disliked her dependence on him. Like a parent, he set about forcing her to do things on her own. She turned then to other women in the women's collective, which helped, but, in college, Marlene was a fawn struggling to get up on wobbly legs.

Although a very successful student who had a lot of pride in her intelligence, Marlene at the end of college was too afraid to assert herself, and, not knowing what she wanted to assert anyway, by default, she planned to follow her boyfriend. She would go where he went and find something to do. She needed more time to get to know herself, and she wanted to do this in the company of someone she trusted. Although uncertain about what to do with herself, Marlene seemed eager to continue to explore. Keenly aware of how she acted in the company of others, she was in search of a picture of herself that could contain both her strength and her vulnerability. She was trying to get herself in focus. She felt far from a home she could not emotionally return to, from parents who seemed to belong to a different world, whom she in no way wanted to emulate. She looked up to her boyfriend and a couple of her close friends, but knew she couldn't be exactly like them either. While she was hearing the call of new ideas—new definitions of women, of society—she didn't know how to place herself among these currents. But she was actively struggling with all of it, debating with herself and with others all the "debatable" issues of religion, politics, ideology, love, women's roles, expression of feeling—all the issues of life.

I was moved by Marlene's struggle and aware that she was intently using the interview to try to say who she was. She told me as we said goodbye that she had told me things she had never told anyone, referring, I supposed, to her doubts and vulnerability. On listening to the interview later, I was struck by how much she was trying to define herself with reference to others' views and beliefs. Even to my opening question of what she would tell of herself to someone who she wanted to know her, she said, "it would depend on who the person is." A part of her was still trying to "fit in," a part was still in search of models on which to pattern herself, and a part of her was straining to find something core in herself on which to build.

Age 33

When I saw her again at age 33, Marlene narrated an odyssey of search that was just then coming to resolution. Marlene had followed her college boyfriend to Boston and took odd jobs while he went to law school. But this relationship soon began to sour because he continued to feel too tied by her dependency on him, a dependency made worse when her mother died shortly after she graduated from college. Desperate for security, she painfully came to the realization that her boyfriend was not going to marry her after all, and she would have to think about making some plans on her own. Marlene then began to consider developing some career goals. Why had she not done anything with her education? she wondered. But she didn't know what to choose. One of her close friends was enrolled in a library science program, and Marlene thought that such a course of study might give her credentials that would get her out of doing temporary secretarial work. She had another friend in California and decided to move out there and enter a library program.

Marlene liked the life in California, its openness, its freedom, and she settled into a contented period of study and friendships. But when she finished her degree, she was unable to find a job. She put together a pastiche of part-time work, one "on the margin of library work," but found that since the "California work ethic was much more fluid" than that of the East Coast, this was an acceptable kind of life. What was most exciting to her during this time was some volunteer work she was doing at a women's health center. Again she had turned to women's issues and to the company of women dedicated to a cause as a source of meaning in her life.

At the same time, Marlene was dating Ben, a man who had plans to emigrate to Israel to set up a residential treatment center for emotionally disturbed children. This reverberated with some old Zionist interests that Marlene had not thought about since high school. And she found in herself a longing to reconnect with her extended family in Israel, many of whom she had never met. The more he talked about his dream, the more Marlene wanted to take part in it. The more she thought about "family," a word tinged for her with longing and loss and hope, the more she realized that "family" somehow went with being in Israel, where Ben also had relatives. She decided to marry Ben and move with him to Israel. The future, at this point, seemed lit by promise.

But the project in Israel was fraught with disappointment. Things didn't happen on schedule, funding that was promised didn't arrive, negotiations with the administering authorities were stalled. They waited for a year, living on a kibbutz. During this time, her father died and their son was born. Marlene had a mild postpartum depression, her emotions were out of control, and she felt terribly isolated and without support.

The Israel venture was turning out to be a disaster. Marlene had longed to settle down, to build a life of stability and community in Israel. Instead, the stress and the frustration of not being able to accomplish what they had set out to do was putting them at odds with each other. They began to argue and blame each other. Marlene began to feel that Ben wasn't serious about making things work out in Israel—maybe he wasn't trying hard enough. After another six months, they began to see that they would have to return to the States.

At this point, Marlene was 30 and recognized that she would have to begin again. Uncertain of any direction, Marlene, Ben, and their son, Simon, began wandering around the country, staying with relatives and friends, trying to decide what to do. Visiting some friends in northern California who lived in a coastal town that charmed them, they impulsively decided to stay. Marlene found a part-time job in the local library, Ben got part-time work in a bank, and they divided the child care. Hoping now to establish the stable family life she had always dreamed of, Marlene and Ben framed their family with an increasing religious commitment; they began participating in the Jewish community and observing more holidays and traditions.

Eventually, Marlene began to volunteer again in a women's health center and reimmersed herself in women's issues. After a year, the library lost its funding and Marlene lost her job. But the women's health center offered her an administrative job that, though far beneath her skills, did allow her to devote more of her time to a crusade that would help women take charge of their bodies.

All this time, her marriage was deteriorating. Ben quit work in the bank, tried some other things that he didn't like, and eventually stopped working altogether. He spent his "work" time—when Marlene was watching Simon—playing music and hanging out in coffee houses. Eventually, he decided to go back to school, but what claimed most of his attention was the opportunity to be involved with other women. Marlene felt that they were sharing nothing but child care. To use her words, "It was all falling apart. I desperately wanted to hang on to what I saw as my family, but it wasn't working out."

Fortunately, Marlene had been taking part in a women's support group, and these women rallied to help her sort out her feelings and accept what she in some way already knew—that she would have to separate from her husband. The "What do *I* do now?" question was more serious than ever before. But her friends helped her regard this new possibility with expansiveness rather than terror. Marlene sensed that it might be her last try.

She had always hovered around the edges of women's health and women's issues. Now she began shaping the idea to focus this interest and transform it into a career. She talked to a lot of people and investigated training programs. Finally, she found one that would train her to be a nurse-midwife, qualified to work in both gynecology and obstetrics, exactly what she wanted. The only problem was that the university that offered this program was in New York. Could she leave her three-year-old son that far away and for that long? How could she even think of taking him along? His father would fight it, and besides, this was a very demanding program of study, too demanding for a single parent. And one thing about Ben: he was a wonderful father. This was an agonizing decision for Marlene, but, in the end, she decided that the time had finally come to make decisions based on her needs. She could see her son on school vacations and in the summer. And if she used the small inheritance she had, she could fund her training with the help of loans. "For the first time, I felt like I knew what I wanted to do. I remember in college feeling so envious of people who were directed and knew what they wanted to do. Then I suddenly felt that sense of direction at the age of 32, and it felt wonderful. Everything started to fall into place."

She took the GRE's, applied to the program she had selected, sold the house, took an anatomy course, and filed for divorce. "I was doing all these things and handling them well. I felt very in control." And off she went to New York. Perhaps for the first time in her life, Marlene had found and expressed her agency, her sense that she could exercise choice and direct her future, and this involved making a courageous and very wrenching decision to leave her young son behind—temporarily.

When I interviewed Marlene at age 33, she was inundated with school-work, which she was happily struggling through. She missed her son and worried about her relationship with him, but was optimistic about the future. In New York, where she was studying, she met a new man, Jerry, and was beginning to hope for another chance at making a family. She felt she had learned from the mistakes of her prior relationships, having been dominated by her first boyfriend and having done too much caretaking with Ben, not fully communicating with either of them. She felt in love with Jerry and believed that they were making a more equal, healthier relationship than she had ever experienced.

At this age, Marlene was very reflective about her growth and felt she could see now where she had been blinded and made bad choices. She felt that she had been motivated by a desire to "hang on to security above all else" and had clung to one man or the other as though they were a life raft. She had hoped that her boyfriend during college would take charge of her, then relied on Ben to define a life for her. As she thought of her years during and since college, Marlene said, "I was floating here and there and bouncing off of what I was getting from other people. My attitude was 'why not' rather than the sense of what to do."

In thinking back, Marlene pictured herself in college as focused on having a family rather than a career (which may have been so but is not how she described herself or her wishes at the time. She may not have admitted this out of shame because she was then joining the feminist discourse). Following this theme, Marlene wondered, looking back from the vantage point of age 33, if she had been in thrall to her deep, often unconscious, wish "to have a TV kind of family," the family she had never had. She thought that perhaps she had been so afraid of a career interfering with that dream that she had "kept myself fluid" in order to be ready to mold into marriage and family. Only when she could mourn the dream of the "perfect family" could she think realistically and clearly about how to fashion a goal. And her feminist women friends were essential to this—they gave her the support to help her "emerge." When she left California, they gave her silk butterflies as a symbol of her metamorphosis. And this metaphor seemed apt: it felt to her as though she had been through a process of emerging, a competent, goal-directed self lying hidden, preparing hesitantly to show itself. "If I can perceive how someone else perceives me, it helps me to pull things together," Marlene said.

Ironically, though, moving ahead independently steered her into her worst fears—it disrupted her family—or, at least, her relationship with her son. But Marlene was hoping for another chance, a chance to "get it all in." Now it seemed possible, even though, as Marlene said, it would "require a whole lot of planning."

Age 43

Perhaps Marlene had mastered planning in all the turmoil she had endured. I found Marlene at age 43 still in New York, working as a nurse-midwife, married to Jerry, and mother of another child, having realized most of what she had hoped for 10 years earlier. But not without potholes along the way. The biggest frustration for Marlene in the past decade had been not being able to conceive, going through every hi-tech fertility attempt, but failing at all of them. That had absorbed most of her attention in the previous decade. Finally, they adopted a little girl as a very young infant, but the adoption did not end their preoccupation with conception as they had hoped it would. Marlene felt that the infertility period was the hardest life crisis she had yet endured. By the time I saw her again, she was settled into the planning involved in raising a toddler and a teenager (her son Simon) and managing a demanding career.

On every front, Marlene had learned to use her new capacity to take charge of her life, to speak her needs and desires, and to pull her life into the shape she wished. Marlene's first job after graduate school "seemed like the best job in the world and it turned out to be a disaster—the wrong job with the wrong person. It was a dream job—setting up a women's health center. Looking back on it, I was ignorant of the political stuff and a little bit naive. So it was a hard experience, but it helped me figure out what kind of place I needed to be in. I left after six months." Given her hopes and dreams for her new occupation, this failure shook Marlene, but she was able at that point to reflect and change rather than to hold on at any cost or to abandon her enterprise in despair. She found another, more suitable job.

Marlene's decision to stay in New York and marry Jerry meant that she and Ben had to work out a bicoastal custody of Simon. They decided to have him spend two years in each household, but after some years, Simon had more of his own say in how he would arrange his life. Reworking their relationship was emotionally wearing, and a brief period of family therapy helped. When I saw her at this period, Simon was enrolled in high school in New York, with a plan to continue to live there. Marlene felt their greatest strength as a family was their capacity to talk together about things. She felt that she and Simon have "a great relationship," that she and Ben were still working out the parenting with respect and harmony, and that Simon had settled into the blended family well. "But it's more difficult than anyone imagines—all the different dynamics of the different relationships."

Marlene at age 43 was content, but she didn't idealize her life. She no longer seemed to require that life be perfect. Mothering a baby at this age was harder than she had thought it would be, even though she badly wanted to do it. "I just don't have the patience I had—the patience I had even when Simon was little. And I'm having trouble with a toddler—the demands. And she's not a terrible kid, but sometimes at the end of the day, if I hear 'Mommy,' you know. . . I just don't feel like I have the patience I should have." Some of this came from Marlene trying to juggle work and mothering. She worked three days a week and continued without a break after her daughter joined the family. But she felt the tug of her professional connection on the one side and her daughter's needs on the other. Daily, she engineered judicious and painful compromises. "I feel all the things I wish I had time to do in terms of work and career. I feel I go to work and see my patients because that's all I can deal with. It's not what I thought I would be doing in terms of going to professional things, things I wish I could do politically. I beat myself up for not doing this and not doing that, and I'm completely exhausted."

Meanwhile, Jerry's work had gotten more involving and was taking more of his time. That left more housework for Marlene, and she often resented this and wished that he were more involved in the family—that he would lose himself playing with the baby for hours the way Ben had. But she basked in Jerry's love, so her complaints were dwarfed by her overall sense of his cherishing her.

Marlene's work as a nurse-practitioner gave her a sense of purpose and effectiveness she always wished for. "I feel like I can help really influence women's lives. Birth control, what are they doing to protect themselves from AIDS? Or they have a partner who is abusing them, who refuses to use condoms and what does that mean for that woman—how does he feel about her? What is that message? How does she feel about herself? I see a lot of women doing a lot of risky things. I think I can really work with people in terms of making some positive changes."

Having created what she had been searching for in her life, Marlene was even more in pursuit of her roots than ever before. She felt increasingly aware of the meaning she had in her parents' lives, and, no longer having them to talk to, she grew closer to her relatives in Israel. Only in this interview did Marlene tell me that she has a half-brother there.

"My parents had such a different life. We didn't have a shared experience— they didn't know what it was like to be in school here or to grow up here, and I used to have this feeling like I was raising myself. Both my parents died years ago and even more so in the last 10 years I feel how their [Holocaust] experience has shaped my experience, my identity. Well, some of it is positive in the sense that it was re-establishing a family again, so I sort of carry the family line. And it feels like a responsibility I gladly take on, the heritage and the memories. My birth continued it on. A lot of it was kind of bad—that feeling I had of being cut off and them not sharing things with me. I don't ever remember them telling me about it but I knew about it. . . . And now that my parents are dead I have all these questions about their family and my family and what happened, and there's no way to get those answers and it's become more and more of an issue in the last 10 years. Part of it is having children, the other part is just trying to seek my roots. I also am at an age that I can remember when my mother was at my age, and I'm trying to grapple with what her experience might have been like, but there's too many holes and too many gaps and I can't quite fill it all in."

More certain of herself and her own life path, Marlene sought more and more to place her life in the larger context of her parents' life and of history. This is one more thread not yet woven fully into the tapestry Marlene was creating. Identity revision for Marlene was a process of letting a part of herself go, then pulling it back toward her when she could see a place for it. She put her intelligence and competence on hold while she sought a secure relationship with a man, then had to leave her son behind for awhile as she reclaimed her ability and prepared for a profession. She couldn't claim her parents or their meaning in her life until she felt a more solid sense of embeddedness in her culture and her life. For her, then, searching and integrating was an ongoing process.

Asked about how she had most changed over the past 10 years, Marlene defined her changes in terms of being able to know and express her feelings. "Sometimes it takes me awhile to recognize a feeling and figure out where it is coming from. I used to just dismiss it or rationalize or ignore, and I try not to do that now. I feel better able to know what I want and need and able to ask for it."

Age 53

Marlene's account of herself at age 53 is a narrative of stability and fulfillment. "Well, I'm working in the same place. Basically doing the same thing. That's been really stable, and that's been great. I mean that continues to be really fulfilling and just a great job. Still a nurse-practitioner doing the same job. And I realize it takes about 10 years to get really competent. So I'm at the point now where it's really comfortable. I don't really come across anything that really throws me. So that little piece of stress is just gone. And I've had patients that I've seen now for 17 years who maybe were teenagers when I first saw them and now it's their third child or second husband or, you know, whatever. Just going through these lifecycle things. So that's great. And it's still part time and that works out really well. And, my son graduated from high school, graduated from college, is now home. He has turned out to be an absolutely wonderful adult. I've loved having him at home, and he's sort of okay with it. It's okay for now. And my daughter is 13, we just had her Bat Mitzvah and she's kind of a teenager and she's always been kind of a handful and a difficult kid and maybe a little better now than she was when she was 3, and, you know, she's sort of developing into a nice young lady. So things are still busy with family stuff, you know, shlepping her around to lessons and stuff, and we're trying to figure out what to do with her for high school. My husband is still doing the same thing. And his career has really taken off, he is very preeminent in his field. And the nice thing that happens is that he gets invited all over the world to give talks. So we have really been to a lot of places—China and Australia, Europe several times, Mexico. And my job is really flexible, so all I need to do is tell them that I'm leaving on such and such a week, so that's all worked out really well. Um, the dog is four-and-a-half—my new baby and she's a very special part of the family. So that's what's been going on with me. It feels like a time of just kind of gently moving through with no great upheavals or major crises."

Marlene was still living in Brooklyn, in a comfortable townhouse. Having more time available now that her daughter was older, Marlene was contemplating doing something more political, more aimed at influencing wider issues, like reproductive rights. With some humor, Marlene told me that her life was actually kind of "boring" these past 10 years in the sense that it has been smooth and without crisis, just "good, really good." There have been the occasional struggles with the kids, but she has weathered those. Her son "was a pretty good kid, but even the good ones, you know, they total your car, you know, sort of those little worries. Is he going to survive high school? Am I going to survive high school?" And her daughter, who is highly willful, continues to try her patience, less than when she was a toddler, but still Marlene feels they are better off when they have time away from one another. She remembers being happy to leave her at daycare and go off to work. She enjoys her more now that she is older and keeps her focus on the "great woman" she hopes her daughter will be. With Jerry, there is some tension about his "work–home balance," but she tries to be judicious in picking the issues to struggle with him about, accepting that his work comes before the family.

Marlene was comfortable during our meeting and I felt her ease with herself (and with me). At this stage, she began her life story in college when, it seemed to her, the world took shape. She spoke of the exciting atmosphere or the late '60s, early '70s—anti-War, SDS, drugs, sex, the Women's Movement—merging her own experience with the experiences of her generation. The thread of her own life story was about figuring out what she really wanted to do, and she sees this experience of searching recreated in her son's current experience. "I wanted to have a real job and do something professional that made sense to me and that I would enjoy and it was sort of the decision kind of delayed 10 years. Some people make that decision in their 20s or coming out of college and I didn't. I didn't have to really." She now narrates that stressful decade as a period of freedom—young and single, free to do whatever she wanted. The major turning point, as she now sees her life, was finding a vocation, making the decision to study far from her son and later creating a new, blended family. The only regret she could name was not having had a larger family, but she acknowledged that she isn't sure how she would have handled that, especially given how challenging she felt that raising her daughter has been. At the time of this interview, Marlene felt her life in balance, her wishes fulfilled.

In a quiet way, Marlene had continued to try to integrate and understand her parents' history, but this part of her identity remained, as she put it, "in the closet." She shared with very few people her parents' traumatic past even as she continued to learn about it. "You know, my parents were Holocaust survivors and . . . and, uh, it's strange now for me to look back and think that at the time it didn't have any impact at all. You know, I had no perspective on it, but now when I look back, you know, there's a lot of painful memories there. Not specific memories, but just um, you know, I look back and I go, you know, that was pretty significant and that's something that I don't venture into a whole lot. . . . I think of it now as coming from a very wounded family. Not in the sense of dysfunctional kind of family, but just in the true sense that my parents obviously had all kinds of tragedies and issues in their lives that I was really not in touch with when I was younger but now when I look back and I think of what they went through, um, it had a greater impact on me. . . . As I've gotten older and I've had children myself I can begin to sort of relate to what it could have been like to have been separated from your family and have your spouse and children, you know, killed and um. . . . I feel like I can begin to feel it now. And, you know, there was always total silence about that."

Marlene told me tearfully about her much-older half brother dying in Israel last year, visiting his children and discovering photos and documents about her father's first (murdered) family. "So there's a lot of old pain and issues about that [sobbing]. But, clearly, when I was growing up, it didn't have that effect. I just felt we were a boring suburban family." I asked about the long-term impact she felt this had. In much pain, she told me how she wished she could have talked to her parents about their experiences: "If they were alive . . . [cries] just a lot of loose ends. . . . I think I definitely realized how much I have not dealt with it. It's a piece I have just sort of pushed away. Definitely has a lot of emotion. . . . Just a lot of sadness. The grief, the loss. . . . That's all I can say now. . . . The sense of always knowing that my parents were Holocaust survivors but never having a clear memory of having the conversation. . . . I always knew not to ask. Not in a conscious way. And I think also, the whole teenage thing about not wanting to be different. So at that stage, there is nothing my parents could even have told me that I would have wanted to sit down and listen to. I think by the time I was old enough to want to explore that, they weren't around."

This painful knowledge doesn't fit with her experience or her memory. "I had a very happy childhood. There was a lot of love in my house and um, you know, I was very aware of the advantages of being an only child at times, which to me was great. Even though now, you know, feeling like it wasn't. And my parents gave me everything they could possibly give me. And I had a great time in high school and enjoyed my friends and felt completely normal."

I did not tell her that, from the perspective of what she had told me years before, her early life was colored by trying to feel "normal," by trying to overcome the distance she felt from her agemates given that her parents were so different from theirs. From my psychological view of her development, this led to her over-reliance on others for self-definition and her long struggle to find her own self. (But I know that we all shape life narratives that we can live with.)

I had asked all of my participants, at each interview, to tell me their two earliest memories. Marlene repeated the same one at each time period, each told somewhat differently:

> *From about age 2½, told at age 21:* Running up and down a staircase in an apartment building—yelling and hearing an echo—a lot of people my parents knew lived there.
>
> *From about age 2½, told at age 43:* In the apartment building where I was born, there was a large entryway and a large marble or tile staircase and when people walked on it, it made this echo-y sound.

As Marlene ages, the echo moves closer to her sense of home, and she moves from actively creating the echo to simply hearing it. Throughout her life, Marlene has had the echoes of her family's past to make sense of, and she has largely distanced herself from them. She tried to keep her focus on the future, making use of all the resources that she could discover. For now, as she ages, Marilyn wants to understand those echoes by trying to think and feel about what it might have been like for her parents to have the lives they had and, by doing so, to locate herself and her own identity in the wider frame of her life history. But, so far, this is a very private matter.

REGINA

Age 21

Regina, in college, was very clear about her career plans, but searching in relationship to everything else. Always having been an A+ student but a shy and awkward child who read a lot, she wanted to get a PhD in sociology and had been accepted to a doctoral program. For financial reasons, she was still living at her family's home in a small rural town not far from the big state university she attended. She was in the process of forming religious and political ideas. Her parents had changed religions when she was in high school, so she didn't have a sense of a family religion and was trying different churches to see what belief system suited her. She was a keen observer of the political ferment of the times but wasn't sure where she could fit with it. The big area of search for Regina was in relationships with men. She felt terribly guilty about her limited sexual involvements, and she related to men hesitantly. She felt unsure of herself as a woman, ambivalent about playing hyperfeminine games, wanting to be respected for her intelligence, but fearing that this would put men off. At the same time, she found herself falling into a pattern of letting a boyfriend think for her; then she would break up with him to date others only to fall back in the same pattern. Or she would date someone for a while and then become disappointed in him. Her favorite book and favorite fantasy was *Jane*

Eyre, the woman who gets the man she loves over those who are beautiful and popular. Her identity struggle in college, then, was one of locating herself in relationships and, secondarily, in beliefs.

Regina derived strength from an intense closeness to and support from her mother. But her mother led an isolated, somewhat socially phobic life and was in no way a model for her. Her father was a distant, fearful figure who took no interest in her until she began accomplishing scholastically. Neither parent had gone to college, but her father respected success. She emulated his rationality, but felt he was cold.

When I saw her in college, I felt that beneath all the conflict she was feeling in college, there was a very solid person, anchored in her conviction of her intellectual ability. She told me she was aware that she was about to leave home for the first time and that, from here on, the future would be "all up to me."

Age 33

When I met her at age 33, Regina had earned a doctorate in sociology and was developing an academic career. She had found a church that espoused a "spiritual humanism which meets my need to escape the emptiness in daily life when it lacks a centeredness, and provides a connectedness to others." Similarly, her political beliefs felt clear as she became increasingly committed to a feminist orientation. She had married Roger, who she met in the first days of graduate school. Through these years, Regina felt herself clearly pursuing a path of her own making, a path that seemed promising and, most of all, right for her. She was trying to elaborate her academic interests and wasn't sure whether, with her strong career orientation, the sacrifices involved in having children were "worth it."

After several years of marriage, she began to feel that Roger was not all that she needed. Although they were "best friends," their sexual life together was sorely lacking. Roger was relatively uninterested in sex, not romantic, and Regina found herself craving more intimacy and passion in her life. In her early 30s, Regina had a turbulent but secret affair that raised soul-searching questions about whether she wanted to stay in her marriage, whether it could be improved, whether she wanted to have children with Roger—or if she should leave and start again. After a long period of psychotherapy, she decided to stay in the marriage and try to make it work, but the doubts and discomfort never fully abated. At this age, Regina had found a clear occupational and spiritual identity but, as in college, was in conflict about how she wanted to be a woman.

Age 43

By age 43, Regina was more settled on a well-marked path. Now the mother of two children under four, one of whom is seriously intellectually and developmentally disabled, Regina's identity was grounded among the markers of work, family, and spirituality. Regina was promoted to professor and had established a national reputation as an expert on women in the criminal justice system. She had found good care for her cognitively challenged son and managed to meet his special needs. Her religious questing led her to convert several years ago to Episcopalianism, a religion that "offers me a deepening of my relationship with God. Religious practice is a way of opening channels within my self to broader spiritual experiences and broader connections with other people." She and Roger built a house in the woods near the university town where they lived. All the pieces of her complex and challenging life felt in place, and this despite the fact that Regina had undiagnosable periods of intense fatigue and pain.

But Regina continued to experience internal cycles of searching, of thinking about redoing her life. At age 43, she described her 20-year marriage to Roger as "loving, committed and stable but profoundly unsatisfying." Looking back, she wondered if perhaps they married out of a need not to be alone. "We were pretty frightened, pretty anxious, and pretty defensive about life in general and maybe we thought that we could protect each other. And we did know each other pretty well at that point in time. . . . I think we fit together as a couple much better now. We've made some major decisions in terms of having a family. I think we work better together in planning our lives, working out daily details, helping each other manage the details of everyday life." They had given up on sex altogether. Regina regretted that she lost the chance to really experience herself as a woman. "It's almost like I had to put everything else on hold if I was going to escape the kind of compromised life my mother had had," referring to her fear of being trapped into traditional female roles. But she was no closer to knowing what to do about her marriage. When I asked her why she has chosen at each period of crisis to remain in her marriage, she said, thoughtfully, "I don't leave relationships easily. And the establishment of a home and family have provided me with a stabilizing influence. We work well together and are friends. But in a deep sense, I don't know."

Age 56

At age 56, Regina was delighted to participate in the interview. She said that she reflects on herself and her life every day, so telling me about herself seemed "consistent"—and it was nice to have someone to do this with. I was astounded by Regina's appearance. Tall and thin, with long dark hair, she looked much younger than her age.

In the intervening years, Regina had become a deacon at her church, and her work was about integrating her academic pursuits with her spiritually framed social justice interests. She was as active in church activities as she was as a professor. The projects she undertook involved her students in community action, trying to work with disadvantaged groups and put theory into practice.

Regina framed her recent years as herself having become a "completely different person." I never fully understood what she meant by this because what she described seemed to me to be a continuous evolution. Looking back, she saw herself up to her late 30s as having been "robotic." She was doing what was expected of her—publishing what was needed for academic advancement, jumping through all the necessary hoops. "I spent a lot of my 30s feeling like a robot, feeling like I was operating behind a mask. My marriage wasn't happy. I was working far too much. I didn't have a life that was meaningful. My paid work wasn't that meaningful. I just felt compelled to work and establish myself professionally. I had to prove to myself—and I didn't get much joy from it. When I would get recognition and awards, there'd be a sense of shock: They liked it. That's all changed dramatically since then. My husband and I went through some extensive marital [therapy] work and we reaffirmed our relationship. So we've been married 28 years now and we've been a couple for 35 years. Then we had children and that was the beginning of the transformation." Having a son with special needs meant "learning a whole new way to do life."

Now, she said she was living more deliberately, more guided by her own aims, making her own choices. Combining her teaching and her ministry had been an act of creativity, and she derived satisfaction from seeing her doctoral students engaged in meaningful projects—and meeting with them for seminars in Starbucks. She was doing things her own way, becoming a mentor for her students rather than a distant, formal teacher.

The structure of her life changed as the needs of her son changed, as they gradually came to better understand his various diagnoses and challenges. He needs constant supervision so, although he is a teenager, she still needs babysitters if they go out. There was a period when he had violent outbursts at home, and they had to learn to manage that. And, at each stage, they had to find appropriate schooling and help for him. I was struck that Regina spoke about all these challenges in such a measured, calm way—they were problems that she solved as best she could. The interview was punctuated by moments in which she recalled things her son enjoyed—a movie, a joke—and it was clear to me that she took pleasure in experiencing the world through his eyes.

Regina's daughter is not such a challenge. She is sensitive and gifted ("She has my soul"), and Regina revels in their close relationship.

Harder to describe, perhaps, was the way in which her spiritual life "has really developed." A new priest at her church inspired her in many ways, including her decision to take the training to become a deacon. This is unpaid work, but she can perform various ceremonies like baptisms and marriages, give sermons, and lead bible study. She feels that she clarified "that this is who I was becoming—that my life was going to be more about service. My work has become less about producing and more about loving and nurturing students and developing projects in the community. . . . And, in our church, a very strong emphasis on caring about each other, tending to people who are in need." For Regina, her spiritual stance has been transformative. "My life was too self-centered and I felt there was something I could do even with my limited energy. One of my personal beliefs is that we are called to contribute the best we can, whatever that is, and my feeling was that I could use my thinking capacity in this direction. My ordination was not about my being this holy person but more about saying that I believe in the Church as an institution that is dedicated to trying to make people's lives better."

The doubts about her marriage and about being a woman that had plagued her in the past now seemed resolved. "The relationship with Roger over the years has become very satisfying as a much deeper companionship. There's still not the passion there, but that's no longer important to me." They parent well together, and they share the projects in the church.

Looking back, Regina now thinks she was depressed for many years—overworking to prove she was okay, functioning well but joylessly. With the help of a good therapist—and medication for both depression and pain—she feels she came to accept herself and to stop having to prove herself in a driven way.

From the time they were in college, most of the Searchers, like Regina, struggle to balance often-warring parts of themselves. Outwardly, they may appear certain and committed, but internally, they must wrestle with inner confusion which, once quelled, only reappears and requires renewed resolution. They may have successful careers, but they struggle against feeling like an imposter and labor to convince themselves that they are doing their best. The deeper, knottier problems of identity lie in relationship, in belief, and in feeling at home in who they are. Their paths, now marked and clear, are nevertheless dotted with doubt and remain open to continual refashioning.

Searchers Who Settled Down Early

For some, the opened-up, questioning, soul-searching period that flourishes in the college environment evaporates as they take their diplomas. Some of the Searchers found that when college ended, the search seemed to end as well. So they headed home—emotionally if not also physically. They had tried their wings a bit during college, but once that ended, they sought firm ground and took the bus to what was familiar. Interviewing them after college, I often couldn't tell whether they were choosing on their own terms or fleeing into what seemed safe—and available. Rather than find answers to the questions they had been asking themselves during college, these women simply turned their backs on them. They resolved the dilemmas of the conflicts between their parents' expectations and their own desires by muting that part of themselves that was finding its own voice. Separation anxiety or guilt often unconsciously overwhelmed the striving for something new. They returned to the world of their parents, sometimes with a small space carved out for their own decision-making.[3]

NORMA

Age 21

Norma, in college, was not a typical Searcher, but she fit this category better than any of the others. People, after all, don't sort themselves neatly into the categories that we psychologists create. She had chosen her university, near to her home, because her high school friends were going there. Neither of her parents were college-educated; her mother was the only one in her family to complete high school. Her mother was "a housewife, because that's what Dad wants." Inspired by a junior high school teacher, Norma had always wanted to become a teacher and was paying her own way through college because her parents didn't see the point of college for a woman. She was engaged and planning to marry soon after she graduated. She had a fairly clear life plan— marry, save for a house, start a family, and return to teaching when her children were in school. She had formed her religious beliefs on her own terms, which, in addition to a strong belief in God, were much like the general disengagement of her parents from organized religion. Completely apolitical, she hadn't voted in the election because she didn't even know where to register. In matters of sexuality she was experiencing some conflict, wanting to follow the "Puritanism" of her family but sleeping with her fiancé "once in a while" and feeling very guilty. She was also questioning the roles of women, becoming aware that women were discriminated against and feeling that this wasn't right. So there were glimmers of independence of mind that suggested that Norma had moved out of the Guardian category, but her goals and beliefs still seemed enough in transition that she wasn't a Pathmaker either.

Age 32

At age 32, Norma had returned to her home town, a small, rural community in Iowa, had married, and was teaching in the local high school. Her political and religious beliefs had not changed but she was more involved in the Church than her parents had been. Her main concern at this age was dealing with what she felt was limited opportunity for career advancement. She had earned a master's degree and received a number of teaching awards and honors—but there was nowhere else to go in her school system. She saw herself teaching the same classes for the rest of her career, and she experienced this as thwarted ambition.

The focal point of her life was her husband, and she tried to organize the extra work she did at school so she was never away from home when he was there. They enjoyed sailing together on weekends. They had been trying to have a child but had not yet succeeded. The rest of her life was centered in her extended family; she had no friends except the other teachers at school. Looking back from age 32, Norma felt that her college experiences were "eye-opening," being "exposed to Blacks, Jews, Arabs, and people from other cultures and beliefs." It was not clear what Norma was doing with these more open eyes, but she experienced the change internally—she had, at least for a time, been in a wider world. Comparing herself to her family at this age, she felt different from them in having modern appliances and "being more impressed with status due to education and money."

Age 43

By age 43, Norma had three children and had moved into a counseling position at school; she took no time off from work after the births of her children, largely for financial reasons, but also because she liked her counseling work. She was still reveling in her "good relationship" with her husband and feeling that she was continuing to grow with him, especially as they expanded to be parents together. "We center all activities around work and the children. It is still a marriage based on common interests, friendship, and love." Their oldest child was born with limited sight and required special care, both socially and medically. She spoke of coming to terms with her parents' eventual mortality.

At this point, Norma was fully engaged in her job and described the stresses involved in keeping peace among warring parties at the school and helping the children she worked with manage difficulties in their lives. Still she felt the tug of ambition and wished to get further education so she could become a principal. But her husband thought that she should be devoting her time to the family and resisted the idea of her getting a doctorate.

Norma felt aware of being an "older mother" and the challenge of keeping up with a three-year-old at her age. This sense of "older" seemed to distinguish her from the others in her town. Focusing on her children felt like a way of coping with the stresses of work. She tried not to bring her work home mentally. But, she said, "I rarely have time alone for myself." While she felt that her views on child-rearing were the same as her parents', she felt she was more lenient with her children than her parents had been with her. "I am a product of my family," she said, and she still turned to them for emotional support. She saw herself as different from them only in her having a microwave, dishwasher, and VCR. Norma had indeed gone home again, but her occupational ambition seemed to me to be a marker of difference, even though she did not identify herself this way. Rather, she saw herself as carrying forward her family's ethic of hard work. At age 43, she looked back at her college years with fondness and a sense that she had gained an "open-minded" view of other people. Looking forward, she was anticipating retirement in 10 years, being more relaxed with a slower pace of life and "having my children grown, happy, healthy, and successful." Reflecting on her life thus far, the greatest satisfaction was "helping my children and the children at school become happy and successful." She recalled with joy the students she had in class who "came back to tell me of the part I had in their accomplishment."

Age 56

By age 56, Norma had become a middle school principal, having gotten a specialist certificate but not the doctorate that continued to elude her. Still, she took pride in her role as a community leader and of having learned about building permits, boilers, parking lots, and all the other administrative matters that fell to her. She was an involved principal, sitting with the students in classes and managing the various interpersonal clashes of her large roster of teachers and support staff. And her open-minded orientation was useful when it came to dealing with differences, the greatest of which were generational; she even had to manage her own "old-fashioned" attitudes.

Norma was planning to retire in two years, although she was eligible already. "I want to be a housewife for a little bit. That would be a new luxury and a new experience in my life." There was so much in the house that she wanted to have taken care of, and there had never been the time. "I could get into doing volunteer work and do some things that I want to do when I want, instead of when I have to." In some ways, Norma seemed worn out by the pace of life she had maintained all these years. "I'm such a wreck during the school year because I leave home at 6:30 and a lot of times I don't get home until 6 o'clock at night and then there are a lot of evening meetings. It's just a very busy, busy schedule. I think I would enjoy a change of pace." I could find no regrets as she contemplated leaving her work. She has been involved in fundraising for a number of organizations and could see herself doing more of this.

Norma has grounded herself in a kind of hard-headed practicality that has led to a number of leadership positions. "I focus on what needs to be done at the time and how can we best get it done, and how does it solve a problem. And that's the satisfaction I get out of it." From the stories she told me about her various activities, I gathered that Norma was someone people relied on to figure out "what goes on in organizations and to help move it along." She seemed to be good at getting people to work together and to smooth over differences. With a lot of modesty, Norma admitted, "Yeah, it's something that I seem to have some strengths in." Sitting with her, I felt this strength—she clearly seemed to me to be someone who could manage difficulties. While balancing her need to be busy with the needs of her family, Norma also strove over the years to "expand my horizons" beyond her school and her family, and the community work filled this need.

Her children were now either in college or about to graduate from high school, and she was pleased with their development. Her middle child was rebellious despite their attempts to keep her too busy to get into trouble. Still, she seemed to be the one straying from home in ways that made Norma uncomfortable. By contrast, her oldest daughter, the one who was visually impaired, was "the one that follows the rules. In fact, she would follow the rules sometimes to the nth degree when sometimes she should relax a little bit. But we try to maintain her independence." Indeed, it sounded to me like Norma and her husband had done an excellent job of helping her get the help she needed and, at the same time, promote her living on her own. So, it seemed to me, Norma had the rule-bound, moralistic outlook of the Guardians but with more flexibility to account for individual needs—and she was able to let go of her children as they strove for independence. But their own lives still revolved around participating in their children's many activities—soccer, sailing regattas, orchestras. "We've always been very involved with our kids in that respect. We give them their space, but at the same time we like supporting them."

Looking back on her life, Norma said, "I think I have accomplished more than I hoped to accomplish. Because going back to when I was a 21-year-old, fresh out of college, if you were to ask me at that point in time: will I have done everything that I have done in my life, I would have probably told you "no." Because you don't see the things that are out there, the possibilities. I think you look at the immediate goal and achieve that goal. And then as that goal is achieved, then you start looking at other things." Indeed, that is the story of Norma's life—fulfill one goal, find a new challenge, all the while maintaining balance with her family's needs. Norma doesn't feel that her values have changed at all since she was five years old. She has just learned to articulate better a morality based on Christian values and live by it. She assesses politicians at election time in terms of their moral stance. At the same time, she has learned to relax her moralism in dealing with people in her school. There are difficult parents, for example, who teachers refuse to work with. "They're not bad people, they just handle the world differently. When they come in and you work with them, and they walk out at least understanding a different point of view."

Norma is still satisfied with her marriage. She tells me that they have had to work through differences over the years and have done so successfully. The biggest challenge has been about the management of finances because she is conservative and her husband is a risk-taker. He likes to gamble for recreation. "I define how much he can gamble and, when he starts winning, we have an agreement. I collect what he invested, and he plays on the winnings. See—I'm the stable, solid bank person"—and this seemed completely consistent with how I had come to know her.

Thinking about herself in the context of the extended family, both her own and her husband's, Norma identifies herself as different from them in terms of encouraging more independence for her children. Both her brother's family and her husband's siblings "are more protective of their children, almost cocooning, protect against the world, don't let them do anything that might expose them to anything that's worldly. Uh . . . whereas our values . . . we've raised them with a good core values system. You know what our expectations are, what we feel is very wrong. Now, we have to have faith that . . . my policy is, I can't do that for you forever. You need to get out and be involved in things and experience the world and not be part of mom and dad." My interpretation of Norma saying this was that the issue of individuation—how far one can go internally from home—has been a lifelong one for her, now experienced in terms of her children. Over the years, her ambivalence about this, although superficially resolved, has remained. While occupationally successful and self-directed, Norma has, in large measure, gone home.

At this interview, Norma told me more about her early life. Her mother was "very strict, kept the yardstick at hand" and did not hesitate to use it if she or her brother disobeyed her. "That nagging fear that was instilled early on was, you know, the punishment thing. I think it is still there. And always will be." Norma added that times have changed and "probably in this day and age, you get hauled into court" for the physical punishment her mother meted out. But there seemed to be no anger or outrage at her mother about this— Norma understood that this was a product of the times, the culture, and her mother's own troubled background. "I think that kind of treatment instilled in me the need to meet her expectations, and maybe because of that, being able to do well in school, doing well at everything I try to do. And, you know, if you're gonna do something, you do it the right way, you do it well." While she is more lenient with her children, Norma credits her mother: "What she did with me also made me a strong enough person to say that I'm the parent." She had always admired her mother and felt she had become much like her— strong, confident, insisting on what she thought was right.

Norma described her father, who could not read, as home very little— always travelling for his work. He had little influence on her and did not mitigate her mother's power over her. At each interview that I had with her, Norma told me about her high school math teacher who encouraged her educational goals and set an example for the kind of teacher she wanted to be. It was only when I met her at this later age that I began to understand how important he was in helping her achieve the individuation that led to her occupational path. Norma went home again and, in many ways, resembled the Guardians, but she had a professional path that was her own and that she managed to integrate with taking her preassigned, but more open-minded, place in the extended family.

Drifting Searchers

The dividing line between the Searchers and the Drifters is a fuzzy one. The groups share an absence of commitments, and what distinguishes the two categories are signs of active efforts to make commitments—some plans, however hazy, some dreams that they try to realize. For some of these women, evidence of searching was some loosening of ties to a childhood self, as we saw in Norma, a loosening that might just have been temporary. But some of the women in this group had no strong ties to a childhood self to loosen. They were women who just adapted to the next task in life, trying to do well at what was set before them, but without commitment to a defined sense of self. Some of these women were caught in internal struggles with self-esteem, with conflict with one or both parents or with emotional upheaval, and they couldn't get in focus the task of defining themselves or who they might become.

Unable to imagine a life that might suit them, these women suited themselves to what presented itself to them. And this strategy had varying outcomes. Some adapted themselves and felt content. Others simply drifted along, often suffering from a life that didn't satisfy them, but doing the best they could—much as we will see in the Drifter group.

LAURA

Laura gave me pause and seemed in a group of her own as a Searcher who drifted into a completely contented life, close to home but not in a Guardian sort of way. Even into late midlife, Laura felt that she never made any critical decisions in her life. Life just kind of happened, but turned out well. Laura felt that her life just flowed, one thing into the next, without her steering it in any particular directions.

AGE 21

Laura was a cute college senior with a little-girl quality about her, but she was trying hard to grow up, thinking deeply about her life and her relationships. She walked with a slight limp that resulted from a deformed foot and early childhood polio, but she did not think of herself as disabled or handicapped. Laura had felt pushed into college by her working-class parents who wanted at least one of their five children to succeed by this standard. Her being in college, she felt, was her mother's "one big accomplishment in life." But once there, she had become interested in her studies and, as graduation approached, was thinking of applying to graduate school in public health. But this wasn't something she wanted to "rush into." She wanted to take time to think it over. She had decided to work for a year to earn money for graduate school and to be able to live on her own in their mid-sized city in Indiana.

As she was graduating from college, Laura was at the beginning of a struggle for separation and autonomy that many of the other Searchers had undertaken long before. She was starting to break away from her mother, wondering how much longer she would continue to go to church to please her mother. She was frightened about sex, but curious and readying herself to define things in her own way. She was clear, though, that she couldn't become sexually active until she left home. "I couldn't make love to someone and then go home to my own bed."

What was most troubling Laura as the end of college approached was that she had never fallen in love. Oh, she had had crushes and infatuations, but nothing ever grew into what she could think of as love. "I hope that one day it will hit me like a brick wall," but she was worried. Despite her talk of graduate school and independence, her frustrated wish for love seemed to be Laura's emotional center.

Laura's family had moved around a great deal while she was growing up, and her younger sister had always been her best friend. More outgoing than she, her sister made friends and was willing to share them with Laura. Deeply, unconsciously, Laura seemed to long to repeat this sense of an intense two-some, bonded against whatever life disruptions might befall them. This was her fantasy of marriage, but she hadn't yet found a suitable man. Her primary concern in the interview was about romantic relationships—she read romances, had secret attractions, imagined herself married even while doing the laundry. She dated, but never felt love, and she was clear she would only marry for love. Worriedly trying to reassure herself, she was reminding herself that one of her aunts, unmarried, had a good life even without marriage.

Midlife

Shortly after graduation, however, Laura did fall in love—with a man she described at age 33 as "an attractive man, a very nice man, a very quiet man, very much like my father and very much like me." They formed an ardent couple and married several months later. At age 33, Laura was centered on her husband and very proud of their relationship. She boasted that they had never had a fight and the only negative thing about their relationship was that they never got enough time together. "I can't imagine anything I would want of marriage that isn't there. I think in every area of my life my husband has a part. He is totally supportive of me in my personal life and with my work experiences. If I'm pissed off at work and can't stand it and say I want to quit, he says, 'Fine, quit.' We are open and honest with each other—if we have something to talk about, something we're worried about, something we're afraid of, we can go to each other and talk about it. We respect each other, and that's a big part of why we're able to have such a good marriage." Although her husband had a similar family background and was raised a Catholic, he had no interest in the church, so Laura gave this up as well.

They had decided they didn't want children. "We sort of baby each other," Laura said. After college, she had taken a job in medical technology, answering the call of a friend who worked there when the service was short-staffed. She was trained on the job and was still there when I interviewed her at age 33—and at age 43—and on into her early retirement in her late 50s. She never defined herself by her work; it was a job, and she did it well, retraining as the technology advanced. She hardly ever missed a day. "If there is a job to be done, you do it—this is what I learned in my family." In the last interview I had with her at age 60, Laura recalled her thoughts about graduate school and told me that she never felt she was smart enough and simply didn't have the drive. At age 33, she had told me that she liked her job but found it somewhat repetitive and boring, doing the same medical tests all the time, and hoped she would be doing something different in 10 years. But in the later interviews, she had simply accepted that this was her work and didn't mention hopes for anything else. When a buyout was offered in her late 50s, she took it, having wearied of the interpersonal struggles at work and also some mysterious panic attacks that had begun to plague her on the job.

Laura lived for and within her marriage, and their needs as a couple took center stage. In their late 30s, her husband had become fed up with the long hours and pressure of his managerial job. In her age 43 interview, Laura explained, "He decided to quit and was going to take a little break before he went back out into the workforce, but what happened was that we both really got to the point where we really liked him being at home. He's a wonderful cook, and all the kinds of things that one has to do at home—laundry, grocery shopping—I'm not really suited for that—I have some physical limitations which make some of those things kind of difficult for me. He didn't mind doing it and so he's still doing it. He works part-time doing odd jobs. This is really nice for me because I really don't do anything other than go to work. He does everything else at the house. I think at the beginning it was a little difficult for me because I was concerned what people would think of him, that they would think less of him. I wasn't concerned that they approved of the way we worked this out, but that they wouldn't think of him as highly as I think he ought to be thought of. He's extremely intelligent, he's a wonderful loving husband and what some people might think who don't really know us—I know that people who know us understand what we're doing, but I didn't want people to think badly about him. I talked to him about this because we talk about everything and he didn't care what other people think. I'm rather happy with the way we've worked out our life and rather proud, to be perfectly honest. We don't feel that he has to go out and get a job so we can make big money. It's not what we're all about." Their needs were simple ones, they had most of what they wanted, and "expensive toys are not that important."

The rest of Laura's life revolved around helping her sisters who had some difficult times. And they had two dogs that Laura feels have "helped me to become a better person. Simply because I'm aware that others have needs and I can satisfy these needs." What she has wanted most out of life is "to be a good person and to be and to have been a loving wife."

In late mid-life, Laura told me she has never been an "out there" person. She and her husband have built a loving haven that they reside in quietly, content just to be together. Since her retirement, she spends her days planning dinner, her husband having returned to work and given the cooking task back to her. Or she plays with their dogs or reads. In her reading, Laura seeks out mysteries or stories about women who have adventures and who take risks. She admires these women. But that is not what she has ever wanted for herself. The center of her life has been her relationship with her husband, insular and sufficient.

In her late midlife interview, Laura told me some details that helped me make more sense of her history. The first was that her mother had had some serious mental illness as she was growing up, which accounts for Laura never having felt close to her. Both of her parents, she felt, were caring and present, but never very involved with her. Second was that because of having had polio as a child, she was given free tuition for college. Looking back, she felt she went to college (the only one in her family) because she didn't know what else to do—and it was free.

I asked her, toward the end of our talk, what her college-age self would think of the woman she had become. "I'd think I was incredibly lucky," she said, tears coming. "I found a man who thinks I'm smart and beautiful and wonderful in every way." For Laura, what else is there to desire?

At our last interview, Laura repeated an early memory, a memory she recalled telling me earlier that gave me some insight into the dynamics of ambition. The memory was "Learning to tie my shoes and being really excited about it. I remember running to tell my mother about it. She was in the basement. I called down to her. But she wasn't as excited about it as I was. I was her fourth of five kids, and I think that this probably had lost some of the charm by the time I had learned to tie my shoes. I do remember feeling disappointed that she wasn't more excited about it."

I was entranced by Laura and liked her a great deal. There was something about her self-containment and evident contentment that left me feeling happy after talking to her. She spoke easily and thoughtfully and seemed fully present. She got tearful when she spoke of something sad and seemed radiant when she talked of what brought her joy. So her serenity didn't reflect emotional constriction. She was just a person that I have never run across before (perhaps few of us have) because she keeps herself to herself—and her husband.

Persistent Inner Knots

Two of the women who had been Searchers at the end of college found themselves too tied in inner knots to form reliable identities. Unlike Laura, their efforts to find a place in the world were met by rejection. By midlife, they had lapsed into states of disorganization in which they were barely able to function, living quite circumscribed lives. By late midlife, Sandra had gotten more settled while Leslie continued to decline.

SANDRA

Sandra, who I described at the beginning of this chapter as filled with conflict and uncertainty at the end of college, was caught between pleasing and rebelling against her father and submitting to and fighting the men she was dating. She was trying to figure out what in herself felt real—and I was shaken by the intensity of the distress she was experiencing in every part of her life as she struggled to make some plans and commitments as a college senior. Sandra was holding out for doing something that felt right to her, not to please other people. In her college interview, she said, "Right now I feel very dependent on my parents. I love them very much and I don't want to hurt them. They've done so much for me. Especially my father. I'm trying to get away from them, but they won't let me. They want to keep me there forever. . . . I want to do something but I don't even know where to begin."

By the time she was in her 30s, Sandra had settled things a bit, but in a self-contradictory way. Just after college, she followed her mother's pattern (which she thought had been disastrous for her mother) in marrying a man 20 years older than herself. She had replaced her father out of a wish to escape him. Not surprisingly, at age 33, she expressed great ambivalence about her marriage. Although it provided her with security, she felt the romance and spontaneity were gone and that her husband was "completely oblivious to my feelings." But she held on for the security and had begun to see other men. She doubted that she would ever want to be tied down to children, but hadn't yet made a final decision.

After college, Sandra began working as an administrative assistant in the business world, using her zealous conscientiousness to succeed. But although she held seven jobs in ten years, none was satisfactory. Either the pay was low or the people were unpleasant or there was no opportunity for growth, and Sandra would move on. At this point in her life, age 33, Sandra still seemed to be searching.

This search led her to psychotherapy, and, at age 43, Sandra felt that her therapy had been the most important aspect of her life in the past 10 years. She sought therapy when she finally acknowledged to herself that she had been bulimic for years. Through therapy, she felt she had come to a new understanding of her life, which involved recognizing that her parents were "seriously deficient as role models. I just became really aware of what had happened to me when I was younger. My parents never beat me or hit me or anything like that. They tried to give me everything I needed materially. My mother is a people-pleaser. And my father is a really angry man. . . . I'm very aware. I just don't know how to act on a lot of it. I come from a family of denial, I come from a dysfunctional family, whatever. . . . I have spent a lot of time trying to pay back, I guess."

Yet Sandra felt unsure of how to make use of her new awareness. After several extramarital affairs that ended badly, she valued her husband more. But the marriage was completely asexual, and she didn't know how to make her peace with that. Her mother began living with them after her father died, and this was a source of intense distress for Sandra. "She and I do a dance of pushing each other's buttons. I'm in the house for three minutes and I'm out of my mind." So her solution was to be home as little as possible. Given her Persian background, she couldn't even consider not living with her mother. "In my culture, when parents get old, you take care of them," she said.

Sandra had a pattern of getting overinvolved in her work, staying long hours. "I'm a people-pleaser like my mother and the office manager has to please everyone. It keeps my mind off my own problems." But she recognized that her people-pleasing was often in the service of her anger. "I'm a very angry person," she said, "just like my father." She had decided not to have children; she was too afraid of trying to raise them, too afraid of her anger.

At age 43, Sandra was just keeping afloat, awash in anger at her parents, particularly her mother. She had had a sequence of unsatisfactory admin-istrative jobs and was in a marriage that was constantly in turmoil. She resented her own sense of obligation to live with and take care of her mother, with whom she had battled throughout her life. Reflecting on herself at age 43, Sandra said, "I have struggled over the years to put my life together as best I can inwardly and outwardly. Outwardly I do a better job. Inwardly its tougher for me. . . . I appear to be strong but every day it's a struggle. I have to fill my life up with all sorts of things to get me through. I work out, I have a lot of friends, I take classes, I do volunteer work. I put myself on a schedule. . . . Whatever it is I can fill up the time with, I fill it up. I am fearful of having any quiet time because I don't know what I'd do with it. I don't know what it is to be relaxed. . . . I think I've been lucky not to fall apart."

When I interviewed her in her early 60s, after the death of both her mother and her husband, I found Sandra more placid and settled in a comfortable relationship, no longer feeling in danger of falling apart. But she was drifting, still hoping to find herself. Sandra had continued her long history of checkered employment, and, even approaching retirement age, she said she still hadn't figured out what occupation she wanted to pursue. Sandra still struggled with her lifelong bulimia and her unresolvable anger at those who had taunted her when she was a "fat child." The essential story of her life, Sandra told me, was being a survivor, just going on—after being the unacceptable fat kid, losing her husband in a tragic accident, and having had overbearing parents. Indeed, she seemed to have drifted into a relatively comfortable niche at age 63, finan-cially secure but endlessly nervous about money, living with a kind man with whom she shared activities but did not want to marry for reasons she couldn't detail. She kept working because doing things for others (however resentfully at times, as with her mother) kept her going. Sandra still felt fundamentally rather lost—but not without hope. She felt she had "evolved" over the years and thought perhaps she might yet find a craft that would give her satisfaction, "but I still don't know what I want to do when I grow up."

LESLIE

Leslie fared less well. Like Sandra, Leslie began to drift just after college, changing jobs frequently, feeling increasingly desperate to find acceptance when she was, as she described herself, "morbidly obese." What anchored her in her 20s was a close relationship with her family, which deteriorated when, during a course of therapy in her early 30s, she revised her understanding of her life history and recovered memories of both physical and sexual abuse. But this resulted in estrangement from her family who denied that such things had happened and were furious at her new version of events. Through much anguish and torment, Leslie, by age 43, was finally able to separate herself from them. Leslie felt that through therapy, "I was able to free myself from the prison of my abusive past," and she set about remaking her life. This process took several years. With the help of a vocational rehabilitation program, she retrained in a data management field and graduated at the top of the class. She liked the work and found that she could accommodate herself to the work conditions without the anger and distress she had always experienced in work settings. "I regained a positive self-image," she said. She and her woman partner, after a turbulent time, acknowledged their commitment to a permanent life together and had a formal wedding ceremony. They bought a house together. They decided not to have children. Leslie seemed to me at age 43 full of insight, and it seemed that she was trying to create a future path that held promise for her.

When I met her at age 55, Leslie was officially disabled, her health was deteriorating, and she rarely left the house. She was living a reclusive life with her partner in an airless house overstuffed with furniture, many dogs and cats— and a welter of birdfeeders out the window. She had been in a mental hospital numerous times. Leslie relied on her partner (but did not define herself as a lesbian) and, when she was able, helped her with her job, which she did from home. The working world had become noxious to Leslie as experiences of rejection compounded, and, at one point, she had lashed out physically at her co-workers. Controlling the expression of her anger had been a lifelong problem, but she felt that, with the help of psychotherapy, she was beginning to master this. Perceived failures in adulthood, experiences with rejection, and struggles with mental illness marked Leslie's view of herself as defective. But she was struggling to overcome these feelings of inadequacy, to learn how to relate to others—and had not given up. She was, at age 55, grounded in her relationship with her partner and the flickering hope that she garnered from her therapy. She was still searching for a way to be someone who could be valued in the world. Indeed, I was struck by the perceptiveness of her understanding of herself, and I was very touched by her perseverance. There was something about how she told me her life story that gave me hope, but I thought she had a long and difficult road ahead.

Both Sandra and Leslie described continuing problems managing anger, which made it difficult for them to contain themselves in a workplace. Fortunate to find partners who could steady them somewhat, they were still hoping to find a sense of direction, even as late as age 63 in Sandra's case. While they resembled the other Searchers in college, these women never managed to stabilize themselves. They blamed their parents even into midlife: they described themselves as always having had "low self-esteem" (in part from being fat), of having had abusive childhoods, and parents who were poor role models. Their midlife concerns were about simply getting through the day or the week. Neither had a sense of having given much to others.

Their stories were sad, particularly sad for me to hear because they had both been in psychotherapy and this had had what, to me, was limited effect. They became women whose identities were centered in a struggle to hold on, not to fall apart, in Sandra's words. Looking back at their college interviews, though, they seemed much like the other Searchers. Like them, they continued searching through their 20s and early 30s, but couldn't ground themselves in meaningful commitments like the Searchers who became Pathmakers. Nor could they return emotionally to their families like the Searchers who went home again. For these two women, home is what they felt had damaged them. They began to drift, much like the Drifters who we will meet next.

Notes

1. I followed 10 of the college-age Searchers to age 33, at which point three had clearly become Pathmakers after prolonged searching and six seemed to have largely returned to a Guardian identity, making commitments by going home again just after college, grounding themselves in the same values and lifestyle they had in childhood. One was still searching(Josselson, 1987). By age 43, I followed eight of these women, having lost track of two of those who seemed to have gone home again. I do not present the follow-up interview of Teresa, who was in acute crisis at the time I saw her (Josselson, 1996).

2. Elders was fired by President Clinton in 1994 for saying that she thought that, in order to prevent risky sexual activity, it might be appropriate to teach children masturbation.

3. See Kroger (1996) for a discussion of these processes.

6

The Drifters

Creating an identity is akin to assembling a puzzle. We all have many parts to ourselves and often contradictory feelings and wishes. We have many sides to our personalities; we are not unitary beings. The challenge of identity formation is ordering the pieces, making a border and relating the pieces to one another into a more or less coherent picture. The Drifters are distinguished from the other groups by their inability to assemble the pieces; they keep their pieces in the box, different pieces emerge at different times, but they never form a picture. In psychological language, this is a form of dissociation—parts of the self kept separate from other parts—and this form of functioning is typical of the Drifters. Unlike the Searchers who feel and articulate their conflicts, the Drifters offer me fragments which I then find it difficult to assemble (as they do as well).

Interviewing the Drifters over these many years, I persisted in trying to see what picture they were creating, and I have come to recognize that there would be no picture. Instead, they told me, interview after interview, about their various pieces. Often, their stories were not very coherent, either for me or for themselves. Why they did what they did was often inexplicable, even in retrospect. Life just happened. They were leaves blown by the winds. Their selves were fragmented. And this fragmentation had a chilling persistence over 35 years even though there were sometimes periods of stability.

Unlike the Searchers, the Drifters in college were not struggling to make commitments or plans as they approached the end of college. Nor were they juggling the pulls of the past and the promise of new forms of experience like the Pathmakers and the Guardians. They had simply stepped out of their pasts and were living only in the present. The future seemed like a far off world as they floated on the currents of the moment. Responsive to their immediate world, open to its novelties, they were expecting to fall into an interesting rabbit hole and lose themselves among its wonders.

The social climate of the late 1960s made just about anything possible. It gave the Drifters as college seniors the space and the permission to lose themselves. They could give free rein to their impulses. They could "drop out," accept being labeled as "hippies";[1] their elders, although perplexed and chagrined, regarded this as typical of the times. But, in every age, there are ways to drift.

Although some of the Drifters seemed charming free spirits, on closer examination, they were really less in control of what they were doing than it might have appeared. Rather than anticipating the place they might take— even a countercultural place—they were expecting that life would somehow happen to them. They mistook the relatively protected world of college for the larger reality of living in the adult world and were therefore at a loss for what to do next. They were avoiding rather than undertaking the work of forming identity.

As a group, the Drifters were among the most talented and privileged women I have studied. As children and teenagers, they all did well in school. They were high achievers who recounted histories of getting A's or of being recognized for their artistic talent. More than half of the women in this group were attending a highly respected private women's college, meaning that they came from families wealthy enough to send them there and were academically outstanding enough to be accepted. Their "drifting" in college was not for lack of talent or skill or resources. They were women of promise who had the opportunity to choose their future.

In addition to having no clear goals, their value systems were equally diffuse. They had cast off their religion of childhood and formed no new ideology—they didn't feel a need for one. On sexual standards, they said confusing things that reflected the absence of coherent frames in which to decide on standards or principles for their own behavior. "It all depends on the situation, the kind of environment you're in," said one. "I just get a feeling for a person and go with it," said another. Pressed to define some pattern or logic to how she decided who to have sex with, one woman thought for a while, then said brightly that she did have a standard: "I wouldn't sleep with anyone who is fat."

At pains to bring their behavior in line with some inner guidelines, they rationalized what they did and, if they felt any guilt, repressed it quickly. Jennifer, for example, spoke at age 21 about a time when she slept with a man she had just met, then wondered the next morning about whether it had been a good idea. "I kissed him and then I figured that if I had gone that far, what difference did it make?" When I asked what this incident meant about her standards or values, she said that she felt that if it was right at the time, then it must have been right later and it's silly to feel guilty.

The Drifters often felt wishes and dreams stirring in them, but the voices of their inner selves were unintelligible, hard to translate into the language of plans, beliefs, or goals. If they imagined a future at all, their hopes were fantasies rather than linked to any action that might translate them into reality.

It took Vicky 20 more years to put her feelings into language when she said, "I feel like an artist without a medium." Indeed, this description would hold for many of the women in this group. Several were in fact majoring in art in college. But all the Drifters had the sensitivities of an artist, seeing the world from a somewhat different perspective, alive to their own responsiveness, but unable to structure this knowledge into identity. Instead, they set about realizing themselves in impulsivity, in the pleasures of the moment, even in the pleasures of despair.

The women in this group are very different from one another. They were all rather lost as college seniors, but lost for different reasons. Some regarded themselves loosely as "hippies"; others were simply having a good time. Still others were angry or deeply sad. The future was something that would arrive some day, but they regarded it with neither fear nor hope. "When the time comes, I'll do something," Debbie explained. They lived as though the present would never come to an end—and, for some, life became a serious of disconnected present moments. After college, most of the Drifters dispersed widely, went on the road to encounter the world.

Some seemed to have fairly serious psychological problems that prevented them from taking on the work of identity formation. Other psychologists who have studied these four groups have found the Drifters to be the least psychologically healthy on a variety of psychological measures. The Drifters score highest on measures of anxiety and in general show themselves to be most likely to withdraw from situations that are frustrating or difficult.[2] Psychologists have regarded this as the most worrisome of the identity pathways, but we have known little about what becomes of these women.

Some Drifters eventually found someone else to assemble their puzzle pieces and were relieved to be free of the task. They could simply live out someone else's plans for them and at least feel at peace. But for most of the Drifters, something would wreck this plan and they would scatter the pieces to the winds once again.

What is most intriguing to me is that the Drifter life path was predictable from the college-age interview. Although they are a varied group, they are alike in becoming midlife women who feel battered and chastened by life.

Drifter lives make the most interesting stories because they have lived closest to the edge and have undergone the most unusual experiences. In their 20s and early 30s, the Drifters changed their addresses, held more jobs, had more abortions, tried more religions, and used more drugs and alcohol than the women in the other groups. They continued to drift—in and out of places, relationships, and projects. But the drama in their lives came at the cost of much suffering. Often, their early adult histories centered on an episode of something important in their lives exploding and then having to put out the blaze and get things right again. Yvonne's life story at age 33, for example, was centered on the trauma of having been abandoned by her partner after the birth of their child who, born prematurely and very ill, died several months later. Erica married a much older man who she knew was dying because she felt she could bring joy and meaning to his last months, but she felt lost after he died. Evelyn had been living in a turbulent and violent lesbian love triangle. In their early adulthood, the Drifters made often hasty choices that they spent their 30s regretting. Why did I have these children? they wondered later. Or why did I never find a partner? Or a career? Or something to believe in and work for? Or, I used to have friends—where did they go?

When I found them again at age 43, I was astonished that, after long-checkered odysseys, most had gone home again—literally. All were at that time living near where they grew up (or, in Donna's case, where her husband grew up). I thought that this signified a search for some foundation on which to build, and most seemed headed in more promising directions. "I still don't know what I really want to do," mused Donna at age 43, "I just go on doing this and that." In this emotional state is where I found most of the Drifters in their 40s—doing *something*, but not at all certain that it's what they ever wanted. Many at this age were still very much anticipating that their real lives would yet begin and were once again trying to start over, hoping for better outcomes.

In this latest round of interviews in their mid-50s, I was sorry to learn that going home had been just another failed attempt, and it did not lead to the internal structure they needed to craft a life that felt meaningful. Except for Debbie, each of the college-age Drifters continued to drift in one way or another and, in their mid-50s, felt unfulfilled in her life. By their mid-50s, the Drifters are more aware of time running out, and they are not much closer to finding themselves. They are not necessarily unhappy, and they feel regret,[3] it seems, only when I ask them to give an account of themselves. Some have life structures, however unsatisfactory, but stability is not the same as committed self-directed choice, and they are painfully aware of this. They continue to live in the present, and planning for the future or setting goals still eludes them. While living in the present can be a reasonable choice for a life, one often heralded in today's times, this was not by conscious choice for these women. It was what was left to them.

The Drifters are, for the most part, self-reflective women, aware of their often-mercurial feelings, who try to make sense of themselves even if the parts don't form a pattern. They are alive to their own responsiveness and to their impulsivity. The reader will (I hope) notice, in their quotations, the ways in which their mode of talking about themselves differs from the other groups—the contradiction, the trailing off, the incomplete thoughts, the stories that make no point. As I write about the Drifters, I try not to impose my own structure on what is often rather formless, but to some extent I have to do so or I would just be showing you, the reader, a lot of unassembled puzzle pieces—which is, in the end, more like what these women live with. Still,

I present these life stories with at least some of the messiness and clutter that characterizes Drifter lives.

In contrast to the uplifting tone of the lives of the other groups, these are, for the most part, life stories of disappointment and frustration. I can't put happy endings on them except to laud these women for hanging on. In Faulkner's words, they endure.

Yvonne

AGE 21

Yvonne grew up on a small middle-western farm where they raised cows for milk, chickens for the table, and grew some of their own vegetables. Her father worked in town as a bookkeeper, and her mother was a cashier in a grocery store. Her earliest memories were of singing to the cows and showing them anything new that she received. Her father was busy all the time, rarely home, and her parents stayed together until she went away to the state college and then they divorced.

She felt somewhat adrift in her family—her mother catered to her oldest sister, her father to the second one, and she was left out. She felt her mother related to her largely by restricting her and grounding her, so she found ways to keep beneath her mother's radar. Her mother had strict codes about going out, what to do with boys, and both of her sisters were very "straight-laced." From Yvonne's narrative of her life at the end of college, it seemed that she had only very loose bonds to her family, suggesting what psychologists call a form of insecure attachment. In this pattern, people tend often to view others as all good or all bad and find it hard to develop a realistic sense of how one's self is related to others.

Yvonne was majoring in art and went to the nearby state college because it seemed like the next thing to do. She had little contact with her family. While she went home to her mother on school holidays, the only time she was in contact with her father was to ask him for money. "It's a financial relationship—like going to the bank."

Yvonne had been interested in art since fourth grade when found she really liked painting; she had some ideas of doing something with design. But what was really on her mind at age 21 was working out her relationships with boys. She was one of the few who didn't plan in college to marry—she said that she didn't want to get saddled with responsibilities and then she could spend all the money on herself. At the same time, her thoughts were filled with her relationships with guys—the one she liked early in college who dumped her, her fantasies about a guy who wasn't interested in her, and her live-in boyfriend who caused her ongoing grief.

When she talked about herself, she talked in terms of being dependent and independent, and this seemed to refer to how much she needed a guy in her life. She wasn't sure about where her own self ended and where she had to bend to the wishes of the man she was involved with. Overall, Yvonne seemed quite confused about how to make relationships with other people.

Each of her parents had a different Protestant religion, and each tried somewhat inconsistently to engage her with their beliefs. Her mother had counseled her to wait until she married to choose a religion, and she thought that probably her beliefs would follow her husband's. She seemed not to recognize the inconsistency here—in that she said that she didn't plan to marry. Still, she thought that if she were to choose a religion on her own, it might be Catholicism. She had been involved in Satanic beliefs for a while (following a guy she was dating) but, she said, it got too "weird" so she left the group.

Her family had no interest in politics and neither did she. Asked if there were any issues she felt strongly about, she said she thought that taxes were too high, but did not elaborate this at all. She had not voted and didn't even know where to vote.

Yvonne's decisions about sex were colored by having been date raped when she was 17. She gave a ride home to a guy who forced her into sex. Since then, she had been having sex with her boyfriend of two years, but their sex life was filled with ambivalence and complication. Often, she cried after sex, wasn't sure if she wanted to do it or not. While she didn't think there was anything morally wrong with sex, she feared getting caught and the shame this would bring. She said, "I hide a lot—think about something else." She was living with her boyfriend, and, recognizing how much her mother would disapprove of this, she felt a lot of guilt and worry. She herself was amazed that she was doing this, "If anyone would have told me last year that I'd be living with a guy, I wouldn't have believed it. Somehow I got messed up along the line."

When she thought of her parents, she didn't see qualities in either one that she emulated. She certainly didn't want to be "busy all the time" like her father. She was trying to work out in what ways they were "dependent" or "independent"—these were important categories for her as she thought about herself. She also evaluated everyone in terms of their bodies—who had a nice one, whose not so nice. She thought of herself and her sisters (and her mother) as having nice bodies, and this had something to do with attracting guys. The people she admired were fashion models. Her heroine was Scarlett O'Hara who she liked because she always thought about herself.

The emotional center of Yvonne's life was her current relationship with her boyfriend who lived with her "sometimes" and to whom she referred as "Dingbat." When he was there, she was involved with him, but when he left, she said she hardly thought of him. In fact, she said she was in love with another guy, but no one knew about her feelings. They were friends, but when she told him that "Dingbat" was living with her, he distanced himself.

"Dingbat" treated her badly. Their apartment had become a kind of commune, four people living there, others crashing there, with a lot of drugs and sex. Yvonne described it as very "messed up," and she felt out of control of the mess. She ended up having to do the dishes and clean. She felt like a housewife there and told me that this, too, was part of her decision never to get married. She expected that she would leave Dingbat eventually, and it wasn't clear to me why she was staying in this situation. She wanted him out of the apartment but couldn't think of how to throw him out without hurting his feelings. The complexities of their relationship, including his bringing other girls to the apartment, kept her from sleeping, and she had been cutting a lot of classes.

Yvonne was resorting to some magical thinking here—she had heard that if you make a wish in a church you have never been in before, the wish will come true. She tried it in junior high, and her wishes came true. Now she tried it with her wish for her boyfriend to leave. If that didn't work, she told me, she could perhaps drink a case of beer and then tell him to leave.

Her experiences with guys changed the romantic hopes of her girlhood. She had imagined love to have no problems, all smiles and being treated like a princess. Now she was trying to "take things the way they are and to play it cool, have to take the bitter with the sweet." She went to see a college counselor in hopes of sorting things out.

At this stage, Yvonne was quite occupied with the complexities of her unsatisfying relationship with her boyfriend, who she both loved and hated and who treated her badly but still came back to her. Although she didn't want to be with him, he dominated her thoughts, kept her from sleeping well. There was constant drama between them, and it was hard for her to focus on much else.

It was hard to really "find" Yvonne during this interview with so many contradictions in what she said of herself. She could tell me what she was doing but when she asked herself why she was doing what she was doing, she came up with no answers. It seemed to me that she was living her impulses of the moment and desperately clinging to a leaky vessel, her sort-of boyfriend. She had no real plans or very real relationships. She didn't seem depressed, but I worried about her. She seemed to have no coherent center and seemed never to have internalized anything solid from her family. It made some sense to me that her earliest memory was singing to the cows. At least she could imagine that they were responsive to her. No one else in her life seemed to care.

Yvonne represented to me a clear example of someone experiencing identity diffusion. Her views of herself and of others were shifting and unstable, and she found herself living out unintegrated aspects of herself, doing things that didn't make sense to other parts of herself. This lack of "making sense" seemed to reflect early problems in attachment that would have permitted her some core sense of self. She was entering adulthood with some serious psychological handicaps, and I could only hope that the counselor she was seeing could help her sort herself out.

AGE 33

At age 33, Yvonne told me about a checkered 12 years. I was saddened by this, but not surprised. She tried to go into art education after college, got a part-time job teaching art to migrant children, and did some substitute teaching, but she couldn't get a full-time job. Then she tried working in the retail world, but there were cutbacks there, too. She had had six different jobs in somewhat different sectors of the economy over 12 years, but none lasted. Many of these jobs were part-time, or filling in for someone on leave, or a job just for a summer. She usually found these jobs through people she knew. At the time I met her again, she was working part-time in a department store, thinking about the possibility of some kind of management training. She really wanted to find some kind of career, something with job security and decent pay. It seemed to her that the sales representatives she came in contact with had a good life, although she worried that all the traveling might leave her lonely. Perhaps there was such a job with less traveling.

The biggest change in her life was that, following a trauma in her recent past, she became a Catholic. In her mid-20s, Yvonne met a guy she liked, and he was pressuring her into joining the Catholic Church. They had unprotected sex, and he promised to marry her if she got pregnant. Indeed, she did get pregnant, but he didn't marry her. She went through the pregnancy alone, working all the while in a small store as a cashier until she was laid off. She gave birth to a daughter who had an abnormality and stayed alive in intensive care for two months and then died. While her baby was in the hospital, Yvonne had a vision of Christ, and this was followed by other mystical experiences. This led her to an intense involvement in the Church and a deep belief in her Catholicism, which, she felt, gave structure to her life. It also gave her an outlet for her artistic interests because she devoted much time to voluntarily doing the calligraphy and posters for her Church.

To an extent, then, Yvonne had followed her mother's advice about adopting the religion of the man she would marry, even though they never married. She did, however, link the intensity of her religious commitment to her grandfather who had built a Lutheran church.

At this age, Yvonne had become more political. She said ruefully that 10 years ago, she would just have voted for the candidate who was the best looking, but now she tried to follow the issues and be aware of what was going on. She was opposed to abortion and welfare: abortion on religious grounds, welfare on the grounds that it was a handout to people who didn't want to work.

Yvonne had become more conservative in regard to sex, partly as a result of her own experience. She had few relationships since the man who left her—she said it was now "hard to have casual sex. . . . Maybe if people are engaged and love each other, sex is okay." But she was vehement about extramarital sex, horrified by going into a bar and finding it filled with married people "on the prowl." She was still hoping for lasting love and expected to treasure it if she found it. And she was very clear at this point that "I don't have to do anything I don't want to do." Given how helpless she had seemed to feel in college, that seemed to be important growth for Yvonne.

She very much hoped to marry, although there was still some doubt. She didn't like the loneliness of being on her own but also had a hard time seeing herself staying with just one person. As she spoke about her dating patterns, I thought she sounded remarkably young. "You either like somebody a whole lot and they don't come around, or you don't like somebody and they do come around. There's somebody I do like, but right now we're ignoring each other." But, after all, Yvonne was coming out of a very difficult time, having taken the father of her child to court for a paternity suit, hoping for a big settlement which, of course, became moot. Asked what she wanted in a love relationship, Yvonne said, "somebody who cares more about you than you care about them." While this comment may have reflected Yvonne's frustration with her unrequited infatuations, it also points to a kind of self-absorption that likely interfered with her having close relationships with people at all. When she spoke about friends and important people in her life, she largely regarded them as people to turn to for advice about her work or her romantic interests.

Yvonne now lived with her mother, having found it difficult to keep up her part of the rent when she was living in apartments with roommates. The financial struggles determined a lot of her choices.

Asked to look back on her life, Yvonne related that in high school and college, she was consistently interested in the same thing—getting a boyfriend and getting married. I was surprised when she told me "I never had anything important happen in my life." And I found it heart-rending when she said, forlornly, "Here I am—I'm still thinking 'I'll get a job, then I'll get married.' That's terrible . . . I'm still thinking . . . that really is." Yvonne's sense of herself at age 33 was that she was stuck, hadn't moved on or accomplished any of her dreams. She remained as mystified as ever about why her relationships with men were so unsatisfying and unpredictable. She tended to meet men in bars, but didn't want to be with a man who drinks or did drugs.

Yvonne's philosophy of life at age 33 was "All I can do is put my best foot forward and pull myself out of the mud." Christ and her priest were the most important people in her life, although she did have several friends to whom she felt somewhat close. Still, it seemed her friendships were short-lived—people always seemed to be moving on. She did not list her mother or sisters as people she felt close to, although she was living with her mother. Her sisters had married. While she got along well with her next oldest sister and enjoyed her nieces, she resented the oldest sister for badgering her about finding a good job. Yvonne and her mother "had their ups and downs," particularly after her mother remarried (a husband who died not long after the marriage). She felt she was getting a bit closer to her father after he remarried, in part because Yvonne liked his new wife.

Throughout this interview, Yvonne stressed the Church as the bulwark of what was good in her life. It provided her with structure and meaning. She was, as she said, still hoping for a career and a marriage, even children, but still taking things one day at a time, seeing what might happen.

AGE 43

When I found Yvonne again 10 years later, she was still living in her mother's house, but her mother spent winters in California with a sister. Yvonne had managed to become a sales representative for several companies. She felt that a lot had changed in the past 10 years, years she described as "not all bad." She was enjoying getting out and meeting people while traveling around three states in her job. Still, she hadn't met a man she could make a relationship with.

An important decision she made was to be in business for herself and get products to sell directly from the manufacturers. Friends came and went but, she said, "I've learned to accept myself more. When I realized I had to solve the problems myself—I couldn't keep going to people asking them for advice because you're going to get different opinions."

In meeting Yvonne again, I was struck by the difference in her appearance. She had gained weight and had lost the youthful attractiveness she once had. Although she was fitfully dieting, she had about 40 pounds to lose. Yet she seemed more focused and was now engaged in a career—selling various "lines" as she put it. Her frustrations had to do with economic give and take: companies that didn't pay her properly, finding products that would sell in her territories, getting along with the companies whose lines she sold, fighting for particular accounts. Yvonne seemed proud of her decision to go out on her own. She had given up the dream of making a lot of money, but she felt she could now make enough to live on.

Satisfaction came from store managers being excited about her products. One particularly moving moment came when Yvonne spoke of her joy of walking through a town and seeing someone wearing something she had brought into a store. This was, for her, a sense of impact, seeing the fruits of her work. But sales is a high stress job. "People can yank the territory, pirate your lines, lots of backstabbing." She found herself often having headaches or being unable to sleep and in tears of frustration a lot of the time. Still, she hoped to continue in this work and hoped the economy improved and gas prices got lower. "My stores are really scared of this economy," she said, and I noted the "my." Yvonne, at this age, at last felt she had something that was hers.

In thinking about marriage, at age 43, Yvonne was now defining herself as "a career woman." She said that a person she would marry would have to understand this, that she wasn't going to sit at home or take a 9-to-5 job. "I like going to bed when I want to, watch what I want to on TV, go where I want to go without making excuses. I can eat what I want, as much as I want. There are many things about being single that I've grown accustomed to that I think I would be hard to live with. If there was a special person who would understand, I would go along with something like that. If it happens, it happens, if not, that's okay, too. Maybe I'll be sorry later." She hadn't completely given up the idea of having children but that, too, was in the category of "if it happens, it happens."

One of Yvonne's sisters has three kids, the other four, and she hoped that in the future her nieces and nephews would come to see her. She had worries about growing old alone.

As has been true at various points in her life, Yvonne had strong romantic fantasies about a man who she worked with, but he was far away and they met only occasionally. "I think he knows how I feel, but I haven't done the things that would encourage him. I want him to do the pursuing." Meanwhile, Yvonne hadn't had a date for several years. She went out with friends, usually "tagging along with couples." Several years ago, she had a long, primarily sexual relationship with a married man and, when she told me this, seemed to have forgotten her vehemence of 10 years ago about extramarital relationships. "We were both going through problems, so I don't feel guilty about this." He went out of business and moved far away, and that ended the relationship. Yvonne still felt angry at married men who posed as single and had developed strategies for trying to identify them before she got involved with someone.

Asked what she looks for in a love relationship at this age, Yvonne said she wanted someone to talk to about what bothers her and she wanted someone who shares her values and political views.

I kept waiting for Yvonne to bring up her faith, the bulwark of her life at age 33. When I finally asked about it, she told me that she had left the Church because she didn't go along with some of the political things that were happening there and the priest she liked had left. As with her other commitments, Yvonne could easily move on. This one, though, I had thought might be more lasting.

Traveling so much and listening to radio talk shows, Yvonne had become quite politically aware and quite identified with the far-right. These were the Clinton years, and she felt that "this country is so screwed up." She was vehement about not using federal funds for abortion, about imported goods, against unions and for "family values." She talked at great length and with much passion about these matters, mainly giving examples about individual people who get more than they deserve at government expense, often people she knew or knew about. Indeed, she sounded a bit like a conservative radio show.

Looking back at her past, Yvonne now understood her life in a different way. She talked of her father's absence from the family and the sense that her mother did the best she could. She wished her parents had been stricter, given her more guidance, and encouraged her to study. (She had forgotten her earlier complaints about how overly strict her mother was, how she was beaten with a belt for not doing the dishes or sassing her mother.) When Yvonne talked about the child she had lost, she thought of it mostly in terms of the loss of self-esteem that came from "being dumped while pregnant" and then having to go in front of the judge. "If that hadn't happened, I might have gone on to another relationship and my career may have been different."

Yvonne had grown more self-reflective at midlife and told me some details about her past I hadn't heard before. When she was in elementary school, years she called "the insulting years," she was kept back a year in school. She thought of her years in high school as dominated by thoughts of boys and friends and the joyful independence of having a car. Early college was "the good time years" in which she partied a lot but thought of herself as becoming more serious by late college. She did not recount her preoccupation with boys at this point, but perhaps she did not remember. She described herself after college as "a lost soul," unable to find a job. Again, she said she "partied too much." She felt there were a lot of issues in these years that she put out of her mind because they were too painful, and she didn't like to think about it. I began to think that there was a whole untold story about "partying" that she had never talked to me about, but I couldn't really know what this was. She said she had never been an alcoholic, but she likes her beers; she likes bars. Partying seems to be some form of having a good time, but she could only really discuss it (or, it seems, think about it) once those years are past.

Since our last meeting when she was 33, Yvonne, at age 43, saw her life story as being about developing a career and trying not to struggle so much financially. She had become closer to her family and put both of her parents, her oldest sister, and two aunts on her list of close relationships. A few friends were also there, people she could turn to for help or to think things out. But she rued the fact that most of her friends from earlier years were gone, and the friends she had were people she pursued to seek advice on her latest job or relationship struggles.

Looking back, she felt she had lost whatever she might have gained from college. Maybe she got a little more independent living away from home, she said, but this may have happened anyway. "I think about all that wasted money. It seems foolish when I think about it now. The people I met in college—I haven't run into them for years."

Yvonne tried to keep moving forward; too much self-reflection was painful. "A lot I put way back in my head and shut my head on it. I think about where I've been during this time. Where's my artwork been? A lot of those years were just lost. I hope to recoup some of my artistic ability. I'm not disappointed. Sometimes I am, but life goes on."

Yvonne used to see an astrologer who kept telling her that life was about her own free will. Finding this will and exercising it was the main thread of Yvonne's life struggles so far. I felt pained for her loneliness. She seemed not to have figured out how to relate to people except to sell her merchandise. In some corner of her mind, she retained the dream of working with art, but she couldn't quite find a way to express this in reality. And her hope for a partner felt completely left to the stars.

After our interview, Yvonne wrote me to tell me that she had decided to start making some paintings to sell along with her other lines. She also began taking drawing classes. It may have been that talking things through with me sparked something in her. She also told me excitedly in the letter that she just received two more lines of products, so things were looking up business-wise. And a friend of hers predicted it all by telling her not to be so negative. She was very grateful to him for his support of her, but added, "I suppose if we spent more time together, we wouldn't be such good friends."

AGE 55

Yvonne was very surprised to hear from me but delighted to meet me. She warned me that she could talk nonstop—and she rather did. It was difficult to interview her because one thought would lead to a seemingly unrelated other thought, and I found myself interrupting her a lot to try to follow the thread of what she was telling me. Her mother having died several years back, she bought her sisters' shares of the house and was now living there alone. She was working as a sales representative for a new company and had been with this company for four years.

The first thing she wanted to tell me about was that, after our last meeting, she began doing screen prints of old mills, had them printed on paper and on t-shirts, and had sold quite a few. But this is secondary to the jewelry, scarves, and cosmetics line she mainly sells. Right off, she began telling me about various frustrations with orders and with production, all of which involve her losing money. The main satisfaction of her job is getting as much money as possible, which is, in any case, not a lot. The competition is stiff, and she always feels in danger of losing customers. She had been fired from a previous job, so holding on to this one was important.

Yvonne told me that I would like the jewelry she sells, that I would like the town she goes to when on her route—and I wondered how she would know what I would like. This was one of the first inklings I had that Yvonne, despite her talkativeness, was difficult to feel connected to. It seemed to me that she might be lacking in a capacity for empathy or a sense of how to deal with differences among people.

Conflict with others has dominated her life. As she began to tell me about getting fired from her last job, it was hard to follow just what this conflict was about. The woman said she yelled at her, but she didn't and she didn't like her products anyway, so after many years, she was just fired. Then she didn't know what to do next, so out of the blue someone she used to work for called her looking for someone else, asked her what she was doing these days and when she told him not much, he offered her another sales job. "My company yelled at me [during the] last sales meeting. He was upset with me, you know and gosh [laughing], I must be Calamity Jane." Then immediately she launched into another story of conflict with the person who rented the other half of her house. No sooner did she rent it to another person than another major conflict occurred, and she had to go to court to have him evicted.

It seemed to Yvonne that, over the past 15 years, people have changed for the worse. "Or maybe it might be me that changed—I turned into a real German like both sides of my family—bull-headed, can't tell me anything—I don't know."

Yvonne is proud that she "got my art back together. When I do my art work, I usually get an award for something that I do. . . . I just got another commission yesterday from the bank in town." She thought about giving art lessons to children, but then got into conflict with someone—and another dispute with someone at the art co-op. People persisted in withholding the money she feels she is due or "yelling at" her for doing things they don't like, like telling people things they didn't want told.

Her mother's death was very difficult for her, and the illness and aftermath led to all-out war between her and her sisters. "I think my mom always protected me from my sisters," Yvonne said tearfully. "I'm so different from them you wouldn't think we're from the same family." I couldn't get clear on what the tension between her and her sisters was about. She said that they didn't think she ever had a real job, but "if there's anyone who has a real job, it's me." They thought their mother had done more for her than for them, but Yvonne felt that she was the one who was there for their mother, even though her sisters live just 10 miles away. Yvonne has formed now a kind of relationship with their father and his woman friend, but her father still prefers her older sister as he always had.

At this time of her life, Yvonne seemed angry at everyone. She was an even more devoted conservative talk radio listener and generally hated all politicians—and most people in general. "I think things are pretty messy all over. I feel sorry for the kids going over to war. Personally, I would have been more aggressive—probably nuked them [laughs]. They're fighting over there. They're all evil, I think they all lie. I don't think Bush lied really, I think he got bad information. I hate politicians, all of them. I think they're just there for the money. I don't think they help people at all." She recognizes that her political views have changed since college, when she imagines she was a liberal. She takes no political action, but her conservative views are a channel to express all the pent-up anger she feels about her life.

Yvonne now narrates a different story of her growth, particularly in college. "I wanted to go to an art school but my folks talked me out of that. They didn't think that is where I needed to go. They thought I needed to go to a university and be a little bit more diversified." It was her mom actually who suggested this since her father showed no interest in her at all. Although she was now in a kind of relationship with her father, she still resented him for having paid no attention to her while she was growing up. At this interview, she told me that he had been "running around" on her mother for years, and I understood better her earlier vehemence about extramarital relationships.

Back to her career hopes: "My mom actually wanted me to go to hair school. But I said I don't like working with wet hair, mom. My sister was a hair stylist, and she thought I would be good at that. I wanted to be an artist and move to Greenwich Village and be a beatnik. . . . I thought I was good enough. I got a wake-up when I got to college. I thought I would take art classes. I was so disappointed when I got to college and found out I had to take math, English, science—my English class, I took it at night school so that would give me something to do at night. I wrote term papers and wrote a sentence and a paragraph, and I was thinking why am I doing this? I had this when I was in eighth grade. I went to somebody there and said 'Why do I have to take all this other stuff? I had all this in high school.'

"I still wish I could have gone to an art institute or whatever. I ended up doing an intensive art degree with education where I'd teach K–12. My mother thought I should have done art as a minor, and, looking back, I think she was right. I should have done something like elementary education and had the art degree on the side. I would have ended up in the school system. I think that that would have been better for me—I'd probably be retired by now. But that's not what I wanted to do. I really wanted to work in the commercial art field—what would be called a graphic designer today. That field is all computerized now. It's gone. It's done."

The drawing classes she took 10 years ago left an impression on her. She admired, actually envied, the teacher who was teaching adults. She recognized that this woman had talent and experience, and Yvonne longed to be like her. She regretted not having pursued her art. "I let it go for a long time. I hadn't done acrylic for 30 years, and I took someone a photograph and he said, 'What? You haven't painted for 30 years,' and I think if I would have been painting for those 30 years, where would I be at?" I asked her why she thinks she let it go. In a barely audible whisper, choking on tears, she said, "I don't know. I just—I thought it had let me down and I thought art's something that will never let you down."

Her memory at this age has her mother encouraging her art throughout her life. Her mother's aunt was a well-known painter, and now Yvonne feels joined to art through them. She had never known her aunt well because, growing up, her own primary family spent their time with her dad's family and only rarely with her mother's relatives. Still, there was one of her aunt's pictures in the house, and she fought doggedly to keep it after her mother's death.

Sadly, at age 55, Yvonne feels not only alone but estranged from people. Last year, she had a fall in the house and worried that she could be there a long time before anyone found her. There is one male friend who she speaks to every few days. Perhaps he'd look for her. "But that kind of scared me back then. I didn't sleep well for a couple of days."

There are a couple of men who seem interested in her, but maybe its just sex they are looking for. In any case, its not a courtship. And Yvonne wouldn't be available anyway. "I can go home from my job and I can do what I want and eat what I want, you know, I don't have to answer to anybody. I don't want to say when I'm going to be home and somebody's going to be sitting there worrying about me. Or if I stop at WalMart for whatever reason, and I can watch what I want to on TV. And I have people to talk to about politics although all my Republican people are dying off." In the years before her mother's death, she began spending more time with older people, people in their 70s and 80s, and she still invites friends of her aunt and other older people for coffee when she feels lonely.

One more thing about Yvonne—something consistent over all these years. At each interview, I ask each woman to tell me about the earliest thing she can remember because these memories usually sound themes that are repeated throughout a life. Yvonne's earliest memory, which she repeated four times, once at each interview, was of going out and singing to the cows and showing them anything she got new. I had puzzled over the meaning of this memory for many years, and, at this interview, I took the opportunity to ask Yvonne to explain to me its significance. "They liked it. They stared at me. I'd go sing to them every day. I'm tone deaf and can't sing a note. My mom used to get mad at me because I'd sing as soon as I got out of bed. They just stared. They just looked at me. They couldn't get away. I always liked cows. I don't know. I just liked to have an audience."

So perhaps that is a central theme that has pervaded Yvonne's life—wanting to find an audience. She needed someone to validate something that was good in her. But somehow her search for an audience seemed only to alienate others and interfered with her ability to form satisfying and meaningful relationships with people—not just with potential male partners, but with family and friends. Even I experienced her as performing for me, talking at me, rather than relating to me. I asked her how her godchild, her favorite niece, the one person she seemed to feel some love for, would describe her, and Yvonne said she would probably describe her as "a basket case." Awash in tears, she could not tell me just what this meant. Some of the tears were for her mother, the person to whom she had been closest throughout her life. Now she is resigning herself to perpetual conflict, has given up on the idea of finding a partner, and seems mostly to want to keep holding on. Her art may be a bright spot, giving her some hope and solace, but she can't quite take hold of it.

I was pained by Yvonne's grief for her mother, which is intense and raw. And I was also pained by her grief for her unrealized life. "I went away to college and thought I'd never come back to this little town. Never wanted to come back and that's where I ended up. I just got lazy. I've lived here all my life, and I'm an old duck. It's my place—my sofa, my TV. I don't participate in too much. I've been in the art club for a while, but I don't care for the girls at the meetings. I'd like to start the art club again and just do painting or drawing sessions. Pay off the mortgage. Take care of my yard, grow my flowers."

I took Yvonne to dinner, having time before my flight. She was wound up from the interview and talked almost nonstop, one story leading to another. Nearly all the stories ended with some kind of interpersonal conflict. Indeed, I was experiencing how hard it was to get into real contact with her and imagined that others in her life must feel the same. I also understood more about how devastated she was by her mother's death. She apologized profusely for her tears and asked me if other people are going through endless mourning, feeling she should be over her grief. But her mother, ambivalent though their relationship was, had been the constant good person in Yvonne's life and now she was, as she was well aware, quite alone. She said she would send me a painting, but she never did.

Over the years, I had been struck by Yvonne's beautiful eyes, large and blue. Once she was pretty. Now one just sees that she is overweight. I was feeling, with her, the diminution of hope, the agony of the idea that she had become "a basket case."

As I tried to puzzle this out, I kept going back to the feeling that there was something about how Yvonne relates to people that has been in her way all along. She is superficially extraverted, but missing some connection. (Consistent with this, her self-rating on the attachment scale is dismissive avoidant.) Friends have come and gone, and I couldn't be sure what "friend" actually meant to her. She is estranged from all her family. Somehow she didn't seem able to emotionally know where other people are or get in sync with them. This may have accounted for her consistent mistakes in choosing male partners—her college boyfriend and the man who left her pregnant and abandoned. This led her to become very cautious of men, living in her fantasies but afraid to engage in the real relationship she also longed for. There are so many points in Yvonne's history where something might have turned out better than it did, but somehow she was unable to follow through on opportunities. Yet I didn't have the impulse to take Yvonne on as a patient or to gently suggest she find a therapist. My sense was that, in her own way, she had accepted who she was. She was surviving, after all, and relieving her loneliness by finding people along the way who would be, however temporarily, her audience. Still, I found myself wishing that something good would fall in Yvonne's lap and that she would be able to embrace it.

In contrast to Yvonne, Donna had moments in her life where it seemed she had taken hold of something and could begin to direct her own growth. But the commitments she tried to make seemed to slip away, and she became lost in a different way from Yvonne.

Donna

COLLEGE

Donna was a particularly smart and talented young woman who excelled in a small elite women's college. The first in her family to go to college, she took pride in her academic abilities. She had some interest in art conservation, but felt that she could do anything she wanted and hadn't yet really figured out what she most wanted to do. She stood out for me among my participants at the time because of her personal life—she had eloped and married after her freshman year, divorced a year later, then moved in with another man to whom she was engaged as a college senior.

In her college interview, Donna could only describe herself in relation to what others wanted of her and whether she complied with or rebelled against their wishes. She married out of rebellion and then regretted doing so. She was drawn to her (ex-)husband because he had clear ideas about how she should be in their marriage. "I just fitted into his desires," she said, then she left him when she realized she didn't want to be the traditional wife he wanted. I was astonished that, two years later, she seemed to remember little of this marriage. Her memory was vague about most of her life experiences. She valued her fiancé, Dan, because he gave her "space" and also fit in with her family. She often spoke of her decisions in terms of what her mother, to whom she was very close but desperately trying to separate from, had told her. I was struck by her earliest memory: "In the third grade, my teacher asked us to write a poem and I was convinced I couldn't write a poem, so I went and copied a poem from somewhere and when she confronted me with it, I denied it." I thought that was a theme of what Donna was doing at this age— trying to copy an identity from somewhere else, all the while denying that she was doing so—and not being comfortable with any possibilities that had so far presented themselves. At this point, though, Donna said that she wanted the freedom to try new things, whatever they might be. I had become accustomed, with the Drifters, even back then, to the folly of my wish for them to give an account of themselves.

AGE 33

By age 33, Donna was quite settled but recounted a complex and confused journey. What settled her was her engagement with a spiritual advisor who led a somewhat cult-like community that she and Dan (to whom she was now married) had joined. They found this community after their marriage almost collapsed following six years in their 20s in which drugs, alcohol, and a philosophy of open marriage were driving them apart. During this time, Donna had been working in photography, and, for several years, she was commuting between Miami and Key West where Dan was working in his family's construction business. She had learned to fly her own plane back and forth. When she decided to move back to live full-time with Dan, she felt she had to give up a good job, a great apartment, and a good salary. "Giving up all these things was not because of any marital problems, but as a result of soul searching and realizing that I ought to get on with the more important aspects of growing together as a couple and a family." Their spiritual leader taught a path of meditation, prayer, chastity, and vegetarianism, and these became the central pillars of Donna's identity in her early 30s. I noted as she spoke that Donna did not say that she wanted a family: instead, that "I ought to get on with it."

Donna had two young children when I saw her at age 33 and was trying to be a full-time mother because this is what she felt her babies needed. Still, she tried to grab what time she could to work on her photography and still accepted a few assignments, finding her work in photography quite fulfilling. She hoped to devote more time and attention to her work once her children were older. She stressed the way in which her marriage was an anchor stabilizing her and credited her husband with supporting all of her endeavors. Motherhood, she felt, was stretching her, teaching her to respond to others' needs and helping her learn about herself. "It exposes you to the good and bad within yourself." Donna was struggling with the demands of being a mother and having "days of not accomplishing anything tangible."

In her interview at age 33, Donna spoke about herself in the language of spirituality, inner peace, and karma, none of which connected very directly with what she was doing in the world—at least I couldn't make these connections. Karma explained many of her decisions. She had been in quest of feelings, of expressing herself, and, although she tried many things, nothing quite sufficed except for short periods of time. Her new religious awareness had created a lot of guilt about an abortion she had had in her early 20s, and no amount of prayer relieved her of that burden. Still, despite a lot of contradictions, Donna seemed quite settled in her early 30s, enlightened by her spirituality and her confidence in the wisdom of her spiritual advisor, as well as bound to the demands of motherhood, commitment to her marriage, and her frustrated wishes to return to her work.

AGE 43

When I saw her at age 43, Donna told me that the past decade had been difficult, and she seemed to me to have returned to her earlier turmoil. She was still primarily involved in raising her now early adolescent children, but not enjoying them or motherhood very much. From time to time, she had home-schooled her daughter. Her most recent passion had been learning to play the viola di gamba, and she was spending a great deal of time practicing and playing with an ensemble.

Turning 40 had been a difficult time. "I absolutely lost everything from being absorbed in being a mother," she told me at the beginning of the interview. "I just felt like an onion being continually stripped of one layer after another of my identity. And really trying to get to focus on who I am." She found herself revisiting her past and trying to make sense of who she had been, asking herself a lot of questions. Why had she married her first husband? Why had she divorced? She could remember so little of this time, as though she had left the happy home of childhood and been thrust into a fog. Why had she had an abortion? And how could she come to terms with a recent miscarriage? "I'm looking at things now with a different consciousness and can't reconcile them with my belief system now. Life just propelled me." She seemed to feel that accepting herself in the present involved coming to terms with a past that she couldn't specifically remember. I thought that she was experiencing and expressing the fragmentation of self that Drifters so often struggle with.

The extent of her inner disconnection was most graphically illustrated by Donna telling me about how she felt while playing her instrument. "It's absolutely like jumping off a cliff. It's the most fearful thing I've ever done . . . , I could visibly see my hands shaking, but afterwards my response was, 'Oh, so that's what happens. I wonder what will happen next time.' And I sit there and I wonder can I play again, and you say, 'I can't play.' There's no connection. It's the most bizarre experience, and I think it is part of starting something when you're 40 and getting up and doing something. You know, you get out of college when you're 22 or 23, and nobody looks and expects something more of you than you're new and that you're green. So I don't know whether their projections or perceptions of yourself or other people. . . . This one woman said, 'I expect that if you get up there and play that you know what you're doing.' And I said, 'But I don't know what I'm doing.' I have to get up there and say 'You know what you're doing.' And I have to continually run my dialogue that

I know how to play—yes, you do—no, you don't." This seemed to be emblematic of Donna at age 43. She was doing things but felt disconnected from what she was doing, and, when she stopped to think about what she was doing, she got mired in confusion. Again, I thought here that Donna was giving voice to what the other Drifters experience as fragmentation and dissociation of self.

The story of the previous 10 years that Donna told me at age 43 contained continuing disjointed episodes. At some point, she had abruptly moved with the children to Italy for six months but could give no account that I could understand of why she had done this. Her response to my question about this gives the flavor of how Donna thought about her choices in life: "It was more the flow into something—more of an intuitive thing. I felt it and moved on it and pieces fell into place and it happened." While there, she spent some time studying the viola di gamba and looking at art. She told me that her husband, who was wonderful about giving her space, supported her doing this.

Over these years, she had also trained as a yoga instructor and an energy therapist, but hadn't done anything with these skills beyond the certification.

Donna had taken membership for the family in a traditional church even though her spiritual life remained with her spiritual community. Home schooling hadn't worked out, she said, but "it was important for me to get it out of my system." When the children were both in school, she had largely given up photography and wasn't sure what she wanted to do. Then she unexpectedly became pregnant. Donna didn't say she wanted another child, but she was "crushed" by the miscarriage. Around the same time, her husband's business was teetering, and they were, for the first time, having financial worries. She had to help her husband in his work in her non-mothering time. Then she had a cancer scare. "I feel like I've been under siege for three years," she told me. Donna was clearly quite stressed and somewhat depressed at this interview. The calm place was her viola di gamba. She was also directing the youth choir at church and building each year an elaborate Christmas village as a fund-raiser. But when I asked her what had been the major good experiences in her life in the last 10 years, she told me "there weren't any." She felt she was still struggling with the question of "what do I really want to do? I just go on doing this and that." The past few years, she told me, had been years of feeling her feelings more intensely—anger and sadness particularly. "I never stopped doing things long enough to know what really makes me happy or feeds me on a deeper level." She thought she might like to reground herself in work, perhaps take on more photography projects. She knew she wanted to feel creative and artistic.

Donna felt that her marriage was a success, glued by their shared spiritual commitment that still involved meditation, chastity, and vegetarianism as well as intermittent spiritual retreats. I could not find a way to ask how she got pregnant if they were practicing chastity, but, as with all such contradictions, Drifters live with them. Perhaps it is like what Donna explained to me later,

"If you eat a hamburger, it is not a failure, but it does not work toward the human capacity to achieve a spiritual goal." With Dan, clashes occurred only "when one of us is being too perfectionistic about something. I don't think he is ever critical of me. This turns my own perfectionism and self-evaluation on itself." Thinking back on the turbulence in their marriage when they were in their early 20s, Donna said, "We followed the times into something we didn't understand very well." Like so much in Donna's past, it was ancient history, poorly grasped, a faded episode of life quite disconnected from the present.

Dominating Donna's concerns at this age were her frustrations with herself as a mother. She felt she had chosen to stay home with her children out of her "perfectionistic" belief that that was the right way, but she felt that she had no training to be a mother and wasn't feeling that she had been very good at it. She hadn't enjoyed motherhood and rarely played with her children. In addition, the financial problems in Dan's family business were creating splits and struggles in his family, and Donna worried about her children getting caught in the uproar and wasn't sure how to protect them.

Also of note at this time was a long story that Donna told of an intense relationship with her viola di gamba teacher, a relationship "of many levels and a lot of love," that ended when this woman abruptly distanced herself and rejected her. I couldn't help but wonder if some of Donna's eroticism and sexuality was emerging here—but I kept these thoughts to myself. What I noted is that this was evidently a source of some of the pain that Donna was expressing through this interview. Beyond her family, whom she lived far from but still felt close to, there seemed to be few people in Donna's life. Friendship, she said, had been hard "because of the feeling thing. When I found environments where I thought I could be myself, I would be fearful of really expressing myself, fearing the judgment." She felt she was in search of the "wise woman—both within and without."

So, at 43, Donna was aware of a need to ground herself and still cautiously hopeful of doing so. She was exploring her inner world, trying to connect to her past and make sense of her life. While she was doing what she needed to do as a wife and a mother, she was feeling emotionally disconnected from these roles, and although her spiritual life gave her structure and moral stability, she was at a loss to know what to do with her sense of fragmentation.

AGE 53

At age 53, Donna was eager to meet me and traveled a long distance to do so. She very much wanted and needed to talk. She was now in pieces, alone and afraid, barely holding herself together. Her long hair was now stylishly short, and she was still slim and lithe. In many ways, she looked young, with something of a teenage air about her. Time seemed not to have touched her, but losses had. "Every way in which I had been attempting to provide myself the context to define myself, went," she told me. For the past 10 years, she told me, she had been living in her "Shadow self. . . . But how could I have a Shadow when I haven't even identified the being who had the shadow?"

Donna was now divorced, and both of her children were in college. She was not working, and all she had left was the large home in which she had lived most of her adult life. Oddly, this left her in the position of being both wealthy and poor, living in a very valuable property but having no income beyond some minimal alimony. Donna's recounting of the past 10 years was fractured by her distress, her wish to tell me all the details, and her hesitance to do so. The interview had the quality of circling around issues, presenting them and revisiting them later. Donna herself seemed not to quite understand just what had happened to her, except that it was all punctuated by panic attacks.

She dated her current life history from her miscarriage, which she had talked about at age 43. She saw this as "breaking a shell that I never knew was there for me. Like into an emotional life. I think that sort of split happened for me in my relationship with my husband, because I think I felt so vulnerable and just. . . . I had been brought up in not having any outward expression of anger or tears, and I couldn't find for so many years after that a place for myself or my husband to receive that. Everything was affecting me, I could cry at anything—somebody else's suffering or my own, and I didn't really understand it, what that was, what that vulnerability was, so I think I tried to understand if I could get that from my husband, find a place to get some comfort with that. And I think I went through the '90s, the decade, probably four different kinds of, I call them affairs, places where I really fell into being extremely vulnerable to other people's needs and energies, thinking that I was going to receive some attention there. A place for that part of me.

"I know also, just before I had become pregnant at age 40, that that was the first year that my youngest was all day in school, and I knew that I was very consciously turning my attention to what I thought was reclaiming my life. I understood that I had become very diffused [here she laughs because she realizes she had picked up my language from *Finding Herself*] in all the things I had done. The home schooling, I could no longer find the same connections so strongly that I had always felt with my photography. I didn't feel anything for going back there. So having done my educational work with the kids, with the school systems, having done a lot of work with the district commission, all these things that were just kind of there ... I knew that I wanted to go to finding myself but I didn't have a clue, and so I know I've kind of entered upon different relationships or fell into things. I remember thinking in the '90s this is my musical mid-life crisis, because I started to be so involved in music and I learned to play the viola de gamba without any intent or awareness of why I was doing it or what would happen. I was still singing in the choir and singing also with another choral group and starting to play percussion in the community band. You know, that was wonderful for me as an

outlet somewhere. It was making a lot of voice [laughs] somewhere at least."
Ironically, among her projects, Donna had also run a community program
that promoted wellness, with invited speakers who tried to help people care
for their "whole selves." She told me about this program with some pride.

Throughout the past decade, she had been primarily involved with her
children and their needs and helping out in her husband's businesses, which
continued to be financially precarious. "I wasn't being compensated for half
of what I was doing when I really needed to be making an income to help out,
and I realized how much I had given over from the time I committed to being
a mother."

Most prominently, though, there was what Donna called "the underground."
Her words give a flavor of how her inner disorganization feels to her, despite her
efforts to analyze and understand her experience. ". . . And then of course the
underground, which was a big part of the undercurrent. Underground were
those affairs where it would pull my heart. . . . When I started to learn to play
the viola de gamba and it began in the teacher–student relationship, and it was
a younger woman—and you know, I think I was in such a vulnerable place
and I had not . . . I don't think had any one-on-one relationship in terms of a
teacher–student and perhaps the just getting one-on-one attention became a
new experience for me, or somewhat fulfilling for me, or something like that.
But ultimately I know that, I look at four different people, you know and I never,
I mean that what I call an affair, just because I really know that I became
absorbed in a good part of myself in that relationship, that's all it ever was, was
a teacher–student relationship. . . . And, yeah, I know I probably would always
love for some sort of mentor to come into my life, and especially in that point of
my life where I needed, where emotionally I was just totally raw and vulnerable,
but really was looking for who I was."

Over the past 10 years, there had been four such relationships, three with
women and one with a man, and all ended in heartache. Did that mean she
had become a lesbian? I wondered. She wasn't identifying herself as such.
I had to ask Donna if these were sexual affairs, and she told me that three of
the four had been. But she was not interested in defining herself as a lesbian.
Even a sexual orientation identity eluded her. She just responded to whoever
seemed to respond to her "with a caring eye." Throughout this time, she had
tried a number of therapies to help her understand what was happening to her
as she became deeply enmeshed in one relationship after another. "I was trying really hard to understand what the dynamic was that was happening that
would seem to kind of short-circuit me into a behavior that I couldn't recognize." She came away from each relationship feeling rejected and despondent.
"Having given myself over so, it was difficult to come back into any sense of
wholeness. I couldn't understand how it made me this consumed. I was still
being mother and a wife, you know, so they were, they were often in a real
closet, but I gave myself away in them."

I asked Donna if she could tell me about what drew her to these people. "I would just give myself over to whatever was there. It was kind of their passion, their life, I don't know. I would jump ship on, not that I had a lot of ship there for a while [laughs]. I think looking for help in getting my identity and my core coupled with someone paying some attention to me."

Now, without family or work, Donna finds it "excruciating." "There's just no, there is no, there's no place for me to go and gain my context from somebody or some other situation." Worse, she said, "the level of deception within myself and my maneuvering that I've been able to witness has certainly made me trust myself less as to any kind of decisions that I might make, seeing that I can make such great blunders."

The divorce was particularly painful, but it, too, is shrouded in fog. My best understanding of what Donna described is that she was involved with a woman (one of her "affairs"), and her husband began living with another woman part of each week, and it somehow all just came apart. "I never in a million years would have thought that I would not spend the rest of my life with Dan. That's who I was. I obviously wasn't thinking anything through by then."

She feels that she had a marriage and children, although these are things she never really had to want, like other women she knew. "I mean I never had to want any of that you know, I never had to go through the risk of wanting something and not having it, but I feel I was very disconnected I guess from . . . whether it was the emotional stuff, that kind of life that I wasn't leading, but so, but that's the way it is."

Some of their estrangement had to do with the chastity mandated by their spiritual path. I already knew that Donna defined sexuality in her own way. And I had learned over the years that she could not describe her approach to sexuality in any way I could understand. So it was no surprise to me that she could have "affairs" with women without asking herself if she is a lesbian. And, evidently, Dan had joined her, after their period of open marriage in their 20s, in a kind of asexual marriage advocated by their shared "spiritual path." People, I had learned through the depth of this study, live in worlds of their own construction, scaffolded by perceptions and values that might be quite foreign to me.

I was also becoming increasingly aware, as Donna spoke of the relationships in which she had desperately hoped for a mentor and a guide, that she had come to the interview in hopes that I could somehow be this mentor that she craved and bestow on her the identity that she sought. I was drawn to her, moved by her struggle, wishing I could help. She was indeed raw and vulnerable and in considerable pain.

Over these years that led to the divorce there had been a tangle of loyalties and battles. She and Dan were allied against his family who were trying to cut (and ultimately succeeded in cutting) Dan out of the family business. There were estrangements and recriminations, blame and self-defense, court battles and threats of financial ruin. In addition, Donna had some serious bouts with pneumonia, and both her father and sister died. Several times, she had distanced herself enough emotionally from Marge, the woman she was most preoccupied with, to ask Dan to try to resurrect their marriage. But it was not to be.

I never had much sense of who Dan is as a person. Donna, very much ensconced in her own reality, was never very adept at portraying the people in her life. At this point, Dan "was completely absorbed in another life that didn't include his children" and saw them rarely. It fell to Donna to help them get into college, to transport them there—and recently to secure a loan at the last minute to pay her daughter, Gretchen's, college tuition. Amidst all the upheaval, Donna was still fulfilling her responsibilities as a mother. But, driving back from taking Gretchen to college, she cried all the way. Once her son left for college, Donna found herself alone for the first time in her life. She has been filled with intense anxiety, doesn't sleep well, and fills her days taking care of the house and gardens, trying at least to preserve the property, the only asset she could salvage from her marriage. Although she has felt pressured (and advised by her mother and brother) to sell this valuable estate and make a new life, "I guess it remained the only kind of ground under my feet with everything else shifting. I do everything, I scrape ceilings, I plaster, I paint, I fix lawnmowers. Yeah, I'm a property manager, and that's kind of finding the place where I can shift from the overwhelmed."

Listening closely to Donna's words, we hear that she felt "consumed," felt she was "giving myself over" and "trying to gain my context from somebody." She was well aware that she looked inside and couldn't find a reliable sense of self, but she couldn't find someone to create an identity for her.

"I could do anything. I'm a person that really doesn't do well with choices. And also just the not knowing, and feeling I'm not in a strong enough place, and I'm not in a place where I want to add any more regrets. I do regret the loss of family, I do regret being alone. . . . I've applied for a few jobs here and there, but it hasn't happened, and I guess my heart hasn't been pulled strong enough to really go after anything. I know that I need to be on my own and to get a connection to myself before I could feel good. . . . I lived here because of Dan. What do I want? Do I love this town? Where are my friends? And you know, coming out of parenting, I didn't have a social life. . . . I wouldn't have friends just to call upon if I wanted to go to the movies on Saturday night, especially after cutting it off with Marge. That had distanced me even more, and that was still somewhat of a closet relationship. I was not really going out and saying: 'I'm a lesbian now.'"

Donna has some connections to people in the church choir, and sometimes this group feels to her like a family. She does yoga and choir and has started painting and drawing in the past few months. A college friend in Maine recently asked her to help with a graphic design project, which Donna accepted as a way of "putting my toe in the water."

When Donna looks back at her early life from the vantage point of age 53, she recalls being a good child who suppressed "any kind of connection with my own self or my own needs." Going to college was "escape" from the demands of being good, but she did so many things she now regrets, referring here to her first marriage and then her abortion in her 20s. When I asked her at this point how she understood her first marriage, she told me that she thinks she was afraid of all the choice and freedom when she went to college, and it was a way of finding some comfort and security. But the marriage had its own threats. "I remember feeling a loss of myself. Nothing like the 40s' affairs, but I know I felt I was losing myself. . . . Leaving that marriage was one of the clearest things I ever did in my life. I left one day, and I never saw him again." For Donna, the best time was in her 20s when she went to graduate school and got an MFA and "did some amazing projects." And there was clarity in deciding to leave her job, live in Key West with Dan, and become a mother. Through this time, in retrospect, she regards herself as having been a strong person. "My very strong sense of knowing exactly what I wanted for the children in their upbringing in terms of everything from music, diapers, just committed to all these things that I don't know where they came from. Things in terms of—we were strongly vegetarian, we have a strong spiritual discipline. I went into studying and doing home schooling with them. I was so immersed in development and really providing teachers and people and experiences for them and really into listening to who they were as individuals and recognizing both as individuals. So, even from the birth, studying and doing my own home birth, I just knew what was right and what wasn't, what was good and what was wrong. The whole home environment for them." And then, in Donna's telling, came the "Shadow self," the confused, frightened, emotionally overwhelmed, and lonely self that asserted itself in her early 40s.

She was still hoping to find a mentor and to find a relationship. I asked if, when she thought about having an intimate relationship, she imagined herself with a man or a woman. She replied, "I would think of a man. But when it did happen, it didn't matter what kind of a body it was in."

As always, Donna narrated mixed images of herself. "Some of what I love about where I am is the childlike innocence about life and possibility and mixing in elements of faith and spontaneity and synchronicity. I want to be flexible enough to allow the magical in life to happen. I can be so incredibly enthusiastic. Giving up possibility is painful and at the other end is too much possibility, and I know there are too many things I can do. . . . The greatest fear of my life is that I will reach the end of my life and I will not have come to express who I am and I will have just wasted. . . ."

Donna had read my books and correctly identified herself as a Diffusion/Drifter. She didn't like either term because both seemed negative to her, but could identify more with the idea of "diffusion." She said that she is aware that she still wants someone to show her the way.

Over the years, Donna had tried various forms of psychotherapy, most of which were of the sort that I consider gimmicky. She found one "Inner Child" therapist who was an anchor for her, but then felt that he abandoned her. Reprogramming therapy, energy therapy, therapy with a Buddhist monk. Hearing the despair and desperation she was experiencing, I started to lose my role as a researcher. I wanted to offer her something and felt that if she were my patient, instead of my research participant, perhaps I could help. I began then to make strong recommendations that she see someone I knew in Key West to be a solid, good therapist. As far as I know, she did not follow through on this. It was hard to say goodbye to Donna. As I listened to the recording, I hear myself at the end of the meeting trying to press food on her for her return journey. Indeed, I deeply wanted to give her something.

Gretchen, Donna's daughter

AGE 21

Beyond pouring out her heart to me, Donna also gave me permission to interview Gretchen who, having just graduated from college, was the same age Donna was when I first met her. I was eager to learn about how Gretchen had experienced her mother, and I also wanted to be able to see Donna from the perspective of someone who knew her both better and differently.

I found Gretchen to be as bright and charming as her mother had been at her age, but clearer, more centered, less diffuse. Like her mother, she was uncertain about her occupational direction and questioning a lot about her future in what seemed to me a searching rather than a drifting mode. She was determined to support herself at this age and, after graduating from college, was working for a gardening company, gardening being something she had a lot of experience with working on her family's property. She was interested in teaching and thought she might try this after she saved up enough money to travel first.

Gretchen continued to follow the "spiritual path" of her family, although this was something that she was actively rethinking. She was learning to deal with people who didn't share her assumptions about support for things like gay marriage or opposition to the Iraq War.

Thinking back on her life, Gretchen described her mother as having been "very, very present" when she was a child, always there for her and encouraging her imagination. She remembers a lot of travel as a child and freedom, from the time she was 11, to travel to other countries and live with a family. As a teenager and into her early 20s, Gretchen wanted to make her parents happy, but this was complicated by their jealousies in their various undefined other relationships.

"I've always been my own person," Gretchen said as she described her relationships with her friends. Many of the stories she told were ones in which she held her own, held on to her differences and her right to her own ideas. What she was struggling with most at this time was claiming her right to her own life but still wanting to make her mother happy. Gretchen credits her mother with having been "at home every day after school. I don't know that I fully appreciated that, because I wanted more freedom, but that's what she did." But it is hard for her to leave her mother on her own. When Gretchen goes home, which she often does, bringing friends to the big house near the sea, her mother expects a lot. "She wants a lot of time out of me, she wants a lot of participation in the house, she wants me to be enthusiastic about moving benches."

Gretchen seemed to me to be quite sensible and mature. She was in a searching phase in terms of her occupational direction, but about everything else, she seemed to have thought things through and made decisions on her own terms, clearly a Pathmaker pattern. And I was impressed by how well she was navigating the strife in her family, telling everyone that she was *not* getting in the middle of any of it.

I was intrigued that Gretchen described her mother as "indefinite." She was quite aware of Donna's identity confusion, and, although it frustrated her, it doesn't seem to have impeded her own identity development.

What troubled me on reflection is that Donna didn't mention Gretchen's successes. To be sure, being a mother, in Donna's view, cost her her identity, but it seemed to me that this was an aspect of her identity that she had realized quite well. And she did recall those early years of parenting as the most stable, structured, and satisfying ones. That she could not fully claim motherhood as a fulfilling identity seemed to also cost Donna her sense of generativity and to rob her of pride in having been a good enough mother.

Vicky

Of all the Drifters, Vicky is one of the least noticeably discontent. She has seen herself consistently as "in transition" from a vaguely remembered past to an indefinite future. But this doesn't seem to trouble her; she creates herself—provisionally—wherever she lands.

AGE 21

As a graduating college senior, Vicky seemed like one of the most psychologically disturbed women in the group. She was depressed and angry, unable to control herself well or make much sense out of her life. She was questioning deeply, thinking about herself and her feelings, but nothing was adding up.

I began the interview with my standard question: "If there were someone you wished to know you, what sorts of things would you tell them about yourself?" Vicky replied, "I'd tell them the way I was feeling at that moment—my mood and why I was in that mood—the way I'm reacting to the things that are happening to me now." As is typical of the Drifters, she defined herself in the moment. Vicky seemed to be flooded by diffuse inner conflict, wallowing in emotions that she could neither master nor interpret and gaining respite from the pain by following friends into drugs, sex, anti-War marches, and generalized protest.

Vicky had been a high-achieving, obedient, and compliant Catholic girl until going to a small women's college, from which she returned after freshman year looking like a hippie and espousing the virtues of the youth and drug subcultures. She worried about what the neighbors in her small rural town might think of her, but decided not to care. Her father was prominent in the community, and she was one of 11 children, so she had always felt that she and her family were noticed and evaluated. As Vicky engaged more in the culture of her college, she became increasingly estranged from her family. They could not understand her. In turn, she was angry at her father for his tyrannical demandingness and her mother for her docile acquiescence to his rule. At the same time, "I was afraid to leave my past." She told me she had stopped going to church, then spoke of how much she really likes hearing Mass.

Vicky's way of experiencing these contradictions in herself was very different from the psychological phrasing of the Searchers. Where the Searchers felt their conflicts as parts of themselves in opposition to one another, the Drifters experienced disparate feelings that didn't seem connected to each other. Vicky felt "afraid to leave" her past, for example, but she was unaware of any way in which she was holding on. "I live day by day," she said, by way of explanation. Recalling herself in high school, she described herself in one part of the interview as having been "obnoxious. I never got punished equal to how bad I was." In another part, she described herself as "I always did everything right." In college, she felt she behaved in too many different ways to adequately convey except to say, "I always have a sense of unhappiness. I wonder if I'm happy to be alive." Unable to reconcile the many parts of herself, she kept them apart and lived with her confusion and a sense of emptiness. Like Donna and Yvonne, Vicky described a dissociated self. "I'm not making any plans," she told me, "I just want to leave things open so anything can happen. It doesn't matter if I make plans anyway because I'd just change them."

Throughout college, Vicky would become deeply involved with a group of friends, but then would feel that she was losing herself and would pull away from them. Much of the time, she felt lonely. Majoring in psychology as a way to learn about herself, Vicky toyed with the idea that she was mentally ill. She wondered if she were really any different from people in a mental hospital and daydreamed about what it would be like to be in one. As she was about to graduate from college, Vicky seemed to me to be headed for disaster.

IN MIDLIFE

To my surprise, however, Vicky pulled herself together (in a diffuse sort of way). At age 33, she told me that she had actively moved away from what she came to think of as "the soul-searching I did in college," regarding it, in retrospect, as "an exhausting waste of time. I don't think there are permanent answers, though there seem to be permanent questions." And Vicky became able to live with that ambiguity, keeping herself in check for the next decades. After college, she got a job in a mental hospital and realized, in retrospect, that she had hoped to change the world, or, at least, to change the way mental patients were treated. By the time she turned 30, Vicky had been continually disillusioned with how things were in reality in the world of work as she found it. She had also become disappointed in her communal living situations, where people would seem to have the same values as she but would turn out to be unreliable or behave in ways she considered unfair. She had also had two love relationships that ended badly. She couldn't understand why her partners acted the way they did, couldn't communicate her wishes to them, and, in the end, simply left or was left.

Lost and confused, Vicky decided to return home in her early 40s in hopes of finding some stability in her life. She took a "desk job" temporarily while she set about "researching possible occupations" in an effort to take charge of her life. In this "temporary" job, however, Vicky gained a mentor. Her supervisor, a woman, recognized her managerial talents and encouraged her. More than this, however, this woman validated Vicky's sense of how things were in the world: that people did cover up and pretend, that organizations often overlook mediocrity and shoddy work, that the best people don't always rise to the top, that people behave irrationally, and so on. Each was a hard-won insight. For the first time, Vicky understood that things she had in some way known about the world matched reality. Knowledge that had seemed forbidden or in error could now be aired. Vicky felt enormous relief to have someone else, someone she admired, confirm what she had always at some level known to be true. She could at last claim her own sanity. And, with this, Vicky was also able to recognize that in her family no one was ever allowed to say what was what. No wonder she had felt so confused! Living near her childhood home gave Vicky a sense of security and structure while her mentor provided her support and validation.

At age 43, Vicky told me about a long and somewhat haphazard sequence of administrative jobs in the human services and industrial fields She was still enraged at the working world and spoke at length about her dissatisfactions with her current job. She resented working for a manager she considered to be incompetent and railed against the fact that (her) good work received no more recognition than the half-baked dashed-off work of her colleagues. She took the role of the "outspoken" one at work, the one who complains, who challenges authority, who questions policy and fights for change. At the same time, she realized that this made her unpopular with some and that she had to put up with the tension of interpersonal conflict. Occupationally, Vicky still didn't feel committed. As with previous jobs, Vicky regarded her current one as a necessary way to make a living. She stayed with this company because she had grown weary of changing jobs every two years, but she still thought of finding some way to express her skills in some work that would be truly meaningful. She recognized that she had talents and was trying to think clearly about how her skills could intersect with the world. She was trying to frame her questions in narrower terms (no longer about "saving the world") and plot her goals in more achievable units. She loved physical activity: perhaps she would like to direct an exercise gym. Perhaps she might start her own business, parlaying her talent for sewing into designing clothes and selling them. Perhaps she might try to live abroad, leading hiking tours through remote areas.

Although Vicky's work was not the center of her identity, her sense of competence at work made it possible to take herself seriously. "I feel like an unsung heroine," she said at age 43. And what she had learned, as she entered her 40s, was about the valor in being able to appreciate and accept the "small changes." No longer interested in changing the world, what was most significant to Vicky is that she had lost weight, stopped smoking, found time for the regular exercise that she enjoyed, designed and made her own clothes, helped her mother care for her now-disabled father, learned to ski, and grew wonderful roses. And that she had learned to speak up and gain the courage to say what she feels and believes. "Some people regard me as a renegade," she said at age 43, "but I regard it as living in the reality that I perceive—and not denying things." And that is what Vicky found had been most heroic about her.

In her late 20s, Vicky had begun living with a man, an old high school friend, who traveled a great deal in his work. She said, at age 33, that her ideal relationship was a "commuter" one. She jealously guarded her own freedom and was fearful of too much togetherness. By the time she turned 40, Vicky felt certain enough of herself and her own boundaries to marry him. She said she valued him particularly for giving her a lot of space. Their understanding when they married was that she would remain free to pursue whatever career she wished even if this meant that they would live apart. (He, too, had uncertain career goals and had been employed in a number of different areas.) He was her companion in hiking and backpacking, and they together carefully chose elements of their living space. She described their relationship as fully reciprocal and equal, sharing chores and responsibilities. They had little physical or emotional intimacy, but she felt she could always rely on him for support. She recognized that she could be demanding and persistent and difficult to live with, and she was grateful to him for his acceptance of her. Neither wanted children. Vicky felt she had done her mothering in raising 10 younger siblings.

Also in her early 40s, Vicky joined an Episcopalian church, which she valued because of its openness and freedom from the rigidities of her Catholic girlhood. At the same time, she enjoyed the familiarity of the Mass and the ritual. She actively participated in church community activities and saw herself particularly as an advocate for women's rights. She also worked on political campaigns for women candidates in local elections and sometimes wondered if she, too, might like to run for office.

All in all, Vicky regarded herself, at age 43, as content. Her hopes for the future were, simply, to be heard. The main thing, Vicky reflected, had been gaining more control of herself. For her, it was "a devilishly persistent process to identify *my* values and make my own choices free of the institutions that earlier in my life had more authority." But Vicky was still casting about trying to center herself.

In some ways, Vicky was still drifting at age 43—but also searching—with a clearer idea of herself, trying to find a place to express herself that would appreciate her. She had increasing stability and control of her life. She had some anchors—her spirituality, her marriage, and her understanding of the world. Her sense of identity was taking shape as she learned both to communicate and to compromise. She didn't know yet if she could find a place for herself in the occupational realm that would suit her, but she felt more certain in her understanding of how she intersects with her world. What she wanted most—and fought hardest for—was to be heard. I expected that, 10 years hence, Vicky would be living in yet another version of herself, another rearrangement of the pieces. I was reassured that the disaster she had seemed headed for in college was averted. Her life course seemed to reflect greater internal organization, and I had hope for her.

LATE MIDLIFE

I didn't find Vicky again until she was in her early 60s—but it wouldn't have made much difference because her peregrinations over the past 20 years had some consistency. Continuity was embodied by her husband who she had followed to five cities over this time as he pursued his own shifting occupational course. Each time they moved—from east to west and west to east—Vicky managed to find work that "interested" her. But she never stayed in any job for longer than two years. Either she lost interest or began to dislike her employer and she left. Evidently, she had enough experience and organizational skills that she always managed to find another nonprofit or small organization that needed someone to do event planning or marketing or office management.

Sometimes she would start with a temp agency and then parlay this into a regular job. Talking to Vicky, I could see that she was smart, articulate, and organized, and it didn't surprise me that she could introduce herself as new in town and people would latch on to her to help them in their various projects.

When I met Vicky in her early 60s, she announced first off that she was "in transition," not currently working for the past six months and trying to figure out what she wanted to do next. The possibilities were widely arrayed—paint, start a home business, teach English as a second language. As she told me the long story of her various jobs, it was clear that she privileged being "interested" in the work. She still hated routine and disliked just sitting at a desk. She wanted to be interacting with people in one way or another. "I don't like doing the same thing over and over again. I like programmatic work where I have my own responsibilities." But, reflecting on her life, she told me, "I realize that I don't fit well into any environment." Sometimes, she said, she feels rather like a chameleon.

When she moved to a new city, she told me, she grounded herself by finding four things: a library, an Episcopal church, a swimming pool, and community organizations. These were, for her, the cornerstones of building community and feeling that she had a place—and thus, a kind of identity. Feeling part of a community, taking part in its activities was important to her. When I spoke to her at this age, she had been living in a small town for the past two years. I asked her how she made a life for herself there. She explained: "I have a woman that I walk with. I am physically active. I like to walk and bike and ski. I don't always like to do things with other people, but sometimes I do. I enjoy doing things with my husband, but it's not like he's the only person to do things with. I don't like organized groups—has to do with growing up in such a large family. It's gaps like that that I haven't completely filled." In each of the places she had lived in the past 20 years, she had found a community. But, when the time, came, she could leave it and find another.

Her connection to an Episcopal church has also been constant across her changes in place and relationships. She enjoys the rituals and celebrations without the dogma. It ties her to her past, although she does not profess a deep faith. It's a place from which to orient herself.

Part of Vicky's sense of consistency was her passion for outdoor activities. She still loved to walk and bike and swim, and living in the West gave her more opportunity to do these things. When she reviewed her life, she told of a long bike ride she had taken at age 24 across the country with friends. This was transformative for her. She felt that the process of organizing it and doing it gave her a sense of her capability. "It opened a world of possibilities and realizing how much I liked being outdoors and doing physical activities. I hadn't thought of myself as being athletic. Being able to deal with what came up. Being resourceful. I learned a number of things about myself, about my stamina and endurance and persistence. No one had ever recognized my strength. It wasn't part of my life growing up." Since then, being involved in physical activity has been a central part of her identity.

Vicky chose as "the high point" of her life meeting and marrying her husband of 25 years. Still, she complained that they don't communicate well and there is still little intimacy. They are good companions, though. They are part of each other's families of origin, and she tries to keep in touch with her many siblings although she can see them only infrequently. When I asked if she was particularly close to any of them, she said it depended on where they were living. Again, I was struck by the way in which Vicky's life is defined by circumstances, even the closeness of her relationships. She engages with what and who is at hand.

Her marriage is stable but distant. She feels they don't have good communication. They live in separate rooms "because we like different kinds of mattresses." She puts her husband third in her list of close relationships, after a sister and a friend of six years, both of whom she rarely sees.

Trying to define herself at this age, Vicky said, "An ongoing characteristic of my life has been following my nose, following my senses and intuition, certainly for a number of decades in my adult life. In terms of occupation, I've always done some sort of volunteer work, and I've used those opportunities to explore particular interests of mine, and I think I'm still doing that. I don't necessarily want to do things I've already done. I think now I'd like to do something more creative or expressive. I try to be broad-minded about it but also to pay attention to my gut, my intuition, things I seem attracted to." Or maybe she'd like to work with elders. "I'm trying to figure out what is the constellation of my skills and interests. . . . I guess I'm sort of stymied by all of this. Not a whole lot interests me." She has not worked for six months, the longest she has been out of work. I wondered why, at age 62, she was still looking for work. "For some income. I still want professional working relationships. The sense of accomplishment." I experienced in Vicky the characteristic amorphousness of the Drifters.

So Vicky's life has continued to drift along, but she is content to see herself, as she labeled an earlier chapter in her life, as "a woman explorer." She seemed quite satisfied with her life, a life in which she had, as she said in college, left things open so anything could happen.

I asked her what had happened to the intense introspection that had bedeviled her when she was 21. She said she sort of remembered that from the first interview. "I must have been distraught," she said. It was clearly a self that she did not recognize any longer. When I reminded her that she had told me at age 33 that introspection was a waste of time, she said, "There are things that need to get done—and for me, getting outside, getting fit, maintaining my strength . . . in the last 20 years, I mean, I've paid attention to that."

The Enmeshed Drifters

Several of the Drifters seemed to have solved the challenge of forming identity by finding someone else to define their lives and make their decisions. What was striking about interviewing them is that they replied to most of my inquiries by talking about other people, and it was nearly impossible to pin them to any statements about themselves. They seemed to have subsumed themselves in others.

When I called Erica at age 58 to make arrangements to meet her, her husband grabbed the phone and insisted that he could tell me better how to get there. He offered to pick me up at the airport and show me around. When I declined these offers, he delivered Erica to my hotel along with sightseeing brochures—and Erica didn't find any of this remarkable. In her view, he was being kind to me, as he was kind to her—except when he was upset and yelled. She worked as a cashier and was mainly interested in telling me about the benefits and leave policies. They did not have children, although she said at some point she had thought it might be nice to have them. What she loved most was animals, but they lived in an apartment that did not allow pets. Sometimes she kept fish. Mainly, during the interview, she told me about other people, especially her husband's relatives whose needs they were often responding to in various ways. If she mentioned an interest, like in art, and I followed it up with a question, she said she hadn't done it in a long time. If she mentioned a close friend, she said she hadn't talked with her in a year. I experienced Erica as a soft, gentle woman with a warm, giving heart and a complete absence of will. She did acknowledge at the end of the interview that she wished she had asserted her own wishes more in her life rather than just going along with whatever others wanted her to do. But this seemed like a detached observation rather than a source of anguish. Erica seemed content, just absent.

Robin, at age 54, defined herself as "a pleaser." Throughout her life, she just wanted to please others, to feel liked. As she was graduating from college, she told me that "my boyfriend is my future, so I don't have to figure out anything else." When this relationship abruptly ended, she coasted through the decades trying to find a relationship, working in administrative jobs in which she was not very invested, until she got together with Hal, a man who "gives me confidence." In her mid-50s, she is content, focused on improving her tennis game, a sport she began playing through Hal, and she evaluates herself and her life in terms of the degree to which she feels liked and accepted by others. "I can't really say that I've worked very hard at getting to where I am. . . . It's almost like, you know, things have fallen into place." When she looks back, she has no regrets but vaguely wonders if, had she had more confidence, she might have married or had children or a serious career. For now, at the age of 54 and after much therapy, just being able to form and express an opinion of her own feels like growth.

Jennifer, from a well-to-do family who went to a private college, married a Methodist minister and made her life as a minister's wife in what she described in her 40s as "an incredible partnership." Her identity was completely entwined with the daily demands and politics of the church community ("in which I'm not any kind of a leader") and her husband's activities. She spoke throughout the interview of herself as "we," including her husband in all her thoughts and decisions. She told me about places he had been as though she had been there, too. Jennifer's large house, in a small Southern town, was completely decorated in gray—gray rugs, furniture, walls, with only a few spots of light colors. And indeed, she was gray to me (although she was wearing a beige outfit), and, I thought, rather gray to herself. Her three grown children called frequently, as did her and husband's parents, and she spent a good deal of time just talking to them about "daily stuff." She said she found her children's lives interesting and liked to do things with them. She raised them, but expressed little passion about them and, when I pushed her on this, was able to say that she probably did a good job. From what she said, it sounded like they were all doing well. Jennifer's life was about responding to others' needs. Like Erica, she seemed content. I invited her to dinner, but she declined. I was encouraged to see that she could say no, but I thought that she had probably had enough of my persistently urging her to reflect on herself. I sensed that asking her about herself was touching on a raw nerve of disappointment, given that she had once regarded herself as a feminist and had made a start on a career she left behind when she had her first child. In her mid-40s, she was still hoping to pick up her career, but in her 50s, hardly mentioned this plan. She seemed to have buried her dreams of independent achievement— or just fully accepted herself and her life for what it was.

I was, however, sorry that Jennifer declined to have dinner with me because I enjoyed talking to her—that is, when we were talking about things other than herself, which she found difficult to do. But we had some common interests, and she seemed genuinely curious about me—and, in musing about this, I realized that I was responding to a profound receptivity I sensed in Jennifer. Her talent was in taking others in and being with them, quite selflessly. I could understand that, as a minister's wife, Jennifer had found a niche in life that suited her well. I thought she might have made a good therapist.

Toward Greater Integration

The Drifters' paths are checkered and complex. They start in college by throwing off all that might bind or contain them, and they spend the next 35 years trying to feel in charge of themselves. Some Drifters, often after bouncing from place to place, return home in search of a lost part of themselves, hoping

to find a feeling of settledness where last they experienced it. Perhaps returning home around age 40 represented some effort to reclaim the past and to
take in something they could internalize and keep for their own. The challenge for the Drifters is one of holding to some foundation from which to start
building a life.

More than any of the other groups, the Drifters live in midlife with a sense
of missed opportunities.[4] "Do I want the second half of my life to be the same
as my first?" Evelyn asked herself at age 43. "I don't. I keep setting up the
same dynamics. I don't want to do it again." Their past decisions often mystify
them. "I look back and I can't believe it," Vicky said. "I wish I had done some
career planning in college," sighed Erica. Donna despairs at age 53 when she
looks around and sees others her age so far ahead. For all their talent, all of
the Drifters who are employed outside the home are working in relatively
poorly paid jobs, often with no benefits, doing work that feels unfulfilling and
not equal to her potential. But, as Yvonne said at age 53, "Those years are lost
but life goes on."

If their work lives are largely disappointing, their intimate lives are also less
fulfilling than they may have wished. The Drifters both crave and fear intense
closeness. Less certain of themselves and their own boundaries, the Drifters
both long to lose themselves in another and are terrified that this may happen.
Many of the Drifters' partnerings have a somewhat Gothic quality, unlike those
of the other groups. Both Donna and Jennifer married men they had known
only two months. Erica first married a dying man, then married a foreign man
who had rented a room in her house. Vicky married an old high school friend
after he proved not to threaten her freedom, and Debbie married her first husband's best friend. Their marriages seem less intimate, less fully resonant than
the marriages of the other groups. They value the feeling of being "in it" with
someone and having someone to share the chores. Some speak of valuing the
sense of being in each other's families, feeling grounded and connected in that
way. Only Jennifer in this group mentions that sexuality is important in her
marriage; among the others, sex is infrequent or unfulfilling. In general, this
group feels they need a partner to manage life better. By their mid-50s, the
marriages that have lasted seem less conflict-ridden than they were at earlier
stages, with both partners settling into a kind of acceptance.

Part of what sustained the Drifters in college was their network of friends.
Most were highly involved in what their friends were doing and looked to
their friends both for structure and to clarify their own feelings. As they pro-
ceeded into adulthood, friendship became more difficult and less stable. Most
talked poignantly in their interviews in their 30s and 40s of losses and disappointments in friendships. The Drifters often found it hard to understand
what was taking place in their relationships. Others' motives were opaque
to them; things just "happened." By their 50s, they expected less of friends,
contenting themselves with occasional companionship.

We are still left to ask what led these women to this particular path of identity. Why has their course been so painstaking? Why was it so hard to structure themselves? While they were in college, the Drifters had forgotten or were trying to forget their past. As a group, they were defined by what they lacked—exploration or commitment in regard to identity. That they were doing neither of these things resulted from an inner world that didn't hold together, that was made up of pieces that didn't seem to fit and a lack of concern about this inner fragmentation. The sense of their childhood or their parents was distant from them, irrelevant. But, in abolishing their past, these women obliterated a core part of themselves, leaving only a space, an emptiness, a receptacle to be filled with whatever they might find. They were living "free"—either out of choice or anger. Few at this time could say much about what their parents were like. Their parents seemed to be shadow figures, ghosts without qualities, there only to be fled. For many different reasons, they were unable to identify with their parents or make use of them as templates for their own identities. In this sense, they represent the polar opposite of the Guardians.

Over time, the Drifters gave quite different accounts of their early lives, which makes it impossible to say which early experiences may have been formative. Their stories of the past change dramatically. Their development remains mysterious because, at each point in their lives that I have talked to them, they tell a different version of their histories. Even the facts of their early lives are transformed as they experience themselves differently. Vicky, for example, as a college senior, told of spankings as a child, of terror of her father. But when I asked her directly at age 43 if she had ever been treated in a way that she might now consider to be physical abuse, Vicky said that she could remember her younger siblings being beaten but never herself. Similarly, Yvonne spoke of having been raped on a date while she was in college, but could not remember this event in her interview at age 43. Donna told me a story of growing up in an idealized close, warm, loving family. At age 33, she expressed gratitude to her mother for "having an open and liberal mind which has enabled me to be receptive to new ways of thinking and doing." But by midlife, she described her family only as having been distant and cold, never really understanding her.

I would, then, be on too shaky ground to try to find the developmental roots of the Drifters' fragmentation. The identity problem is more difficult for them because they seem to internalize so little that felt good from their childhood, some good that felt foundational. Thus, they were starting from a blank slate, hoping that good things for them would appear in the future. From what I knew of them in college, the task before them seemed to be inventing themselves rather than reshaping bit by bit. With so much possible in the absence of valued existing structure, nothing was very realizable. With so little that felt good taken in from the past, the building blocks were not there.

The Drifters got stuck in the sense that they *could* be anything at all. There was little inside that felt fundamental or core against which to match or test external possibility. Being one thing or another, believing this philosophy or following that religion, all were equally likely. "Instinct" and "feeling" seemed to be reasonable sources of action. As a result, the self remained at the mercy of inner impulses and external claims.

When I interviewed them in their early 40s, I was more hopeful that their efforts to ground and consolidate themselves at that period of revision might bear fruit. They seemed to be realizing that they needed to pull themselves together sooner rather than later. Debbie, who had at ages 21 and 33 repeated the idea that she might make herself into something she hadn't yet even imagined, was, at age 43, more realistic about possibilities in the world. Her world had become defined, and she accepted its terms, however grudgingly. When they were 43, they were setting aside glorious dreams of what "might happen" and enduring the pain of disappointment. They seemed to be setting some goals. Midlife seemed to offer them another opportunity. By their mid-50s, though, these projects had failed. Vicky, who found "a good boss" and had a number of promotions in a company that she managed to stay in for eight years, felt that she was finally developing a career when the company went bankrupt. Donna fell in love with a woman who seemed to love her in a way that she wanted to be loved, but the relationship ended in rejection and suffering. Yvonne, at 43, was trying to do some artwork but found no receptive audience. These women returned to accepting what was at hand, giving up the identity quest altogether—or, perhaps, putting it on hold once again.

By their mid-50s, the opportunities are thinning out, as they are well aware. They don't know where time has gone and are trying to accept themselves, as best they can, as they are. Where the other groups are occupied in late midlife with their generativity, the Drifters do not feel generative, do not proudly talk about what they have offered to the world. If they define themselves at all, it is in terms of what they like: Vicky likes being outdoors, Donna likes to organize her garden, Yvonne likes to listen to Conservative talk radio. I suppose that these are identities of a sort.

Only Debbie, among the Drifters, was able to forge a path in this later decade, and I give her a chapter of her own.

Notes

1. I do not mean to suggest that all "hippies" were Drifters. Some were Searchers or Pathmakers, depending on what it meant to them to be living this lifestyle; see Keniston (1960, 1968). But it was an easy avenue to drift into and along, since impulsivity, risk-taking, and restlessness were part of the norm (Braungart, 1980).

2. See Bourne (1978).

3. Laura King (King & Hicks, 2007) has written eloquently about the growth-promoting forces of regret as reflected in the relationship to lost possible selves. The Drifters, however, do not seem to have clearly imagined possible selves to have lost.

4. Wink (1996) described a similar subgroup in the longitudinal Mills sample as "hypersensitive," based on their scores on the California Q-set. These married, working women showed interpersonal difficulties that kept them from a sense of security and comfort in an intimate relationship. Wink notes their failure to "develop a resilient and cohesive sense of self" (p. 66) and their decline in personality resources through middle age, although they were indistinguishable in personality characteristics in college. Citing Kohut, he attributes this to unresolved issues of narcissism stemming from early life that didn't become apparent until these women were in their late 20s. His findings are consistent with my own in that the women in the Drifter category became more doubtful of themselves and had less support as they aged, perhaps due to more general difficulties in interpersonal relationships.

7

A Drifter Who Created a Path

DEBBIE

Of all the women I interviewed as college seniors, Debbie charmed me in an unforgettable way. She was a free spirit, highly articulate, and filled with energy and passion. I might have thought of her as a "hippie," but she wouldn't have labeled herself that way because Debbie rejected all descriptions that seemed to curtail her freedom. She said she just wanted to be "fully myself," and she had explored many possibilities to experience herself in as many different ways as she could. She had been involved with mysticism, sexual freedom, and mind-altering drugs. She had lived and studied in England and reinvented herself there. "In England, I could be anyone I wanted to be. I kept changing my name." Her quest was to feel intensely alive, living her inner experience and her feelings. Finding a place in society was not on her mind.

Asked if she planned to marry or have children, she said, "I don't think about it—it seems so far away. But I wouldn't like to live by myself for the rest of my life." In regard to occupation, Debbie said, "I don't know what I want to do—join the circus, a gypsy camp, I don't know." She was majoring in English literature because she liked to write. But she was very critical of education as she had experienced it, and she had some strong ideas that education ought to be more conducive to creativity. She thought she might like to start a day-care center in Vermont and run it according to radical methods of education. But this was a fantasy, not something she was trying to make happen. "I'm terrible at planning," she said. "I don't do long-range things very well. When the time comes, I'll do something." Her approach to her life was, "I just trust my instincts." She said that, like others, she had gotten involved in political demonstrations, petitions, and marches, then decided "the whole thing was absurd." She fell in the Drifter category because she had no plans and had set up no clear choices. She was perhaps searching in her own way—experiencing and thinking deeply about her experiences, but in a scattered fashion. Still, she was clearly the most self-aware and animated of the Drifters.[1]

Debbie was raised in a highly traditional Irish Catholic family in Boston. With an extended family all living nearby, she barely knew, growing up, that there were other ways to live. In high school, she had obeyed her parents' strict rules but was fascinated by the kids who didn't conform. She always had many friends and a boyfriend, did the things that were expected of her, and tried to live up to her older sisters who were very successful in everything. But she deliberately chose a college different from the one her sisters attended, wanting to strike out on her own path. Already very attentive to who she was and who she was becoming, she didn't want to be a carbon copy of anyone. Perhaps I was drawn to her because, of all the women I have been following, Debbie was most consciously aware of her self and what it meant to be who she was, whatever that might be.

A successful businessman, Debbie's father was dominating, critical, and demanding and was unhappy at her lack of goals. Her mother was a devout member of their church and devoted her life to her children and their well-being. Debbie thought of her as always being very good, never doing anything that is wrong. "She always thinks the best of people. She was a good mother, a good wife, everything." But Debbie couldn't feel that she was anything like her mother. When she came to college, Debbie threw off all the ties of her childhood, and she seemed to do this without guilt. She felt she wanted to "make a Debbie which has nothing to do with my mother or father." To use her words, "I said to myself, 'I'm just going to be me. I'm going to start with a clean slate.' And what I started to put on it were all new ideas, and all these ideas were ones opposite to what my parents believed and slowly what's happened is that I'm feeling incomplete and I realize that what's happening is that I'm adding on a lot of the things which they've told me and I'm taking them as my own and coming more together with them." This last statement is a lovely description of the adolescent process as we generally understand it and is to some extent true of many people's sense of what their adolescence was about. In Debbie's case, it was more true than in most. She leaned farther out over the edge: there was little that she didn't test.

Debbie said that she didn't trust words enough to allow them to define her. The bedrock of her self, she said, was "That I'm honest. I think I'm a good person to have a relationship with because I'm an honest person." And I saw the essential honesty in Debbie. She wanted to see life and see it clearly. She saw hypocrisy around her and resisted forcing herself into prearranged roles. She held onto her voice and her own perceptions, no matter what.

I felt deeply for the intensity of Debbie's identity dilemma at this point. With so many pieces of herself to fit together, she seemed to be living them sequentially. Her devotion to casting aside the worldview and values of her family, her sense that she could identify with neither of her parents and did not want to follow her sisters left her with maximal freedom but an absence of internal structure. Indeed, she could "be anything," but how would she know if choices fit something core and essential in her beyond her feelings of the moment?

AGE 33

I expected that I'd have a hard time finding Debbie 12 years later. Fortunately, I had her mother's phone number who told me that she had moved to San Francisco and gave me her new address. I found Debbie at age 33 ready to tell a picaresque of adventures that constituted her past decade of living. Indeed, she had lived in seven different cities in the past 12 years. I was touched at how fervently this very intense woman tried at this time to communicate to me the complex story of her development over the past 12 years. Debbie felt, at this age, very removed from her college self, which seemed to her now to have been quite "naive." Looking back on herself in college, she said that she remembered "vaguely wanting to talk with people and help them via counseling or therapy." But, she declared, "I was naive then and I didn't really realize how much education and training were necessary for that sort of work." I reflected to myself, somewhat ruefully, that Debbie at 21 would never have accepted a judgment that she was naive. Several times during this interview, Debbie commented that she had no idea what she might have said about the questions in college—so far away did that self seem. Ironically, I felt that I knew the college age Debbie better than she did. She summarized herself as having been part of the "drop out, turn on, tune in" generation.

Although marriage had seemed "so far off" to Debbie in college, she in fact married a year after graduation. She met Brett when they were both doing LSD. "That's the kind of relationship Brett and I had. Everything was very magical and energized and everything very high—very all possibilities and everything was very adventurous and open and everything was like sparks flying and nerve-ends opened and life happening [sighs] ... and then what happened I think is that we both began to grow—and during the next two years I began to grow in a different direction. Brett was an artist and he was a quintessential artist—a mind-expanding drug-taker, limit-destroying life-adventurer, and I became tired or something, and I didn't want to be smashed into a million fragments and didn't want to stay up all night and take drugs and didn't want to have sex with other people and in groups, and I didn't want Brett to have sex with other women." And so, after several more years, they eventually separated and divorced. While together, she and Brett lived in various cities, in the United States and abroad, always with a life full of intensity. "It didn't seem to matter whether the intensity was in the direction of pain or joy. The intensity was there, and I felt that was real."

Although the relationship was frustrating and disappointing, she didn't want to end it. She did everything she could to try to make the marriage work. In all, the marriage lasted six years. After their final separation, Debbie felt she had nothing but herself. "I felt I was separating myself not only from Brett but from my family because Brett was my family. I also felt that I was symbolically separating myself from my original family because they could not accept divorce. I had no job, no friends, but I felt I needed to stay and resolve things by myself. I started with me in this one-room apartment, and I felt very broken and I felt that I began to make myself anew."

Throughout these years, Debbie had been employed on and off in a number of jobs. But what she really felt she was "doing" during this time was reading books, meditating, writing in her journal, doing Yoga, recording her dreams, sitting in cafes, and "making one or two friends."

One of these friends was Bob, a friend of Brett's, also an artist but more settled and less self-destructive. After some time, she moved in with him and, just before I found her at age 33, married him. After more moves around the country, Debbie began teaching part-time in a Montessori school. She liked her work in that she felt she was trying "to guide children toward the creation of their own selves." For the first time, Debbie seemed to have found work that was meaningful to her. She had persisted in her effort to make something of herself. But her commitment to her work remained tempered. When she thought about her future, she thought she might like to continue teaching in a Montessori school or running one or teaching others how to teach. But, she added, perhaps she might be a parent and not working, or perhaps she might be doing something "I haven't even thought of yet."

I was fascinated with these words and how they echoed what Debbie had said in college. Perhaps the future would hold something she hadn't even yet thought of. Despite being more settled, trying to live within the structure of her marital and occupational commitments, Debbie still held on to her sense of unknowable possibility. She could still have a life she couldn't even imagine.

When she described her marriage, I noticed how Debbie stressed the friendship and mutuality in her relationship with Bob, omitting any mention of the intensity she had experienced with Brett. Indeed, she said she wanted to be "more on an even keel."

Debbie married Bob because she was beginning to feel ready to have a child. And she knew that her parents could never accept her having a child outside of marriage. Her mother was so traditional that she still hadn't told anyone at home that Debbie was divorced. And, of course, she could not bring Bob home as long as they were just "living together." So, with a more traditional aspect of herself again surfacing, she and Bob married.

Debbie had begun to try to get pregnant, but without success. She worried that four previous abortions may have prevented her being able to conceive. But she knew what she wanted. "I want to be a mother, to experience myself with Bob and a child, to experience family anew."

At age 33, then, Debbie was trying to settle down, within the boundaries of her own choosing, still trying to live life in terms of her own inclinations and perceptions. She was still resisting "being" a role or a job, committing herself instead to fully living her experience, whatever that might be, but now without mind-altering drugs. "I was more concerned with living my life and unfolding as a person than pursuing an occupation or career," she said. She was still awaiting the emergence of future, possible selves. "Although I am 33," she said, "I remain somewhat vague and unknowing as to what I may 'be' in my future." And yet, I felt I heard in Debbie a fundamental strength, rooted perhaps in some complex tie to her family, which allowed her to take risks with herself, to play with merger and intensity, with other states of awareness and consciousness, to ground herself in some basic reality while taking flight with her feelings. Reflecting on herself, she said, "I feel that in the past five years or so, I have become more conscious. Before that, I feel that I was following some kind of path, but it was dimly lit because I was moving in a particular direction, moving toward something but I don't know if I could have described what that something was. I was using some inner senses for direction, but using them not very consciously." The theme of feeling more conscious, more deliberate, more in control of her destiny is what Debbie highlighted at this time of her life. And she sounded mellowed. Still lively, still questioning, but more willing to accept. As she got older, alternatives got more concrete for her. She had the same goals but understood them in a new way. She was clearer on what action would be required from her to get to a new destination. Life felt more embodied, less magical. And this was concretized in the idea of having a child.

AGE 43

Ten years later, it was again only through her mother that I found Debbie. And I was astonished to find her living just around the corner from her family home. Had she just "gone home" again? I wondered. After all that?! And, in some significant ways, Debbie had. I didn't meet Debbie at this time because one of my graduate students lived quite close to her and Debbie was willing to be interviewed by her instead, with me later listening to the tape. Both of us were very moved by Debbie's effort to find words for her effort, as she put it, to "find herself." At this point, Debbie had been in therapy and was studying psychotherapy as part of a master's degree in social work, so she now had psychological language and a professional interest in women's development. And—still being Debbie—she often questioned the questions, pointing out that she could never give an adequate account of herself; life and emotional experience was simply too multilayered.

A year after my last meeting with Debbie, her daughter, Miranda, was born. And being a mother was transformative in opening a new part of herself. It seemed to me that it was perhaps the first role Debbie ever had that was clearly defined in terms of its demands. "Because I was a mother—it's so cliche, but it was for me a very profound, very meaningful experience. I decided I wanted to be a mother who was home. That was a choice I made. This made it difficult for my husband. We had both worked part time. We each liked to do other things, so we made sure we didn't work too much, but what happened was that I was home *a lot* with Miranda, like 24 hours a day as happens with mothers who decide to stay home, and he worked a lot and what happened is that we got into traditional sex roles. That had never been our style previously. So having Miranda changed me in a number of ways, and it changed my relationship with Bob. I resented being the person who was home all the time although that's what I had chosen when I said I would not work. I hadn't clearly seen the picture of what it might mean.

"Having a daughter was an experience of falling in love with a whole new person. It gave me the chance to love someone unconditionally. She didn't have to do anything but I just loved her. I liked to hold her, sing lullabies, watch her all the time—it was wonderful but it was also overwhelming. Again, it was my own personal style. One doesn't have to do this 24 hours a day, but I didn't know another way to do it. I chose to do it in this way—it was exhausting because you don't sleep. Then it's like you're sitting in your house all the time alone with a baby."

Debbie found herself in a "trap" of her own making. She clearly and consciously chose to be a full-time mother, to give herself fully to this role—24 hours a day. And at the same time, she deeply resented having to do this. She regretted losing her friends. None of her friends had children, and Debbie found that childless people had limited patience with spending time with an infant or toddler. And Debbie wouldn't leave Miranda with a babysitter—she only wanted her to be with people who loved her. As Debbie talked about this, she spoke with a combination of ruefulness and defiance. She was both critical of herself for ever having thought in this way but also proud of herself for having wanted to cherish and protect Miranda so completely.

The hardest part was how strained her relationship with Bob became. "All the sudden you've turned into a parent and that's not what you set out to do. You start to feel like you're a married couple like your parents, and that's not what we ever tried to be. It's how many tasks can you do and how many can I do and somehow you get it all done." And although they tried to talk about how things had become, neither could find any solution, and eventually they each just hoped that somehow things would get better. They moved back to San Francisco where Bob's' family was and where they still had friends.

But, by the time Miranda was four, Debbie felt like she was "drowning. I felt I had no life, I was being sucked up by being Miranda's mother. It was my own choice—you don't have to let a child suck on you—literally or anyway else. I see other mothers. I guess this is how I wanted to be a mother—who knows, maybe it was my own need to have that kind of a mother—come here, take anything you want from me. Miranda breastfed until she was three—it was a very physical manifestation—here take whatever you need as long as you need. It was also very wonderful—wonderful to see someone take from you what they need and look up at you all happy and smiling but its also overwhelming if you don't have things coming in to renourish you."

And Debbie felt she had almost nothing coming in. Her marriage was getting progressively worse. She and Bob rarely spoke. Debbie was always with Miranda, and, when she and Bob did have time together, she felt they "really didn't like each other that much anyway." Debbie felt angry all the time, but didn't know who to be angry at. She spent hours wondering how she had gotten trapped. Finally, she entered therapy to figure out what could be going on.

Debbie didn't really come to understand why she needed to box herself in as she had, but her therapist did help her recognize that Miranda could survive with less attention and constancy from her. She began then to think about what some of her own needs and interests might be. She knew she wanted to do something creative, perhaps to write. For the first time since Miranda was born, Debbie got a babysitter for her and enrolled in a writing class.

As she wrote her stories, Debbie realized that she was using her writing to look at herself and to gather together different pieces of herself. But there was no magical happy ending here. Anne Sexton fought her way out of drowning in motherhood by writing, but hers is perhaps a Cinderella story. For so many women with talent, the road to making a living through creativity is blocked. Debbie's writing, like so many others' good writing, found no welcoming audience.

When she thought about returning to school, the old rebellious part of Debbie intervened and objected. "School was the straight world. I was going to make *myself* into something. I wasn't going to get another degree to say who I was or who I could be." Again she returned to the idea of "making myself into something," and again she was stuck on how to translate this amorphous idea into something tangible and realizable.

"I asked myself what I had made of myself so far. And the answer was: I had this child, I loved the child. I didn't like my husband, we never talked to each other. What was I doing? I didn't know. I didn't feel like I had made myself into much—or maybe I started to feel like, okay, you made yourself into a mother and you've done it very thoroughly for four years and now what else?" For the next couple of years, Debbie tried to solve this by focusing on Bob and helping him clarify his goals. Blocked in thinking about what she might do next, it was more comfortable to be concerned about what Bob should do. She could see that he, too, felt trapped, hated his job, hated his life. Eventually, instead of starting school herself, she persuaded Bob to go school part-time to earn a teaching certificate.

Debbie missed her mother and sisters, began longing to move back to Boston. She wanted Miranda to grow up near them. She hoped that once Bob was qualified to teach, they could move back there—which is just how things turned out. Just weeks before her 40th birthday, she and Bob and Miranda packed up their possessions, and Debbie went home.

They lived (uncomfortably) with her parents for the first year, then bought a house down the street. Part of what she termed her "conscious" decision to move back home was a wish to finally feel comfortable around her father. She had always felt like the "black sheep" of this high-achieving family and hoped that, at last, she could be accepted. "I got divorced, I looked like a hippie. They always had jobs, I never had jobs—I worked as little as I could so I could have time for myself—I'd be a waitress, I worked in a bar, I was a Montessori teacher, but only part time"—she could spell out her father's dim view of her.

Debbie had always enjoyed being with her mother and sisters, and now everyone was, in some ways, back where they started. Debbie was able to use the structure of home to rebuild herself. When Miranda began first grade, Debbie felt ready to think seriously about her own next step. At first, she tried running some mothers' support groups, helping new mothers think about issues in mothering, something she felt she had come to understand quite well. But she came to see that if she wanted to make some money or be taken seriously, she would have to get a degree. Both of her sisters are social workers and both are therapists. Debbie decided that she, too, would study for an MSW.

So, 20 years later, Debbie returned to school. And she began school with much fear and trepidation. Would she be able to write the papers? Could she manage to pass the tests? For the first time, Debbie's doubts about her own capabilities were clearly visible. Now it was not her rejection of "the system" that was at issue, but her fear of "the system's" rejection of her.

It was hard for Debbie to adapt to the traditional orientation of her graduate school. In the first year, she had all A's but felt as angry about that as she had in college. "Schools give you A's for saying back what the teacher says. All schools say they want you to be creative, but they really don't. For a long time, the reason I didn't want to go back to school was that I felt the structure and the way schools teach was not what education means. I want to grow more psychologically. I didn't want a bunch of information. I wanted it to come from inside of me." But Debbie was maintaining herself in the educational system, despite her criticisms of it.

She also made compromises in her expectations of marriage. "Bob and I never had a marriage made in heaven. When things don't go right, I want to talk about it. What is going on here? Bob's way is that relationships have ups and downs, and it will pass. It's so archetypal. I hate to even say 'I want to talk' because he ways 'You always want to talk.' But sometimes I get so angry or so sad that I have to. I can't believe that he can't see the need or that he doesn't think that it's better after. It's like one of those books—I have to do the emotional work for him. Just recently, we've had one of those. I feel at rock bottom and I bang on him, pull something out of him, something out of me and then I feel better." She realized that Bob had a difficult life as well. He hated being an entry-level teacher, missed his artistic life, which he enjoyed but recognized he could not make a living doing. Debbie realized that he, too, felt in a trap of his own making, much as she felt in those early years with Miranda. They frequently discussed separation, but always decided to continue to work it out, particularly because of Miranda. Perhaps one day, she said, she will walk out the door. But she stayed.

One of Debbie's great disappointments in her marriage was the lack of physical closeness. She felt more erotically alive and sensual than Bob, who was usually too tired or too distant for physical intimacy of any sort. Debbie thought about having an affair. She wouldn't shrink from this on moral grounds, but rather from fear that this would complicate her life.

Their marriage was limping along, sometimes with contentment, sometimes with intense anger. "Maybe I don't know what love means. What the hell is loving? He respects me, he lets me be who I am. He supports me, he seems to respect me in any way I want to grow. That seems important to me. Does he pick me up and twirl me around when he comes in? No. Is that important to me? I don't know. Would I like someone who gives back massages more? Probably. I could ask him more and I do, but then I get mad at him that I have to ask."

Miranda continued to be the keystone of her life. Debbie got tearful as she described her. "She's a wonderful child—she's intelligent, curious, and kind to the other kids—she's creative." And to describe her daughter as "creative" was, as I knew from following Debbie this long, the highest accolade. Expression of creativity is what Debbie has always sought—in her effort to be her own creative product ("to make myself into something") and now in her effort to nurture Miranda.

But, as Miranda grew, the relationship got more complicated. It was hard for Miranda to adjust to Debbie being away and not being available to her whenever she wanted. Miranda expressed her resentment and loss in a number of ways that were painful to Debbie. Now nine, Miranda was beginning to explore her own independence and often did this secretly, refusing to allow Debbie to know what she was doing or thinking. Most difficult, however, was Debbie realizing how often she was angry at Miranda for not being how she wanted her to be. "I'll ask, 'So how was camp?' 'Fine. Mom, please don't ask any questions. You ask so many questions.' She's kind of rude sometimes. That's hard. I don't want her to be rude. But I don't want her to be stuck being a nice little girl. I don't want her to be a good little girl like I was, but I don't want her to be rude either." Debbie hated her father's criticism of her, and yet she recognized that she heard herself being hard on Miranda. "Because I have other things to do, I don't want her dumping her books anywhere. Or take a shower—hang up your towel." So, most recently, Debbie was struggling to find herself as a mother of an independent daughter.

She tried to think about what in her life has been for herself and what for others but got lost in the intricate maze of this question. How can she tease them apart? Relationships had always been central to Debbie. "Loving people and being connected to people are very important to me, and a lot of what I've been doing in the past is that." And Miranda helped her access treasured parts of herself, gave her the right to "be funny and silly and creative." But now, having a husband, having a daughter, Debbie said with great passion that what she wants to do is "to work on being in the world and being what I want to be besides those things. I want to be a mother and a lover and also something else. . . . I'm trying to wake up and try to figure out who the hell I might be and certainly having relationships is part of that."

Debbie had less time to express her spiritual side since Miranda was born. While she continued to feel that life is soulful, her life seemed too full of the practicalities of homework and schedules to allow for meditation.

Thinking back on her primary family from the perspective of her 40s (and a good deal of therapy), Debbie concluded that "enmeshment was the mode of being." Individuality was treason, and independence was desertion. "Boundaries are not heard of in my family. If I go to my parents' house and ring the doorbell, my father is insulted. 'Why are you ringing the doorbell? This is our house—all the houses are supposed to be like our house.' I had to go away first because I felt like I was going to suffocate here, like I couldn't be myself so I had to get away—I felt too confined here. I had to put miles between us. And now I want to come back so I could understand how to do it and be right here and be separate *but* I don't want to be separate—I want to be attached. . . . I love the connectedness—this is what I grew up with. I loved the cousins and the aunts and uncles, and I know what a sense of strength and belonging comes from all that. But I'm me and I'm separate. I'm not them." And she had come to tolerate that they saw her as the failure.

Thinking of her future, Debbie hoped for yet more control of things. "I'd like to become more conscious of myself, to make some more conscious decisions. I'm a pretty intuitive person—I've gone along my whole life kind of like on my feelings. I'd also like to add to that some conscious choices as well." I thought that what she meant by this was that, at this age, she was trying to connect her choices to real external possibilities, to tolerate what felt like it didn't fit her exactly and to make herself into something recognizable to others. Debbie still stood out to me as highly conscious of herself, her feelings, and her inner experience, yet she seemed less captured by them, more oriented to what was outside herself. Feelings, she seemed to have learned, were evanescent, and she was now in search of something more durable. Having experimented with selflessness in motherhood, she was actively in search of making a solid self. For the first time, I thought, Debbie had entered a period of exploration and search, 20 years after the Pathmaker group had done this.

What I was learning from Debbie at this age was about the complexity behind what seemed to be, on the surface, choices between motherhood and career. Debbie was finding her way through this thicket with a very particular identity structure, one that was both fluid and vulnerable to totalistic immersive solutions. Feeling intense love for her daughter meant submerging herself and resenting it at the same time. Having not consolidated a satisfactory identity structure before becoming a mother, there was little to integrate with motherhood, and this was a consequence of her fragmented identity. Now, with the most intense period of motherhood behind her—and clear that she didn't want to risk "drowning" a second time—Debbie was poised to try to organize a more workable identity, this one rooted in her connection to her family, to the field in which her sisters worked, a field that had always piqued her interest. At age 43, Debbie no longer proclaimed that she might make herself into something she hadn't yet imagined. Her world was now defined, and she seemed to be accepting its terms.

AGE 53

To my chagrin, Debbie was reluctant to agree to talk to me again (the only one of the whole group to have these reservations). I reminded her of how important she was to me because I had learned so much from her, and I promised that we could talk about what troubled her—and that I was sure I could learn from it. When we met, I discovered that Debbie had finished her social work degree, done postgraduate study, and was now in psychoanalysis where she could explore herself in depth. She had recently reread all that I had written about her and had been in fervent imaginary conversation with me about all that I got right about her and all that I got wrong. This is mainly what she wanted to talk about. She pointed out to me that I couldn't possibly get all of her (which, of course, I knew), that there was never enough time to talk about all the important things that mattered so deeply to her. *Who am I?* was a question that had plagued her since college, and how could I answer a question like this when she couldn't? I knew she was right about this and invited her to collaborate with me on writing about the issue of what it means to write about another person. (So far, we haven't followed up on this.) I tried, though, to explain that I was trying to understand the Drifter pathway of identity using her as an example, rather than trying to understand her as I would if I were her therapist. Debbie understood this, but it disturbed her nonetheless, made her feel vulnerable and objectified.

Although Debbie acknowledged that "drifting" had been an apt word to describe her own life path, she objected to being in what seemed to her like the least healthy group. Not only did she still vociferously object to being in a category of any sort, this particular category felt to her like being placed surreptitiously in the lowest reading group in elementary school. I could see her point. I meant no disrespect to her, and I deeply regretted causing her pain. Perhaps she recognized how much I liked and valued her, so she agreed to tell me about her recent years.

What I learned of Debbie's growth in the past 10 years is that she had stayed the course, working as a therapist in a mental health center, trying to feel confident enough to open her own practice. Her psychoanalysis was helping her understand her early development and the difficulties she had throughout her life in separation and individuation. She often wondered why it took her so long to accomplish what she had, why she didn't manage it decades earlier like most of her peers. But she was accepting of having followed a twisted path. Debbie was also in dialogue with her younger self, the one who wanted to "join a gypsy camp," trying (as I had) to understand the many forces, both internal and external, that led her to an insistence on refusing available alternatives. She described Miranda, now 20, as artistic and creative, and hoped that she would take an "alternative path, but one that will be more focused and clear than mine was."

Miranda's leaving home for college was painful, but Debbie also found herself more relaxed, and she noted that her relationship with Bob had improved. Maybe, she thought, this had something to do with her analysis. Perhaps she had become less judgmental and attacking. She now could think of herself as happily married, and she felt that she and Bob would stay together. She had also come to value more her family's traditions and heritage, something she had disavowed. At age 53, she was very happy to have brought Miranda up in this community of family and family history. She was clearly very proud of Miranda but not sure what her own contribution had been. She loved Miranda's poetry. They had always made up poems together when Miranda was little; she always read poems to Miranda. Was there some line she could draw here to connect the dots? In her typical questioning fashion, Debbie could not be sure.

As we talked, I was impressed by how much Debbie had read, how deeply she had thought. And I agreed that psychological concepts were not adequate to the complexity of actual experience. Still, I thought how fortunate it was that Debbie had found psychoanalysis—a place where she could explore and contain the intricacies of her self. I, at least, no longer doubted that she had found a meaningful path that she could follow. She showed me that Drifters, too, could become Pathmakers—with a lot of effort, insight, good fortune, and—maybe—good therapy.

Taking no chances this time, I asked Debbie to read what I have written this time. I was delighted that she approved.

Notes

1. The distinction between the Searcher and Drifter categorization at late adolescence turned on evidence of trying to formulate some kind of identity, an attribute that can be hard to rate. In retrospect, Debbie was right on this line, and, in my first analyses of the identity statuses, I had labeled her a Moratorium/Diffusion (Josselson, 1973)—that is, a searching Drifter. Being on this line might represent more psychological strength than was present in the other Drifters. There were two others in this subcategory, but they are not among those I have followed.

{ 8 }

Paths to Fulfillment

REFLECTIONS ON ADULT GROWTH
AND DEVELOPMENT IN WOMEN

In this concluding chapter, I focus primarily on the women who were initially or became Pathmakers[1] because they exemplify fulfillment in midlife and offer most opportunities for more general comments on women's development. These are the women who created identities that they chose on their own terms after some period of exploration and who embody, in my view, the most mature and healthy adulthood. It is from them that I think we can learn about the optimal paths of women's development and consider how the stages of adulthood unfold.

As I have witnessed, reviewed, and analyzed the unfolding of these complex lives, I have understood that the age decades each have their own themes. In their 20s and into their early 30s, women are focused on competence, the growth of a sense that they can take meaningful places in the world and be recognized as the people they want to be. In their 30s and into their early 40s, they ask themselves if their lives are going in the directions they wish and if they feel themselves to be the people they wish to be—this becomes the age of revision. By their mid-40s, they are living the commitments they have made and are, into their 50s, reaping the fruits of what they have sown, enjoying what I see as an age of fulfillment.[2]

When these women speak about their growth and challenges in the period of life from their early 40s into their mid-50s, their focus is on both internal change and external engagement. They experience their lives and their relationships in more complex terms, in shades of gray, with multiple influences.[3] They have greater awareness of their embeddedness in social forces that are larger than they are and greater appreciation for human imperfection. Their adult development reflects subtle changes in how they see the world and themselves. In terms of inner growth, they highlight becoming more aware of and expressive of their feelings, gaining insight into their past and achieving greater self-understanding. The years of making the pieces fit together, holding responsible work roles, taking care of their marriages, raising children, and mastering the changing demands of motherhood seemed to them to have necessitated a kind of emotional suppression. They reined themselves in so as not to rock boats, but they only could see themselves doing this in retrospect. Many asked themselves if they were living authentically—or, as Regina put it, "like a robot," with a well-crafted mask to impress others, to prove themselves. In the period from their mid-40s to early 50s, they grow more self-reflective, more attuned to their inner life, and are more authentically themselves. They have more of a sense of how they were a product of their families and unique life histories. They develop new ways of understanding things they already know, and they know themselves in new ways. The liberation of advancing age opens a range of feelings that intrigue them, and they quest for a self that feels both more whole and more real. Part of the fulfillment of this age is making more space for their emotional responses, particularly in their relationships, but also as private awareness of parts of themselves that were relegated to the shadows. In their 50s, these women are passionately engaged in their lives, alert for new opportunities for self-expression, savoring experience.[4] The nagging self-criticism of their earlier years has abated, and they relish the opportunities for self-expansion and for mutuality in their interactions with the world. As they turn inward to better understand themselves, they also expand the possibilities of expressing themselves in their worlds.

When she was 43, Regina told me a dream that I thought symbolized the stage of revision for all the women in my study: "I dream that I'm in a big house where I've lived for quite some time. And all of a sudden I learn that in the center of the house—it's almost like between floors—there is a whole suite of rooms that I never knew was there. It's hidden from sight and the only way that you can have access to this suite of rooms is through a cobwebbed spidery staircase that's narrow and dark, but I go up through the staircase— or maybe its going down, I don't know—and I find myself in this suite with huge rooms. Everything is suffused with this golden light, and my reaction to all of this is delight. I think 'there's room for everyone here' and I never knew it was here. I've thought about that dream a lot lately. I don't yet know what these rooms are going to be like to actually live in them, but I know that they are there." This dream captures the essence of the process of revision, as I understand it, in women's lives. Revision is like discovering rooms that have always been there, hidden inside, accessible through the previously darkened and unused regions of the self—but taking care to make room for everyone who matters. By the time they are in their mid-50s, though, these women, having explored the rooms, are satisfied with their metaphorical houses, improving and expanding what is there, touching up. They have built their life structures and are actively harvesting the rewards. As I interviewed them, some remarked that I might find them boring at this age, aware, as I was, that fulfillment is harder to articulate than the dramas of conflict and change.

The external changes and challenges they emphasize in their lives focus on having impact and meaning for others—being generative. Assured as they age of their competence and authority, they are attuned to the effects of their investments in others and in the projects to which they have devoted themselves.[5] They become more empathic, and their thinking becomes more complex. They increase in their understanding of how the world works and the place they may take in it. They relish feeling needed by others; increasingly, this defines who they feel themselves to be.

This is the trajectory of the Pathmakers, the largest group of women, including those who became Pathmakers after the end of college. The Guardians live largely fulfilling lives in their 50s, but their lives are more constricted than the Pathmakers, marked by a rigidity that leaves them open to disappointment, especially in their children. The Drifters, as we have seen, just continue to ride the waves as life progresses, adjusting rather than growing.

The dominant themes of these women's lives up to their mid-40s, which I described in detail in *Revising Herself*, were competence and connection. From their mid-30s to 40s, women were revising their understanding of themselves in relation to others and trying to find balance between self-expression and responsiveness to others, consolidating their confidence in their talents and proclivities and still experimenting with ways of being in the world. In this ensuing decade, the mid-40s to mid-50s, the theme of generativity takes a more central role on the stage of their lives, notable in the lives of the Pathmakers and notable for its relative absence in the lives of the Drifters.

Identity as Psychological Structure

Identity, whether at the close of adolescence or after, and regardless of its content, becomes an internal psychological structure that undergirds adult development. This identity structure is largely unconscious and functions to integrate the various aspects of experience including roles, values, wishes, beliefs, worldview, and relational ties. The sense of conviction in identity, which grows over time, reflects a relatively secure and affirmed awareness of a place in the world that results from searching for self-definition. Identity is multiple in the sense that all of us take up various roles in different spheres of our lives and have different subidentities perhaps, but Identity in the sense that I am describing it here as a structure, organizes and synthesizes these parts into something coherent that feels like a more or less unified self.

Identity as a psychological structure relates the disparate parts of the self into some more or less coherent organization, leaving room for different kinds of self-experience, even contradictory ones. The importance of some period of exploration, which loosens the childhood structure, lies in the challenge of managing the experience of disequilibration, with its accompanying anxiety and guilt.[6] In moving away, internally, from the realm of parental dependence, new levels of freedom and integration become possible. Sometimes this is propelled by inner necessity and sometimes by new experience that cannot be assimilated to old psychological structures. This process of transformation can be either gradual or abrupt (although it is the abrupt ones that make for good stories and are most often depicted in books and movies). The loosening of childhood structures provides the flexibility necessary to carry forward adult development. What these women learn through the process is both to assimilate their new experiences to their existing views of themselves as well as to change their ways of thinking and feeling to accommodate and make new sense of experience. In this way, they grow internally through their interactions with the world. Through learning to traverse disequilibrium (which always feels upsetting), people learn to take risks with the self as they experiment with various ways of being in the world, engage in intimacy, and find outlets for generativity. Put simply, we learn to bear feeling uncertain about ourselves as we try new things—and we allow ourselves to change. But this disequilibrium has to be carefully titrated. Too little, as in the case of the Guardians, leads to rigidity and a staunch effort to make the world conform to expectations—and too much leads to identity diffusion, a center that does not hold.[7] Flexible decision-making, self-directed, that results from traversing the disequilibrium is empowering and becomes a template for the later choices of adulthood. Having mastered the disequilibrium once makes it possible to do so again.

The experience of "identity crisis" comes into consciousness when there is a sense that the parts don't fit together—a new experience of disequilibrium. This, in adult women who have successfully traversed the identity formation period, invokes the need for revision such that some harmony among the parts can be restored. Revision can take place internally, in regard to feelings and values; interpersonally, in regard to others; or externally, in regard to goals. Identity is dynamic, always in process, but it nevertheless maintains coherence. Identity, as I have said, is like a kaleidoscope with finite parts (although some can be added) that rearrange themselves into somewhat new but related patterns.

Necessary to resolving the adolescent identity formation task is the capacity to integrate ambivalence. Often with much anguish, these women give up the quest for perfection. They learn to tolerate the gray areas of life and to create a dialectic between change and acceptance. While this is true of all the Pathmakers, we see this clearly in Marlene's case as she learned to embrace what she could create and let go of what she could not control. Throughout her interviews, she could acknowledge the negative aspects of her life—her disappointment in her husband's overfocus on work, her struggles with her children—but these were put in perspective and accepted as things she had to adapt to. Like the others who began as Searchers in college, she learned that not all problems can be fixed and gradually shed her earlier idealism and insistence on perfection—but without cynicism or depression. (This pattern was in contrast to the Guardians' insistence on things going their way or the Drifters' getting angry when the world didn't conform to their expectations and moving on to the next thing.) The Pathmakers, in their ability to integrate ambivalence and accept imperfection, are able to enjoy what is good and acknowledge what isn't. These are the psychological advantages they reaped from working through the dilemmas of identity formation.

As we have seen, those who were or became Pathmakers have cycles of revision, at least through their 40s, where aspects of their lives that feel unsatisfying require reworking. Having traversed this in late adolescence, they are able to bear the disequilibrium once again. They change careers, get divorced, reorient their mothering to accommodate the emerging needs of their children, get more education or take up new interests. But here, too, there is complexity because the Pathmakers, although they are largely self-reliant, are also the most interdependent. They move forward in step *with* others in a carefully orchestrated dance. The daydream that Andrea told me when she was in college rather foreshadows development for this whole group of women, the dream of being in the exciting, spooky, scary castle looking for the treasure, but "as long as I'm with someone, I don't get scared." This combination of agency and company, venturesomeness and collaboration, kept in balance, is the dance by which women move forward in their lives.

As we have also seen in progressively tracing the development of those who became Pathmakers, the crucial developmental shift was in individuation, a painful psychological separation from a childhood self and the safety afforded by the parents of childhood, a shift that, for most of them, took place during late adolescence but for some was delayed into their 30s. With the resolution of this necessary individuation and the formation of identity came a sense of agency and personal authority, a feeling that "I can do things—and I can do them on more or less my own terms." Individuated agency forms the core of identity, and, when it is absent, there is an experience of loss of control to external factors.[8] When I saw these women in college, they were just finding their footing. But this did not imply standing forever on their own. Instead, it involved forming a core of self-knowledge and self-direction that was then invested in others. They developed a sense of competence based on others' validation of their efforts; they set goals based on the impact they could have on others' well-being. The identity they formed created investments and meaning-making that changed over time. They expressed themselves in commitments to significant relationships and generative projects, both familial and public, such that, in mid-adulthood, the boundaries between identity and intimacy and between identity and generativity are blurred. Identity becomes foundational and informs intimacy and generativity that, in turn, modify the contents of identity but not its basic structure in the personality. Erikson theorized what these women seem to discover in living: that we are most ourselves when we mean the most to those who mean the most to us. Identity is never finalized, but it moves from life's center stage, shifting, often subtly, in the face of new commitments that evolve from the later adult challenges of intimacy and generativity.

Identity, Connection, and Generativity

One overarching question I have had throughout the years of this project has been whether Erikson's model of adult development—in which the identity stage is followed by the intimacy stage and then the challenge of generativity—would apply to women. By looking so carefully and deeply at these lives, we see how identity becomes infused with intimacy and how both identity and intimacy expand to generativity, which then serves as the touchstone of fulfillment in middle adulthood.[9] Yet there are very fuzzy boundaries among these stages for women. And I have learned that we have to expand the consideration of intimacy by treating it more broadly as "connection to others." A woman's primary bond to her life partner is indeed central, but other relationships are important sites of the performance of identity as well.

As adult development proceeds, identity becomes intertwined with intimacy, the relationships of love that anchor identity, the "we" that the woman embeds herself in. Important relationships support, enlarge, and bound identity. In women (and perhaps in men, too), identity is deeply relational. It evolves to be "who I am in the world *with* others"—especially, but not exclusively, a *particular* other.[10] Too often, we, as a culture, equate identity with occupational role, but this simply does not fit these women's experience. Recall the image of Emily, ensconced in her lavish judicial office, telling me without pause that the most important aspect of her life is her husband. Does this then imply that a woman needs a man to have an identity? Most certainly not—but an intimate relationship is identity-defining, even identity-enhancing. Although few of the women I studied are without partners, it is apparent to me that a woman needs other people who are significant to her to feel a sense of her meaningful place in the world.

In their interviews at age 55, though, the theme of expectations of others, so prominent at age 21, still powerful at age 33, less so at age 43, had all but disappeared. Women were no longer responding primarily to what others wanted them to be but actively choosing who they wanted to be for and with others.[11] A noteworthy shift at midlife is that validation of the self moves to the next generation; no longer seeking approval from parents, women derive a sense of worth from their meaning to their children, students, mentees, and other recipients of their efforts.

As adulthood progresses, identity is subsumed in generativity—"who I am in the world for others." To reach a picture of their identities, I might just as well have asked these women, "To whom/what do you make a valued contribution?" Their answer would tell me who they feel themselves to be. We see this most starkly by contrasting the Pathmakers and Guardians with the Drifters. Lacking an organized identity structure, the Drifters founder with intimacy and largely fail at generativity. Without a clear sense of who they "are," they find it difficult to meaningfully relate themselves to another or to draw sustenance from their partners. And, with the disruption of intimacy, they cannot fully engage in generative involvement in midlife (although they take stabs at it). The Pathmakers, by contrast, with an internal structure that directs their relation to the world they co-create with another person, come to express themselves in midlife in generative interconnection with the people who have become meaningful to them. In their mid-life years, generativity creates their sense of fulfillment[12]. Identity, Erikson theorized, has as its psychological virtue, *fidelity*, commitment to something that joins the self to the world. What we see in these women's lives is the enactment of that fidelity, their bonds with and loyalty to those values and goals that reflect the ways in which they have joined themselves to their social worlds.

Women's lives are entwined with others in ways that enrich rather than diminish their identities. To conceptually oppose investment in self and investment in others is both misguided and damaging, but it is a message that is repeated often in the media and in popular constructions of womanhood. What the women of this study have experienced and learned is that self and others unfold in a complex balance, mutually enhancing. Identity in women is deeply relational as the self realizes itself through meaningful interaction with others—and these interactions buttress a valued sense of self.[13]

As adulthood progresses, the question of "who am I?" gives way to "how are my relationships with others enriching my life and theirs?" Identity in midlife is decentered as generativity becomes the realization of self. As Millie phrased it, "You find yourself by giving yourself away." This does not, however, imply submission to others or merger with them. Giving oneself away means investing deeply in the growth of others, feeling responsible to them, being needed (but not overly so). Care, as Erikson thought about it, is the hallmark of generativity—care for the next generation, both literally and figuratively. Generativity is about creating something in the world that will ripple forward. The adult moves beyond self-absorption (which Erikson considered a form of stagnation) and connects to the well-being of others. Care structures identity; people orient themselves in the world to what they care about—and, most often, care is rooted in relationships to others.[14] Women realize themselves within a relational web, trying to enhance the well-being of those they care for and care about—and reaping the emotional rewards. Their sense of significance comes from their caring and care-full engagement with the world. What changes over time is the *quality* of their connection to others, the ways in which they love, protect, and affirm. Care, generated by love, overcomes the ambivalence that attends obligation.

The stories that these women narrated to illustrate their sense of meaningful engagement with their world were generative stories, often small stories that represented their sense of having impact. Alice spoke of students to whom she had said something simple who came back years later to tell her that she had changed their lives. Emily, lauded for her role as a judge, treasures the letters she has received from claimants who felt that her decisions helped them. Fern, noticing that her physical therapy patients went hungry, brought them food. Laura, one of the least generative women in the group, told me about feeling good just being able to help lost people find their way through the hospital. What struck me about these generative stories were that they were freely chosen moments of offering something to others—or recognizing that one had. Such moments are experienced as meaningful investment in others rather than obligation. As these women age, generativity moves from role (wife, mother, teacher) to a deeply felt virtue of care.

Understanding the psychology of women has involved liberating our thinking from a lexicon that prized autonomy, independence, separation, and self-realization, terms that were central to a psychology of men. For women, autonomy is expressed as agency in relation to others, independence becomes interdependence, separation involves reconnection, and self-realization presumes a context of others. American cultural myths of adulthood, however, do not make the achievement of adult commitment, fidelity, intimacy, and care seem meaningful and heroic.[15] Yet, complex negotiations about responsibilities of care for others (and for the self) anchor the ongoing experiences of everyday life.

Over the years, these women have educated me to the relational grounding of identity. They told me clearly, back in 1970, that their identity was embedded in the people who mattered most to them. In some ways, these women have continued to tell me the same thing over the course of 35 years. Even in their 50s, in response to my request for them to tell me what has been important, particularly in their development over the past 10 years, their interviews are dominated by interactions with and stories about the people in their lives. Their "identity" is lodged in the people who embody their worlds—their spouses and children and other family members and also their students, patients, clients, co-workers, and others with whom they interact. As they paint their lives for me, they draw people. Their most profound learning is about their relationships. Our theory of identity, they have taught me, must include a vision of the individual developing more differentiated forms of connection with others while also cherishing movement toward self-realization (in relationship to others). Individuation is toward greater belonging and sharing. Identity is the place we take with partners, parents, children, colleagues, extended family members, friends—and maybe even strangers in brief but meaningful encounters. We are most ourselves as we are meaningful for others.

When I wrote *Revising Herself* in the early '90s, I still felt a need to defend women for the relational basis of their identity, as though I still thought that this would denigrate them in some way. Times have changed, and I no longer feel I have to argue the point. Indeed, men now seem to be moving in a direction of claiming their right to the joys of emotional bonds to others, to demand paternal leave and more family-oriented work hours and to resist being defined by their professional roles. As the decades have passed, women's models of being in the world—relationally—are not only respectable, but lauded.

Women's Work

For everyone, the workplace offers opportunities to feel effective, valuable, and meaningful in the world. As Vicky, one of the Drifters with a very checkered work career, put it simply, "I get satisfaction out of somebody saying 'Thank you—you've been so helpful to me.' I get a charge from that. I don't know why, but I do." Such moments are undoubtedly gratifying for everyone, but work goals change over time and what feels rewarding at one stage may be less so at another. As women mature in their work roles, what they expect from their occupational endeavors enlarges.

While nearly all of the women I have been following are in the workforce, the meanings of work to them vary widely—from central to their identity to quite peripheral.[16] As at age 43, just over half are *vitally* engaged in their work in their mid-50s, primarily the Guardians and those who were or became Pathmakers, for whom work is an anchor of identity. The others, primarily the Drifters, never found a hospitable occupational niche for themselves and settled for doing "jobs." Where work is central to identity, it serves either generative purpose or relational connection (or both). But many women struggled with disillusionment in work in perhaps the same way that their mothers might have struggled with disillusionment in marriage. For many, work did not provide them the satisfactions they might have hoped for, and they railed against bureaucracies and difficult superiors who frustrated their efforts.

When I first met them as college students, they were imagining themselves in grownup roles, wondering, sometimes worrying, about how they would be received in the world of work. Would they be taken seriously? Would they be up to carrying out meaningful tasks? When I interviewed these women in their 30s, they were developing a sense of competence, looking to advance in whatever they were doing, growing in skill and sophistication and moving forward. When I interviewed them in their 40s, the period of revision, they were actively struggling with their disillusionment in their work worlds. Now that they had achieved a sense of competence, the bureaucratic demands and the politics of their workplaces were causing them frustration, and they were wondering if there was a better way or better place to express their passions in their work. Over the course of midlife, they all became more realistic—or disillusioned—about the satisfactions the working world could offer them.

Over the decades, work seemed to evolve in its psychological meaning. At first, as young women taking on adult roles after college, they were oriented to approval from their superiors, to discovering if they could "make it" in their chosen work worlds. Many sought or found mentors who helped orient them and develop the skills and knowledge necessary to succeed. They responded to recognition, daily, sensitive to how they were viewed by people senior to them, wanting to know they were at least "good enough." In the next decade, from their mid-30s to mid-40s, some changed occupations or moved into new roles in the same ones, and here ambition and possibility became more prominent. They were now eligible for higher level roles with greater responsibility and authority, and they had to decide whether or not to bid for them, taking seriously the question of just where they wanted to go in the workplace. At this point, they seemed to weigh the possibilities of greater fields for action against the risks. When Maria, for example, who had enormous prestige in her role as Director of Nursing, toyed with the idea of applying for a higher position, she feared losing her livelihood in a system that often let higher paid, higher level managers go. "I was offered another job at a considerably higher salary, and I really struggled with the decision, but I knew that the responsibility was going to be enormous, the place was a mess, and I knew that it would take a long time to build everything up. I weighed where I was and the comfort level there and I said, no, I don't need to do that now. . . . My husband saw the more money and he said go for it, but. . . . The other thing would have been leaving the people here who mean an awful lot to me, and I just kept weighing back and forth and this place won out. I've thought about moving up to a vice-president level. Sometimes I think that from that position I might have the ability to make more positive changes. But the other side is—is this a group of people I can work with? I don't know."

As careers mature and stabilize, emotional bonds with co-workers secure identity. Work roles provide a place in a social network and a feeling of belonging. This is part of why changes in occupation are difficult. It is not only the nature of the work that changes, but the social and emotional structures that in part anchor occupational identity.[17]

By their mid-50s, most of the women who had careers as important identity anchors were secure in their places and finished with ambition to move up some hierarchy. Their focus was on what impact they were having on others, how they might influence people or systems in meaningful or lasting ways. They were invested in their work to the extent that they felt they had the authority to do what they wanted to accomplish in their roles. No one used the word "legacy"—this may have been too grand a word, but I understood their concern to leave a personalized mark.

Work identity goes far beyond the name of a role to include the individual stamp a woman puts on it. Work roles give one a sense of worth and inclusion in the social world. But identity is manifest in particularity, in how one invests in these roles. While developing their competence in early adulthood, these women wanted, above all, to be taken seriously by those they worked for and with. They had to move from being a student or beginner to becoming seasoned and knowledgeable. But all of these women mightily resist institutionalization, desiring to find self-expression in how they engage in their work. They are women who have honed their values and strive to keep them fresh and alive. Alice enjoys her role as supporting students in their confrontations with the school administrators—an unofficial role that is not defined by "teacher," and Regina relished supervising her graduate students in coffee shops. Clara wants no "negative signs" in her library. Norma had to learn about building parking lots in her role as principal because this is what the community wanted at the school. Andrea, when the medical world no longer supported her values about the delivery of care, began volunteering to treat homeless people—outside the purview of managed care. Putting one's own stamp on taking up a work role mark the sites of growth in identity and generativity. In these decisions, identity becomes individualized and unique to the person.

These women, by their mid-50s, are no longer thinking about changing their career paths, but they are considering retiring—some time in the now-foreseeable future. They are setting up a choice between continuing with what they are doing or having a life outside the workplace. For some, early retirement is a perk of their systems, so they could retire sooner rather than later (as Grace and Laura did at 60 and Norma was planning at 58). They are wondering if the generative opportunities of work outweighed the hassles. In general, though, they have accepted the politics of the systems in which they work and have found ways to do their work meaningfully within them. They are beating their heads against the walls less, having carved out comfortable and effective ways of doing things and accepting the limitations. Those women who have been in long-time careers now have seniority or more responsible positions and seem to be carrying out their missions as much as possible on their own authority, so they are less painfully frustrated than they were a decade earlier. Some have found ways of fulfilling their goals outside their systems or changed their venues. Andrea, dissatisfied with the commercialization of medicine, increasingly volunteers her services and is actively thinking about doing something else entirely. Maria left the public system in the past decade and went to a private practice more in keeping with her values. Millie was looking for ways to teach and pass on her religious values outside the confines of her own church.

Those most passionate about their current work are those who have moved into new roles in the past decade, trying to master fresh challenges—Clara in her library, Emily in her court, Debbie just embarking on a social work career. The women with long-term career paths, clear on their skills and values, were mainly struggling with how best to bring their now well-honed work identities in line with the systems in which they worked. Although often feeling stymied, most weren't yet ready to give up this aspect of their lives. Harriet, describing her teaching career, said, "I'm very comfortable with what I'm doing. I'm very well-respected—that allows me to sit back and relax a little bit as to how I feel about myself professionally. You start out as a teacher, the parents are older than you are. Now they're almost half my age. It's just a very different feeling. . . . I love the kids, I love the teaching. I would have retired years ago if I could have afforded it because I'm just tired of the paperwork and the meetings and all the auxiliary things you have to do . . . you get knocked down by all these other things that take you away from the places where you can have some effect." And, Harriet asks herself, what would she do if she weren't teaching, articulating a question that all of these women seemed to have asked themselves.

As was true in the age-40s interview, some stressed loving their work because they loved the people with whom they worked, with the relationships as important—sometimes even more so—than the work itself. Helen, a teacher, told me she "loves the kids," but then described her work life focusing on the social engagement with her team—the fun they have during lunch and the opportunity to be close to women of different ages. She is eligible for retirement but continues teaching because school is a respite from the stresses of home and the care of her parents and in-laws whose health is rapidly declining. Erica likes her work as a cashier because "the people there are really nice."

Strikingly, no one seemed motivated by success in financial terms. Money and power were simply not primary incentives for the women I have followed. Nor was stark ambition. With all the current cultural conversation about why there are not more women CEOs, the answer from the women I have studied seemed clear. Perhaps they are different in some way from others, but none saw herself as existing within a hierarchy she was trying to climb. The "alpha male" competitive spirit was foreign to them. If they wanted to "move up," it was only if they saw this move as affording them more influence or impact on some goal they cherished.

For those without clear occupational goals, work was a financial necessity and they evaluated work opportunities in terms of how they would feel in positions of working toward others' goals in the corporate world. Nancy, looking for work after being laid off from her previous administrative job, said, "I was looking for a job with some money and responsibility, fairly close to home, something that was going to feel comfortable. I wanted a place that felt homey, department-wise, comfortable, sort of how the culture was." How they would *feel* day to day in the workplace was paramount. And there were daily satisfactions. Sandra, working serially over time in what she terms "support roles," told me, "I'm very devoted to what I do at work, whether it's a small thing or a big thing. My motivation is being competent . . . I like being viewed as the go-to person . . . I get a charge from that."

Although work lives varied in terms of importance in the identities of these women, all spoke of a *sense of accomplishment* in work. This could be an overall sense of meaning or the joy of realizing a more time-limited and narrow goal. Many found that sense of accomplishment came also from either volunteer activities or personal projects.

With children grown and work pressures lessened, many are engaging more in personal pursuits. Betty is weaving and painting; Alice is planning a garden and learning about canning; Emily is organizing ever more lavish dinner parties; Grace is writing short stories. They are enlarging their sphere of what they *do* and looking outside of the paid work world for the satisfaction of expressing themselves.

Identity and Intimacy

The identity structure, once formed, opens up to and is infused by intimacy. Love becomes a context for the experience of identity, both bounding and enlarging it. Values and goals are re-examined in the context of an increasingly cherished other person who, loving in return, appreciates and buttresses the woman in the expanding world in which she expresses herself. Autonomy grows in the context of connection as women discover how the world responds to them and choose who they wish to include in the social world they are creating. Connection grows in the context of autonomy as the self learns to make more differentiated, and therefore more intimate, relationships. Our experience of identity rests on a sense of fit between self and the social world, on the expectation that the environment will, at least much of the time, be in tune with us.[18] A love relationship is a safe haven in which the most authentic self can be articulated (and further discovered).

By their mid-30s, these women think of their own identities as co-constructed with their husbands. They refined their identity projects in light of the person to whom they committed themselves so that the sense of "I" enlarged to a feeling of "we." In no way did I see this as involving submission or subjugation. Instead, the women I have studied emphasized the importance of their partners in supporting their efforts, cheering them on, soothing their frustrations in the outside world, and joining them in household management to free energy for their occupational pursuits. In turn, their own identity included supporting their partners in their pursuits. Each partner committed not only to the permanence of the relationship but to developing the other's strengths—despite the compromises that may be entailed by the commitment. Betty had to modify her occupational plans (which involved satisfaction as a physical therapist) to accommodate her retired husband who wanted to travel and live in the countryside. They worked out a compromise that would accommodate both of their wishes. In addition, partners enlarged these women's worlds, bringing them into contact with people, projects, and concerns that extended their worldviews and provided other spheres in which to engage.

For some women, the realization that they could not be the person they wished to be in their love relationship meant divorce and another search for a partner who would fit better. Alice and Andrea, among the college-age Pathmakers, and Marlene who found her path later, all reworked their relationships to suit their identities but also revised themselves in the context of the new, more satisfying partnership. Regina, whose identity search centered around the way in which she wanted to experience herself as a woman, struggled to stay in an unhappy relationship but eventually revised herself and her needs so that she found a way to appreciate and more fully love her husband.

Relationships grow and change, and identity is expressed in the quality of connection with those one loves. Intimacy, like identity, is a process that is never finalized. While in their 40s, women were still wrestling with how they wanted to be with their partners and how they wanted their partners to be with them; by their 50s, they seemed to have made peace with their ways of being as a couple, and their interviews were marked by less complaint and discontent. Many women, reflecting on their lives, felt that something they were most proud to have accomplished was a loving marriage, proud that their love for their partner had overcome whatever difficulties they had had along the way. They described their marriages as filled with mutual companionship, understanding, and support. Many described their husbands as their "best friends." But they didn't idealize their marriages. Most stressed that there were problems they had to work out or live with. They lived in loving marriages that survived illness, gambling, infidelity, impotence, workaholism, and unemployment.

Some felt they grew in their marriages under pressure to make needed changes in themselves, to become more tolerant, for example, or more accepting of difference. For some, learning in midlife centered on learning to better express their feelings in their relationships; this was a developmental challenge for women who had succeeded through suppression of emotional experience. Many had to work out changing sexual needs with their husbands as erotic and sensual experience for both partners changed over the decades.

In their 20s and 30s, many actively struggled to understand what love is and might be. By their 50s, they better know both how they love and how to let themselves be loved, but there are still discoveries to be made about the intimacy of their couple. Marriages did not stay static over 30 years—and there was no typical marriage. Living together is an ongoing process of learning to make decisions together, and this may involve more or less actual togetherness. Negotiation often centers on times and spaces for togetherness and times and spaces for separateness. Some women appreciated their husband's separate activities, which left them time for their own individual pursuits; others wanted more of their husband's time and involvement with them, whereas others wished their husbands would need their availability to them less. Some couples were re-finding each other after children had left home. Some couples had become asexual with more or less mutual agreement; others relished their still-passionate sexual engagement. Most of the women seemed even more satisfied with their marriages as they aged. Their identity had become lodged in a sense of "we," which included acceptance of whatever dissatisfactions there were. The couple had become the foundational unit for the structure of their lives, and the women I have followed spoke about themselves as inseparably part of this unit.

Successful marriage as central to a woman's sense of fulfillment is a reality of women's lives that our contemporary culture rather dismisses. For one thing, our literature has never adequately depicted this phenomenon. Perhaps it would be too boring, as Carolyn Heilbrun suggested. Marriage as a safe haven, as a containing structure to a life with the pleasures of interconnectedness and sharing, is too quotidian, too prosaic, too mundane for the literary imagination. In contemporary psychology, there is much focus on abusive marriage, marriages that contain conflict and drama. What is not represented are Betty and Bill, he carrying the logs for the house they are building, she stripping them, him putting them in place.

The companionate shape of the Pathmakers' marriages seemed a valued invention, so different, in these women's views, from the marriages of their parents. Women who told me that their husbands were their best friends had both joy and pride in their voices. These were women, after all, who came from families where roles were stereotyped, who saw their fathers as uninvolved in the family, gruff, critical breadwinners who expected caretaking from their wives. They saw their mothers as enslaved to their household chores, powerful perhaps in regard to the children, but subservient in all other ways. No wonder some of these women were so delighted to tell me that they relied on their husbands to do the cooking! Unlike in their families of origin, these women contributed significantly to the family income, half earning as much or more than their husbands, and that profoundly shifted the balance of power (although no one said it like this). No one was staying in a marriage out of economic necessity. Where they sensed in their parents' marriage the complex dynamics of dependency that ensued from an economic arrangement that led to various forms of dominance, resentment, retribution, and emotional distance, they wanted to construct in their own marriages a liaison of love, respect, and mutuality. The achievement of an egalitarian marriage that felt like a supportive partnership, which most realized, was very much part of their sense of fulfillment—and of their identities.

For the Drifters, women who did not emerge from the identity challenge with an organized identity, the intimacy "stage" was a different experience in contrast to the Pathmakers. Without a solid core of identity, they tended to make marriages with fragmented parts of themselves, often hastily. Erica twice married men she had known only a month. Or they married men with whom they could re-enact painful, usually highly critical, relationships with one of their parents. Some tried to substitute intimacy for identity, leaving it to their partners to define them—a strategy that worked for Jennifer but not for others. The Drifters' marriages were, unsurprisingly, troubled, marked by persistent battling or withdrawal. The deficits in identity formation set their efforts at intimacy on shaky ground.

Those who remained Guardians made stereotypic rather than intimate marriages. They chose men who would enact their version of the role of husband and who allowed them to supervise (or even dictate) their behavior in this role. The Guardians, clear as they are on right and wrong ways to live life, defined the terms in their marriages. Strikingly, in their interviews, the Guardians tended to refer to their husbands as "my husband" whereas the Pathmakers referred to their husbands by name. With the Pathmakers, I got a sense of the people their husbands were. With the Guardians, I knew them only as "husbands."

Marriage, then, is a central site of identity, both as an arena of identity expression and as an anchor for who else a women is in the world. It can either stabilize or destablilize a sense of self, and it becomes an integral part of self-experience. A marriage is a unique creation and, like identity, is dynamic and evolves to suit the needs of both partners. We learn much about a woman's identity by hearing the story of her marriage. Self and other are inextricably knit. Among these life stories, marriages range from almost completely intertwined to ones that are interdependent, with large spaces for individual pursuit. In their mid-50s, some women adore their husbands, others tolerate them, more or less lovingly. Whatever the design of the marital relationship and the quality of the affective bond, their marriages are simply part of who they are.

Identity and Motherhood

For those who became mothers, motherhood not only added a role to identity but provided another anchor point from which to experience themselves in the world. It connected them to the social world in a new way because they had to engage with the larger society in terms of the well-being of their children. They chose where they would live in part out of consideration of their children's schooling. For many, needing a field of endeavor outside of tending their children drove them to greater commitment to their occupational work. Clara, for example, found that she needed her work for intellectual stimulation to balance the often tedious care of young children. Others reworked their occupational commitments so they could be more flexibly available to their children.

All of those who became mothers spoke of how having children changed them as people. They had to refashion how they felt and behaved in relationship to others, how they expressed their love and anger. They had to decide, however inconsistently, how they would take up their authority as a parent. They had to rethink their values as they came to understand themselves as models for their children.[19] Many spontaneously contrasted their own mothering styles to their own mothers and to their sisters or cousins, mainly in terms of the freedoms they did or did not afford their children, the rules they chose to enforce and how they managed discipline.

Many women found that being a mother was an opportunity to rework their inner experience of their own mothers, and this promoted their own growth. Being a mother of the same age at which they could remember their own mothers engendered compassion and, often, forgiveness.[20] They could let go of old anger and feel internally freer. Some found that they could reclaim early identifications with good aspects of their mothers and feel enriched. All along, I have found that the early relationship with their mother is central to identity formation in women, and internal struggles with her to claim an independent self continue into middle adulthood. So many of us remember our mothers saying to us when we were children and angry at her, "Wait until you have children of your own—then you'll understand." The women I have studied demonstrate that there is truth and wisdom in this. Still, all of these women believe that they have *been* better mothers than they had.

Identity and Others

In order to get a snapshot of the social worlds that these women live in, I had asked each woman, at each interview, to make a list of the 10 people she felt closest to in the world. By their 50s, these lists were dominated by family members, with most listing only three or four friends.

To my surprise, friendship was less important than I expected. Most of the women told me, regretfully, that this is what they had to let go of to focus on their work and have families. They missed the joys of friendship, but couldn't find the time. Nearly all of the women listed friends on their "close relationships" lists, but didn't talk about them much as they described their lives. Friends were usually there, but not central. (On the other hand, I didn't focus on this much, as I had in a previous study of women's friendship.[21]) Friends tended to be people from their work worlds that they socialized with—or people who were there to help or be helped by in an arrangement of mutual availability in times of need. As Emily, who is married without children, described it at age 43, "Friends used to be listeners for my dating problems. Now I need them more for dinners out and socializing. I'm also happier on my own now, and my husband is my best friend. Or I do things with them that my husband doesn't like—like shopping or eating sushi or going to a spa." For those who maintained intimate female friendships, it was either with very old friends, often from college, who lived far away and were rarely seen or, most commonly, with their sisters. It seemed that these women leave little time for the self-indulgence that downtime with friends would represent. Instead, their meaningful friendships outside their families center on shared engagement in generative projects—at work or in their communities. Companionship and friendship emerge from common purpose.

Earlier in their lives, friends stabilized their identities by validating them as who they felt themselves to be. The significance of friendship was at its peak in their 20s, when identity was still forming and firming. As they age and feel more certain of themselves, they no longer need friendship as much for this purpose. Although anxiety and change are diminished in the late 40s and early 50s, friendship can still serve as a sounding board. Harriet, for example, mentions her close friends as people she talks to about her struggles with her daughter. Overall, though, these women's friendships in late midlife tended to be casual or companionate, bounded and momentarily satisfying, rather than deep and intimate.

Identity and Generativity

Generative investment involves compassion, time, and effort to enrich the lives of others. As these women began to take up ever more responsible roles in the work world, their attention slowly and subtly shifted from "how good am I doing?" to "what good am I doing?" Their sense of purpose evolved around having positive impact on others. By their mid-50s, no one spoke of narcissistic ambitions simply to have "higher" roles, even those who were most accomplished in the usual terms. If they wanted to move up in their work hierarchies, it was usually to have more impact on how best to do their work. Rather than being occupied with validating their competence, as they had been in their 30s, they wanted to have influence and to see that they were effective. Alice resisted continued invitations to become a school principal because she liked the impact she was having on her students and didn't like sitting in meetings. Maria left a high-status role as director of nursing in her hospital when she felt that the bureaucratic suffocation prevented her from carrying out her sense of purpose. For Clara, who prized harmonious relationships, it was a struggle to take up a director's role. She had to persuade herself that the good she could do for students as a library director outweighed the pain she would feel when people were angry at her for (inevitably) making decisions that were unpopular with some. These women were driven by generative purpose rather than ambition.

Generativity also involved a deepening commitment to the welfare of their families. For those women who became mothers, the challenges of generativity were to parent well in the way that they understood good parenting, to create independent children who would always be attached to them but could find their own way in the world. These are the overarching goals. Yet, on a daily basis, generativity comprised the creative improvisations that motherhood entails, the stamina and dedication, including maintaining a sense of humor in light of all the anxieties. Motherhood is a centrally important site of generativity (but not the only one). Of the 11 women who were Pathmakers either in college or later, all but two had children, and all of these had two children. (By contrast, of the seven Drifters, only two had children.) By late midlife, these mothers in their mid-50s were taking joy in the success of their children (and, thereby, their own successful generativity) and adapting to being a mother to adults. The growing maturity of their children, especially as children left home to create their own identities, was both a loss and a liberation. They now knew their children as *people* and were no longer occupied with how to mother them, although they were grappling with how to maintain adult relationships with them. At the time of this mid-50s interview, most of their children were between late teenage and the late 20s, and the nature of motherhood had changed. Many women, in response to my opening question of "Tell me about what has been important for you in the past 10 years?" began with their children, indicating that they still located themselves first and foremost as mothers. But the quality of their descriptions had changed. They had grown more into engaged observer roles, were less actively involved or trying to influence (unlike the Guardians who stayed overinvolved with managing their children's lives as their parents had done with them). They mused over their children's choices, took pride in their successes, stayed available for counsel or commiseration, but were actively letting go. Many women spoke of renewed joy in their children, some of the best times being when their children came home—for visits.

Throughout their adult years, the dilemma of generativity was to achieve balance—to be giving without being overly self-sacrificing, taking care of the self while taking care of others. Cultivating a sense of humor seemed important here, a way of taking distance from what often seemed to be overwhelming need from others. These women relished being needed—but not too much. And they were called upon to respond to needs that are unpredictable. I am reminded of Marlene's wry observation about parenting her teenage son: "but even the good ones, you know, they total your car, sort of those little worries. Is he going to survive high school? Am I going to survive high school?"

The most telling examples of balanced generativity came from those who had children with special needs. I still can't fathom how Betty and her husband managed to take their highly compromised son on international biking trips—and keep up with his schooling. And Regina maintained her high-achieving career and her commitment to her son with many special needs.

The need for balance in taking care of self and others at the same time arose each day for each of these women in myriad decisions. This seemed to be the essence of each woman's "work." They learned to multitask and prioritize. Sometimes they leaned too far in the self-sacrificing direction and then corrected for this. (I heard little about overly leaning in the self-indulgent direction from this group of highly conscientious women, but I suspect there must have been moments of this, too.) Balance was a bit like a seesaw—not achieved, just attempted over and over again. When the goals are clear, the problems become a matter of logistics.

For women who did not have children, generativity was more diffused. They were perhaps more attentive than the women who were mothers to what they were offering to their spouses. They carried their investment in the next generation to their nieces or nephews, and they were responsive to the need of members of their families and their friends. (This was true of the non-mothers who were not Drifters—Emily, Andrea, and Laura. Drifters were relatively stagnant in regard to generativity.)

Women drew strength and enjoyment of life through what they contributed to others. Being needed by others affirmed their identity.[22] And, by midlife, it seemed to me that identity melded into generativity, phrased as "I *am* my sense of purpose—and that is invested in the well-being of others." Erikson said that the hallmark of identity was a sense of fidelity and the hallmark of generativity was the sense of care. By midlife, woman are most *faithful* to what they have chosen to *care* for—and, when this is successful, it feels to them self-enhancing rather than self-sacrificing.

Just over half of all the women I have followed still had mothers who were living. Where their mothers remained a dominant force in their emotional lives at 30 and 40, most had made peace with their mothers by their mid-50s and no longer occupied themselves as much with whether their mothers did or did not approve of them. They had grown more insightful about their relationship with this centrally important figure in their lives and had resolved their ambivalence in the direction of acceptance. As Regina described it at age 54, "My mother is very critical and opinionated and tries to take over whenever she visits. She doesn't really understand what our lives are like. I finally came to understand that my mother is incapable of empathy. She can be sympathetic but can't put herself in your shoes, she can't do that—that was always true—she supported me in a distant way." Many of the Drifters and those who remained Guardians were still in thrall to their mothers, either focused on their anger at her or their need to please her.

The women of my study all wanted to give back to their parents. Several told me of taking their parents on trips to places their parents very much wanted to visit. Others spoke of their embeddedness in family rituals—holiday celebrations, weddings, or, if distance allowed, simply being together. Many were caught up in family squabbles and tried to make peace among siblings or between siblings and parents—their own and their spouse's.

Identity is embedded in an almost tribal belonging. For these women, their "tribe" is their extended family of origin, including, most often, the family they have married into. Women located their experience in relation to these important others, contrasting themselves sometimes in terms of values or worldview, but more often speaking of their commitments to the welfare of and relationships with their parents, in-laws, and siblings. Most, especially in midlife, included in their sense of embedded identity a nod to their ethnic origin. Many had immigrant grandparents (or great grandparents), and ethnicity dictated certain codes of behavior or rituals, so the sense of being Greek or Italian or culturally Jewish located their sense of identity in a generational heritage, one they may have moved away from but still locate themselves within.

The relational arena of adult relationships with parents is often misrepresented in both psychological and popular literature. Most often, this is denoted by the necessity of taking care of aging, needy parents, but there is a wealth of adult relationship with healthy, active parents as well. Being with their parents offered them opportunities for generativity in the form of family meals, visits, shared outings, and engagement in the lives of their own children. These women recognized that they were bringing pleasure to their parents (and in-laws) and ensuring meaning in their lives, an opportunity for another expression of their generativity.

In their mid-50s, those with still-living parents (mainly mothers) were actively monitoring their parents' health and capacity to care for themselves, providing help where necessary or preparing themselves to do so. Those whose parents had died spoke of their grief and either their pleasure in having cared well for them or, in a few cases, guilt at failing to do so well enough. Caring for ailing parents usually awakened old sibling issues as they negotiated with their siblings about who would do what, how, and when. It was not a problem they shouldered alone.

Another important aspect of the intersection of identity and generativity in midlife for these women is enlarging identity to include themselves in the cycle of generations.[23] Women who were Pathmakers or Searchers in college had been eager to individuate from their parents, to create themselves as far as they dared from their families. Incrementally, as midlife progresses and they become aware of themselves as guides for the next generation, they begin to link their own identities to their origins, celebrating rather than disowning familial patterns or traits. Andrea, for example, had always decried her "traditional" mother for holding her back in so many ways, but by midlife was speaking of her mother as the source of her own adventurousness. Alice, who felt she had little in common with her parents, was in later midlife planning to take up canning vegetables as her father always had. Many reclaimed a generational ethnicity which in some ways they no longer really shared, exploring the ways in which they could claim "Italian" or "Armenian" aspects of an identity that they had wanted no parts of when younger. Marlene, whose tragic family history had been largely hidden from her, was in the process of trying to unearth and revisit it in her 50s. Identity, then, expands to include one's place in the cycle of generations.

As women grow into their 50s, generativity expands beyond the personal toward taking care of the future in terms of community and systems. With children more independent, generative purpose enlarges to passing on values more broadly, and it is this aspect of generativity that is likely to expand into the next decade. Partly as a result of work roles and partly in response to inner maturation, women become concerned with how to have impact in wider spheres. Marlene is considering working more systemically on women's health issues—beyond treating her own patients; Clara wants to influence the role of libraries on college campuses; Sandra is recognizing her fund-raising capabilities and deciding which organizations she wants to devote her time to. The sphere of generative influence magnifies as women see their potential place in wider systems.[24]

Agency and Compromise

Over time, from late adolescence through midlife, these women gain in agency, a self-directed sense of being able to do things in the world. Increasingly, they can have impact on the people toward whom their occupational efforts are directed. And they agentically make decisions about how they will comport themselves as mothers or in their family relationships. They choose how they will spend their remaining time, what other interests to pursue. Their agency expresses who they choose to be in the world—that is, their identity. At the same time, they increasingly learn the art of compromise, the capacity to rework plans and goals in light of circumstance—but not too much, not too fully. In part, they find a way to get what they want, but they also develop the ability to want what they get. This capacity to experience ambivalence and settle it on the positive side distinguishes the midlife Pathmakers from those who remained Guardians or were or became Drifters. The Pathmakers were able to modify themselves and their stake in their worlds while retaining a central core. They held their goals flexibly and got as close as they could. When life delivered something they hadn't foreseen or even wanted—a developmentally challenged child, an ill husband, an inhospitable economic climate—they found ways to embrace what was essential to them. They acknowledged their disappointment and carried on. The Guardians, by contrast, kept trying to make the world conform to their insistence that it be a certain way. The Drifters just remade themselves to fit into whatever circumstances of the moment seemed to demand of them. The growing core of wisdom in the Pathmakers was developing insight into what they could change (in themselves, in others, and in their institutions) and what they had to find a way to accept.

I admired the strength at the core in most of those who were or became Pathmakers, a strength that derived from a clear sense of identity, from knowing who they had become in the world and valuing their chosen ways of being in their world. And I acknowledged also their sense of regret, of paths not taken or compromises they had to make. Emily, who cherished her husband and her high-profile successful career, nevertheless admitted her regret at never having had children. And Andrea, who had staked so much on her career, regretted coming to a dead end because of funding and the changed medical world. Everyone had some difficulty to manage—special needs children, divorce, occupational dead ends, unemployment, fertility problems, tragedies in their extended families. Maturity, even happiness in maturity, involves transcending regret and pain to value one's own particular life course[25]—rather than dwelling on what might have been.

I come up against the impossibility of taking a stand about another woman's life; I have no ground on which to judge them. They take pleasure in different things and feel fulfilled in myriad ways. Many live with regret and accept that they will be unfulfilled in some areas of life. Most would agree with the wisdom of Maria's perspective at age 55: "I've learned not to expect too much from life and just to take each day as it comes and to enjoy, you know, the little joys and little successes that—I don't know, to me there's not one big goal at the end—not one big prize at the end. But it's like, you know, life is a series of bumps in the road, but you just keep moving forward and, uh, you accept, you know, what life gives you, really. There've been a lot of positive things, there've been a lot of ups and downs. And I think that's what everyone's life is. I don't think anyone's life goes a hundred percent smoothly." Wisdom, for these highly agentic women, has been found in acceptance of what they could not change.

The Limits of Identity

We might also ask, based on these interviews over time, how far identity can expand from the roots of childhood. Our culture and our literature are filled with stories of women (and men) who seem to make adult selves out of materials that they glean just from the culture at large, quite distant from where they began. This is our cultural mythology of "you can be anyone you want." Real lives, though, are a blend of something old and something new. All of the Pathmakers, women who forged a life on their own terms, can be seen as either creating new selves or falling not that far from the tree, depending on the perspective one takes. All of these women, daughters of stay-at-home mothers, had careers (and most raised children at the same time). In that sense, they lived lives quite different from their mothers'. Most were raised in religiously focused homes, and most had moved away from the religion of their childhood—another important difference. Economically, most were living somewhat more comfortably than their parents had. Because most of these women were the first generation to go to college, they were also in more professional worlds than their parents had been, in white-collar versus blue-collar occupations and social worlds. Politically, most said they were more liberal than their parents.

Yet most of these women felt themselves still very much part of and identified with their parents. They emphasized that, although their lives were very different from their mothers', they had the same basic approach to raising children. Most of those who grew up in small towns made their own homes in small towns; the city girls nested in cities, usually different cities from where they grew up. The less notable aspects of identity, but nevertheless important ones, were continuous—the kinds of foods they liked to eat, the entertainment they enjoyed, the family celebrations that structured the calendar. For some, a shared sense of ethnic background was an important part of their identity that might not be apparent to acquaintances or co-workers, was an identity link to their families—a sense of "being" Irish, Italian, or Jewish. Few of the late midlife women stressed their differences from their families of origin because they emotionally experienced the continuity.

Many of these women came from families who encouraged them to go to college and explore the world, and they began college with a sense that they could "be" whatever they wanted. But they were nevertheless bounded by who they already were. Identity is not created from a blank canvas. The process of identity formation and identity revision over time involved modifying an existing picture. The most dramatic changes come during the college years, but change over time, as we have seen, involves reworking sections of the already existing painting, adding elements, removing sections and starting over, retouching, rearranging. Over the course of 35 years, the painting looks different but is clearly the work of the same artist who has a unique style and sensibility.

The interviews I have conducted draw a portrait not only of the individual but of the world she understands herself to be living in—in some ways, this is the essence of identity. The woman not only takes a place in the world, but structures a world that feels like her own. Talking to me involves telling me about her world, the gallery in which she locates her own canvas. For some women, it was frustrating to tell me about her world because its basic features were foreign to me—the locales, the local institutions, the local customs and activities, the primary people with whom she interacts. The sheer localization of identity was illuminating to me—and sometimes surprising. For me as an academic who lives a binational life, the globe is my neighborhood (which has its own limitations since I hardly know my actual neighbors). For most of these women, life is much narrower than the grand aspirations I might have imagined for them. Home, workplace, and (in some cases) church are the arenas for the performance of identity. In small towns, what church you attend is an important marker of social identity. Thus, for many women, church affiliation marks not religious belief but which subgroups in the community one affiliates with.

Most are aware of "the news," but their lives seem to them untouched by larger political forces except as they affect economic realities. Having interviewed these women in the 1970s, 1980s, 1990s, and 2000s, I was very attuned to changes in the times and larger world. While these women were at the forefront of the changes wrought by the feminist movement, most did not see it as a defining context for their lives. Those who did were the few who felt discriminated against in the workplace or the ones who became the first women to take up particular professional roles. By the 1980s, women were prominent in public and professional life, and, by the first decade of the 21st century, equal opportunity for women was widely assumed to be a right in the United States. These women had the advantage of taking part in the world outside their homes, unlike their mothers, and it became an assumption of life rather than something to be noted. I reread all the interviews for references to the sociopolitical context, but could find only economic considerations that reflected their awareness of the impact it had on them. If these women are politically engaged or active at all, it is in local issues that directly affect their families or their work goals. Only a few have traveled abroad, so there is little personally meaningful sense of other countries or cultures (except as part of familial origin). Identity is an awareness of who one is not. These women are white and American, but these identity elements are taken for granted and not conceptualized as aspects of who they are. The meaningful "not-me's" that counterpoint identity are much closer to home—the local "others" who have different values in terms of family or work.

Although many of these women had heard "you can be anything" from their parents as they went off to college, most created—or recreated—lives quite similar in concern to those they began with. They were revolutionary in terms of the change they effected in women's roles, most of them quite adamant about expecting to enact a function in the workplace and be treated fairly there. Most would say that, although balancing raising children and realizing their professional goals was a challenge, there was never a serious question about giving up their professions. Moments of doubt, times of feeling overburdened, perhaps, but no serious questions. These are stories of realizable, rather than outsize dreams. In college, they told me they wanted meaningful work and loving families. Many created that. As they aged, these dreams fleshed out: they wanted contentment, material comfort, a sense of accomplishment and dignity, the respect of their peers, and a feeling that they were having meaningful impact on others. This is what they have largely achieved. And this is what has brought them fulfillment.[26]

Fulfilled but Not Finished

I have understood and portrayed these women in late midlife as living out their sense of fulfillment, and I want to stress that this is dynamic rather than static. They are still very much engaged in solving the next puzzles of their career commitments or family needs. And they seem to be operating from a position of satisfaction rather than deficit. They may feel they have nothing left to prove in their careers, no ladders they yearn still to climb—but there is much they still want to do. Retirement for most of them feels far in the future, and they trust that they will know when the right time arrives and that they will find meaningful ways of reinvesting their time and energies. They actively seek to expand their relationships with their husbands and to understand themselves better. Most of them, with children either in college or about to leave home, are moving quietly to the sidelines of their children's lives, alert to times they may be needed but trying not to intrude their own needs too much. Some are eagerly thinking about what it will mean to them to be a grandmother, the next major familial role for them to define for themselves. Their lives continue to unfold in a dynamic flow of interaction. These women in their mid-50s seem to have learned to live in the present, not impulsively like the Drifters, but savoring the moments, enlarging their vision from the point of view of "now," satisfied with the lives they have built and hoping for it to go on and on. None has a life untouched by sorrow, disappointment, or regret, but these they used to strengthen themselves, integrating unrealized dreams as part of the larger picture. They take responsibility for the choices they have made. Looking back, they nearly all say they feel "lucky" even while they acknowledge that they were in large part the architects of their lives.

George Vaillant, in his longitudinal study of men,[27] found that generativity in middle adulthood predicted successful aging in later life. There is every reason to suppose that this is true of women as well. The challenges of examining, evaluating, and honoring commitments have given the women I have followed strength, agency, and purposefulness, attributes that will serve them well as they give up roles, take on new ones, and continue to make meaning in their lives. I hope to be able to continue to follow them to see how their development so far affects how they encounter and cope with the opportunities and challenges of advancing old age.

Lessons

The primary enlightenment from this long study is that what happens in late adolescence has profound impact on the adult life course. Those who were Pathmakers at the end of college have led largely fulfilling and productive lives into their mid-50s. Those who were Drifters mainly continued to drift. What can we, as a society, do to support optimal identity formation in our young people? Once the initial identity structure is crystallized, the conditions of its formation are largely lost to conscious memory. But this prospective study, following women as they grow and develop, demonstrates the nature of the pathway, even if the women themselves cannot detail it from midlife. The experience and influences of college are melded into the identity structure like various hues mixed together to make a new paint color. The university provided the needed period of exploration for identity to be reworked from childhood identifications and to be created as a new aspect of the self. The whole social milieu, with its diversity of people and ideas, temptations and opportunities, is at the service of the hatching adult. The current skills-focused discourse on what universities should offer completely elides this centrally important developmental function that universities serve. And, I think, universities can and should be more proactive in reaching out to those who are drifting. Drifters don't "grow out of it."

The opportunity for revision in their late 30s and early 40s afforded these women possibilities to make new commitments to generative pursuits, either at work or in their families. These reshaped identities scaffolded their sense of fulfillment in their 50s. In the early years of the 21st century, revision of identity has become not only sanctioned but promoted for women, a cause for celebration and social support, the fruit perhaps of the revolution in the place of women in American society. This is perhaps another way in which we can view these particular women as pathbreakers. They won for themselves, and for other women, the right to choose again, to remake themselves into the women they wanted to be—and this is a quest that continues into their sixth decade and beyond.

Notes

1. I include in this group Betty, Alice, Andrea, Clara, Maria, Regina, Marlene, Millie, Emily, Grace, and Debbie. Studies of adult development show that a third to a half of the adult population reaches a level of ego development that would be equivalent to an integrated sense of personal identity in the Eriksonian sense (Kroger, 2003, 2007; Kegan, 1995). My group of 26 women, of which 11 are Pathmakers in midlife, is consistent with these findings on larger samples.

2. Helson, Soto, and Cate (2006) conceptualize three phases of middle age based on a longitudinal sample of college women about 12 years older (a study known as "the Mills study") than those in my study. In the ascendant phase, roughly age 27–45, women are most likely to show achievement-related identity conflicts, whereas in the executive phase (45–61), the woman reaches maximum status and responsibility. Affective control increases. Time demands are heaviest, leaving little time for leisure. These authors also summarize other research on the phases of middle age that largely parallel the conception I offer here. Across a wealth of publications on the longitudinal study of the Mills women, the 50s seem to be the age of greatest well-being. Women in their early 50s show increased confidence, decisiveness, comfort with the self, and commitment over the past decade of their lives (Helson & Wink, 1992). Those women who showed the most self-directedness at age 43 were most likely to increase on measures of impulse control and agency in their early 50s (Wink, 1996).

In a study that included both cross-sectional and longitudinal data about women 12 years older than those I have studied, researchers found the early 50s to be women's "prime of life" in that life satisfaction was highest in this period (Mitchell & Helson, 1990). They attributed this to a number of factors, including better health than an older cohort, the "empty nest" with the advantages of living with a partner alone, and engagement in the present with a sense of control over one's life. Stewart, Ostrove, and Helson (2001), using measures from three different cohorts of women who were 3–12 years older than the women I have studied, found that "identity certainty, generativity and confident power" (p. 23) were experienced as more prominent in women's scores in their 40s than in their 30s and rated even higher in their 50s than their 40s. They concluded that women's scores on these measures were more a function of age than historical period or particular experiences in social roles.

3. The work of Gisela Laboivie-Vief and her colleagues has detailed the changes in cognitive and affective complexity that develop over the adult years (Labouvie-Vief, 2005; Labouvie-Vief & Medler, 2002).

4. Increases in positive emotions over the course of midlife, using large samples, have been well documented; see Helson, Soto, and Cate (2006) for review.

5. Other scholars have referred to this as "confident power" and note it as a hallmark of well-being in midlife; see Stewart and Ostrove (1998) for review.

6. I am grateful to Jim Marcia and Jane Kroger, with whom I developed this and many other ideas in this book.

7. Berzonsky, Rice, and Neimeyer (1990) and Berzonsky and Adams (1999) found differences among the four identity statuses in terms of self-construct systems. College-age identity achievers (Pathmakers) in both studies displayed the highest levels of self-differentiation and self-integration, whereas moratoriums (Searchers) had high levels of self-differentiation with limited integration. Foreclosures (Guardians), by contrast, had undifferentiated but highly integrated self-protocols.

8. This is Daniel Stern's (1985) observation about agency in early development as well.

9. See also Stewart and Ostrove (1998) who suggest that "the early formation of a strong personal identity enhances the likelihood of development of 'executive personality' in middle age. This, in turn, may foster efforts to express generative impulses in the larger social world outside the family" (p. 1189).

10. I began this study not with a purposive sample, but a randomly selected one. All but one of these women married (or were in committed relationships) and all but two were married at the time of the age-50s follow-up. I do not think that marriage is necessary for movement to generativity, but I cannot present such cases because the women I studied did not follow this path.

11. Helson and McCabe (1993), in a longitudinal study, found that whereas women in their 20s had clear ideas about what others expected of them, women in their 50s thought that other people no longer had expectations about what they should be doing and thus felt free of interpersonal fetters in planning their lives.

12. There are a number of excellent papers about generativity in McAdams & de St. Aubin (1998). See also Mayseless (2016) for further discussion of the dynamics of care.

13. Nearly all researchers who have intensively studied women conclude that interconnection is the foundation of identity (Franz & Stewart, 1994; Gilligan, 1982; Miller, 1976; Chodorow, 1978; Hulbert & Schuster, 1993, among others), yet psychology persists in thinking about identity in individualistic terms.

14. Researchers doing empirical studies of generativity have found that highly generative adults emphasize themes of love, friendship, communication, and community and have warmer and more complex depictions of others in their life stories; see McAdams, Hart, and Maruna (1998, pp. 7–43).

15. See especially Swidler (1980). Miller (1976) concludes that the greater capacity for relatedness in women is a developmental achievement higher than autonomy, representing a different and more advanced approach to living.

16. Other studies of women similarly find that work is seldom named as the most central or satisfying activity in women's lives. Being with family usually comes first. (See Hulbert and Shuster [1993].) Women's autobiographies also tend to emphasize affiliation and interdependency over achievement, in comparison to men's autobiographies (Gergen & Gergen, 1993).

17. See Flum (2015).

18. SeeWinnicott (1965) and Kohut (1987).

19. See Noddings (2013) for a discussion of the ethical dimensions of motherhood. The experience of motherhood leads also to increases in ego resiliency (Paris & Helson, 2002).

20. Josselson (1998).

21. Apter and Josselson (1999).

22. Valory Mitchell (2007) presents a case study of a woman who was likely a Drifter, marked by an insecure attachment style, until she had children. The love she discovered she was able to give to her children led her to develop a sense of competence in her occupational world and from there to a capacity for intimacy with a new partner. This demonstrates that the three adult tasks of identity, intimacy, and generativity are interdependent and can be mastered out of order. This is also apparent in Debbie's case in my own study.

23. Erikson, Erikson, and Kivnick (1986) elaborate on this theme.

24. George Vaillant, who did an intensive longitudinal study of a cohort of Harvard men a generation older than my participants, theorized two stages of generativity, a second one he called "Keepers of the Meaning" to represent a concern with "conservation and preservation of the collective products of mankind" (Vaillant, 2002, p. 48). I don't see

this as a separate stage in my own data, but he was writing when his participants were two or three decades older than mine—and he was writing about men.

25. See King and Hicks (2007).

26. Mitchell and Helson (2016), in their longitudinal study that extended from college through age 70, similarly concluded that "satisfaction and fulfillment are wedded to the experience of strong feeling, even passion, in the pursuit of deeply meaningful goals; that is, to a strong sense of purpose in life—whether it be a passionate interest in work, volunteer activity or one's garden, or a deep commitment to the unity and welfare of one's family, or a profound relationship which may support years of care-giving, or a need for self-development. Purpose in life can invigorate, transform regrets into challenges, can help us navigate our limitations, even accept our losses by honoring the depth of their importance (p. 228)." The women in their study who consistently had the highest scores on a measure of Purpose in Life were also higher than other women in the personality trait of Conscientiousness.

27. Vaillant (2002). Vaillant (1993) also showed that women who achieved generativity at age 60 were more likely to demonstrate better adaptation to old age than those who had not achieved generativity. A survey-based longitudinal study also showed that women who are higher in generativity in midlife show more signs of successful aging at age 62 (Versey, Stewart, & Duncan, 2013).

{ AFTERWORD }

Many of the women I followed have, at some point, been aided in their development by psychotherapy, sometimes intensive, sometimes short-term to help them traverse an obstacle. These women were self-aware enough to recognize that they needed some help sorting themselves out or gaining insight into something that was awry in their lives. Often, it was distress in their relationships that led them to outside help (Emily, Grace, Andrea, and Alice), and their therapy helped them to rework parts of themselves and aspects of their early histories that had hampered them in their growth. The majority of those who became Pathmakers had some psychotherapy along the way, not to alleviate symptoms but to promote growth or solve relationship problems. Therapy catalyzed the adult identity formation process by freeing them from repetitive bondage to past patterns and by helping them to understand their own needs better.

I can't help but wonder if this is one way in which I may have subtly influenced them. Talking to me over these years at least gave them an experience of talking about themselves with a psychologist—even though I scrupulously avoided taking anything like a therapist role. Still, just having this brief encounter with a psychologist may have made psychotherapy seem less foreign to these women who do not operate in a psychological world. It was also still fairly normative in the 1980s and 1990s among educated women to seek therapy. And these are goal-directed women who, if something is in their way, find resources to help them traverse the obstacle. Psychotherapy is one such resource. Before the dominance of symptom-focused care, seeing a therapist was part of the cultural milieu for educated women. For the women I have followed, therapy was an intervention, help over a hump—and not *the* major influence in their development. It was an aid on their road to self-acceptance, self-expansion, and empowerment. And in no way do I think that this engagement in psychotherapy makes these women less "normal"— in some ways, it perhaps makes them more so.

In the end, I cannot know how I might have affected these women by swooping in and engaging them to talk intimately about themselves every decade or so throughout their adult lives. They tell me I haven't meant all that much—not to insult me—I know they have enjoyed talking to me and reflecting on themselves—but to point out that they are engrossed in living their lives and what I see or think just doesn't really carry a lot of weight. As it should be—and I believe them. I do know that they have deeply affected me.

I have spent hundreds of hours poring over what I know about them, trying to understand them, trying to find patterns and reasons, trying to assess how well psychology manages to theorize women and what is omitted or distorted.

Most are women I would never have gotten to know in the course of my own life, and they have taught me about the many different ways in which women live their lives, the ways in which their roots form the soil in which they grow and the ways in which they courageously venture toward other possibilities. I admire them all for their perseverance in their efforts to grow, to find meaning, to love as well as they can—and to fulfill themselves.

{ APPENDIX }

A full account of the Sampling Methods and Data collection procedures as well as the full questionnaires and interview protocols are available in *Revising Herself.*

Participants:

Between 1971 and 1973, I randomly drew names of senior-year college women from the student directories of four colleges or universities. I interviewed 60 women until I met the criterion of having 48 women who would be distributed as 12 in each of the four identity status groups. At the time, Pathmakers were over-represented - there were more Pathmakers than were included in the final sample. It was harder to find Drifters, in part because they were least likely to keep appointments and had to be pursued.

In that universities tend to have characteristics unique to themselves, I interviewed women from three very different kinds of institutions, all middle to upper range in terms of their academic standing: two large state universities, a large private university and a small women's college. Most students lived on campus but many lived at home. Many also held part-time jobs and paid for all or part of their own tuition.

In 1983, I attempted to locate the 60 women who I had interviewed in the previous decade. Because many had moved or changed their names, and their educational institutions had no record of them, I was able to locate only 40. Of these, two were deceased. Five refused to participate. Therefore, 33 people constituted this second group.

In 1993, I succeeded in locating 30. All agreed to participate.

In 2003, when the women were 53, I began travelling around the country to interview them. They were so spread out and my time was limited, so this phase lasted for 10 years in which I met with and interviewed 23 of them. When I began to write, I tried to find more with an intention of interviewing the remaining three women virtually. In this phase, I found and interviewed 26.

Method

In the first data collection, I contacted each woman by letter and then by phone inviting her to participate. I described the study as an investigation of the psychology of women. Seventy-five percent of the women I contacted agreed to participate.

I interviewed each woman beginning with Marcia's Identity Status Interview, which took between a half-hour and an hour. Interviews were taped and later rated by myself and Susan Schenkel, who was an advanced graduate student also studying identity formation using the identity status format. We agreed on 90% of the ratings. Those on which we disagreed were rated by a third person and we grouped participants into the identity status which had received two ratings.

I also interviewed participants for one and one-half to two hours using an open-ended semi-stuctured protocol that elicited material about the participant's early life, relationships with parents and friends, significant internal (and external) conflicts as well as information about her experience of herself.

In the first follow-up contact in 1983, participants were either interviewed for 3–4 hours in person or sent and asked to respond to a comprehensive questionnaire. This was usually followed by a lengthy interview either in person or by phone. Most of the women vaguely remembered that they had participated in some study in college, but many did not. In the intervening years I had had no contact with them. Often, at this time, I had to persuade and cajole them to participate—they were suspicious about revealing themselves to someone they weren't sure they knew. The times had changed as well—it was a less trustful age. Some were hesitant at the beginning of the interview, but then warmed to the task and seemed to enjoy the opportunity to reflect on their lives with an interested, empathic listener. I did the majority of face-to-face interviewing at this time, although two women were interviewed by my students.

In the second follow-up in 1993, all remembered me. In some cases, in the late 1980s, I had sent people who had requested it copies of a paper I had published about the study. Two or three had come across *Finding Herself* and read it. In 1984, a year after the first follow-up, I sent each woman a Christmas card to thank her again for her participation and to urge her to be sure to let me know of any address changes she might make. Beyond this, I had no contact with them in the interim. I was delighted to find that these women were not only willing, but often eager to participate once again. Some went to a lot of trouble to come for interviews. Others offered to meet in their homes, offices or vacation houses. Again, I personally did most of the interviewing while seven of my graduate students did others. Some women were not available for face-to-face interviews, so again we worked by questionnaire, tape and/or telephone. In-person interviews lasted 4–5 hours.

The third follow up spanned the years 2003–2015 because I travelled to meet each person. In the last years, I interviewed 3 women virtually. People were very welcoming to me at this point—we felt a bit like lifelong friends.

In this phase, the interview was quite unstructured. I began by asking each woman about her reactions to being in the study, raising the question of whether she thought it had affected her life in any way. (Many of them had previously requested a copy of *Revising Herself*.) I did this to make space for any concerns she might have had about what I had written and also to confront directly the supposition of many of my colleagues that their participation in the study was shaping their lives in some way. I then asked each woman to "Tell me about the last 10 years or so—what has been most important to you, what changes have there been?" I followed the narrative each offered, asking for more detailed stories and also made sure to cover the main areas of endeavor, relationships, politics and religion that we had discussed earlier.

The overall principle in all of these data collections was for me to get to know each woman as intensively as possible. Rather than follow some rigid format, I modified both procedures and questions in the service of gaining as much knowledge of each one of them as I could. Each woman has given me written permission to use her material, suitably disguised, in my work.

{ DISCUSSION QUESTIONS }

1. Which group was easiest for you to relate to and why?
2. Which group do you think you would have been in at the end of college? Now?
3. What were the most important identity-defining decisions in your life?
4. Which important changes in your identity did you choose to create, and which were imposed on you by events? In other words, how much have you been the architect of your life?
5. How has your identity been affected by those you are closest to (intimacy) and those you care for (generativity)?
6. How has the feminist movement enabled you to be the woman that you are?
7. How do you think the challenges of identity formation are different for later generations of women?

{ REFERENCES }

Apter, T., & Josselson, R. (1999). *Best friends: The pleasures and perils of girls' and women's friendships*. New York: Crown.

Bacha, A. (1992). *Fertility of American Women: June 1992*. U.S. Dept. of Commerce, Bureau of the Census.

Bakhtin, M. (1981). *The dialogical imagination: Four essays*. Austin: University of Texas Press.

Berzonsky, M. D., & Adams, G. R. (1999). Reevaluating the identity status paradigm: Still useful after 35 years. *Developmental Review, 19*(4), 557–590.

Berzonsky, M. D., Rice, K. G., & Neimeyer, G. J. (1990). Identity status and self-construct systems: Process X structure interactions. *Journal of Adolescence, 13*(3), 251–263.

Brockmeier, J., & Carbaugh, D. (Eds.). (2001). *Narrative and identity: Studies in autobiography, self and culture*. Amsterdam: John Benjamins Publishing.

Bruner, J. (1990). *Acts of meaning: Four lectures on mind and culture* (Reprint edition). Cambridge, MA: Harvard University Press.

Bruner, J. (2003). *Making stories: Law, literature, life*. Cambridge, MA: Harvard University Press.

Chodorow, N. (1978). *The reproduction of mothering*. Berkeley: University of California Press.

Cohler, B. J., & Hoestler, A. (2003). Linking life course and life history. in J. T. Mortimer & M. I. Shanahan (Eds.), *Handbook of the life course* (pp. 555–575). New York: Kluwer Academic Press.

Collins, G. (2009) *When Everything Changed: The Amazing Journey of American Women from 1960 to the Present*. New York: Little, Brown.

Erikson, E. H. (1980). *Identity and the life cycle*. New York: W. W. Norton.

Erikson, E. H., Erikson, J. M., & Kivnick, H. Q. (1989). *Vital involvement in old age*. New York: W. W. Norton.

Fadjukoff, P., Pulkkinen, L., & Kokko, K. (2005). Identity processes in adulthood: Diverging domains. *Identity, 5*(1), 1–20. doi:10.1207/s1532706xid0501_1

Flum, H. (1994). The evolutive style of identity formation. *Journal of Youth and Adolescence, 23*(4), 489–498.

Flum, H. (2015). Relationships and career development: An integrative approach. In P. J. Hartung, M. L. Savickas, & W. B. Walsh (Eds.), *APA handbook of career intervention* (pp. 145–159). Washington, DC: APA Books.

Franz, C. E., & Stewart, A. J. (Eds.). (1994). *Women creating lives: Identities, resilience and resistance*. Boulder, CO: Westview Press.

Gergen, K. J., & Gergen, M. M. (2001). Narratives of the self. In L. P. Hinchman & S. K. Hinchman (Eds.), *Memory, identity, community: The idea of the narrative in the human sciences* (pp. 161–184). Albany: State University of New York.

Gergen, M. M., & Gergen, K. J. (1993). Autobiographies and the shaping of gendered lives. In N. Coupland & J. F. Nussbaum (Eds.), *Discourse and lifespan identity* (pp. 28–54). Sage Publications, Inc: Thousand Oaks, CA.

Giddens, A. (1991). *Modernity and self-identity: Self and society in the late modern age* (1st ed.). Stanford, CA: Stanford University Press.

Gould, R. L. (1979). *Transformations: Growth and Change in Adult Life*. New York: Simon & Schuster.

Helson, R., & McCabe, L. (1994). The social clock project in middle age. In B. Turner & L. Troll (Eds.), *Growing older female: Theoretical perspectives in the psychology of aging* (pp. 68–93). Newbury Park, CA: Sage.

Helson, R., Soto, C. J., & Cate, R. A. (2006). From young adulthood through the middle ages. in D. K. Mroczek & T. Little (Eds.), *Handbook of personality development* (pp. 337–352). Mahwah, NJ: Lawrence Erlbaum Associates.

Helson, R., & Wink, P. (1992). Personality change in women from the early 40s to the early 50s. *Psychology and Aging, 7*(1), 46.

Hoare, C. (2001). *Erikson on development in adulthood: New insights from the unpublished papers* (1st ed.). New York: Oxford University Press.

Hulbert, K. D., & Schuster, D. T. (1993). *Women's lives through time.* San Francisco: Jossey-Bass.

Josselson, R. (1973). Psychodynamic aspects of identity formation in college women. *J Youth and Adolescence, 2,* 3–52.

Josselson, R. (1987). *Finding Herself: Pathways to Identity Development in Women.* San Francisco: Jossey-Bass.

Josselson, R. (1996). *Revising Herself: The Story of Women's Identity from College to Midlife.* New York: Oxford University Press.

Josselson, R. (1998). On becoming the same age as one's mother: Intersubjectivity and ego development. In P. M. Westenberg, A. Blasi, & L. Cohen (Eds.), *Personality development: Essays in honor of Jane Loevinger* (pp. 237–253). Mahwah, NJ: Lawrence Erlbaum.

Josselson, R., & Lieblich, A. (2001). Narrative research and humanism. In K. J. Schneider, J. T. Bugethal, & J. F. Pierson (Eds.), *The handbook of humanistic psychology: Leading edges in theory, research and practice* (pp. 275–288). Thousand Oaks, CA: Sage.

Kegan, R. (1995). *In over our heads: The mental demands of modern life.* Cambridge, MA: Harvard University Press.

Keniston, K. (1968). *The Young radicals.* New York: Harcourt, Brace and World.

Keniston, K. (1960). *The Uncommitted.* New York: Harcourt, Brace and World.

King, L. A., & Hicks, J. A. (2007). Whatever happened to "What might have been"? Regrets, happiness, and maturity. *American Psychologist, 62*(7), 625–636. http://doi.org/http://dx.doi.org.fgul.idm.oclc.org/10.1037/0003-066X.62.7.625

Kohut, H. (1977). *The Restoration of the Self* (Reprint edition). Chicago: University of Chicago Press.

Kraus, W. (2006). The narrative negotiation of identity and belonging. *Narrative Inquiry, 16*(1), 103–111.

Kremen, A. M., & Block, J. (1998). The roots of ego-control in young adulthood: Links with parenting in early childhood. *Journal of Personality and Social Psychology, 75*(4), 1062–1075.

Kroger, J. (1995). The differentiation of "firm" and "developmental" foreclosure identity statuses: A longitudinal study. *Journal of Adolescent Research, 10*(3), 317–337.

Kroger, J. (1996). Identity, regression and development *Journal of Adolescence, 1996*(19), 203–222.

Kroger, J. (2003). What transits in an identity status transition? *Identity, 3*(3), 197–220.

Kroger, J. (2004). *Identity in adolescence*. New York: Routledge.

Kroger, J. (2007). Why is identity achievement so elusive? *Identity, 7*(4), 331–348. http://doi. org/http://dx.doi.org/10.1080/15283480701600793

Kroger, J. (2014). Identity development through adulthood: The move toward "wholeness." In K. C. McLean & M. Syed (Eds.), *The Oxford handbook of identity development* (pp. 65–80). New York: Oxford University Press.

Kroger, J., & Marcia, J. E. (2011). The identity statuses: Origins, meanings, and interpretations. in S. J. Schwartz & K. Luyckx (Eds.), *Handbook of identity theory and research* (pp. 31–53). New York: Springer.

Kroger, J., Martinussen, M., & Marcia, J. E. (2010). Identity status change during adolescence and young adulthood: A meta-analysis. *Journal of Adolescence, 33*(5), 683–698.

Labouvie-Vief, G. (2005). Self-with-other representations and the organization of the self. *Journal of Research in Personality, 39*(1), 185–205. http://doi.org/http://dx.doi.org/ 10.1016/j.jrp.2004.09.007

Labouvie-Vief, G., & Medler, M. (2002). Affect optimization and affect complexity: Modes and styles of regulation in adulthood. *Psychology and Aging, 17*(4), 571–588. http://doi. org/http://dx.doi.org/10.1037/0882-7974.17.4.571

Lieblich, A., & Josselson, R. (2013). Identity and narrative as root metaphors of personhood. In J. Martin & M. Bickhard (Eds.), *The psychology of personhood: Philosophical, historical, social-development and narrative perspectives* (pp. 203–222). New York: Cambridge University Press.

Linde, C. (2001). The acquisition of a speaker by a story: How history becomes memory and identity. *Ethos, 28*(4), 608–632.

Marcia, J., & Josselson, R. (2013). Eriksonian personality research and its implications for psychotherapy. *Journal of Personality, 81*(6), 617–629. http://doi.org/http://dx.doi.org/ 10.1111/jopy.12014

Marcia, J. E. (1966). Development and validation of ego identity status. *Journal of Personality and Social Psychology, 3*, 551–558.

Marcia, J. E. (1993). The ego identity status approach to ego identity. In J. E. Marcia, A. S. Waterman, D. R. Matteson, S. L. Archer, & J. L. Orlofsky (Eds.), *Ego identity: A handbook for psychosocial research* (pp. 3–21). New York: Springer–Verlag.

Marcia, J. E. (2010). Life transitions and stress in the context of psychosocial development. In T. W. Miller (Ed.), *Handbook of stressful transitions across the lifespan* (pp. 19–34). New York: Springer Science + Business Media.

Mayseless, O. (2016). *The caring motivation: An integrated theory*. New York: Oxford University Press.

McAdams, D. P. (1988). *Power, intimacy, and the life story: Personological inquiries into identity* (1st ed.). New York: Guilford.

McAdams, D. P. (1997). *The stories we live by: Personal myths and the making of the self* (1st ed.). New York: Guilford.

McAdams, D. P. (2001). The psychology of life stories. *Review of General Psychology, 5*(2), 100–122. http://doi.org/http://dx.doi.org/10.1037/1089-2680.5.2.100

McAdams, D. P. (2013). The psychological self as actor, agent, and author. *Perspectives on Psychological Science, 8*(3), 272–295. http://doi.org/10.1177/1745691612464657

McAdams, D. P., & de St. Aubin, E. (Eds.) *Generativity and adult development*. Washington, DC: American Psychological Association.

McAdams, D. P., Hart, H. M., & Maruna, S. (1998). The anatomy of generativity. In D. P. McAdams & E. de St. Aubin (Eds.), *Generativity and adult development* (pp. 7–43). Washington, DC: American Psychological Association.

McAdams, D. P., & McLean, K. C. (2013). Narrative identity. *Current Directions in Psychological Science, 22*, 233–238.

McLean, K. (2008). Stories of the young and the old: Personal continuity and narrative identity. *Developmental Psychology, 44*, 254–264.

McLean, K. C., Pasupathi, M., & Pals, J. L. (2007). Selves creating stories creating selves: A process model of self-development. *Personality and Social Psychology Review, 11*, 262–278.

Miller, J. B. (1976). *Toward a new psychology of women*. Boston: Beacon.

Mitchell, V. (2007). Earning a Secure Attachment Style: A Narrative of Personality Change in Adulthood. In *The meaning of others: Narrative studies of relationships* (pp. 93–116). American Psychological Association: Washington, DC, US.

Mitchell, V., & Helson, R. (1990). Women's prime of life: Is it the 50s? *Psychology of Women Quarterly, 14*(4), 451–470. http://doi.org/http://dx.doi.org/10.1111/j.1471-6402.1990.tb00224.x

Noddings, N. (2013). *Caring: A relational approach to ethics and moral education* (2nd updated ed.). Berkeley: University of California Press.

Paris, R., & Helson, R. (2002). Early mothering experience and personality change. *Journal of Family Psychology, 16*(2), 172–185. http://doi.org/10.1037//0893-3200.16.2.172

Polkinghorne, D. E. (1988). *Narrative Knowing and the Human Sciences*. Albany: State University of New York Press.

Schenkel, S., & Marcia, J. E. (1972). Attitudes toward premarital intercourse in determining ego identity status in college women. *Journal of Personality, 40*(3), 472–482. http://doi.org/http://dx.doi.org/10.1111/j.1467-6494.1972.tb00074.x

Sheehy, G. (1981). *Passages: Predictable Crises of Adult Life* (30th Anniversary ed. edition). New York: Ballantine Books.

Singer, J. A. (2004). Narrative identity and meaning making across the adult lifespan: An introduction, *Journal of Personality, 72*(3), 437–460.

Stern, D. (1985). *The interpersonal world of the infant*. New York: Basic Books.

Stewart, A. J., & Ostrove, J. M. (1998). Women's personality in middle age: Gender, history, and midcourse corrections. *American Psychologist, 53*(11), 1185.

Stewart, A. J., Ostrove, J. M., & Helson, R. (2001). Middle aging in women: Patterns of personality change from the 30s to the 50s. *Journal of Adult Development, 8*(1), 23–37. doi:http://dx.doi.org/10.1023/A:1026445704288.

Versey, H. S., Stewart, A. J., & Duncan, L. E. (2013). Successful aging in late midlife: The role of personality among college-educated women. *Journal of Adult Development, 20*(2), 63–75.

Whitbourne, S. K., Sneed, J. R., & Sayer, A. (2009). Psychosocial development from college through midlife: A 34-year sequential study. *Developmental Psychology, 45*, 1328–1320.

Wink, P. (1996). Transition from the early 40s to the early 50s in self-directed women. *Journal of Personality, 64*(1), 49–69.

Winnicott, D. W. (1965). *The family and individual development.* Oxford, England: Basic Books.

Vaillant, G. E. (2003). *Aging well: Surprising guideposts to a happier life from the landmark Harvard study of adult development.* Boston: Little, Brown and Company.

Zucker, A. N., Ostrove, J. M., & Stewart, A. J. (2002). College educated women's personality development in adulthood: Perceptions and age differences. *Psychology and Aging, 17,* 236–244.

{ INDEX }